# UNSUNG

# UNSUNG
## A History of
## Women in
## American Music

CHRISTINE AMMER

*Contributions in Women's Studies, Number 14*

GREENWOOD PRESS
WESTPORT, CONNECTICUT • LONDON, ENGLAND

Library of Congress Cataloging in Publication Data

Ammer, Christine.
    Unsung.

(Contributions in women's studies; no. 14 ISSN 0147-104X)
    Bibliography: p.
    Includes index.
    1. Women musicians.    2. Women composers.
    3. Musicians—United States.    I. Title.    II. Series.
ML82.A45        780'.92'2 [B]        79-52324
ISBN  0-313-22007-7

Library of Congress Catalog Card Number: 79-52324
ISBN: 0-313-22007-7
ISBN: 0-313-22909-0 (paperback edition)
ISSN: 0147-104X

First published in 1980

Greenwood Press
A division of Congressional Information Service, Inc.
88 Post Road West, Westport, Connecticut 06881

Printed in the United States of America

10 9 8 7 6 5 4 3 2

To all women musicians, then and now

# CONTENTS

# AUTHOR'S NOTE

In the mid-1970s America's bicentennial prompted celebrations of national achievement in many areas of endeavor, including music. At least two ambitious surveys of American music were undertaken by commercial record companies, yet the only woman composer represented on any of several dozen records issued was Mrs. H. H. A. Beach. The implication was that there had been no other women composers.

In 1975 I was asked to introduce to a concert audience the Quintessence, a wind quintet made up wholly of women. To prepare my introduction I looked for background information about women instrumentalists and discovered, after a few days of research, that almost no such information was readily available. Again, the implication was that there had been no women instrumentalists. But here, at least, there was a perceived discrepancy: The school orchestras in which our children play invariably include as many or more girls than boys, whereas the symphony orchestras we see consist predominantly of men.

Several years of research showed that women indeed have been writing and performing music for as long as men have. But, owing to the social climate of earlier times, their work went unnoticed, unpublished, unperformed, and was quickly forgotten. This book is a history of the role played by women in American music, as performers, composers, and teachers, during the past two hundred years. The musicians included are instrumentalists, conductors, and composers; singers have been omitted because, for a variety of reasons, considerable information about them is widely available.

Although this book focuses especially on the lives and work of outstanding individuals, it does not pretend to include all the women who have been active in American music. Such an exhaustive survey remains to be done. Moreover, in contemporary music it may not even cover all those who will be regarded, with adequate hindsight, to have been the most important of our time.

I am deeply grateful to the many persons who have answered questions and made suggestions, criticisms, and corrections and, in particular, to those who have assisted the vast amount of research that went into this book. Among those who merit special thanks are Roberta Bitgood, American Guild of Organists; Willa Brigham, Henniker, New Hampshire; Constance T. Ellis, Augusta, Maine; Neva Garner Greenwood, Falls Church, Virginia; Dr. Calderon Howe, New Orleans; Anne Hull, Westport, Connecticut; Professor Walter S. Jenkins, Tulane University; Virginia Koontz, Sacramento; Ruth Lomon, Lexington, Massachusetts; Katherine D. Moore, Knoxville, Tennessee; Patricia Morehead, Toronto; Barbara J. Owen, Organ Historical Society; Professor Harrison Potter, South Hadley, Massachusetts; William Strickland, Westport, Connecticut; Professor Milos Velimirovic, University of Virginia; Dr. Frances Wiggin, Maine Federation of Music Clubs; the staffs of the music divisions of the Boston Public Library and New York Public Library; Esta J. Astor, Maine Historical Society; R. Jayne Craven, Public Library of Cincinnati and Hamilton County; Rosalinda I. Hack, Chicago Public Library; Marjorie McDonald, National Federation of Music Clubs; Wayne D. Shirley, Library of Congress; Judith Wentzell, Portland (Maine) Public Library; James B. Wright, University of New Mexico Library; scholars Adrienne Fried Block, Laurine Elkins-Marlow, Carol Neuls-Bates, and Judith Tick, who have done valuable research on women in music; and composers Beth Anderson, Karen Phillips, Julia Smith, and Nancy Van de Vate, who have been extraordinarily active on behalf of their fellows. This book has been vastly improved through their assistance and advice; its errors and shortcomings are solely the author's own.

# UNSUNG

# 1 THE FIRST FLOWERING —AT THE ORGAN

...then if there must be a Singing, one alone must sing, not all (or if all), the men only, and not the women. And their reason is: Because it is not permitted to a woman to speake in the Church, how then shall they sing? Much less is it permitted to them to prophecy in the Church. And singing the Psalms is a kind of Prophecying.[1]

So wrote the Reverend John Cotton in his 1647 tract in defense of psalm singing, describing the arguments of those early Puritans who felt that true Christians should sing to the Lord only within their own hearts. Unlike them he believed that singing is both harmless and beautiful, and that the entire congregation, male and female, should worship the Lord in song. Presumably some others agreed with him. But for the most part the early American colonists, if they did not actually oppose music, paid scant attention to it. Music was all right in its place, but its place was miniscule indeed. To the sober and practical settler, it was a luxury, a "frill," a view held even today by some public school educators who would eliminate it from the curriculum. This sentiment was expressed in a letter from Leonard Hoar, who later became president of Harvard College, written to his nephew Josiah Flynt from London in 1661. Hoar wrote that he would not bring his nephew a fiddle because music was a waste of time; he would, however, bring instruments for Josiah's sisters, "for whom 'tis more proper and they also have more leisure to looke after it."[2]

The same strictures did not always apply to vocal music, for the colonists did sing. It is not known today exactly what they brought with them from England in the way of secular music, but congregational singing was and is a part of many Protestant church services, and there is a clear record of the psalters (psalm books) that they used. Indeed, among the first books ever printed in British North America was the Bay Psalm Book, a translation of the psalms made by Puritan ministers in 1640 and published in many subsequent editions.

In the typical congregation, however, there rarely were enough books to go around, and even if there had been, few if any of the members could read music. Consequently, by the later 1600s most churches in America used the practice of lining out; that is, the minister or deacon or clerk would read aloud each line of a psalm before it was sung by the congregation. The dozen or so melodies that were used for all the psalms were familiar. However, they had been learned long ago and transmitted by rote, so that in time distortions inevitably crept in.

By the 1720s it was well recognized by those who had any training or ear for music that most congregational singing was abysmally bad. In 1721 the Reverend Walter described psalm singing as "a mere disorderly noise... sounding like five hundred different tunes roared out at the same time, and so little in time that they were often one or two words apart."[3] Walter was one of a few concerned individuals who about this time began trying to remedy the situation. They published instruction books for reading the notes, and some instructors set themselves up as "singing masters" and began to conduct "singing schools" where they taught the "rudiments of Vocal Musick."

The singing masters traveled from town to town, using a room in someone's home or in a tavern or the local school for a classroom. Practically all of them pursued another trade, their music representing but a sideline. The typical singing school met two to three evenings per week for three months or so, after which the singing master moved on to another town. The master taught the fundamentals of vocal performance, especially tone production, note reading, and ensemble singing.[4]

There was no question but that singing schools were coeducational. Indeed, their enormous popularity was due chiefly to the fact that they gave young people a legitimate excuse to meet together during the evening, ostensibly—and also actually—to learn to read music and sing from the tune books. They thus provided a rare opportunity for social intercourse and courtship that could hardly have occurred without the presence of both sexes.

The singing school originated in the New England colonies but rapidly spread up and down the length of the Atlantic coast, and it soon gave rise to the first school of native American composition. From the 1720s to the 1770s numerous new collections of church music had appeared, but they were largely compilations of English hymns and anthems. The singing schools fostered a growing demand for new tunes and new tune books, and in time many of the singing masters themselves obliged by composing songs for this purpose. Between about 1750 and 1825 literally thousands of pieces were written, by William Billings, Daniel Read, Andrew Law, and countless lesser-known men. Many of these tunes are spirited, original, and beautiful, and although for a time they were considered crude and unsophisticated, they are earning new admiration today.

The best products of singing-school training entered the ranks of organized church choirs, to provide sturdy leadership for faltering congregational singing. At least, this was true for the male pupils. Not many girls and women were permitted to sing in the eighteenth-century church choir, and in those Episcopal churches where singing was part of the liturgy they were excluded entirely.

Solos by women singers were not unknown, but they had no place in church. Operas, chiefly in the form of the popular English ballad opera (of which the most famous is and was John Gay's *Beggar's Opera*), were being performed in New York, Charleston, and other American centers during the second half of the eighteenth century, but they were viewed more as theatrical performances than as music. A number of English singers became well known through such performances, and by the late eighteenth century a few, such as Mrs. Oldmixon, Miss Broadhurst, and Miss Brett—all English—were considered fine musicians.

Ballad operas were not the only musical import during the late 1700s. Portions of the oratorios of Handel and Haydn and works by Gretry, Stamitz, and Mozart began to be heard increasingly. Concerts of instrumental and vocal music, presented sporadically from the 1730s on, became more frequent, and during the last decade of the eighteenth century a large-scale immigration of professional European musicians took place. One of the most talented of the new arrivals was J. C. Gottlieb Graupner, a German oboist who had played in Haydn's orchestra in London. He came to Prince Edward Island in the early 1790s, went in 1796 to Charleston, where he married, and finally settled in Boston in 1797 or 1798. His wife, Catherine, was a talented and highly experienced singer, who as Mrs. Hellyer (or Hillier) had made a successful career in English ballad opera. Catherine Graupner soon appeared on the concert platform beside her husband. A program presented by Graupner on May 15, 1798, in Salem included two solos by his wife with instrumental accompaniment, as well as a song by a Miss Solomon, a duet by Mrs. Graupner and Mr. Collins, and a quartet by three gentlemen and Mrs. Graupner. In subsequent years Catherine Graupner became one of Boston's leading soloists, and upon her death in 1821 the principal Boston music journal (the *Euterpiad)* said that "for many years she was the only female vocalist in this metropolis."

The inadequacies of existing choirs and choral groups became all too apparent when they attempted the newly imported choruses of Handel and Haydn, or anthems by Purcell, Blow, and Arne. The music was simply too ambitious for even the most gifted of the singing-school graduates. As a result, musical societies began to be formed for the express purpose of learning and performing more difficult and larger works, such as Handel's *Messiah* and Haydn's *The Creation*. Free from the restrictions imposed by religious worship, these groups could, in theory, include women. In fact, however, they did so only by express invitation rather than routinely.

One of the earliest organizations was the St. Cecilia Society of Charleston, South Carolina, founded in 1762; it had 120 members who were permitted to invite ladies.[5] The Stoughton (Massachusetts) Musical Society was founded on November 7, 1786, by residents of Stoughton, Canton, and Sharon (neighboring towns just south of Boston). It proved to be somewhat less exclusive than most: Women were invited to take part in the singing of choruses, although they were not actually considered members, a rule that remained unchanged for a century. Likewise, the Handel Society of Dartmouth College, founded a few years later, met weekly to prepare the best musical works attainable. Members were chosen after an examination and counted their admission an honor; ladies were admitted only as "honorary members."

By far the most influential of the numerous societies formed during the first half of the nineteenth century was Boston's Handel and Haydn Society, which today claims to be the oldest still in existence. It was formally organized on April 20, 1815, with a constitution signed by thirty-one gentlemen (after a series of meetings held in Graupner's Hall). The chorus of the society was made up of members of the choirs of nine Boston churches, presumably the cream of the crop. Although women were not then—and long were not—admitted as members, the tradition of permitting them to sing began with the first concert. On December 25, 1815, a chorus of ninety men and ten women performed the first part of *The Creation* and selections from Handel's works. By 1817 the chorus had been enlarged to 150, of whom 20 were women.

Allegedly there were sound reasons for excluding women singers. Since women were not supposed to lead, in melody or elsewhere, the men sang the melody, usually in the tenor, as well as taking the alto (or counter) part, while the harmony assigned to the women was necessarily sung an octave higher. Consequently, as one contemporary critic described it, "Our ears were assailed with females singing thirds and fifths above the melody or treble. This custom ought to be abolished, being inconsistent with the true principles of choral harmony. Soprano voices should invariably confine themselves to the melody."[6]

Although several early church music compilers had given the melody to the soprano,[7] the older custom deplored by the critic persisted widely. His advice was not heeded by the Handel and Haydn Society for some years, and lesser, more provincial choruses probably were even slower to come round. In 1827, when Lowell Mason conducted the society in portions of Mozart's Requiem Mass, the ranks of the women singers were reinforced and they finally got the treble part; moreover, a few women altos were allowed to join the two or three countertenors who normally sang the alto part. By 1830 the society had about 100 male singers and 25 "female assistants"; the latter were not members and took part by express invitation only. The overall balance of parts produced by this proportion takes little effort of imagination: The bass voices undoubtedly drowned out the sopranos. The famous nineteenth-century critic John Sullivan Dwight commented a few years later, with admirable restraint, that the parts were "poorly balanced."[8]

In view of this obvious prejudice against women musicians, it is all the more remarkable that in 1818 and again in 1820 the Handel and Haydn Society should offer the position of organist to a woman, one Miss Sophia Hewitt. In her late teens at the time, she declined the first invitation but accepted the second, and, for the next decade, she worked for the society as organist and accompanist. She was the only woman they ever employed in this capacity, before or since. Moreover, at times during this period she also served as organist at two of Boston's principal churches, Chauncy Place Church and Catholic Cathedral, the only woman to fill such an important position.

Although the role of women in vocal music had been clearly defined by the colonists, their position with regard to instrumental music was more ambiguous. Instruments had been abhorred by the early Puritans, who would not permit any instrument in church. Nevertheless, by 1713 an organ was imported from England, and the following year it was installed in Boston's King's Chapel.[9] It was one of the first organs in North America (there may have been earlier ones in New York's Old Trinity Church and Philadelphia's Gloria Dei Church[10]). Whether due to high cost or lingering prejudice, relatively few other churches acquired organs, and in 1800 most church choirs still were accompanied, if at all, by flute, bassoon, and "bass viol" (cello). In 1815 only four Boston churches had organs, though that number was doubled by the following year.[11]

As for home instruments, according to John S. Dwight's estimate[12] fewer than 50 of Boston's 6,000 families owned a piano. Keyboard instruments—harpsichords and later pianos—had long been considered genteel enough for ladies to play. Indeed, by extension they came to be regarded as somewhat effeminate. Thus the ad placed in the *Columbian Centinel* in 1799 by Mrs. P. A. von Hagen, a Dutch organist who had recently moved to Boston from New York, respectfully informed the ladies of Boston that she was prepared to teach them the harpsichord and piano forte, as well as voice and organ.[13] Presumably gentlemen would have no interest in such pursuits. But such instrumental playing was almost exclusively confined to the home. During the eighteenth century, just about the only participation by women in public concerts was as singers, and even that was relatively rare. The Handel and Haydn Society did not engage a soprano or alto soloist for some years.[14] Thus a piano performance such as that by Miss M. A.

Wrighten in Boston on October 3, 1795, of *The Battle of Prague* was a distinct novelty.[15]

Presumably Sophia Hewitt had unusual qualifications to be offered a position by such a prestigious organization as the Handel and Haydn Society. However, the facts concerning her life are sparse, and even the exact date of her birth has been lost.[16]

A great deal more is known of her father's history, and from it something of Sophia's early life may be pieced together. James Hewitt, born in 1770 in Dartmoor, England, entered the Royal Navy while in his teens but took a dislike to it and became a musician. He soon became leader (principal violinist) of the orchestra at the court of King George III, and allegedly King George IV presented him with an Amati cello. In 1790 he was married to a Miss Lamb, but both his wife and an infant daughter died a year later; in 1792 he was persuaded to come to New York and lead the orchestra of the Old American Company, a theatrical group organized by John Henry (of Hallam and Henry).

Very soon after his arrival in New York, Hewitt announced his first concert, which according to current custom was to be a "benefit" for himself and four other newly landed musicians. The program for this event, held on September 21, 1792, attests to Hewitt's sophisticated tastes; included were a Haydn overture, a quartet by Pleyel, and a symphony and flute quartet by Stamitz. Among the "novelty" items offered was an *Overture in 9 movements, Expressive of a Battle,* composed by Hewitt himself.

During the next few years, Hewitt was extremely active in New York as a violinist, composer, concert manager, and publisher (he bought the New York branch of Benjamin Carr's Philadelphia music-publishing firm in 1798). He composed the music for what is believed to be the very first native American ballad opera, an anti-Federalist piece named *Tammany,* with a libretto by Mrs. Ann Julia Hatton, sister of the English actress Mrs. Siddons and wife of a New York musical-instruments maker. It was first produced on March 3, 1794, and the composer, who presumably also led the orchestra in the premiere, was hissed, booed, and even physically attacked by pro-Federalist members of the audience. The work was hailed by the anti-Federalists, however, and whatever his true political sentiments may have been, Hewitt became famous (or infamous) for this opera.

He also found time for courtship, and in 1795, at New York's Trinity Church, he was married to Eliza King, the daughter of a British army officer. The second Mrs. Hewitt was an educated woman. She had studied in Paris, where she had resided during the French Revolution, and had come to America with her father, who had an estate to settle there. She was not a musician, at least not professionally. There is no record of her joining in her husband's musical performances, a collaboration that might have been expected, since Hewitt had an unusually open attitude toward women musicians. Shortly after coming to America, he had collaborated on a book of songs for piano or harpsichord with Mrs. Mary Ann Pownall (1751-96), an English actress, singer, and composer who also came to America in 1792 with the Hallam and Henry Company. The book was advertised in a number of newspapers in 1793, and the following year Mrs. Pownall and Hewitt produced another book, *Six Songs for the Harpsichord.*

When the children of Hewitt's second marriage began to come along, it was Hewitt who undertook their musical education. The Hewitts had four sons and two daughters, all of whom eventually became involved with music. Sophia Henriette was the oldest, born in 1799 or 1800.[17] A child prodigy, she first performed in public at the age of seven: In a concert put on by her father at New York's City Hotel on April 14, 1807, she played a piano sonata. She played again in February and April of the following year, and she continued to appear in public on various occasions until she was twelve. Reportedly she was always warmly received.

Despite his many activities in New York, Hewitt decided to move to Boston, probably in 1812. He had visited that city earlier, having led an orchestra there at the beginning of the 1808-9 season (on September 26, 1808). This probably was the orchestra established and conducted by Gottlieb Graupner, who, as John Sullivan Dwight put it, "formed the nucleus of the first meagre combination which could be called in any sense an orchestra"[18] sometime in 1807 or 1808. In any event, the following year (1809) Catherine Graupner sang the premiere of a song of James Hewitt's, "How Cold and Piercing Blows the Wind"; so it is probable that Hewitt and the Graupners were acquainted.

In June 1810 Hewitt returned to Boston. He played in a concert on June 26, in another in August, and on October 2 he "celebrated his return to Boston" with yet another concert, in which his daughter Sophia performed a piano sonata by Pleyel.

By this time Graupner, whose activities included music publishing and a music store in Franklin Street, had organized his sixteen-man instrumental group, the Philharmonic Society, in which he himself played double bass and conducted. Formed early that year, the society began as a quasi-social group that met weekly to perform Haydn's symphonies. Hewitt, however, was not invited to play with them. Indeed, at least one writer presumes a growing rivalry between him and the Graupners, and believes that considerable coldness developed.[19]

Perhaps Hewitt presented a threat to Graupner's established rule over Boston's concert life. Or, more probably, audiences were dividing their time among a greater variety of events, and to the extent that Hewitt added to the competition he was unwelcome. In any event, by 1812 Hewitt had two regular jobs in Boston: He was organist at Trinity Church, and he was in charge of music at the Federal Street Theatre. And in 1814 Sophia again appeared in public, playing Steibelt's piano concerto, *The Storm*. Of this performance the *Repertory* reported: "It is far beyond our ability to do her ample justice....the spontaneous bursts of applause which followed are the best tribute of praise. We never witnessed a performance on the Piano Forte which could compare with it."[20]

Sometime during the next few years Sophia is thought to have moved back to New York, where she taught music at Mrs. Brenton's Boarding School. She also occasionally sang at the New York Oratorios (concerts) and often performed at the concerts of the Euterpian Society. She had studied organ with Dr. George K. Jackson, and in New York she took harp and piano lessons with Mr. Ferrand and Mr. Moran.[21]

On August 28, 1817, Sophia was back in Boston, where she performed the piano part of a Trio by Henri Joseph Taskin and Pleyel's *German Hymn* with variations for piano and flute, as well as singing a song composed by her father, "Rest Thee, Babe," and several glees (a popular form of part song). In December she appeared with the Handel and Haydn Society in New York, and the following year the society offered her the position of organist for the first time, but for some reason she refused.

The society had had considerable turnover in organists. Its first organist, Samuel Stockwell, died in the course of the second season. Sophia's teacher, Dr. Jackson, would have been a logical replacement, but he asked too high a fee when invited to play for a *Messiah* performance, and so Samuel Priestly Taylor was invited to come up from New York. In 1817 Taylor agreed to come to Boston for a fortnight to play the organ at the final four rehearsals and three concerts for the sum of $200 plus expenses, which also was a steep price. In the end Samuel Cooper became organist for the remainder of the season, at the end of which Jackson's services were again sought. Reportedly Jackson demanded full control of the society if he was to deal with it in any capacity, which meant he would have to be named president. Instead the society offered the job to Sophia Hewitt and, when she declined, reappointed Taylor.

That Sophia should have been considered an acceptable substitute for either Jackson or Taylor was high praise indeed. Jackson (1745-1822), born in Oxford, England, had been a choirboy at the Chapel Royal, sang at the Handel commemoration in London (1784), and received the degree of Doctor of Music from St. Andrews College (Scotland) in 1791. Five years later he came to America, landing in Norfolk and gradually working his way up the Atlantic coast. He settled in New York as a teacher but in September 1812 he moved to Boston. Within weeks he was made organist at the Brattle Street Church. A crusty character, the 300-pound organist was banished to western Massachusetts during the War of 1812 because, never having become an American citizen, he was officially an enemy alien and therefore not allowed to remain near Boston Harbor. In 1815 he returned to Boston and was organist successively at King's Chapel, Trinity Church, and St. Paul's, quarreling with each before moving on to the next post. Nevertheless, during these years he was regarded as Boston's outstanding musician and teacher, having written a treatise on theory and published several collections of choral music, as well as compositions of his own.[22]

Taylor, a much younger man (born in 1778), had also begun his musical career as a choirboy in England but was already playing the organ by the age of twelve. He came to America in 1806 and the following year was appointed organist of Christ Church in New York. He subsequently directed "Oratorios" (concerts) at St. Paul's and is credited as being the first to introduce Anglican chant to New York. Taylor accepted the Handel and Haydn Society's appointment in 1818, but in January 1820 he resigned; however, he considerately offered to remain until a replacement had been found.

By that time Sophia had appeared a number of times in Boston with the Philharmonic Society, which regularly assisted at the Handel and Haydn performances, as well as in recitals and other events. Her father was living in New York during 1818 and 1819,[23] and possibly other members of the family joined him there during those years. Sophia made at least three appearances in New York in 1818. But by spring of 1820 she was again living in Boston, as seen from the following advertisement in the April 1 and April 8 issues of the *Euterpiad*:[24] "Miss Hewitt begs leave to inform her friends that she teaches the Piano Forte, Harp, and Singing—Her terms may be known by applying at Mrs. Rowson's, Hollis Street, or at the Franklin Music Warehouse, No. 6 Milk Street." On April 13, 1820, Sophia performed a piano concerto in a concert for the benefit of a Mr. Granger (probably the violinist M. Granger of the Philharmonic Society), which was presented under the direction and patronage of the Philharmonic Society. At the same concert the society's leader and Sophia's future husband, Paul Louis Ostinelli, performed a piece for solo violin.[25]

Ostinelli was, according to one writer, a graduate of the Paris Conservatory. The same writer says the violinist made his Boston debut in 1818, but at least a year earlier he was already playing second violin in a thirteen-man orchestra led by Graupner at a Handel and Haydn concert. On September 7, 1818, Ostinelli gave a concert—this may have been his debut as a soloist—and at a second concert given the following week a composition of his own was performed. This second concert also featured the first performance in Boston of a work by Beethoven (the particular work is not named); by coincidence, the second such performance was of Beethoven's Piano Sonata in A-flat, op. 26, by Sophia Hewitt on February 27, 1819, and allegedly she never played Beethoven in public again.[26]

By June 1820 Sophia had been joined in Boston by at least one other Hewitt and had moved. A series of advertisements in the *Euterpiad* announced her new address at No. 32 Federal Street, "where she will be happy to instruct a Class of Scholars either on the Harp or Piano Forte."[27] On September 9 Sophia was accompanist for a recital by Mrs. French, who was at least as notable a soprano as Dr. Jackson was an organist, and on September 26 she was formally engaged as organist to the Handel and Haydn Society. About the time of her appointment, one critic noted that she was 'the leading professional pianist of Boston....Her ability as an organist may be estimated from the fact that the rehearsals and concerts of the [Apollo] Society she played the most elaborate accompaniments from copies which had been sorely neglected by the proof reader."[28]

There is some question as to how much Sophia was paid. Harold Earle Johnson, author of the society's most recent history, had said in an earlier book that her predecessor, Samuel Taylor, was paid $87.50 per quarter but that the society paid Sophia only $62.50 and later reduced this sum to $50 per quarter. However, this reduction allegedly was due to rising costs and reduced attendance at concerts, and the orchestra's fees were correspondingly reduced.[29]

If these salary cuts actually were made, it must have been during the first year of Sophia's employment. The earliest receipts of the Handel and Haydn Society still in existence date from 1819, but the first for an organist is dated November 6, 1821, signed by Sophia Hewitt, for receiving $50 for one quarter's salary as organist (July 23 to October 23, 1821). Trinity Church, an early leader in Boston's music, paid its organist $100 per year in 1800 and raised this to $200 about 1810, and "through a succession of distinguished ministrations on the organ by James Hewitt [c. 1812-16] and the thrice-eminent Dr. Jackson [c. 1817] the salary remained the same."[30] It seems unlikely that the Handel and Haydn Society's offering would be very different. Its orchestra members were paid $40 each for the entire season (some receipts signed by Louis Ostinelli attest to this figure), so that it appears quite reasonable that the organist, who had to play at weekly rehearsals as well as at special (extra) rehearsals and concerts, would be paid $200 per year. In any event, that is what Sophia was paid from July 1821 to October 30, 1830. At some time during this period Sophia also was organist at Chauncy Place Church and the Catholic Cathedral, but there is no record of when, or of how much she was paid.

Obviously she did not consider herself fully occupied, for in the *Euterpiad* during the November, December, and January following her engagement with the Handel and Haydn Society she announced her willingness to teach piano, organ, harp, and singing. Since organs were even scarcer in Boston than pianos, it is likely that either the society or one of the churches let her use its organ for this purpose.

There is no further evidence of Sophia's activities during 1821 other than salary receipts from the Handel and Haydn Society. The next year, however, was to be one of her busiest. On April 27, 1822, the *Euterpiad* announced a public benefit concert for Miss Hewitt, consisting of instrumental and vocal music presented "with the assistance of the Gentlemen of the Orchestra and many Amateurs of distinction." The editor goes on to say that she "takes rank, in her line, with the first of the profession, and as a Pianiste is confessedly among the most attractive to a general audience." Even discounting the florid turn of phrase then current and the fact that Sophia was a steady advertiser in this journal, the writer's admiration seems sincere. The next issue of the journal carried her biography—one of a series of biographies of distinguished contemporary musicians—in which her keyboard artistry is described:

Her Playing is plain sensible and that of a Gentlewoman; she neither takes by storm, nor by surprise, but she gradually wins upon the understanding, while the ear, though it never fills the senses with ecstacy, drinks in full satisfaction.[31]

The concert took place the following week to a full house, and on May 25 the *Euterpiad* carried the expected good review, expressed with becoming restraint: "The efforts of Miss Hewitt to produce an evening's entertainment worthy of the liberal patronage she experienced on the evening of the 14th were highly satisfactory." In the same issue Sophia ran an advertisement thanking her friends and the public for their patronage, and the members of the "Societies"—the plural suggests not just the Handel and Haydn Society but one or more others—and the orchestra for their liberal assistance.[32]

At least one gentleman of the orchestra must have been especially helpful and was rewarded a few months later. On a Sunday in August 1822 Sophia and Louis Ostinelli were married.[33] Sophia had taken to heart Mr. Parker's description of her virtues: "...the present instance [i.e., Miss Hewitt] proves sufficiently that the public exercise of a talent is not incompatible with the grace, the ornament, and all the virtues of domestic life."[34]

At this time the newlyweds were the stars of the younger musical world. Sophia was held in the highest regard. Ostinelli was leader of both the theater orchestra and the Philharmonic Society, and gave lessons in violin, Spanish guitar, lyre, and singing at their home at 32 Federal Street, as well as offering to accompany (on the violin) any of Sophia's pupils who should require it. The couple was in demand for recitals and soon began to travel about New England. In October they went to Portland, Maine, to perform in the church of the Reverend Dr. Nichols, the old First Parish Church of Portland, in which an organ had been installed the preceding spring. Sophia was to play the organ, and Ostinelli to lead the orchestra and introduce the solos on the violin, while members of Portland's Beethoven Society (founded in 1819) and other "Amateurs" were to assist.[35] Most likely Ostinelli had considerable conducting experience from his work as leader with the Handel and Haydn Society; although the society's original by-laws (later revised) said the president must also conduct, both chorus and orchestra tended to follow the time indicated by the leader.

The following year Sophia was the first to perform on a new English organ purchased for $550 by the South Parish Church of Augusta (Maine). The records here say that she had married "but a few months before" and that the Ostinellis were still on their wedding tour.[36] However, if they did undertake an extended tour of New England, it is not indicated in the receipts of the Handel and Haydn Society, which show no interruption of Sophia's salary. On the other hand, she may have been excused from some rehearsals during a wedding trip without losing any pay, and in fact the signature and handwriting on one receipt, dated May 1, 1823, and acknowledging payment for January 23 to April 23 of that year, differ somewhat from the others, so perhaps someone else collected her salary for her. Interestingly enough, except for two later receipts signed by Sophia (as Sophia Ostinelli), the remainder, through 1830, are signed by her husband. Obviously this was customary at the time, since married women had no legal rights, could not own property, and had no money of their own. The receipts for a number of married vocal soloists were also signed by their husbands.

On September 25, 1823, Ostinelli played in another concert at Portland, Maine, performing two pieces for violin. The writer says that at this time Ostinelli was considered without equal in America, would perform only "fine music," and tells a story to the effect that Ostinelli, when once asked to play for dancing, cut the strings of his violin rather than perform.[37] How New Englanders reacted to such a dramatic gesture is not related, but the anecdote certainly underlines the fact that Ostinelli was a serious musician, of a different breed from the country fiddlers who played dance music.

There is a gap in musical reviews of the Ostinellis for the next few years, but in 1826 the Salem *Register* tells of a last concert by Mrs. Mangeon, a well-known singer who, like many another before and since, gave a number of "last" performances toward the end of her career. On this occasion she was assisted by Mrs. Ostinelli, Miss Eberle (another singer), and several gentlemen. Mrs. Ostinelli played a Concertante on the piano and provided piano accompaniment throughout.[38]

In 1827 Sophia's father died. James Hewitt had been estranged from his wife for some years, during which he had moved about (family records reportedly mention his involvement in several southern theater companies). He was seriously ill for the last months of his life and wrote several heartrending letters to his second son, James Lang Hewitt (1807-53), then a music publisher in Boston. He died in either New York or Boston, the former seeming more likely.[39] He left a large number of original compositions—keyboard pieces, waltzes, battle pieces, rondos, teaching pieces, and, especially, marches.

By this time the Ostinellis had a child, their first and, so far as is known, their only one. It was a daughter they named Eliza, and she was born in Boston, perhaps as early as 1824 but possibly later (no record of her birth survives). Again there was no interruption of Sophia's salary from the Handel and Haydn Society; presumably she continued to perform during at least part of her pregnancy and following her confinement. No portrait or written description of Sophia survives either, but some years later a former neighbor recalls the family during this period and describes Ostinelli: "He was of middle stature or a little under, rather stout, with broad shoulders, and carried his head a trifle one side, the result of professional habit, and moved with an elastic step. His features were good and the expression of his countenance lively."[40]

On April 20, 1828, Sophia gave another benefit concert in which the Handel and Haydn Society assisted. The audience was large and enthusiastic, and the performance judged to be "of the first order."[41] Sophia's reputation seemed firmly entrenched. Nevertheless, by the late 1820s American musical tastes were becoming more sophisticated. Not only were the standards for performance rising, but formal musical training, especially when acquired in Europe, came to be greatly admired. In this respect Sophia's training, if not her execution, was found wanting. It was not "scientific," which was the current term of highest praise for a musician. At least, some members of the Handel and Haydn Society found her lacking in this regard, as did the highly influential Lowell Mason.[42] As a result, according to the society's records, their treasurer, a Mr. Coffin, who was reelected August 2, 1830, "used his influence" to have Mrs. Ostinelli replaced by a German organist named Charles Zeuner.

This move aroused the great indignation of Sophia's friends, who, in a letter signed by thirty-eight members, remonstrated against it on the ground that she had filled the situation "with ability and success for eleven years" and hence ought not to be dispossessed by "a German professor of music...whose qualifications...however scientific...cannot, we presume, be placed in competition with one who has presided so long and faithfully, and with so much satisfaction to a majority of the Society."

The protest was to no avail. The society's board narrowly declined to reconsider (by a vote of 7 to 5), and Zeuner was formally engaged on September 24, 1830. However, the board gave Sophia a double ticket (admitting two) to the society's concerts and rehearsals and offered her the free use of Boylston Hall—which was rented by the season—for a concert at the end of the season.[43]

Heinrich Christoph Zeuner (he later changed his name to Charles) certainly did have more "scientific" training than Sophia. Born in 1795 in Eisleben, Saxony, he not only could play the organ well but was said to "understand orchestral effects" and be skilled in both the theory and practice of instrumental and vocal music. In Boston, where he arrived in 1824, he was regarded as one of the best-educated musicians in America. Perhaps in part to underline the wisdom of the society's decision, Zeuner composed an organ concerto, for organ and full orchestra, which was performed at the Handel and Haydn concert of November 20, 1830.[44] Nevertheless, the society did not consider his scientific training worth more hard cash than Sophia's (or perhaps, as one present-day member of the society has suggested, Yankee instinct correctly told them they could get a foreigner for less). In any case, they paid Zeuner exactly the same salary as Sophia, $50 per quarter.[45]

Sophia did not avail herself of the board's offer of Boylston Hall, at least not immediately. About this time she may have returned to Maine, for one writer says she succeeded Charles Nolcini as organist of Portland's First Parish Church, and in turn was replaced by Mrs. Sarah H. Gilman in 1832.[46] However, the Boston City Directory lists her in 1830 and again in 1831 as having a Musical Academy, first on Norfolk Avenue and later at 3 Morton Place. There is no subsequent Boston address for Sophia, suggesting she moved away in 1832.

During the next few years Sophia continued to appear in Boston regularly, if not frequently. On February 12, 1831, she performed in a benefit for James Kendall, and on April 21, 1832, a benefit for her was held in which the Tremont Theatre orchestra took part. The summer of 1832 she toured the Canadian Maritime provinces with flutist William Hanna, and in September she was back in Boston, teaching piano, harp, and voice, even though the directory lists no residence for her at that time. On May 12, 1833, she gave still another benefit in Boston, at which the Handel and Haydn Society sang selections from Haydn's *Creation* and Beethoven's *Mount of Olives*.[47]

Little is known about her remaining years. In July 1833 in the *Eastern Argus* of Portland (Maine), she announced her return to that city and her willingness to give piano and voice lessons at her residence at B. C. Attwood's, Congress Street.[48] This ad continued to run through December. Whether she then returned to the Boston area or remained in Maine is not known, but on August 5, 1834, she appeared in Boston in a benefit for Mr. Walton, the last concert of hers for which there is a record. One writer maintains that Sophia moved to Portland because of marital difficulties, became organist at the First Parish Church there, and also taught to support herself and her daughter.[49] Indeed, the last-but-one record of Sophia dates from May 1845, when the First Parish Church paid Mme Ostinelli $31.25 as organist (a quarterly payment, perhaps). The only other record of Sophia is of her death, which occurred in Portland in 1846, when she was forty-six.

One reason for this paucity of information is that most of the official records of Portland were destroyed in a great fire in 1866. Hence there is no record of a will for Sophia, nor an obituary in the surviving local newspapers. No compositions of hers survived either, although it is safe to assume that she produced some. All organists of her time had to realize the actual chords and embellishments in music for which only a figured bass was supplied. During her early years with the Handel and Haydn Society, it published several books of vocal music with keyboard accompaniment, but if Sophia had any hand in these, she was not given credit. Most likely she also composed teaching pieces for her pupils.

Louis Ostinelli, from whom Sophia was separated for at least the last decade of her life, continued to be active in Boston until 1843. He was leader of the Tremont Theatre Orchestra, the city's outstanding ensemble, and was called on to play with many other artists, off and on from the late 1820s until 1842. He also served as orchestral leader for a number of other groups, including the Billings and Holden Society (1836-37, 1840), the Boston Academy of Music (1841-42), and the Handel and Haydn Society (1842-43).

The Ostinellis' daughter, Eliza, became a singer. Some Boston gentlemen subscribed enough money to give her the requisite European education, and on November 26, 1843, escorted by her father, Eliza sailed for Naples. In Italy she studied under several well-known teachers, and in 1847, a year after her mother's death, she married an Italian cellist, Count Alessandro Biscaccianti. Her American debut took place on December 8, 1847, at New York's Astor Place Opera House, as Amina in *La Sonnambula*. In May 1848 she sang in Boston with the Handel and Haydn Society in two concerts, and she soon became an established favorite, appearing with a number of groups from 1848 to 1850.[50] Henry Wadsworth Longfellow described her as "a fine little woman of genius, with her large eyes and coquettish ways."[51] In 1849 and again in 1851 Eliza appeared as soloist with the Boston Musical Fund Society, performing arias by Verdi, Bellini, and Donizetti. In 1852 she was in San Francisco, where she received glowing reviews and is said to have raised the staggering total of $1 million for various charities. The following year she was in Lima, Peru, and presumably she spent the next few years touring. In 1859 she returned to Boston and gave a concert at which her husband assisted on the cello. Again she was enthusiastically received. During this visit, she was quoted as saying that, contrary to widespread belief, her father (Ostinelli) was not dead but was enjoying good health and residing in Italy.[52]

Thereafter, however, Eliza's fortunes declined.[53] She returned to Europe, and in 1896 she died impoverished at the age of seventy-two, at the Rossini Foundation Home for Musicians in Paris.[54]

So far as opening a new field for women organists was concerned, Sophia Hewitt Ostinelli cannot be said to have had much influence. By 1830, when the Handel and Haydn Society fired her, the Boston Directory listed twenty-five musicians (including organists) living in the city, and seven music teachers or "professors." Although the number of women organists increased nearly as rapidly as the number of nineteenth-century American churches that acquired organs, they did not win fame or fortune. The large, rich city churches continued to hire men, and concert organists were few and far between. In 1885 one writer said that "Lady organ players are becoming noted in England," and cited two women who performed at a recent exhibition in London.[55] The implication is that they were still a rarity.

Some years earlier, however, one woman organist, Mrs. Lillian S. Frohock, achieved some renown in the concert hall, in Boston and elsewhere. From July 1864 to November 1866 she gave regular organ recitals at Boston's Music Hall, playing works by Bach, Haydn, Mozart, Schubert, Schumann, Mendelssohn, and Chopin, and alternating with such renowned organists as Benjamin J. Lang, W. Eugene Thayer, and John Knowles Paine. She reportedly gave a successful concert in Brooklyn, New York, in 1869.[56] At some point she went to study in Germany, then the Mecca of well-trained musicians, and the *Musical Record* notes her return in 1878.[57] And a decade later, a writer reminisces that Mrs. Frohock had been a remarkable organist. She played every Saturday afternoon, he recalled, at the Music Hall, and also was organist at the Arlington Street Church.[58] Still another writer of the 1860s tells of knowing two "lady organists" who earned as much as $500 per year for two Sabbath services and taught during the week, supporting themselves and their families.[59]

But in 1901 a major article about women organists and choir directors stated that, of the many hundreds of women who officiated as church organists throughout the United States, very few had ventured into the concert hall. Moreover, the important city churches persisted in hiring only men. The conservatories were then (and now) training women organists, but they did not find prominent employment.[60]

Leonard Ellinwood's excellent book on American church music, with its large appendix of biographies of church musicians, names only three women, two of them organists.[61] One is Caroline Lattin Beardsley (1860-1944), who began as a church organist at the age of twelve and in 1883 became organist and choir director of the Second (United) Congregational Church in Bridgeport, Connecticut. From 1909 on she simultaneously held this post with another at the B'nai Israel Temple in Bridgeport. An expert sight reader, she was much in demand as an accompanist. During the 1920s she organized an annual Lenten recital series at the United Church to which she brought many distinguished organists.

The other woman is Mary Cherubim Schaefer (b.1886), who was born in Wisconsin, joined the Sisters of St. Francis in 1903, and nearly two decades later (in 1922) got her bachelor of music degree from Marquette University. Meanwhile she had been organist and choir director of St. Lawrence's

Church in Milwaukee (1904-9) and director of music at St. Joseph's Convent (1909-24). She founded and directed St. Joseph's Conservatory of Music (1924-33) and its College of Music (later called Alverno College of Music). From 1938 on she devoted herself entirely to composition, especially of Masses, motets, and hymns. She also wrote a number of books, including *Liturgical Choir Book* (1939) and *The Organist's Companion* (1945).

Very few other women organists are mentioned in the literature. In 1878 Clara Conant played Schumann's Fugue on B-A-C-H in Worcester, Massachusetts, becoming the first woman organist to perform publicly in Mechanics Hall; she also had appeared in the Worcester Music Festival of 1873.[62] The *Musical Herald* of May 1886 reported a graduate organ recital at the New England Conservatory by Miss Nellie P. Nichols, who "can claim rank as an accomplished organist."[63] In the first decades of the twentieth century there were Carrie B. Wilson Adams (1859-1940), born in Ohio and later a long-time resident of Indiana, an organist, choral conductor, and composer who wrote many anthems, several cantatas, and some church operettas; Mary Chappell Fisher, a church and concert organist born in Auburn, New York, who edited the organ department for a special women's issue of *Etude Magazine* in 1909 but did not single out one woman organist of note; and Patty Stair (1869-1926) of Cleveland, a church and concert organist and composer who was the first Ohio woman to become a Fellow of the American Guild of Organists. She taught at the Cleveland Conservatory for twenty years. Her compositions include two light operas, an Intermezzo for orchestra, and some fifty songs, anthems, and instrumental works for violin, piano, and organ. Her *Berceuse* was performed by violinist Maud Powell (see Chapter 2).

In February 1925 the *Etude* reported that the woman organists of Boston had formed a Women Organ Players Club, the first of its kind. It also noted, in the following (March 1925) issue, that when the American Guild of Organists was founded, in 1896, it had only 4 women among its 145 members, but now, in 1925, of its 536 Associates 250 were women, and of 192 Fellows, 48 were women. (The first woman to become a Fellow, by passing an examination, was Gertrude Elizabeth McKellar, in 1904.) Nevertheless, not until the 1970s did the American Guild of Organists elect its first woman president.

The most distinguished American woman organist of more recent times is Catharine Crozier. Born in Oklahoma in 1914, she began to study violin, piano, and organ at an early age, making her first recital appearance as a pianist at the age of six. She was awarded a scholarship to the Eastman School of Music, where she studied organ with Harold Gleason (whom she later married), and then did graduate work with, among others, the French virtuoso Joseph Bonnet. In 1938 she was appointed to the Eastman organ faculty, and in 1953 she replaced Gleason as head of the organ department.

Following her debut before the national convention of the American Guild of Organists in 1941, she appeared in countless recitals, in concert with orchestras, and over radio and television stations throughout the United States, Canada, and Europe. From 1955 to 1969 she was organist of Knowles Memorial Chapel at Rollins College, in Florida, and then she moved to California. Throughout her long career Crozier continued to teach, both privately and at numerous American universities, and she served on the jury for numerous international organ competitions. In 1962 she was chosen, along with E. Power Biggs and Virgil Fox (the two most distinguished American men organists) to play the inaugural organ recital at Philharmonic Hall (at New York's Lincoln Center), and two years later she played a solo recital there. In 1975 she performed a concerto with orchestra at the inauguration of the organ in Lincoln Center's Alice Tully Hall, and the next year she returned to play a solo recital there. Of this last, the *New York Times* reviewer said that Crozier may be an "honored veteran among organ players" but "she can still run rings around much of her younger competition, not only in interpretive style but in sheer technique as well."[64] In 1979 she received the International Player of the Year award of the American Guild of Organists.

Of course, as church organists (who often combine organ playing with the job of choir director), women remain legion today. Since only a tiny percentage of churches are wealthy enough to pay well, the job of church organist is close to the bottom of the professional pay scale. In practically all churches, moreover, the job is part time, thus paying even less. A national survey conducted by the American Guild of Organists in 1973 revealed that, of those church organists holding a degree in organ or sacred music, unmarried men earned some 60 percent more than unmarried women ($5,300 per year versus $3,300). According to Beverly Scheibert, writing in the August 1976 issue of the *Diapason,* women still were being excluded from the larger church positions, which are generally filled through word-of-mouth advertising. And lest one think that married status was somehow relevant, married men with *no* music degree were earning substantially more than women with years of costly training ($3,800 per year on the average).

In 1909, an organist who was writing about the prejudice against women organists said—very optimistically, it now seems—that this bias was fast disappearing:

Unfortunately for the women organists, the average audience accepts as necessarily good the indifferent work of many men organists, but the women must play doubly well to be appreciated, and then—most wonderful of compliments!—"She plays as well as the men do!" It is nearly time that the ears should judge of a musical performance. They are the only competent judges.[65]

# 2 THE "LADY VIOLINISTS" AND OTHER STRING PLAYERS

"Shall ladies play the violin?" Ridiculous, said many. Unsuitable, ungraceful, unladylike. According to one late nineteenth-century writer, "The picture of an angel fiddling a solo, be it ever so divinely, is an ideal incongruity, and invokes laughter."[1] How surprising, then, to read in the highly respected John Sullivan Dwight's *Journal* in 1877 that not only is the violin "the most gentlemanly of instruments" but also "it is equally the most womanly."[2] And only a month earlier, the critic of a major Boston paper reviewed a recital of Julius Eichberg's violin pupils at the Boston Conservatory and warned, "Well might the orchestral fiddlers cry out at the sight of Mr. Eichberg's twenty-four lady violinists at work on his concerto yesterday, 'We are ruined by cheap female labor!'"[3]

From the ridiculous to the sublime took less than a half-century. In 1850 a woman violinist was a rarity in Europe as well as in America. By 1875 at least two women, Czech-born Wilma Normann-Neruda (later Lady Hallé) of England[4] and French-born Camilla Urso of the United States, were ranked with the great male virtuosos of their time—Henri Vieuxtemps, Olé Bull, and Joseph Joachim. In 1884 the *New York Sun* ran a piece called "Boston's Girl Fiddlers," which claimed that although the taste for violin playing among ladies had started only about five years earlier, at present 400 to 500 ladies were studying the violin and countless others had advanced enough to pursue the instrument on their own.[5] By the turn of the century, the American musicologist Henry Lahee said that the violin had become, in the past forty or fifty years, a fashionable instrument for ladies and "correspondingly popular as a profession for those [ladies] who are obliged to earn a living."[6] Moreover, in recitals in New York, Boston, Chicago, and other American cities with an active musical life, it is apparent that women violinists, both as soloists and as accompanists, were fairly commonplace by 1900, and a number of them were well established as violin teachers.

How did this change come about? By the mid-nineteenth century Puritan prejudices against musical instruments had been largely overcome, to be sure, and not only in church. The principal home instrument, then as today, was a keyboard instrument, first the harpsichord and later the piano. When families could afford an instrument and the leisure required to play it, girls were taught music much as they were taught embroidery or French, as one of the social graces. The accepted instruments for girls were those that could be played in a demure seated position, that is, the keyboard instruments (not including the organ, whose pedals required an ungainly posture) and the harp. Efforts to learn the violin, flute, or even the organ were frowned on as unsuitable, even as late as 1874.[7] And in 1901 George Lehmann reminisced, "Only a little more than a quarter of a century earlier...the mere thought of a refined young gentlewoman playing the violin, either in private or in public, was indeed intolerable."[8]

Public performance, of course, was scarcely encouraged. True, as early as 1824 a concert at St. Mathew's Church in New York featured Mrs. Fagan, a singer, accompanied by Mrs. Geaufreau, a harp player,[9] but it is safe to assume that neither of these ladies was considered quite respectable—though a harp, to be sure, was not so terrible.

Why the harp should have been considered appropriate, and even "feminine," is a bit of a mystery. Yet one of the earliest solo performances by a woman on a non-keyboard instrument was that of harpist Mrs. Blessner, in Boston, on November 8, 1846. Her appearance created a sensation, and she was acclaimed by a very large audience.[10] To this day, though men harpists exist, orchestras reluctant to admit women players of any other instrument will often—even as a rule—employ a woman harpist. The Fourteenth National Conference of the American Harp Society, held in Boston in 1977, had about 375 registered participants, among whom women outnumbered men five to one.[11]

Further, though the harp clearly has its limitations as a solo instrument, one of the most successful touring recitalists of her time was Maud Morgan (1864-1941), a New York harpist who made her debut in 1874 in a recital with Olé Bull and others. During the 1880s, she frequently performed together with her father, the organist George W. Morgan (1823-92). Moreover, though harpists at this time usually participated in popular concerts, Maud Morgan largely confined herself to serious music. In 1924 she celebrated her golden jubilee at Carnegie Hall in New York, marking fifty years of performance on the concert stage.

If piano and harp were the only generally acceptable instruments for women, the appearance of women violinists must have been startling indeed. Yet the *Musical Gazette* of April 26, 1847, states without further comment that "Messrs. Covert and Dodge have given several concerts in Boston and vicinity assisted by two Misses Macomber, from Maine. One of these ladies plays the violin and the other the violoncello."[12] Perhaps these performers could be dismissed as amateurs. But only five years later, in 1852, a ten-year-old girl violinist inspired both New York and Boston critics to lavish praise on her performance of standard works by De Bériot and Grétry, Paganini and Viotti. And even at ten Camilla Urso was no amateur. She had been performing before a paying public for several years, and during the remaining half-century of her career she was to inspire hundreds of other girls to take up the violin.

Who was this prodigy? Camilla Urso was born in Nantes on June 13, 1842, the oldest child and only daughter of a Sicilian flutist, Salvatore Urso, and a Portuguese singer.[13] Her father played in theater and opera orchestras, and on Sundays served as church organist. At the age of four Camilla began to go with her father to the theater when he was performing, and at not quite six she began, after a year of insistent entreaty, her first violin lessons, with the theater orchestra's concertmaster, Félix Simon. The general reaction to the child's lessons was a blend of amusement and outrage. Nevertheless, Camilla first appeared in public at a benefit concert for the widow of the orchestra's bassoonist, who had died suddenly, and she was, after initial guffaws, a resounding success.

Realizing that their daughter was unusually gifted and urged on by her teachers, Camilla's parents moved the family to Paris and tried to enroll her at the Conservatory there. At first they could not even get a foot inside the door. The normal enrollment age was ten, and no girl had ever been admitted. Finally, after nine months of delay the family could ill afford— Signor Urso could not find work in Paris, and his wife had to take in sewing and washing—the Conservatory director, the opera composer Auber, agreed to hear Camilla play. After this audition, the eight-year-old was admitted immediately.

Camilla spent three years at the Conservatory in all, but from time to time she had to make concert tours in the provinces in order to earn money. By the time she left, at ten, she had been awarded the coveted first prize in violin and offered a three-year tour of the United States under the sponsorship of an American businessman named Faugas, who offered the child $20,000 a year. Accompanied by her father and her Aunt Caroline, Camilla sailed for New York, only to find that the concerts planned for her had been undersubscribed and the businessman allegedly forced into bankruptcy (though he may have been a swindler as well).

The Ursos found themselves stranded. Fortunately, Madame Marietta Alboni, a renowned Italian contralto, was then in New York and, hearing of their plight, she kindly arranged a concert for Camilla. The glowing reviews in the influential *New York Herald* led to a Boston concert sponsored by piano manufacturer Jonas Chickering. One thing led to another, and engagements followed in New York, Philadelphia, and again Boston.

In April 1853 Camilla, not yet eleven years old, was invited to join the Germania Musical Society of Boston on a two-month tour that took them as far west as St. Louis and south through Ohio. In June, Camilla returned to New York and then joined soprano Henrietta Sontag for an eighteen-concert tour that took them down the Ohio and Mississippi rivers to New Orleans. Her touring career throughout the United States continued until 1855, when she abruptly retired to private life, settling in Nashville, Tennessee, and not playing in public (except for a few charity concerts) for the next seven years. Charles Barnard, Urso's biographer, ventures no explanation for the retirement. No doubt there was public speculation that at thirteen the child prodigy had, as so often happens, burned herself out.

But in 1862, at the age of twenty, Camilla Urso returned to New York and resumed an active career. John Dwight, who had extolled her first Boston appearances, again praised her warmly for her performance with the Boston Philharmonic under Carl Zerrahn in February 1863. "She played divinely," said Dwight, "but one wishes she would play better pieces."[14] She was playing the (then) standard violin works of Alard, Simon, Artot—composers deservedly forgotten today—as well as a Vieuxtemps concerto.

For the next two seasons Urso toured the United States and Canada, performing with all the major orchestras as well as giving recitals. In 1865 she returned to France for a year, and *Dwight's* quotes a review of her performance of the Mendelssohn Violin Concerto with Pasdeloup's renowned Paris orchestra that describes her as simply magnificent. The following season she repeated this work with the Harvard Music Association in Cambridge, leading Dwight to call her playing "a marvel of art."[15] It was this rendition that led the principal "members of the Music Profession of Boston"—among them conductors Carl Zerrahn and Benjamin J. Lang, composer John Knowles Paine, cellist Wulf Fries, and several dozen other men—to write her a signed testimonial that stated (in part): "It is not enough to say it was a wonderful performance for a woman; it was a consummate rendering, which probably few men living could improve upon."[16]

Beginning about 1868, Urso began to spend her summers in France, and at some point around this time she married a Frenchman, Frédéric Luer, who became (or already had been) director of the touring Camilla Urso Concert Company. It was customary during this period for a small group of musicians to band together and tour from city to city (and country to country), giving concerts. Usually such a group would form around one star performer, whose name was the principal drawing card, and, depending on the nature of the star's specialty (voice, piano, or violin), it would include several singers (enough to perform operatic duets, if not quartets) and one or more violinists and pianists. (If the star was a pianist, a second pianist might be engaged to accompany the singers or violinist.) The rationale of this practice was to provide variety for the programs, since it was felt that few audiences, particularly in smaller towns and rural areas, would tolerate an entire evening of violin or piano solos, or even a solo singer.

Camilla Urso herself had decided views about what constituted a proper program and the artist's duty to educate the public. In an interview published in 1874, she is quoted as saying, "It would be rash, I am certain, to give programs composed purely of classical music to audiences untutored to it...but a few choice *'morceaux'* of the masters should be introduced in every program, and this policy, which I have followed for years, will prove a beneficial result to the cause of good music and elevate the taste." And elsewhere in the same issue, the magazine printed a program Urso had arranged for the coming season:

> Kreutzer, Trio from *Night in Granada* (vocal)
>
> Chopin, Polonaise, op. 53, no. 8 (pianist Auguste Sauret)
>
> Fesca, "Winged Messengers" (song)
>
> Mendelssohn, Violin Concerto (with piano reduction of the orchestra parts)
>
> Flotow, Duet from *Stradella* (men's voices)
>
> Beethoven, Violin Sonata (not specified)
>
> Handel, "Rejoice Greatly" from *Messiah* (solo voice)
>
> Leclair, Sarabande and Tambourin for violin solo
>
> Mendelssohn, Song (not specified)
>
> Verdi, Trio from *Ernani* (vocal)[17]

Of course, for concerts in major musical centers and for performances with large orchestras, Urso's own repertory included all the major works for violin that were then being played—the concertos of Mozart, Beethoven, and Mendelssohn, Vieuxtemps and Bruch and Rubinstein, as well as the special repertory displaying the violinist's technical facility—the bravura works of Paganini, Tartini's notoriously difficult Devil's Trill Sonata, and the like. Moreover, she often premiered the works of her contemporaries, such as the violin virtuoso Joseph Joachim.

Unlike most violinists of her day, Urso would play only from memory. In January 1869, appearing with the Harvard Musical Association orchestra (a group that performed regularly from 1865 to 1880 and is considered the forerunner of the Boston Symphony), she played only the first movement of Beethoven's Violin Concerto because she had not yet memorized the rest.[18] She then played the entire work at her Testimonial Concert later the same month, and repeated it with the New York Philharmonic. Also in that month she was made an honorary member of the Philadelphia Philharmonic Society, a signal honor since the orchestra did not, of course, include a single woman violinist. Later in 1869 Urso went to San Francisco, where she put on a benefit pageant to help that city's Mercantile Library and raised a huge sum for it.

Urso was always very conscientious about her work. In 1874, an extremely busy year for her, it was reported that "every day she takes an hour for slow and patient practice in making long sustained notes, in order to obtain a strong pure tone. Then she plays scales and finger exercises of all kinds for two or more hours, and then such sonatas and other great works as she uses in her concerts. Everything is played slowly, carefully, and thoughtfully."[19] And fourteen years later, by now a veteran of thirty years on the concert stage, Urso still says, "I ought to practise even now six hours a day in order to retain my art. I never bring out a new concerto without devoting six months' study to it. First I learn the violin part and next the other parts. Then I have other parts brought in, so that the entire score is virtually filled in."[20]

That Urso found time for serious practice and study is a testament to her strong constitution, for her schedule was extremely hectic. Take, for example, the 1873–74 season, which she began as the featured star of the Worcester (Massachusetts) Music Festival in late September. In Worcester the only local performers in public concerts until about 1870 were men, but visiting women artists had been well received since the 1840s.[21] The annual Festival, which dated from 1858, was long one of the most notable in the country. In 1874 it was conducted by Carl Zerrahn, whose reign there eventually spanned thirty-one seasons (1866-90).[22] About 1870 the Festival began to feature star performers[23]—musicians of international reputation—and most of the great singers, pianists, and violinists of the latter nineteenth century performed there at one time or another (as did harpist Maud Morgan).

In 1873, at her first appearance at Worcester (she was to return in 1878), Urso performed the Mendelssohn Violin Concerto and Paganini's *Witches' Dance.*[24] In October and November her company, which at that time included several singers, and pianist Auguste Sauret (brother of violinist Emile Sauret), and her husband, director Frédéric Luer, performed in Boston a number of times. The January issue of *Dexter Smith's* monthly magazine then lists the company's forthcoming schedule: December 16, Ithaca, New York; December 18, Hudson, New York; December 19, Rondout, New York; December 22, Pittsfield, Massachusetts; December 23, Westfield, Massachusetts; December 25, Middletown, New York; December 30, Meriden, Connecticut; January 1, Newport, Rhode Island.[25] Bearing in mind that the musicians were traveling in coal-powered railroad cars in midwinter, this could hardly have been a comfortable undertaking. The next major commitment of the season was a series of four "Concerts Classiques," all in Boston, which presumably were confined to serious music. The first two took place as scheduled, on February 23 and March 9, but the last two had to be postponed for a time, because Urso had a serious accident in which her hand was injured. But by May 25 she apparently was able to play again.[26]

Subsequent seasons were at least as exhausting. In June 1879, for example, the *Musical Record* reported that in the season just ending the Camilla Urso Concert Company had appeared in more than 200 concerts in 15 states, 2 territories, and Canada. It had traveled more than 15,000 miles, beginning in Massachusetts and going west as far as Denver. The gross receipts totaled more than $100,000, the maximum for a single concert being $2,789.50.[27] That fall Urso went to California, and from there embarked on a lengthy tour of Australia and New Zealand. In Sydney alone the company gave 27 concerts at which Urso played 171 times (58 compositions by 37 different composers).[28] By late August she was back in New York and performed in various East Coast cities throughout that fall. And in December she planned yet another tour, this time a three-month junket through the South, together with singer Marie Nellini and the Mendelssohn Quintette Club, a Boston chamber group (all men).

From time to time Urso would settle down briefly to teach, notably in Boston in 1884, where she attracted violin students from all over the United States and Canada even though she was continuing to fill engagements in and around the city,[29] and in 1890, when she settled in New York City, at first intending to start her own violin school but then joining the faculty of Jeannette M. Thurber's National Conservatory of Music of America.[30]

At the fifth concert of the New York Philharmonic Society in 1893 Urso performed the premiere of a violin concerto by Edward Lassen, and the reviews indicate that her ability had not diminished with middle age. The highly respected critic H. E. Krehbiel said that the concerto was not a great work but that it was beautifully performed. "She belongs in the rank of the foremost of living artists," he said. "In her case the idea of sex, which so often obtrudes itself and modifies critical judgment, is never thought of... she does not play like either man or woman, but like a sound, noble, earnest and inspired musician."[31]

And what of Camilla Urso's own views concerning women violinists? As early as 1883 she said that women as a rule play in better tune than men, with greater expression and certainty than the average orchestral musician.[32] Nevertheless, she considered the rewards insufficient, for in an article published in 1891 she said, "My life is made up of hard work, and under the circumstances I should say to young girls who are thinking of becoming professional violinists, 'Don't.' Solo playing and teaching are all that are open to women violinists now-a-days."[33] The implication is that a soloist's life, with constant tours, was very difficult indeed, but the only alternative, and perhaps a financial necessity, was teaching. A steady orchestra job with a good organization, such as the Boston Symphony or New York Philharmonic, was infinitely preferable, because one was paid to play and need not travel constantly.

Even in 1891 the pay of a first-class violinist was good, and an orchestra position was a great opportunity. It placed the player before the public, which brought in more pupils at higher rates. The best first-violin players in Boston, for example, earned between $5,000 and $10,000 per year (in today's terms, equivalent to at least $75,000 per year). No wonder, said one writer, that women were looking forward to this field, and no wonder that men preferred to keep it to themselves![34]

A couple of years later, addressing the Woman's Musical Congress at the Chicago World's Fair of 1893, Urso said outright that women should be admitted to theater orchestras—by far the biggest employers of musicians in the United States before the days of movies, radio, and television—in order to earn a living, and because they were not hired many good women violinists were out of work.[35] (In May 1893 Urso had been appointed a member of the Advisory Council of the Women's Branch, World Auxiliary on Music.) Five years later Urso again firmly said that women should play in orchestras on an equal footing with men.[36]

As it happened, Camilla Urso herself never managed to amass enough money to retire. Indeed, during the last years of her life she occasionally appeared in vaudeville shows, and she was harshly criticized for stooping so low. But some took her part. George Lehmann said she deserved the widest sympathy for accepting such opportunities to redeem her broken fortunes,[37] and another reviewer, having seen her during a one-week engagement in Cleveland in 1900, said, "She maintains the dignity of her art perfectly in this new departure, and is literally bringing good music to the masses."[38] She died in New York on January 20, 1902.

Inspiring as Urso's example may have been to American girls of the 1870s, it is doubtful that a single woman virtuoso—even if she was Camilla Urso—could have given rise to a whole wave of girl violinists. For one thing, teachers had to be willing to take on girl students, and there is no reason to suppose that American music teachers and schools were any more ready to do so than the Paris Conservatory was in 1850. But one person did believe girls should study the violin, and as it happened he was an extremely dynamic and dedicated violin teacher. He encouraged girls to perform, individually and in groups, and they flocked to him and his school from all over the United States.

This man was Julius Eichberg, born in 1824 in Düsseldorf, Germany, educated in Germany and at the Brussels Conservatory (under Fétis and De Bériot, among others); he immigrated to the United States about 1856. By 1858 Eichberg had moved from New York to Boston, where his brother was established as a merchant, and in October of that year he became director of music at the Boston Museum, which held periodic concerts although sometimes of dubious quality. (In 1860 *Dwight's Journal* noted that it was a pity that Eichberg, who was very talented, had such a humdrum job, for he really deserved better.[39])

But Eichberg seems to have been content, for he stayed on at the Boston Museum until 1866 or so. During this time, he did a considerable amount of composing, both music for strings and a number of comic operettas. The first and most successful of these, *The Doctor of Alcantara,* was introduced at the Boston Museum in 1862. It was followed by *The Rose of Tyrol* (1863) and later *The Two Cadis* (1868). Productions of these operettas took Eichberg away from Boston from time to time, but in December 1867 he returned and was appointed concertmaster of the Boston Symphony under conductor Carl Zerrahn. This appointment was presumably of brief duration, for by 1868 Eichberg was director of the newly founded Boston Conservatory of Music, and shortly afterward he also succeeded Zerrahn as superintendent of musical instruction in the Boston public schools, two posts in which he was to exert enormous influence on music education.

In June 1868, at the first "exhibition concert" of the Boston Conservatory, Eichberg and his daughter performed a Beethoven Serenade for violin and piano, and from that time on the recitals and concerts presented by Boston Conservatory students attracted wide audiences and, considering the fact that they were, after all, student recitals, received a great deal of attention from the press.

Eichberg was an enthusiastic teacher. He wrote a very popular violin method book and saw to it that his students participated in many concerts. He also appears to have exercised his "equal rights" policies almost immediately, for by 1871 his pupils included the first of what was to be a remarkable series of talented girl violinists, young Persis Bell. In that year, at the age of thirteen, she performed at the Worcester Music Festival, where allegedly "many preferred her even to Camilla Urso."[40] She continued to appear in Boston Conservatory recital programs until February 1875. Sometime during the next few years she married another violinist, Leandro Campanari, moved with him to Cincinnati, and in 1882 returned with him to Boston, but she appears to have abandoned her own career after marriage.

In the December 1874 recital of the Boston Conservatory, Eichberg's own Concertante for four violins with piano accompaniment was performed by twenty-four violin students, nineteen boys and five girls. This occasion marked the first appearance of three young women—Lillian Chandler, Lillian Shattuck, and Lettie Launder—who formed the nucleus of the first all-female string quartet, which not surprisingly called itself the Eichberg Quartette. On February 9, 1878, together with Abbie Shepardson, they gave the first string quartet performance John Dwight had ever heard from four young ladies, with Shattuck playing first violin, Shepardson second violin, Chandler viola, and Launder violoncello. Dwight said of them, "They were well matched; tone and bowing both were excellent; and Haydn's genial *Variations on the National Hymn of Austria* were on the whole quite satisfactorily interpreted."[41] The quartet gave several other concerts that spring, and in fall 1878, at the Worcester Festival, it performed the Andante and Presto from Mendelssohn's Quartet no. 4 and also Eichberg's Concertante for four violins. This performance prompted the following remarks from the *Evening Gazette* reviewer:

A violin seems an awkward instrument for a woman, whose well formed chin was designed by nature for other purposes than to pinch down this instrument into position. Nevertheless, we cheerfully bear witness that four bright damsels in a row, all a-bowing with tuneful precision, is an interesting and even a pretty sight.[42]

Somewhat less coyly, the New York *Music Trade Review* reported, "Their playing was noticeable for its unity, precision, and fine quality of tone, careful phrasing, and intelligent conception."

More telling, perhaps, is the fact that the Eichberg Quartette was invited back, and it played in the Worcester Festival of 1880. Meanwhile the quartet had performed in New York, getting an excellent review in the *New York Times,* and in Philadelphia, where it also was favorably received. However, one of these reviews includes a cryptic comment. Said the *Musical Record* Philadelphia correspondent, writing under the pseudonym Scintillo, "We are glad to see one more avenue open to women....Those who can solace themselves and others with music ought to be content, even though deprived of the *vote.*"[43]

Julius Eichberg was very much aware of his minority stand. In an article on "Lady Violinists" published in 1879, he said that one would think that this instrument, requiring little muscular strength but great adroitness and agility, would have attracted women from the beginning, but even as late as 1842 only a few ladies took it up. Shortly after that date he, Eichberg, had as fellow students under De Bériot two young girls, Teresa and Maria Millanollo, who were fine violinists.[44] Their success, Eichberg went on, inspired others to take up the instrument, and today there are so many fine lady violinists that string orchestras will soon be recruited from this constantly increasing number.

While we take a pardonable pride in the many fine players of the male sex who sought our advice and studied with us for years, we should be remiss in failing to credit our female students with at least an equal degree of talent, industry and success. We gladly espouse the cause of women's right to play upon all the instruments of the orchestra and to bring all their fine faculties to bear upon the proper rendition of our great symphonic works.[45]

It is obvious that Eichberg gave his female pupils an extra measure of devoted attention, an early example of affirmative action, as it were. Some of them rewarded him well, pursuing active and successful careers. The Eichberg Quartet continued under that name (though dropping the terminal *te*), with somewhat different personnel, into the 1890s. In 1882 it returned to Boston after a year's study in Berlin under Joseph Joachim; at that time Launder had replaced Shepardson as second violin, and Emma Grebe was playing viola and Laura Webster cello. Their repertory now included the quartets of Mozart and Haydn, and they undertook a very successful tour that took them as far north as Nova Scotia and New Brunswick and also to the Deep South. By 1886 Launder had been replaced by another Eichberg pupil, Alice Gray Lathrop of Fredonia, New York, but the other three members remained. In 1891, the quartet, still intact, gave some highly successful concerts, playing Haydn and Beethoven in Boston, a city which then had the stiffest competition in the quartet arena (represented by the Kneisel and Adamowski quartets).

Eichberg died in 1893, but his legacy lived on. At the turn of the century Lillian Shattuck and Laura Webster both were established string teachers in Boston. Another Eichberg pupil, Edith Lynwood Winn, was not only a prominent violin teacher but became an outspoken champion of women musicians, frequently writing in national music journals.

Two of the best pupils of Eichberg's last years continued as soloists and chamber players. Olive Mead (1874-1946) had begun her studies at the age of seven with Eichberg and went on to study under Franz Kneisel. She performed as a soloist with major orchestras in the United States and Europe for about a decade. Late in 1903 she founded the Olive Mead Quartet, whose other members were Vera Fonaroff, Gladys North, and Lillian Littlehales. They performed regularly in New York City until 1917, giving two or three concerts a season. The other was Georgia Pray Lasselle, a cellist, who at first appeared largely with amateur groups like the Beethoven Club and Chromatic Club but eventually joined the American String Quartette, with which she performed until about 1910. And still another Eichberg pupil, Caroline Nichols, went on to form a highly successful all-woman orchestra (see Chapter 5).

Although none of Eichberg's pupils achieved the world renown of Camilla Urso, his work gave impetus to others. At least four other American girls born in the 1860s went on to successful careers as solo violinists. All of them went to study in Europe, and one of them, Maud Powell, achieved an eminence almost equal to that of Camilla Urso.[46]

Maud Powell[47] was born in 1868 in Peru, Illinois. She took piano lessons early and at eight or nine began studying the violin with Henry Fickensher in Aurora and then William Lewis in Chicago, soon afterward appearing as an "infant prodigy." At thirteen she was taken to Leipzig to study under

Schradieck. She next went to the Paris Conservatory, where she was the first of eighty applicants to be admitted (for only a dozen openings) and studied under Dancla. Heard by Joachim at some concerts in England, she was persuaded to complete her European studies with a year under his tutelage in Berlin. In 1885 she made her debut with the Berlin Philharmonic in Bruch's Violin Concerto in G minor. Later the same year she made her American debut, with the New York Philharmonic, followed in close succession by concerts in Brooklyn, Orange (New Jersey), and Philadelphia.[48]

One writer later (in 1901) said that Powell's success was not immediate,[49] but that would be difficult to verify from either the number of her engagements or the reviews she received. In April 1887, when she made her debut with the Boston Symphony in the Bruch Concerto in G minor, a reviewer said, "She must have frightened the first violinists just behind her....Such breadth of tone, such boldness of attack, and such clear double-stopping are seldom heard."[50] In that year Powell signed a three-year contract for an American-European tour managed by L. M. Ruben, beginning that October in New York. And in November 1890, beginning her fourth concert season under Ruben's management, another reviewer said she was without a peer of her own sex in her profession.[51]

Three months later, in February 1891, Powell performed a Violin Concerto in G minor written for her by Harry Rowe Shelley at the Brooklyn Academy of Music, and in April 1890 she appeared as soloist in Theodore Thomas's farewell concert in New York. (Thomas had been the first conductor in the United States to engage her, she had made annual tours with his orchestra since her debut, and he was now leaving New York for the Chicago Symphony.) In June 1891 it was announced that she was to perform in seventy-five concerts with Patrick S. Gilmore's band in the coming season. In 1892 she toured Germany and Austria as *the* representative American violinist with the New York Arion Society, conducted by Franz van der Stücken, and the following year she was soloist at the Columbian Exposition (World's Fair) in Chicago, the only woman among the violin soloists. On that occasion she also read a paper on "Woman and the Violin" before the Women's Musical Congress, and together with the composer she played Mrs. H. H. A. Beach's *Romance* for violin and piano (which had been dedicated to her). The following year (1894) she organized the Maud Powell String Quartet (with Joseph Kovarik, second violin, Franz Kaltenborn, viola, and Paul Meirsch, cello), which went on a worldwide tour.

By 1898, however, the quartet had disbanded and Powell resumed her solo career, traveling throughout the United States. She once made a thirty-week tour as soloist with Sousa's band, often giving two concerts per day, leading one writer to say, "She has beyond doubt given more violin recitals in this country than any other native violinist."[52] She also made extensive tours abroad. On one of these, she met H. Godfrey ("Sunny") Turner, son of an English journalist and former manager of London's Empire Theater, whom she married in 1904. Turner then became her manager,[53] and the couple settled in New York. Later that season she appeared as soloist with the Pittsburgh Orchestra, along with Fritz Kreisler.

In January 1907 a noted violin critic said that Powell was the only American woman violinist who continued to improve year after year and who was of unquestionable international note, always adding to her repertory. That season she had introduced a new concerto by Sibelius (which, in the reviewer's opinion, could not be redeemed even by her fine performance).[54] Powell was always interested in presenting new works; during her long career, she performed the American premieres of concertos by Arensky, Bruch, Dvořák, Lalo, Saint-Saëns, Sibelius, and Tchaikovsky,[55] and also introduced numerous works by American composers, among them Mrs. H. H. A. Beach (see Chapter 4), Marion Bauer (see Chapter 6), Henry Holden Huss, and others.

Powell's activity did not slow down with middle age or with marriage. Some time during the early 1900s, probably in 1904, she became the first violinist ever to make phonograph recordings, and eventually she made several dozen records for the Victor Talking Machine Company. In the 1905-6 season she made a South African tour, and until 1910 she made alternate European and American tours each year; thereafter, however, she remained in the United States. She played everywhere, not just in large cities but in small towns and at colleges and women's clubs. Though these engagements inevitably brought her smaller fees, she felt she had a mission in carrying music to those who did not ordinarily hear top-rank artists. In 1907 and again in 1910 she was soloist at the Worcester Festival. In 1911 she introduced a new concerto by Max Bruch at the Norfolk (Connecticut) Festival. She also gave at least one concert per season in New York, from 1909 to 1918, and throughout World War I she entertained troops at military camps and hospitals. In addition to all these performances, she wrote articles and made some excellent transcriptions for violin and piano. (Other than these and some arrangements, the only music Powell composed was a cadenza for the first movement of the Brahms Violin Concerto, op. 77.)

As early as 1893, in her speech before the Chicago Columbian Exposition, Powell predicted that more and more women would take advantage of the opportunities open to violinists. The concert stage, she said, was as open to them as to women singers, and the field of instruction was naturally theirs, since they usually were more sympathetic and conscientious than male teachers.[56] Fifteen years later she was invited to edit the violin department in a special issue of the *Etude* devoted to "Woman's Work in Music" (the first woman to do so in the twenty-six years of this monthly's history), and she did such an outstanding job that her material was continued in the subsequent issue.[57]

The opportunities for the talented woman violinist were now unlimited, said Powell in 1909. Girls play in quartets, in orchestras, or earn their living by solo playing (though for the latter she emphasized that not every talented violinist could expect to have a brilliant stage career). To prove her point, Powell cited the fact that the Buffalo Symphony Orchestra had had Nora Clench at its first-violin desk more than a decade earlier, that the Women's Symphony Orchestra of Los Angeles, with Cora Foy "in the concertmaster's chair," had existed for sixteen years, and that there were several "ladies' orchestras" conducted by women, as well as some all-women's string quartets. "The field of orchestral playing is open to women," she declared. "I see no reason why women should not be regularly employed if they wish to be....If women really want orchestral work, they will get it. Prejudice of the American masculine mind is easily broken down. The 'Union' accepts women members."

Powell's knowledge of this blissful state of affairs was not firsthand—she herself never applied for an orchestra job and, as a soloist, was not even required to join the musicians' union. Indeed, her statements were far from accurate. The reason for the large number of "ladies' orchestras," which are discussed more fully in Chapter 5, was that they represented practically the only opportunity for women instrumentalists to engage in orchestral and even ensemble playing.

In practical matters concerning her instrument, however, Maud Powell was reliable by the most stringent present-day standards. Her ten rules for practicing are unimpeachable: concentrate; play in tune; practice scales religiously; practice all difficult passages slowly; practice long bows slowly for good tone; memorize; keep in mind a piece's overall structure while practicing individual passages and phrases; play a piece in its entirety for any willing listener before a performance; hear other violinists and apply that kind of listening to your own work; stay enthusiastic.

Her emphasis on musicianship was equally unequivocal. She believed all violinists should be able to play the piano well enough to manage piano scores and so understand the overall structure of a composition. She advised them to think out their interpretation away from their instrument. And she believed that one should not alter the composer's meaning, especially in the classics. Thus, for example, she felt that the young Mischa Elman, genius though he was, should not take such liberties as he did with the Beethoven Violin Concerto. "Beethoven is scarcely a vehicle for emotional self-expression. Rather is this concerto an art expression of perfect line, perfect poise, perfect beauty, a noble thought...to be approached in a spirit of complete self-abnegation."[58] Powell developed this idea further in an article published about a year before her death. Discussing two schools of violin playing, the Belgian and the French, she said that the one emphasizes the virtuoso performer (sometimes at the expense of the music) and the other the music itself. In this connection, she praised the young Jascha Heifetz, whom she had then heard just once, as an exponent of the latter school.[59]

True to her wish that she play the violin up to the last minute of her life, Maud Powell died on January 8, 1920, at the age of fifty-one, while on tour.[60] Her extensive library, including violin works with notes in her own writing, was given to the Detroit Public Library. In her will she bequeathed her beloved Guadagnini violin to "the next great woman violinist." (Turner presented it to Erica Morini a year later, almost to the day, on the occasion of Morini's debut in Carnegie Hall.)[61]

A fellow student of Powell's in Leipzig in the fall of 1882 was Geraldine Morgan. In fact, meeting the two girls prompted the American composer Sidney Homer (who was in Leipzig at that time with his wife, the contralto Louise Homer) to comment later, "This was the beginning of that wonderful succession of women fiddlers. All honor to these pioneers with their great courage and great art."[62]

The same age as Maud Powell, Morgan was born in New York, the daughter of John Paul Morgan, founder of the Oberlin Conservatory of Music and organist at Old Trinity Church. Morgan studied under Leopold Damrosch in New York and then went to study with Schradieck in Leipzig, accompanied by her mother, a composer and translator of songs.[63] From Leipzig Morgan went on to study with Joachim in Berlin. She remained there for eight years and became the first American to win the German crown's Mendelssohn Prize, in 1886. She made numerous successful tours in Europe and Great Britain and became famous especially for playing Bach's Double Concerto with Joachim at the Crystal Palace Concerts in London.

In 1892 Morgan returned to the United States and made her debut with the New York Symphony in Bruch's Concerto in G minor, using a Stradivari violin lent her by Joachim. In New York she became the founder and director of the Joseph Joachim School of Violin Playing, based at Carnegie Hall, which advertised itself as the only school in America authorized by Joachim himself to teach his method. She also founded the Morgan String Quartet, which gave two quartet recitals in New York in 1901. Like the Maud Powell Quartet, it included only one woman, Morgan herself, along with Eugene Boegner, Fritz Schaeffer, and her brother Paul Morgan. The same year she married Benjamin F. Roeder, and the couple had one son born in 1906. Morgan continued in solo performances after her marriage, appearing once or twice a year in New York until about 1910. She died of cancer in New York on May 20, 1918.

Two other New York-born violinists of this era, Nettie Carpenter and Arma Senkrah, deserve mention, although both had much briefer careers than either Powell or Morgan. Nettie Carpenter, born in 1865, also went to Europe at an early age. The *Musical Herald* of December 1882 reports that "she has been playing in London with much success; she is only twelve years of age." Carpenter went on to study at the Paris Conservatory, winning the first prize for violin there in 1884, and she proceeded on a circuit of highly successful European and American tours. She toured, at various times, with the Anton Rubinstein, Josef Hofmann, Marcella Sembrich, and Adelina Patti companies, among others, and she was a favorite of the Spanish virtuoso Pablo Sarasate, with whom she studied for a short time in Spain. In 1891 she married Leo Stern, an English cellist. Her public career came to an end with this marriage, which did not last very long, and it never really was resumed.

Arma Senkrah was born in 1864 in New York as Arma Levretta Harkness, and later decided to spell her name backward on the theory that foreign-sounding names had more appeal to English-speaking audiences. (Apropos of this, the *Musical Herald* of March 1888 relates that when she asked the eminent pianist-conductor Hans von Bülow for his autograph, he wrote in her book, "Homage to Senkrah, from Snah von Wolüb.") Taking exotic pseudonyms was not a female idiosyncrasy; the English violinist John Dunn, for example, took the name Ivan Donoiewski.

Her mother took Arma to Germany at the age of nine, and three years later, at twelve, she went to Paris, where she so impressed violin professor Jean-Delphin Alard that he had her admitted to the Conservatory even though the entrance examinations had ended and the classes were filled.[64] She studied under Massart and Vieuxtemps, and also with Wieniawski at the Brussels Conservatory. In 1882 she made her debut at the Crystal Palace in London, and in 1884 and 1885 she made several tours of Europe. In the fall of 1888 several American papers announced her marriage at Weimar to a German attorney named Hoffmann and her subsequent retirement to private life. She did indeed give up her very promising career, and twelve years later, on September 4, 1900, she gave up her life as well, for at only thirty-five years of age she shot herself, allegedly because her husband was infatuated with an actress.[65]

Almost a generation younger than Senkrah and also trained in Europe was Leonora Jackson, born in Boston in 1879.[66] She studied under Joachim in Berlin and received the Mendelssohn Prize in 1897. For several years she toured Europe and then returned to New York, where her first appearance, at an open rehearsal of the New York Philharmonic on January 5, 1900, got only a lukewarm reception. W. J. Henderson said, "She elected for some inscrutable reason to play the Brahms Concerto," and went on to vilify her bad judgment in choosing this work, as well as that of the "totally inexpert women who gave her a musical education" and who presumably convinced her that she had "already scaled the Alps." But he grudgingly admitted that her bow arm was "the best I have ever seen among women," that her tone was big, and there were some good points to her phrasing. Nevertheless, he concluded that she had "no business to play the Brahms concerto for any one but a teacher."[67]

At least part of the reason for this bad review was the fact that Leonora Jackson's "imminent" return from Europe had been annouced a number of times during the previous two years but had been repeatedly postponed because of lucrative European engagements. Thus several New York papers began to talk of her as feeling "too high and mighty" to perform in her own country. Clearly this view was not universal, for Jackson proceeded to tour the United States with considerable success. In March 1900 Herbert E. Hall of the *Musical Record* said she received a most cordial welcome everywhere, and that since her New York appearance with the Philharmonic she had played with the Chicago Symphony, Cincinnati Orchestra, Pittsburgh Orchestra, again at Chicago, at Atlanta, for the Evanston (Illinois) Musical Club, Minneapolis Philharmonic Society, and St. Paul (Minnesota) Schubert Club, followed by an engagement at Springfield (Massachusetts), eight appearances with the Boston Symphony Orchestra (at Fall River, Boston, Baltimore, New York, Brooklyn, Philadelphia, and Providence)—in short, a schedule worthy of Camilla Urso! Further, said Hall, she had dates booked at Orange, Poughkeepsie, Nashville, Akron, Cleveland, Grand Rapids, Chicago, St. Louis, Cincinnati, Louisville, Ann Arbor, Detroit, "and so on west in the late spring." (On the other hand, Theodore Thomas, with whose orchestra she had played the Brahms concerto in January 1900, refused to reengage her, saying she simply was not good enough.[68] And Thomas had no prejudice against women violinists per se, having frequently employed both Urso and Powell.)

The following year, 1901, Jackson gave more than 150 concerts, and in October 1902 it was said that she had given 184 concerts that season and would go to Europe for the next two seasons to study, part of the time in Berlin. August 1903 found her in Prague, studying with Otakar Sevčik. She returned to the United States and in 1907 married a Brooklyn realtor, Michael L. McLaughlin, and retired from concert life. They were later divorced, but on October 12, 1915, she married Dr. W. Duncan McKim, a widower considerably older than she, and settled in Washington, D.C. Thereafter she gave up her career, except for occasional private recitals in her home to benefit worthy charities; she never taught. She died in 1969.

Somewhat less prominent but proficient enought to appear as soloists with major orchestras in Europe and America were a number of other American violinists from this era. Marie Nichols, born in Chicago in 1879 and trained in Europe, settled in Boston around the turn of the century and pursued a very successful career as both touring soloist and teacher. Dora Valeska Becker, born in Texas in 1872, studied in New York and then under Joachim in Berlin, making her debut with the Berlin Philharmonic in 1890. She made several successful American tours, and introduced a number of important violin works to American audiences. Maine-born Elise Fellows White (1873-1933) studied and performed in the Boston area, and also in Vienna, and made extended concert tours of the United States and Canada until the beginning of World War I. She also composed songs, violin pieces, and choral works. Jeanne Franko, born in New Orleans, studied with Vieuxtemps and gave many concerts in the New York area in the 1880s and 1890s. In 1895 she formed a trio with Celia Schiller, piano, and Harold Kronold, cello. She married Hugo Kraemer and continued to teach and perform occasionally. She died in 1940 at the age of eighty-five, having outlived her two violinist brothers, Sam and Nahan, and her two sisters, Rachel and Thelma (the latter was the mother of bandmaster Edwin Franko Goldman).

As doors began to open for "lady violinists," women also became attracted to the cello, though never to the extent that they embraced the violin. The principal cello teachers of America during the late nineteenth century were both based in Boston, Joseph Adamowski of the Adamowski Quartet and August Suck, cellist with the Boston Theatre and longtime member of the Boston Symphony. Suck claimed to be the first to teach the cello to girls in the United States, but in view of Eichberg's record this claim seems a little belated. The Eichberg Quartet had as its cellist Lettie Launder and later Laura Webster, and Georgia Pray Lasselle also made a name for herself. In January 1889 the *Etude* announced that Lucy Campbell of Boston had been awarded a share of the Mendelssohn Prize at the Berlin Royal Conservatory, the first cellist of either sex ever so honored.

A decade or so later a Swiss cello virtuoso, Elsa Ruegger, came to the United States on a tour that took her to New York, Pittsburgh, Cincinnati, Detroit, Cleveland, and St. Louis. She played concertos with various large orchestras, and also sonatas, receiving universally good reviews. Another European cellist, May Mukle of England, performed the Saint-Saens Cello Concerto at the 1908 Worcester Festival. Although neither woman had the international stature of an Urso, both presumably inspired young American students who heard them.

Three women cellists of some note were Beatrice Harrison and Naomi Hewitt, who were known in New York and Boston between about 1913 and 1935, and Canadian-born Zara Nelsova, who toured for eighteen years with her sisters Anna and Ida as the Canadian Trio, studied with Pablo Casals, and moved permanently to the United States in 1953. In 1979 Nelsova gave a New York recital that showed she had, after four decades on the concert stage, lost none of her verve or artistry. One other cellist of international reputation was the young Englishwoman Jacqueline du Pré, who, after a brilliant beginning in the 1960s, contracted multiple sclerosis while in her late twenties and was forced to stop performing.

As chamber musicians, however, women cellists and violinists have done somewhat better. The reasons are obvious. A solo career requires an extraordinary talent and also a certain charisma that will continue to attract audiences. Violin and cello recitals have never been as popular as piano recitals, and to appear as soloist with an orchestra sets up a series of further requirements, not the least of which is enough money to pay a whole orchestra. Chamber music, on the other hand, can satisfy an audience's desire for a group of performers and at the same time lessens the need for a single performer to satisfy in every respect. On the other hand, the chamber literature requires greater musical sophistication from the audience.

In the course of the later nineteenth century women string and keyboard players did perform in chamber ensembles, and not only in the large eastern cities. As early as 1885 a Mrs. Trowbridge of Detroit and her daughters Mary and Clara, all three violinists, gave several concerts in Ohio, according to the Ohio correspondent of an important music journal.[69] In April 1888 Baylor College, in Belton, Texas, had a new all-female string quartet directed by Professor G. H. Rowe (whose wife was the quartet's cellist), and this ensemble was said to be the first of its kind in Texas.[70]

It could be argued, perhaps, that these were basically amateur or at best only semiprofessional groups. Nevertheless, by the late 1890s American conservatories and music schools (of which there were five large ones in Chicago alone)[71] were turning out enough violinists to create a demand for performance opportunities, and indeed Chicago then had three resident professional string quartets (all male). Some of the all-women's chamber ensembles that had succeeded the Eichberg Quartet by the turn of the century were the Scharwenka Trio (Jennie Ladd Parmelee, violin; Ida Mead Holden, cello; Elma Horne, piano), which performed in Boston; the American String Quartette, which included Georgia Pray as cellist and survived, with varying personnel, until about World War I; the Carolyn Belcher Quartet (Carolyn Belcher and Anna Eichhorn, violins; Sara Corbett, viola; Charlotte White, cello), also of Boston, which performed around the same period; the New York Ladies Trio (Miss Pilat of Austria, violin; Flavie Van den Hende, cello; Hilda Newman, piano); and in the Midwest, the Mrs. Hahn String Quartet (Mrs. Adolf Hahn[72] and Mary Louise Wright, violins; Ada Parke, viola; Nina Parke, cello), which gave its first concert in November 1900 in Home City, Ohio, and the Chicago Ladies Trio (Catherine Hall Thatcher, violin; Elizabeth Pickens, cello; Anna Weiss, piano).

Also prominent in New York from about 1910 to 1917 were the Edith Rubel Trio and the Gisela Weber Trio. In the 1920s New York had the

Marianne Kneisel String Quartet (Marianne Kneisel and Elizabeth Worth, violins; Lillian Fuchs, viola; Phyllis Kraeuter, cello), organized by the daughter of Boston Symphony concertmaster and founder of an important early string quartet (the Franz Kneisel Quartet, 1886–1917), and the Durrell String Quartet (Josephine Durrell and Edith Robound, violins; Anna Golden, viola; Mildred Ridley, cello).

From the time that Boston's all-male Beethoven Club (consisting of two violins, viola, bass, and flute) admitted cellist Georgia Pray in 1890,[73] women occasionally joined all-male chamber groups. Both Maud Powell and Olive Mead had founded their own quartets, in which each was the only woman. But there were others. In the late 1890s Chicago had the Studio Trio (Miss Marion Carpenter, violin; Mr. Day Williams, cello; Mrs. Annette H. Jones, piano) and Boston the Currier String Quartet (Frank Currier and Marie Schumacher, violins; Bertram Currier, viola; Charlotte White, cello). In New York Adele Margulies, a pianist and prominent teacher, formed the Margulies Trio (with Leopold Lichtenberg and Leo Schulz), which gave concerts every season from about 1905 to 1918, and in the 1920s there was the Musical Art Quartet, all men except for cellist Marie Roemaet-Rosanoff; the Boston Quintet, with cellist Alma LaPalme (a pupil of Charlotte White's); and the Curtis Quartet, made up of faculty members from the Curtis Institute, in 1929 all men except for first violinist Lea Luboshutz (1885–1965; a former pupil of Eugene Ysaÿe's and sometime soloist with leading orchestras).

During the course of the mid-twentieth century, however, the gains made by women violinists between 1870 and 1920 appeared to be largely lost. Up to the late 1920s Canadian-born Kathleen Parlow (1890–1963), a pupil of Leopold Auer's whom the Russian master considered a "genius," was still touring the United States and Canada, as she had since 1910, but from 1929 on she devoted herself almost entirely to teaching.[74] And there was Ruth Pierce Posselt, born in 1914 in Medford, Massachusetts, who appeared for some years as a child prodigy and then returned to the concert stage in the early 1930s. She won the Schubert Memorial Prize in 1932 and undertook a European tour that year, but despite enthusiastic reviews her appearances after this were relatively rare. (She married Richard Burgin, who was concertmaster of the Boston Symphony from 1920 to 1962, and appeared with him at least once in the orchestra of the Opera Company of Boston in 1979.)

In the 1930s and 1940s, however, with only one exception—Erica Morini—there were virtually no women violinists of international renown on the concert stage, and fewer and fewer appeared in prominent chamber groups. Although World War I had created some demand for women string players to replace men away at war, they all gave way to the returning men, and World II did not seem to have the same impact.[75]

Economics certainly must have had something to do with it, but the question of women's versus men's earnings has long been a murky one. In 1900, for example, violin teacher Edith Lynwood Winn maintained that female pianists and violinists received as much compensation for their services as men, and therefore men regarded women performers as economic rivals.[76] Only eight years later—too short a time for a total turn-about—pianist Olga Samaroff held that she could get as many or more engagements as a male performer simply because her fee was lower than a man's.[77]

Whatever the real truth is—and the American Federation of Musicians vehemently denies any occurrences of discrimination, financial or other-wise, against its members on account of sex—it is only since the late 1960s that women have resurfaced in prominent professional chamber ensembles (string quartets, trios, and chamber orchestras). By the mid-1970s the personnel of both Alexander Schneider's Brandenburg Ensemble and the Chamber Music Society of Lincoln Center was nearly half women. Of the major American string quartets of the late 1970s, only the Composers Quartet (half and half), the Cleveland Quartet (one woman), and the Primavera Quartet (all women, winners of the 1977 Naumburg Chamber Music Award) were bucking the trend. In the mid-1970s at least four all-women's trios were formed, the New York Lyric Arts Trio (Mary Blankstein, violin; Wendy Brennan, cello; Gena Raps, piano); the Caecilian Trio (Sally O'Reilly, violin; Beverly Lauridsen, cello; Annie Petit, piano); the Walden Trio (Gwyndolyn Mansfield, flute; Maxine Neuman, cello; Joan Stein, piano); and the Jubal Trio (Lucy Shelton, soprano; Sue Ann Kahn, flute; Susan Jolles, harp), winner of the 1976 Naumburg Foundation Chamber Music Award.

Some women musicians deny that economics has anything to do with it. Erica Morini, the only woman violinist of her generation to pursue a long-term successful career as a soloist, believed that most women "lack the concentration, the will power, and the willingness to sacrifice everything to art which is absolutely necessary if one is to become a fine artist." Although just as many women as men are born with a great talent for music, maintained Morini, most lack the single-minded drive and determination to bring their talent to fulfillment.[78]

Morini herself, born in Vienna in 1904, first studied the violin with her father and then with Otokar Sevčik at the Vienna Conservatory. She made her debut at Leipzig under Artur Nikisch's baton, and she later performed with Felix Weingartner and other famous conductors. She made her American debut at Carnegie Hall in January 1921, and critics said this seventeen-year-old girl would take the place of Maud Powell, who had died almost exactly a year earlier. Indeed, in May 1921 Powell's husband lent (or gave) Morini his wife's valuable Guadagnini violin for her American[79] tour (but see note 61). Thereafter Morini toured for several years in the United States, returned to Europe for a time, and then settled permanently in the United States. She married Felice Siracusano, but the couple had no children, Morini believing it impossible to combine a family with her career. From the 1960s on she devoted herself more and more to teaching. In 1976, at seventy-two, she gave a New York recital for the first time in ten years, and reviewers praised her excellent but unobtrusive technique and consistently beautiful tone; one called her recital one of the most musically satisfying events of the season.[80]

By the mid-1970s a new generation of women string players had emerged. Texas-born violist Karen Phillips was performing widely in solo recitals and with major orchestras, and the literature for her instrument was being augmented by a number of compositions written especially for her. (See also Chapter 10.) Korean-born Kyung-Wha Chung, who shared the Leventritt violin prize with Pinchas Zukerman in 1967, was carving out a career as a soloist. Rumanian-born and Israeli-bred Miriam Fried became, in 1971, the first woman to win the prestigious Queen Elisabeth of Belgium Competition and subsequently was performing with major orchestras and in recitals all over North America and Europe. Ani Kavafian, for several years a member of the Chamber Music Society of Lincoln Center, was a winner in 1977 of the Avery Fisher Award, entitling her to a concert with the New York Philharmonic, a cash award of $1,000, and six engagements with other American orchestras.[81] Her younger sister, Ida, also a violinist, made her debut as a recitalist in New York in 1978 and was warmly received.[82] Nevertheless, the men violinists of the same generation—Pinchas Zukerman and Itzakh Perlman, among others—still were performing far more frequently on the concert circuit, as had been (and still was) the case with the men of Morini's generation (Jascha Heifetz, Isaac Stern, et al.).

The tradition of the "lady violinist"—a label, it is safe to say, all of these young women would reject—was not totally dead, but it was considerably attenuated. Of course, by far the largest number of opportunities for string players is in the orchestra, but the road there, as will be seen in Chapters 5 and 10, has also been a rocky one.

# 3 SEATED AT THE KEYBOARD

Sit in a simple, graceful, unconstrained posture. Never turn up the eyes or swing about the body; the expression you mean to give will never be understood by those foolish motions....However loud you wish to be, never thump....Aim more at pleasing than at astonishing....Never bore people with ugly music merely because it is the work of some famous composer, and do not let the pieces you perform...be too long.

*Harper's Magazine,* September 1851[1]

The preceding advice, addressed to "Musical Misses," indicates without a doubt that playing the piano was one of the social graces of accomplished young ladies of the mid-nineteenth century. Women had been playing keyboard instruments for a very long time. The frontispiece of the earliest and most important printed collection of English virginal (harpsichord) music, *Parthenia,* dating from 1612 and 1613, pictures a young woman at the keyboard, and in the eighteenth century, as harpsichord and clavichord were replaced by the piano, women moved quite naturally to it.

As with the voice and other instruments, public performance was another matter. In the Puritan mind it was too closely allied to theatrical productions and therefore sinful. At the very least a musician appearing in public was no more respectable than an actor or actress. However, perhaps because children were not considered "people," this stricture apparently did not apply to them. What was not appropriate for a lady, even a young one, might still be countenanced in a little girl. Whatever the reason, the earliest public keyboard performances by women in the United States were those of child prodigies, or at least, of exceptionally gifted children.

Sophia Hewitt had made her debut in New York in 1807 at the age of seven, and she continued to play in public throughout her childhood. She was only eighteen and an experienced performer when the Handel and Haydn Society first offered her the job of organist. Another very young keyboard player of the early 1800s in Boston was the little daughter of the Russian consul, Mlle Eustaphiève (later Mme Peruzzi), whose father played in Graupner's band.

One of the first recorded keyboard performances by a young woman was a subscription concert advertised in the Boston *Columbian Centinel* of November 21, 1792, which included "A Sonata on the Piano Forte by a Young Lady."² A few years later came Miss M. A. Wrighten's performance of the much abused *Battle of Prague* (the most popular of the so-called battle pieces, in which the music imitates the sounds of battle) in Boston in 1795.³ This was a year after Elisabeth von Hagen had moved to Boston from New York and offered to teach piano, harpsichord, organ, and voice to young ladies.⁴

Other than Sophia Hewitt's appearances as both a soloist and an accompanist during her years in Boston, public performances by women pianists were rare until about 1850. Several accounts survive of a concert at New York City Hall on May 10, 1830, by the Musical Fund Society, at which Miss Sterling played Herz's *Grand Variations on "Ma Fanchette est charmante"*; the *Mercantile Adviser,* lavish to the point of bombast, said that "the keys of her piano seemed gifted with vocal powers." Miss Sterling apparently continued to perform this piece, along with Moscheles' *The Fall of Paris* (another battle piece) during the next five years.⁵

In the 1840s two other young women pianists attracted attention. One was Josephine Bramson, whose farewell concert at Boston's Melodeon got a rave review in the *Evening Transcript* of January 3, 1846. The other was a seventeen-year-old Englishwoman, Jane Sloman, who had moved with her parents to New York in 1839 and gave eight very successful concerts in Boston in November and December 1841 (she returned in 1842 and 1844 as well).⁶

Presumably some other women pianists performed for the American public between 1800 and 1850. However, none could be classed as a virtuoso performer of the kind that increasingly dominated the concert scene in Europe. By 1836 Clara Wieck (Schumann) had been named Imperial Chamber Virtuoso by the Hapsburg court, and Marie Pleyel (1811–75) had long since created a sensation in Belgium, Austria, Germany, and Russia. Of comparable caliber (both in ability and popularity) was the first American piano virtuoso, Louis Moreau Gottschalk (1829–69), who, after a few years in Europe, made his first triumphant tour of the United States in the 1853-54 season. By then the American public was ready to embrace a brilliant soloist, and if the music performed tended to sacrifice more lasting qualities for flamboyancy and technical bravura, that disturbed American audiences no more than it did the Europeans who thronged to hear Liszt perform the works of Moscheles and Herz and the like, with only an occasional Beethoven sonata sandwiched in.⁷

The American public got its wish in 1862 with the arrival of an eight-year-old Venezuelan girl, Teresa Carreño, who for the next half-century was to thrill audiences all over the world. A grandniece of Simon Bolívar and the daughter of a minister of finance ousted by revolution, Teresa received her first lessons from her musical father.[8] She made her New York debut on November 25, 1862, at Irving Hall, on a program with violinist Theodore Thomas (better remembered for his fame as a conductor) and others. She played a Rondo by Hummel (together with a string quintet) and pieces by Thalberg and Gottschalk. Gottschalk, when he heard her play, said he would teach her whenever he came to New York (his heavy touring schedule did not permit regular lessons). During the next two months, she gave five more concerts, and then made her Boston debut on January 2, 1863. It was followed by some twenty concerts in the Boston area, whereupon Carl Zerrahn invited her to play Mendelssohn's *Capriccio brillante* with the Boston Philharmonic Society orchestra. She accepted, although she had never seen the work, and learned it in three days. The critics were ecstatic in their praise—all except John Sullivan Dwight, who admitted that he was not partial to child prodigies but allowed that this one might prove interesting.

In March the Carreños went to Cuba, and in April Teresa made her Havana debut. She returned to the United States in the fall. Soon after she played for President Lincoln at the White House, for an encore improvising on the President's favorite song, "Listen to the Mockingbird."[9] (She was to return to the White House fifty-five years later, to play for President Woodrow Wilson.) On December 22, 1863, Teresa celebrated her tenth birthday in Boston by giving a concert with Benjamin J. Lang (noted pianist, organist, conductor, and teacher; see Chapter 4), where she played two of her own compositions, *Impromptu* and *La Emilia Danza.*

For the next couple of years Teresa remained in the United States, but in March 1866 she and her family sailed for Liverpool, to pursue her career in Europe. In May she went to Paris and, now a ripe twelve-year-old, made her debut at the Salle Erard and became a protégée of the influential Madame Erard herself. Teresa met Rossini, who gave her letters of recommendation, and also Liszt, who offered to teach her free of charge in Rome (an offer she did not accept).

Among other musicians Teresa met during this period were the composers Gounod, Auber, and Berlioz, the publisher M. Heugel, who began to publish some of the compositions she somehow found time to produce, and the singer Adelina Patti. In part through Patti's influence, Teresa at fourteen began to study voice. For the summer of 1868 she returned to London, where Anton Rubinstein heard her play and offered to teach her. In later years she always said the deepest influences on her career had been Gottschalk, who had first introduced her to classical music; Liszt, who had told her to cultivate her own individuality and not follow blindly the paths of others;[10] and Rubinstein, who called her "his sunshine" and became, she felt, her true guide and mentor.[11]

Her tours as a teenager came under the management of the great impresario Maurice Strakosch. When the Franco-Prussian War broke out, Teresa was stranded in London, unable to return to France. Needing work, she turned to Strakosch's bitter rival, Colonel Mapleson, who booked her for an extensive tour of England as well as for the famous London Promenade Concerts (at that time conducted by Sir Arthur Sullivan). It was during this period, in 1872, that Teresa was suddenly called on to make an impromptu opera debut in Edinburgh. The singer who was to play Queen Marguerite in Meyerbeer's *Les Huguénots* fell ill, and Teresa quickly had to learn this difficult part and replace her.

In the fall of 1872 Carreño began an extensive American tour (as pianist) with the singer Carlotta Patti (Adelina's sister), the aging tenor Mario, and violinist Emile Sauret. The company went to New York, Canada, Boston, and Charleston. And the following year (1873), at the age of nineteen, she married Sauret and settled in London, where their child, Emilita, was born on March 23, 1874. In June the young couple gave their first joint concert, and in fall she and her husband began another American tour, leaving the baby in London with a Mrs. Bischoff. This tour took the Saurets as far as the Pacific coast and ended in New York. At its end the marriage was falling apart. Sauret returned to England alone, and Teresa, remaining in America, agreed to let Mrs. Bischoff, by now very attached to Emilita, adopt her child.

Too downhearted to begin another tour, Carreño went to Boston and looked up an old friend, the voice teacher Hermine Rudersdorff, who hired her as an accompanist and agreed to give her voice lessons. After a year, on February 25, 1876, Carreño made her formal operatic debut as Zerlina in Mozart's *Don Giovanni* at the New York Academy of Music. Several New York and Boston performances followed, and the reviews were quite favorable. But she now decided that her voice was not good enough after all and she would return to the piano.

The part of Don Giovanni in Carreño's debut was sung by the Italian baritone Giovanni Tagliapetra, who soon afterward became her second husband. The couple settled in the New York suburb of New Rochelle and had three children (Lulu, 1878-81; Teresita, born 1882; and Giovanni, born 1885). Between babies Carreño performed and toured. Although she would have been happy to retire at this point, her husband turned out to be a compulsive gambler (as well as a drinker and philanderer), and she had to function as the family's principal financial support.[12]

On one of her tours, in the spring of 1883, with conductor Leopold Damrosch, Carreño introduced Grieg's Piano Concerto, a work with which she was associated for the rest of her career and which she helped make popular in America. The following year she gave the premiere performance of Edward MacDowell's second *Suite Moderne* in a concert in Chicago.[13] MacDowell had come to Carreño for piano lessons in 1876, when he was only fourteen, and she became his lifelong friend, encouraging his compositions and performing them frequently all over the world. He later dedicated his Concerto in D minor to her.

Carreño herself also continued to compose. The *Teresita Waltz,* written shortly after her third daughter's birth, became one of her regular encore pieces, and the sheet music for it had a steady sale in both America and Europe for many years. She also wrote a serenade, waltzes, fantasies, ballades, and other piano pieces, and a hymn for the Bolívar Centennial (of Venezuela) in 1883.

Carreño's schedule during the 1880s was very full. She played at the Worcester Festival four times (1880, 1885, 1887, 1888), a record number of appearances for a single artist. She toured Canada and the United States a number of times, both with and without her husband. In 1885 she returned to Venezuela, where she was received as a national heroine. She was invited to return the following year, not only as a pianist but as the organizer and director of an Italian opera company. She left most of the organizational details of this assignment to her husband, who apparently lacked the talent for it, for when the Teresa Carreño Opera Company opened its season in Caracas, it was immediately beset with difficulties. The public became hostile to the company, the conductor and assistant conductor both walked out, and for some weeks Carreño herself took up the baton and conducted performances of *La Favorita, La Sonnambula,* and *Lucia de Lammermoor.* This was her first and last experience on the podium. It also signaled an irreparable rift in her second marriage.

Upon her return to the United States Carreño continued to perform widely, her popularity undiminished. The pyrotechnical displays of her earlier years were by now giving way to a more balanced musical approach. Thus one respected critic said of her, in January 1888, "Her touch is inclined to be a little too percussive but the eminently musical qualities of her style overbalance this. Earlier in her career she sacrificed much for mere effect, but she plays now more soberly and certainly more intellectually."[14]

Nevertheless, Carreño herself was not wholly satisfied. In 1889, with her second marriage ended, she decided to go to Germany and test her mettle there. Fearful that the Germans would not appreciate her kind of playing, Carreño nervously planned for her German debut with the Berlin Philharmonic on November 18, 1889. She played the Grieg Concerto with the orchestra, and then played alone a Liszt polonaise and Schumann's twelve *Symphonic Etudes.* Despite her fears, she was an instant success. Critics raved over her "unconventional" playing and her dramatic temperament. Hans von Bülow, the great German pianist who was turning more and more to conducting and usually had little use for women as musicians, said she was the most interesting player of the present day. There could be no higher praise.

For the next seven years Carreño made Germany her home base, from which she toured all over Europe. In May 1891 she concluded a three-month tour in which she had performed nearly every night, leading one writer to say, "Only an American woman could do such an enormous amount of work;...and everywhere is tremendously successful."[15] The Budapest papers called her the "female Rubinstein." Her passionate interpretations gave rise to a number of other sobriquets, chief among them "Valkyrie of the Keyboard" and "Lioness of the Piano."

The principal other pianist of Europe at this time was a Scottish-born pupil of Liszt's, Eugene D'Albert, and in 1891 the two virtuosos finally met for the first time. Eleven years her junior, D'Albert was a small man, whereas Carreño was generally described as imposingly statuesque. These differences apparently did not matter, and by fall of 1891 they had set up housekeeping together. They settled in Dresden, Carreño brought her two children from France to join them, and in 1892 she and D'Albert were married. In September 1892 their first child, Eugenia, was born.

D'Albert was a splendid pianist, but he believed himself to have an even greater vocation for composing. Carreño encouraged him, and she gave the premiere of his second piano concerto, under his baton. Unfortunately, the critics praised her playing but not the concerto or its composer. Repeat performances of the work had the same result, and D'Albert, never easy to get along with, accused her of undermining him. In September 1894 their second daughter, Hertha, was born, but they were divorced soon afterward. Carreño installed her four children in a house on the Kurfürstendamm in Berlin, and to support them she kept on performing. During the next season, she gave some seventy concerts, traveling throughout Europe, and she also returned to composing; she completed her String Quartet in B, which was quite warmly received. She continued with her strenuous schedule, touring during the concert season and spending summers with the children in the mountains. She also became more serious about teaching. She developed a fine set of technical exercises, which, however, were never published. A number of her articles appeared in music journals around this time, and she published one small book on how to use the pedals to achieve different tone colors.[16]

In January 1897 Carreño began a five-month concert tour of the United States, opening with the New York Philharmonic in Rubinstein's Concerto in D minor and moving on to Chicago, Boston, and Milwaukee. At forty-three Carreño was a mature artist. She still could thrill audiences with her fiery interpretations of Romantic music—Chopin and Liszt and, of course, Grieg—but she also could play Mozart and Beethoven properly. Indeed, von Bülow said she was the only woman pianist who could play Beethoven well; she could play intelligently but also had the requisite virtuoso technique and brilliance.[17] In April 1897 the *Musical Record* reported that her tour had been an enormous success. She was compared to Paderewski and called the "goddess of the pianoforte." She in turn advised young Americans to exhaust all the possibilities of study at home before going to complete their musical education abroad.

In 1898 Carreño was back in Germany with her children. In that year, always a champion of contemporary American music, she gave the German premiere of Mrs. H. H. A. Beach's Violin Sonata in Leipzig (with the first violinist of the Halir Quartet). In 1899 and again in 1900 she returned for two more big tours of the United States. On these she frequently combined her appearances with orchestras—in Chicago, Cincinnati, Pittsburgh, Cleveland, Boston—with separate solo recitals, so that she was often giving four or five performances in one city within a few days. She was still performing enormous programs. On November 27, 1900, for example, a program of hers in New York included works by Mozart, Beethoven, Chopin, and Schumann, among others. That same month she played Tchaikovsky's Concerto in B-flat with the New York Philharmonic, prompting the prominent New York critic W. J. Henderson to call her "the Cleopatra of the keyboard. She has more temperament than the other two pianists [Dohnhányi and Gabrilowitsch] put together," although, he went on to say, "she is not always discreet. But it is hard for flaming temperaments always to be discreet, as readers of biographies of musicians well know."[18]

And Carreño bore him out. On June 30, 1902, she scandalized the public yet again, not only embarking on her fourth marriage but choosing her erstwhile brother-in-law, Arturo Tagliapetra, brother of Giovanni (who had died some years earlier). But this marriage proved to be a very happy one.

Now in her fifties and presumably no longer needing the income so badly, Carreño nevertheless continued to tour all over the world. In 1906-7 she undertook a lengthy journey to Australia, New Zealand, and across the United States (where Richard Aldrich of the New York Times said, in January 1908, that she still abounded with vitality and was especially fine in performing the Schumann Symphonic Etudes and a Brahms Rhapsody). In 1909 she began another two-year tour of the United States, New Zealand, Australia, and South Africa. In January 1913 she was in London to perform MacDowell's Celtic Sonata in celebration of the jubilee of her first public appearance. And in 1913-14 she was again in America.

Carreño continued to tour Europe throughout much of World War I and attracted huge audiences, but late in 1916 she gave up her home in Berlin for good and moved with Arturo to New York (both were U.S. citizens). She intended at last to cut down her concert schedule—in 1916 alone she had given seventy-two concerts in Europe, traveling from Rumania to Spain—and devote herself more to teaching. But in the spring of 1917 she was on tour again, this time in Cuba. The tour was interrupted by her illness, and in June she returned with her husband to New York. Within a few weeks she was dead. Some twenty years later, her ashes were returned to Venezuela, where a memorial concert was given in her honor.

Her funeral in New York was attended by many famous musicians, and she was widely eulogized. One obituary notice seemed to say it all: She was first and foremost a pianist, the greatest of her sex, with a brilliant technique, always good taste, and Latin fire. As a person, she was characterized by great kindliness, charm, and common sense. In sum, Carreño had been a great artist and a great woman.[19]

Actually, there is no way of knowing how good a pianist Carreño was by modern standards. She left no recordings. She did at one time make some music rolls for player pianos, but these she later disowned. Apart from the surviving reviews and statements from other musicians, from which we still must discount the inflated bombast current at the time, we are left only with her advice to other pianists. In one article published shortly before her death, Carreño told young pianists to avoid commercial motives; they could never compete with player pianos in technique, so they must emphasize beauty of expression. To accomplish this, a relaxed body was essential above all. She recalled that Edward MacDowell, when he had first come to her as a boy, was very stiff, and she had tried to help him relax his arms and hands.

Later, some of Carreño's former pupils recalled some quite specific advice she had given. One remembered that Carreño always told her to press the tone out of the piano, not to hit the notes but to squeeze them. Use a relaxed hand and wrist, she said, and rely on the weight of the whole arm for power.[20] Another recalled her emphasis on controlled relaxation (not just letting go), and her opposition to keyboard mannerisms.[21] This advice is as sound today as it was then.

Although Carreño was less outspoken than Camilla Urso regarding the opportunities for women performers, her enormous success undoubtedly had an effect on other young women. After the Civil War the appearance of women pianists in public became less of a rarity in America. The concerts of the Boston Philharmonic Society, given regularly from 1844 to 1863, frequently included women singers, and in 1860 they featured their first woman pianist, twenty-year-old Mary Fay, as soloist in the Mendelssohn G-minor Concerto and two movements of Chopin's Concerto in E minor. Fay returned in 1862 to play in three more concerts with the society. The following year, on April 11, 1863, Eliza Josselyn made her debut at a Boston Philharmonic concert, playing the Mendelssohn concerto and a Liszt transcription of *Rigoletto*.

The New York Philharmonic Society first employed a woman pianist, Mme Eugenie de Rhoade (or Roode), in 1856, and in 1857 Mme J. Graever performed with the society no fewer than three times. Thereafter, no woman instrumentalist appeared until after the Civil War, when Alide Topp played twice in 1867, Anna Mehlig twice and Mrs. Davison once in 1869, and Marie Krebs once in 1870.

Topp, Mehlig, and Krebs were German, and Krebs in particular achieved great renown in Europe. All three pianists were admired by conductor

Theodore Thomas, who, when he took his orchestra on tour, brought each of them along at various times between 1870 and 1874, to perform concertos with the orchestra and also solo works. Also during this period, the Worcester Festival featured its first woman pianist, Flora Alger, in 1874.

One other European, London-born Madeleine Schiller, was active around this time. After a brilliant debut at the Gewandhaus in Leipzig, she married Marcus Elmer Bennett of Boston and lived in the United States from 1873 on. She, too, frequently played under Theodore Thomas in New York through the 1870s and early 1880s.

By 1880, judging from contemporary journals such as the *Musical Herald,* local concerts frequently included a woman pianist, and not just to accompany singers (accompanists were listed separately) but to perform in her own right. Competent as these performers may have been, none achieved the stature of a Carreño. It was not until the late 1870s that an American rival did appear on the scene, Julia Rivé-King. In fact, in 1881, when Carreño was on tour in Chicago, critics compared these two performers, and they concluded that Carreño was the greater genius but Rivé-King the better artist. A few years later the music critic John C. Freund wrote, "The other day Mme. Carreño, Mme. Rivé-King, and Miss Bloomfield, all three remarkable pianists of different schools, met and had a chat together."[22] It would be illuminating to know just what they said.

Rivé-King was definitely a different sort of artist from Carreño—not in terms of recognition and acclaim, although her career was confined largely to the United States. She seems to have been more of a musician's musician. In May 1875, when at eighteen she made her first appearance with the New York Philharmonic Society in Liszt's Concerto in E-flat and Schumann's very difficult *Faschingsschwank aus Wien,* the orchestra and conductor Carl Bergmann joined the audience in giving her a standing ovation. By April of the following year the notoriously restrained (for that time) *Dwight's Journal* acclaimed her as America's first pianist and compared her with both von Bülow and Rubinstein.[23] In the late 1870s Theodore Thomas was said to regard her as the finest American pianist. The span of her career was even longer than Carreño's—she made her official debut about 1873, in Europe, and in 1936 she was still teaching in Chicago.

Julia Rivé was born in Cincinnati in 1857.[24] Her father, Léon Rivé, was a painter. Her mother, the French-born Caroline Staub Rivé (1822–82), was an eminent voice teacher who had studied with Manuel Garcia and composed some music herself. Julia first appeared in public accompanying her mother, and by the age of eight she was an accomplished pianist. Around 1870 she was taken to New York to study with William Mason and S. B. Mills, and in 1872 to Europe, where she studied with Carl Reinecke at Leipzig, Blassman at Dresden, and Liszt at Weimar. She made her debut in Leipzig under Reinecke's baton, playing Beethoven's Concerto no. 3 and

Liszt's Rhapsody no. 2. The audience was astounded that she could manage both of these two very different works so well. A European concert tour was arranged for her but was abruptly canceled when she was called home by her father's death in a railway accident. This marked the end of her European career.

That winter Rivé appeared in Cincinnati, and in December 1874 she made her Chicago debut with the Apollo Club; a few months later came her New York debut. In fall 1875 she was back in the Midwest, giving ambitious recital programs such as the following one in Indianapolis on November 25, 1875: Beethoven, Sonata, op. 111; Schumann, *Etudes symphoniques;* Mendelssohn, *Rondo capriccioso;* Schubert, Sonata, op. 120; Chopin, Rondo in E-flat major; Liszt, transcription of the Allegretto from Beethoven's Symphony no. 8; Raff, *Grand Waltz de Concert.*[25]

In February she returned east to play Beethoven's Emperor Concerto with the New York Philharmonic, and in July she gave a series of highly successful recitals in Philadelphia. In August she was in Cincinnati, playing Bach, Mozart, Beethoven, Mendelssohn, Schumann, Wagner, Chopin, and Liszt. The following year, in April 1877, it was said that she had given 300 concerts that season, playing simply everywhere, from tiny towns to major cities. In one week in Chicago alone she played before a total of 6,000 persons.[26] In June 1877 she married Frank H. King, her manager, in Milwaukee, whose 1877–78 season she opened in September with a "grand testimonial concert."

So far Julia Rivé-King's career does not sound too different from Carreño's—child prodigy, early study with a musical parent, later study with great masters, highly acclaimed debut, a hectic concert schedule scarcely interrupted by marriage, ambitious programs. But as a performer and, one must conclude, in personality, Julia Rivé-King was considerably different from Carreño. For one thing, she never catered to her audiences; no flashy curtain raisers or encores for her. She played programs as difficult for unsophisticated audiences as those she played in the big cities. She herself strongly preferred Beethoven to Liszt (who, however, was never dropped from her repertory). Somehow, said *Dwight's* midwestern correspondent in 1877, she had found the secret of being popular without lowering her standards. One clue to her success was her modesty and simplicity. She once wrote a friend, "You praise me too much. I do not deserve it yet, though I hope to some time. I am still too young to have fathomed so great a master as Beethoven, but I love him above all others."[27]

Like Clara Schumann (and unlike most contemporary pianists), Rivé-King memorized all the works she played, and her memory was considered prodigious. Her technique, apparently, was excellent, but she never sacrificed musicianship for the pyrotechnics of a brilliant performance. "Her style," said another critic, "is devoid of any suspicion of sensationalism, and although always refined is never insipid. It combines, indeed, native delicacy with true artistic fervor."[28]

Relatively early in her career Rivé-King discovered her bent for teaching. In 1878 she was already holding master classes for advanced pupils during the summer, and though she was well able to support her career with performance alone, she always took time to teach. She also turned to composition, of both original works and transcriptions of other pieces for piano. At a concert with the Harvard Musical Association in February 1879, she played the Chopin E-minor Concerto and her own transcription of an organ prelude and fugue by Haberbier-Guilmant, of which one reviewer said, "For facility and brilliancy of execution, sure touch, powerful and yet delicate method, Mme. King [ranks] among greatest artists." The same writer admired her technical fluency but said she lacked soulful sentiment.[29]

She was, we may safely conclude, more of the eighteenth and twentieth centuries than of the nineteenth, at least in execution. Compared to the passionate Carreño, the "Valkyrie of the Piano," Rivé-King was an intellectual, a classicist. But as a composer she was a child of her time. At her April 17, 1879, Farewell Recital (for that season) in Boston, she played her transcription for piano of two movements of Mendelssohn's Violin Concerto—a composition that would only have been undertaken in her day—and John Dwight loyally said it was a "musicianly and clever piece of work."[30] She also transcribed for piano Vieuxtemps's *Ballade et Polonaise de Concert, Grande fantasie* (based on Bizet's *Carmen*), and some Scarlatti sonatas. Her original compositions include *Polonaise héroique* (dedicated to Liszt), the tone poem *Bubbling Spring,* an Impromptu in A-flat, and a number of salon pieces, including some for four hands.

Rivé-King continued to tour, playing recitals and with orchestras. In September 1880 she formed the Rivé-King Concert Company, together with several singers and a violinist, which toured widely for the 1880-81 season. Such tours were not without their hazards. In the spring of 1881 Rivé-King was injured in a collision on the Wabash line and sued the railroad for $700,000. (The suit was settled two years later, Rivé-King receiving $4,250.[31] By then she had abandoned the company, which appears to have been active only that one season.)

In fall of 1881 Rivé-King played the Saint-Saëns Concerto no. 2 in G minor at the Worcester Festival (on her next appearance there, in 1894, she played the Tchaikovsky Fantasy for piano and orchestra, op. 56, and for an encore a Rhapsody written especially for her by Saint-Saëns).[32] She had announced that she would, after traveling almost constantly for seven years, spend the 1881–82 season in New York, teaching a few advanced students and filling occasional concert engagements.[33] New York appears to have been her home until 1890, insofar as such an inveterate traveler could be said to have a home. The summer of 1882 found her in California and

Oregon, and in spring 1883 she undertook the first of a number of extensive tours with Theodore Thomas and his orchestra, which Frank King had helped arrange. They appeared, over a period of two and a half months, in thirty cities, from Baltimore to San Francisco. The company consisted of sixty men, five singers, and Rivé-King. In the spring of 1884 she was on still another coast-to-coast tour with Thomas and was booked for concerts in Baltimore and other eastern cities for the fall. Sometime during the next year Rivé-King collapsed and was forced to retire for a time to recover her health. She had played more than 200 concerts with Thomas alone, and an estimated total of 1,800 concerts since her debut.

By the spring of 1885, however, Rivé-King had recovered and was on the road again, touring the South and West. *Freund's* of May 1885 reported that she was getting rave reviews everywhere, had performed brilliantly in Chicago, and had moved on to two recitals in Louisville, where the program included her own *Mazourka des graces*. The following year she undertook another long tour of the South and West. Apparently she took more time off in 1887—no long spring tour is reported—but she was active again in the 1887-88 season. Critic James Huneker, in an evaluation of pianists published in the *Etude* in January 1888, described her: "A finished technic and a very large tone are her principal characteristics. A reserve...has led many critics to declare that her playing lacked fire and passion...she has both in plenty....Madame King is a great pianiste."

In 1890 Rivé-King moved back to Chicago, though her traveling continued. In the spring of 1891 she was again touring the larger cities, but in the 1891–92 season she appeared as a regular soloist with the Chicago Orchestra. For some reason (perhaps illness) she was not one of the six women pianists engaged to play at the Chicago World's Fair in 1893. She performed at the Worcester Festival in 1894, then gave a series of orchestral concerts and recitals throughout the East and West during the 1894–95 season, and toured with Anton Seidl's orchestra in 1896, 1897, and 1898, but reviews of her concerts are sparser during the late 1890s. Her reputation, however, had not diminished. In 1899 in an article in the *Etude* on American virtuosos, J. S. Van Cleve called her the greatest woman pianist of American birth, ranked her with Carreño and Bloomfield-Zeisler, and said her repertory was unsurpassed except perhaps by von Bülow and Rubinstein.[34] By then she had played a total of about 4,000 concerts, 500 of them with orchestra.

In February 1900 Frank King, ten years her senior, died. Plainspoken and seemingly uncultivated, he had in reality been a warm, kindhearted man, extremely knowledgeable about pianists, pianos, and piano music, and an excellent advisor to his wife. From that time on Rivé-King devoted herself largely to teaching, appearing only rarely in performance. She joined the piano department of Chicago's Bush Temple of Music early in the 1900s and remained there until a year before her death. In May of 1929 the *Etude* reported that Rivé-King, "a great favorite of the last generation and one of the first American women pianists to win fame," had given a recital in Chicago on February 27, and despite her age (seventy-four) she was still an admirable performer. In August 1932 she is mentioned again; she is described as the most brilliant American female pianist of the period 1885–1900 and one of the few remaining of Liszt's pupils, still actively teaching in Chicago. She died in 1937 at the age of eighty-two, having given two recitals as recently as the fall of 1936, and was buried, according to her wish, in her husband's grave in Cincinnati.

Despite her long career and her extensive tours throughout the United States, Rivé-King was rather quickly forgotten. Or perhaps her more measured, intellectual approach to the keyboard never won her as many admirers as flashier performers seemed to attract. Fannie Bloomfield-Zeisler, on the other hand, also a midwesterner by upbringing and just a few years younger than Rivé-King, was still remembered, at least in name, by a few older musicians in the 1970s. She, too, had a career that spanned a half-century, and it is said that in sum both she and Rivé-King were more successful than most American men pianists of their time.[35]

Fannie Blumenfeld was born in 1865 in Bielitz, Silesia (Austria), but her family moved to Chicago before she was two and changed their name to Bloomfield. She showed musical talent at a very early age and studied first with Bernhard Ziehn and Carl Wolfsohn, both respected Chicago teachers. In 1877 Madame Annette Essipoff,[36] the great Russian pianist, was on tour in Chicago and heard the child play, and she told her parents to send to her to Vienna to study with Leschetizky.

The Bloomfields took her advice, and Fannie studied in Vienna for five years, from 1878 to 1883. In 1883 she made a successful debut there and then returned to the United States, making her American debut in Chicago late in 1883. In January she appeared with the Beethoven Society of Chicago, under Carl Wolfsohn, and John C. Freund said, "She has a marvelous technique, phrases beautifully, plays with fire and passion, and is altogether the most deserving young pianist...in many a long year."[37] The *Chicago Tribune* and other papers concurred. She went on to score similar successes in Milwaukee, St. Louis, and Baltimore. The following season she played with the Boston Symphony under Wilhelm Gericke and then in New York, and was warmly praised by all the critics, although the peppery A. L. of *Freund's* said of her performance of Weber's *Concertstück* with the New York Symphony (under Walter Damrosch) that it was a pitiful waste of talent to perform this work at all.[38]

In October 1885 Fannie Bloomfield married Sigmund Zeisler (1860–1931), a Chicago lawyer, and appears to have taken some months off from touring. But the 1886–87 season found her on the road again. She gave a recital in Baltimore, where she was said to be "the finest pianist heard in Baltimore for some time." In December she appeared in New York, again

with the Symphony Society under Damrosch, and she was active in the Midwest the following spring, performing a number of times in Chicago and
other cities.

By this time Bloomfield-Zeisler was a seasoned concert artist. Her style of
playing was more like Carreño's than Rivé-King's. James Huneker said, of
her, in April 1887:

Here was something rare in pianism, particularly from a woman. Breadth, color,
fire, variety of tonal shading, and an intensity of attack that was positively *enthus-
ing*....Crudities of style and conception there were abundant traces of, but time is
fast mellowing them, and her noble sonorous touch in cantabile playing is one of the
most delightful things to listen to. It is violin playing on the piano. Her playing of the
Rubinstein D minor Concerto can never be forgotten by the writer. The vehemence
of the attack (like a stealthy panther laying in wait for its prey), the *élan* of the last
movement, and then the sensuousness of tone in the Romanze will long linger as a
musical memory of the most precious sort.[39]

Interestingly enough, Amy Fay, herself a fine pianist and established
teacher, later said of Bloomfield-Zeisler's performance of this same, hair-
raisingly difficult concerto, "She dashed it off like a mere bagatelle."[40] A
few months later Huneker again wrote of Bloomfield-Zeisler:

She is a pianistic genius...but sadly lacks in the matter of self-control. She runs away
with herself, but then the vivid power of her playing, her command of color, and her
incisive, though somewhat hard, touch almost reconcile one to this great defect....At
all events she is always an interesting artist.[41]

In August 1888 Bloomfield-Zeisler and her husband sailed for
Southampton, beginning a six-month European tour. She went to Bayreuth
and to Vienna to visit Leschetizky[42] and Mme Essipoff, and the latter persuaded her to appear with her in a joint performance in London. In March
1889 Bloomfield-Zeisler returned to America and resumed her active career,
appearing with a number of major orchestras. In July 1890 she appeared in
Detroit at the fourteenth annual convention of the Music Teachers National
Association (MTNA), the only notable woman on their entire three-day
program. Accompanied by her husband, she presented an essay on the
piano and a talk on women and music. In the latter, according to a later
report,[43] "she admitted the limitations of femininity but maintained that in
music their work was marked by powerful masculine force." (That was one
way of getting around the age-old argument.) Further, she acknowledged
that women had not yet achieved any extraordinary compositions, but
maintained this was because their emancipation was too recent, and there
had not been enough time for their development as composers. She ended
by predicting great future accomplishments for women in this area.

The 1890–91 season was a very busy one. Bloomfield-Zeisler played Chopin's Concerto no. 2 in F minor at the Worcester Festival, receiving marvelous reviews. She was soloist with the Boston Symphony in a Saint-Saëns concerto in Baltimore and played the Rubinstein G-minor Concerto in Washington, D.C. In January and February she appeared with the New York Philharmonic Society, and she repeated the Chopin concerto with the Boston Symphony in New Haven and with Thomas at the Music Hall Concerts in Chicago. Generally acknowledged to be "among the first pianists in the country,"[44] she was chosen in July to be one of the three examiners in piano for the American College of Musicians, a newly formed organization intending to give accreditation to music teachers; she was the only woman examiner they employed that year. (See also Chapter 11).

The following year she appeared several times with Thomas's orchestra, playing the Chopin Concerto no. 2 and giving the U.S. premiere of Saint-Saëns' Concerto no. 4. (A couple of years later, at the height of the Dreyfus Affair, she was to play the same concerto in Paris, at a time when Saint-Saëns had just refused to preside over the recently organized Musicians Union there, and consequently the performance was roundly booed.[45]) The following season she made an extended western tour with Thomas and his orchestra, and she also helped, along with voice teacher Sara Hershey Eddy, organize the women's music section of the Chicago World's Fair of 1893, at which she herself performed the Schumann Concerto in A minor, and also appeared in Beethoven's Triple Concerto (with Max Bendix, violin, and Bruno Steindl, cello).

That fall she again went to Europe, but following a concert in Vienna early in 1894 she collapsed from nervous strain and canceled all her appearances for a time. The tour proved successful nevertheless, and the following season she undertook another, sailing for Europe in October (1894) and performing in Germany, Austria, Hungary, France, Italy, and England. In 1895–96, however, she remained in America. One reviewer said she created "almost as much interest wherever she plays as Paderewski," and noted that, although Paderewski confined himself to playing only three or four concertos per season, she would play not only the Rubinstein D minor, Saint-Saëns D minor, and Chopin F minor concertos, for which she was already famous, but the Schumann A minor and Beethoven E-flat concertos as well.[46] By July she had made some fifty appearances, twelve of them with orchestra, and had made plans to tour the Pacific coast the following season, where she would give some thirty recitals in two months.

This schedule, although busy, does not seem especially arduous compared with those of Urso, Powell, and Carreño. But Bloomfield-Zeisler also was raising three sons and expressed pride in the fact that she was neither giving up her art nor neglecting her home. Some conflicts undoubtedly arose from time to time, even given her relative wealth and an era of faithful servants, and her life could not always have been easy. Nevertheless, she continued to perform. On March 24, 1900, she celebrated the twenty-fifth anniversary of her debut at the Central Music Hall in Chicago. Around this time she began regularly to spend summers in Europe, in some years either going early (in late spring) or staying late (through fall) in order to take part in the concert season there. She appeared with the major European orchestras—the Berlin Philharmonic, the London Symphony, and the Lamoureux Orchestra of Paris, among others—and also gave solo recitals. In 1903 it was announced that she would head the piano department of the Bush Temple of Music in Chicago, which presumably would keep her closer to home and make her a colleague of Rivé-King's.

In February 1905 the cover story of the *Etude,* by William Armstrong, was entitled "Mrs. Bloomfield-Zeisler on Study and Repertory." Some of her comments in this interview are illuminating. Mozart, she said, was very difficult to play well; every flaw shows, and one cannot be sentimental—the implication being that bravura can cover up flaws with some other composers. Bloomfield-Zeisler loved to play Grieg, especially his *Ballade,* and also Tchaikovsky. She tried to include some contemporary pieces in all her recitals—works by Schütt, Poldini, Moszkowski, Godard, Chabrier— but she neglected to mention any woman composer, not Mrs. Beach or even Cécile Chaminade (some of whose piano works were, for a time, in the standard repertory). Clearly her approach had much in common with Carreño's, who was most famous for her performance of the Grieg concerto and also promoted contemporary composers, most notably MacDowell but also others. And her repertory was huge. She once gave eight recitals in the space of eighteen days in which no work was ever repeated.[47]

As for teaching, Bloomfield-Zeisler said she could not really describe her method in general, since she preferred to take up one problem at a time. Leschetizky had been a great teacher because he had not tried to impose any one method or technique on his pupils but had treated each as an individual, attempting to help them bring out their own, individual styles. Her aim appeared to be the same. Earlier, in a number of short articles published in the 1880s, she had been more explicit on subjects such as expression in piano playing (not only touch but the different kinds of tone produced, and shading, or phrasing, affect expression), the use of the pedal, and other particulars.

We learn still more from an article published some years later by Theodora Troendle,[48] who had been her pupil and then her assistant in Chicago from 1913 to 1920. Bloomfield-Zeisler, she said, was famous for her bell-like pianissimo, was extremely good at using the pedal to vary tone color, and insisted on memorizing everything, at least in part because she herself was extremely nearsighted. Among her dicta to pupils, the most important were: (1) avoid fast, unfirm, or uneven practicing; (2) do not overlook the usefulness of the metronome, but differentiate between faulty time and faulty rhythm; (3) haste makes waste, so practice slowly and carefully; (4) pedaling and phrasing differentiate the gifted amateur from the true artist; (5) when learning a piece, concentrate on one phrase at a time; (6) consider carefully all criticism and advice, and make sure it really does apply to you before using it constructively; (7) success comes from charm, and true charm is the product of sincerity and simplicity; (8) quality is more important than quantity. Like Leschetizky, she emphasized a loose wrist and fingers made strong through training, especially with the exercises of Czerny (Leschetizky's old teacher).

A few other interviews provide some interesting insights. In 1908 Bloomfield-Zeisler said that a foreign debut still was necessary for an American artist in order to win acceptance at home.[49] As for the state of music in America, she believed that Chicago, New York, and Boston all had better music than Vienna, and what was more, performers were paid approximately five times as much in the United States as they received in Europe. On the other hand, the pace of the American tour was much faster. "In one week," she said, "one appears in five [U.S.] cities as widely apart as Novgorod, Berlin, Vienna, and Paris."[50]

In 1910, a veteran of thirty-five years on the concert stage, her ability was still undiminished. "Her style of playing," said one critic, "is vigorous, clear, and yet capable of great tenderness. She is at her best with the modern masters. She is in the front rank of modern virtuosi of either sex."[51] She was still undertaking large tours, too. In 1912 her six-month European tour took her to Dresden, Vienna, Munich, Hamburg, London, and Paris, and included both orchestral concerts and recitals. This, however, was the last of her major tours abroad.

For the next fifteen years Bloomfield-Zeisler devoted herself principally to teaching in Chicago. On February 25, 1925, she gave a farewell concert in celebration of the fiftieth anniversary of her debut. Two and a half years later, after a period of ill health, she died at home of a heart attack.

Two other nineteenth-century women pianists, Amy Fay and Adele Aus der Ohe, must be included here, one because she was also an influential teacher and writer, and the other because, although a German, she made many American tours and for a time settled in the United States.

Amy Fay was born in 1844 in Mississippi.[52] Her mother, Charlotte Emily Fay, was a fine pianist, and Amy began to play by ear and compose from the age of four. At five her mother began to give her formal lessons, which continued for a time. But when Amy Fay was twelve, her mother died. Meanwhile, her older sister Melusina had married the son of a Harvard professor and Amy later went to live with her in Massachusetts. There she began to study Bach with John Knowles Paine and to attend classes at the New England Conservatory. She also studied in New York. At the age of twenty-five she went to Europe, where she studied for a year with Taussig in Berlin, for three years with Kullak, and for a summer with Liszt at Weimar. Liszt reputedly considered her one of his most promising pupils.

In 1875 she returned to the United States (after a total absence of six years) and made her debut with the Mendelssohn Glee Club in New York. She then returned to Massachusetts, where she performed with the Theodore Thomas orchestra at Sanders Theatre in Cambridge, and at the Worcester Festival of 1878, where she became the first performer to play an entire concerto (rather than just one or two movements). John S. Dwight called her style brilliant and hard but not poetic.[53]

Late in 1878 Fay moved to Chicago, where she divided her time about equally between performing and teaching. She devised a kind of lecture-recital called "Piano Conversations," in which she discussed pieces first and then played them. In 1890 her younger sister Rose became Theodore Thomas's second wife. In that year Amy Fay moved to New York, where she remained active in giving lecture-recitals, teaching, and working in music clubs (including a dozen terms as president of the Women's Philharmonic Society of New York, founded by her sister Melusina in 1899). She died in 1928.

The principal reason for Fay's importance is not her ability as a performer, lecturer, or even as a teacher, but a book she wrote about her studies in Europe. Entitled *Music Study in Germany* and originally published in Chicago in 1881, it consists of her very vivid impressions and sharp observations of an American music student's life abroad. Since European study was still considered a *sine qua non* for American musicians, the book had a much wider audience than might be expected. It went into about twenty printings, as well as being translated into French and German. In 1891, a decade after original publication, a writer on music books was still saying, "Perhaps no book on musical topics is more widely read than Amy Fay's 'Music Study in Germany.'"[54]

Germany was, for most of the nineteenth century, considered by Americans to be the wellspring of good music. The finest musicians, orchestras, conductors, and teachers, it was widely believed, were either German or German trained. The personnel of American orchestras was largely German. Practically all American musicians of note went to Germany to study, and, as Bloomfield-Zeisler pointed out, a foreign debut was considered indispensable. Amy Fay thoroughly enjoyed and profited from her six years in Germany, and she said that girls were freely admitted to the study of piano there. In the end, however, she advised no American to go to Europe to study music, since the United States now had William Mason, William H. Sherwood, Julia Rivé-King, and many other fine teachers.

One of the piano students Fay had heard in Germany was Adele Aus der Ohe, about ten years old at the time and a pupil of Kullak's son. Fay reported that she heard the child play a Beethoven concerto perfectly and was astounded at the ability of one so young.[55]

Adele Aus der Ohe was born in Hanover in 1864, the daughter of a university professor.[56] By the time Fay heard her, she had been studying with Kullak in Berlin for three years. At twelve she became a pupil of Liszt's and studied with him for seven more years. Not surprisingly, she became especially noted for her interpretations of Liszt's works.

In 1886 she made her American debut in Liszt's first Piano Concerto in New York, and she undertook extended American tours for each of the next seventeen years. She was especially in demand as a soloist with the Boston Symphony, with which she performed fifty-one times between 1887 and 1906. She also frequently appeared with the Brooklyn Philharmonic, New York Philharmonic, and Chicago orchestras, and she played at the Worcester Festival in 1887, 1889, and 1898. Her repertory was exceedingly large—she played concertos by Chopin, Liszt, Tchaikovsky, Schumann, Beethoven, Rubinstein—and by 1889 she had the reputation of earning more than any other pianist in the United States (and, said one correspondent, "she deserves to").[57]

Not everyone admired Aus der Ohe's style. Huneker said she had a strong touch, reliant technique, but was deficient in musical disposition, and "has a large following among those who prefer physical power to poetry."[58] But another writer said of her rendition of Beethoven's Emperor Concerto, "We knew her great technique, her brilliancy, her dash and magnetism, but to see her abnegate all self-assertion, and carefully and conscientiously reproduce the composer's thought without any effort at effect, was a welcome surprise. She is a great artist."[59]

Aus der Ohe also gave recitals and played chamber music; she appeared a number of times with the leading string quartet of the time, the Kneisel Quartet, in Schumann's Piano Quintet, op. 47. In May 1891 she took part in the festival to dedicate Carnegie Hall in New York, performing the Tchaikovsky Concerto in B-flat minor under the composer's baton. She repeated this work, again with Tchaikovsky himself conducting, with the Boston Festival Orchestra in Philadelphia and Baltimore. In 1897 she filled in for the pianist Moritz Rosenthal, who was ill, in a company tour for which he had been engaged, and she played the identical works that he had planned to play. In the same year, her own Suite in E major for piano was performed at the nineteenth annual MTNA convention, and she played it again in a New York recital the following year.

In 1904 it was announced that Aus der Ohe was moving to the United States permanently, although she continued to perform in Europe as well. In 1909 she was given the title Royal Prussian Court Pianist, the first woman so honored by Emperor Wilhelm II. Soon afterward a crippling illness forced her to retire. She returned to Germany, and in the runaway inflation following World War I her savings became completely worthless. The war's end saw her living impoverished in Berlin, and eventually the *Etude* published an appeal for contributions to a relief fund for her.[60] On this she managed to subsist until her death in 1937.

One other American woman pianist appeared fairly regularly from about 1900 to 1925. She was Augusta Cottlow, born in 1878 in Shelbyville, Illinois. She studied with Carl Wolfsohn in Chicago and made her debut there in 1888 or 1889, followed by a New York appearance in 1891. She then went to Berlin to study with Busoni, and made a number of European tours. Her next appearance in the United States was in 1900 at the Worcester Festival, where she played Tchaikovsky's B-flat minor Concerto. She returned there in 1908, playing MacDowell's Concerto in D minor. She seems to have toured and played without interruption until about 1910, and then returned to Europe, where in 1912 she married Edgar E. Gerst of Berlin. She returned to the United States in 1917 and gave regular recitals in New York until the early 1920s. In 1925 the *Musician* published her memoirs, *My Years with Busoni.* She died in 1954.

By 1900 women pianists were not a novelty, in Europe or in America. However, though they constituted by far the majority in music schools and conservatories and vastly outnumbered men as teachers, relatively few women pianists became influential, either through performance or through teaching. Even disregarding nationality, names such as Artur Schnabel, Walter Gieseking, Rudolf Serkin, Artur Rubinstein, Vladimir Horowitz, and Mieczyslaw Horszowski, and, in more recent times, Van Cliburn, Glenn Gould, Claudio Arrau, Emil Gilels, Alfred Brendel, Mischa Dichter, Eugene Istomin, Gary Graffman, Garrick Ohlsson, John Browning, Eugene List, Peter Serkin, Daniel Barenboim, and Vladimir Ashkenazy are much more numerous and readily recognizable than the handful of women pianists known internationally during the same era (Olga Samaroff, Guiomar Novaes, Myra Hess, Lili Kraus, Gina Bachauer, Alicia de Larrocha, Rosalyn Tureck). And of this last group, only Samaroff and Tureck are Americans.

Olga Samaroff was born in 1882 in San Antonio, Texas, and was named Lucie Mary Olga Agnes Hickenlooper.[61] Her first piano teacher was her grandmother, Lucie Palmer Loening Grunewald, for whom she was named, but she later decided to take a more euphonious and exotic name (Samaroff was actually the name of another branch of her family). European study was still considered essential, so she went first to the Paris Conservatory, where in 1894 she became the first American girl to win a scholarship for piano classes, and then to Berlin, where she studied with Ernst Jedliczka. She also studied at the Peabody Conservatory in Baltimore with Ernest Hutcheson, and composition with Otis Boise. While still in her teens she married a Russian, Boris Loutzky, and retired from performing, but the marriage was annulled after three years.

Returning from Europe, she wanted to make her debut as a concert pianist, and in September 1904 she asked Henry Wolfsohn, the leading New York manager at the time, to handle it for her. Wolfsohn refused because she had no European notices to her credit, and she could not afford to return to Europe to acquire them. Her family, not wealthy to begin with, had lost all their property in the terrible Galveston flood of 1900 and had moved to St. Louis. Wolfsohn suggested that she take a gamble, hire an orchestra, and perform at Carnegie Hall. For this occasion she changed her name to Olga Samaroff and, risking the sum total of her funds, hired Walter Damrosch and the New York Symphony Orchestra for January 18, 1905. She played two concertos, Schumann's in A minor and Liszt's in E-flat, as well as a number of solo pieces by Chopin. The gamble paid off, and thereafter she had no trouble getting other engagements with orchestras in the United States. In 1906 she went to London to give her first solo recital, and in the same year Charles A. Ellis of Boston, manager of the Boston Symphony Orchestra and a select group of individual artists, became her manager.

Samaroff was delighted with Ellis, for he got her the highest fees any woman pianist had ever earned, $500 to $600 per concert. Women were generally paid less than men, and, Samaroff later wryly said, they were therefore considered a good bargain by organizers of subscription concert series and of private musicales. During this period, a Metropolitan Opera star might earn $3,000 a performance, but no woman pianist ever earned more than $600. (In 1908 Carreño was engaged for a series of concerts at $400 per performance, which she considered munificent.[62]) What was more, as Bloomfield-Zeisler had said, American fees were higher than European ones. Samaroff also said that she believed this discrimination in pay had been changed by Myra Hess after World War I, and she hoped her information was accurate.

In any event, Samaroff remained with Ellis until 1911, when she married Leopold Stokowski, then conducting the Cincinnati Orchestra, and gave up her concert career ("Just like a woman," Ellis reportedly said). The following year Stokowski became conductor of the Philadelphia Orchestra, and by 1914 Samaroff decided to resume her own career. In 1917 she went to play the Saint-Saëns Concerto in G minor at the Worcester Festival, accompanied by her husband, and several accounts of this occasion note that she was now fully recovered from some unspecified serious illness (perhaps a nervous breakdown).

During this period, she began to write about music, and several of her articles appeared in the *Etude* and other journals. From these and from a number of books she wrote in the 1930s and 1940s, it is evident that Samaroff was a serious musician. In an article on "Self-expression at the Keyboard," for example, she stressed that understanding the music is quite as essential as feeling, and that true artists avoid sentimentality and exaggeration.[63] She made a large number of recordings for the Victor Talking Machine Company, and the royalties from these enabled her to buy a house at Seal Harbor, Maine, where she spent summers and later invited her favorite pupils.

In 1923 she and Stokowski were divorced, but they remained on friendly terms. She left Philadelphia for New York, where she spent the winters in rented apartments and summers in Maine. For about two years she was quite successful in giving recitals, but in 1925 she fell and injured her arm and shoulder, tearing ligaments. She had to cancel all her engagements, and this proved to be the end of her concert career. Meanwhile, however, she had signed a contract to teach piano at the newly formed Juilliard Graduate School, where her colleagues included her former teacher, Ernest Hutcheson, as well as Josef and Rosina Lhevinne and other notable masters.

Shortly after her accident, Samaroff was offered the job of music critic for the *New York Evening Post,* to replace Ernest Newman. She held the post for two seasons, but resigned when the paper refused her request to expand the department.

Upon leaving the *Post,* Samaroff decided not to resume performing. She loved teaching and wanted to help young musicians, as well as continue with her writing. In 1928 she helped found the Schubert Memorial, a foundation to help give young musicians opportunities for performance with a major orchestra. It established an annual contest whose winner had the privilege of performing a solo work with the Philadelphia Orchestra at a regular subscription concert. In 1935 the winner was one of Samaroff's most gifted pupils at Juilliard, Rosalyn Tureck, who that year made her debut with the Philadelphia Orchestra. (By this time Samaroff was no longer associated with the program.)

In addition to teaching at Juilliard, Samaroff began in 1929 to commute regularly to Philadelphia and teach an advanced piano class at the Philadelphia Conservatory of Music. One of her pupils there was Eugene List, who at thirteen was granted a fellowship to the school and under her tutelage became a successful concert artist.

In the 1930s Samaroff increasingly began to lecture extensively on music appreciation and published a number of books on the subject, the most important of which was *The Layman's Music Book* (1935), later enlarged and revised as *The Listener's Music Book* (1947). In 1936 the U.S. State Department sent her as the official American delegate to the first International Congress of Musical Education in Prague, Czechoslovakia. Two years later she was the only woman among twenty-one delegates to Belgium to serve on the international jury of the Concours Eugene Ysaye. She also received the honorary degree of doctor of music from the University of Pennsylvania. She died in 1948.

Her own success notwithstanding, Samaroff had no illusions about the difficulties faced by women in a highly competitive field. Discussing the status of women musicians in her autobiography, she quotes a story about three wandering musicians in medieval Europe, two men and one woman. In summer they traveled from town to town, performing where they could. In winter the two men retired to a monastery where they earned their keep by copying music manuscripts, while the woman had to earn her living as a prostitute. Women musicians in Samaroff's time were not always driven to such extremes, but there is no doubt that lingering prejudice was still operative.

One way to overcome the difficulties—to get an edge on the competition—was to specialize. A brilliant Polish pianist, Wanda Landowska (c. 1880–1959), did just that. Partly through expeditious timing and partly through her enormous talent and hard work, Landowska, virtually single-handedly, revived the baroque harpsichord and its music. She was not the first to think of rebuilding and reviving this instrument, but she became the first great twentieth-century performer on it, and she gave impetus to its rebirth. She herself taught many others how to play it, and she inspired outstanding contemporary composers (among them De Falla, Stravinsky, Poulenc, and others) to write for it, both orchestral music and solo works. Long before she died, Landowska's name had become practically synonymous with the harpsichord, and it has remained so to this day.

Samaroff's pupil Rosalyn Tureck also chose to specialize, not in an instrument but in a composer. In October 1977 she celebrated the fortieth anniversary of her first playing the complete forty-eight Preludes and Fugues of J. S. Bach's *Well-Tempered Clavier* and his *Goldberg Variations* in New York. That first performance, when she was only twenty-two, took place in a series of six concerts in New York's Town Hall. The anniversary concert began with a single long concert at Carnegie Hall, at which Tureck played the *Goldberg Variations* first on the harpsichord (as the composer had intended) and then repeated them on the piano, "with a touch and technique she has devoted her musical life to perfecting."[4] This concert was followed by five more at which she played the forty-eight Preludes and Fugues. Indeed, Tureck had at various times played Bach on harpsichord, piano, clavichord, organ, and even on an electronic keyboard instrument known as the Moog Synthesizer. She performed Bach all over the world and became as much identified with this composer as Landowska was with the harpsichord.

Tureck was born in Chicago in 1914. She began to play the piano at four and started lessons at eight, making her debut with two solo recitals a year later. She studied first with Sophia Brilliant-Liven, who had been a pupil of Anton Rubinstein's, and then with Jan Chiapusso, a great student of Bach who first aroused her interest in the baroque composer. He encouraged an intellectual approach to Bach, and Tureck began to study the harpsichord, clavichord, and organ in order to gain a better understanding of baroque performance practice. At fifteen she was giving all-Bach recitals in Chicago, and the following year she went to New York to study at Juilliard, where she became a pupil of Olga Samaroff's.

In those days the music of Bach was far from being either well known or popular with audiences. In fact, in a newspaper interview in 1977 Tureck said, "I can remember...having people ask me, 'Who is Goldberg?'" She went on to say that the study, teaching, and even the performance of Bach had improved enormously in the last 30 years.[65] Much of that was a result of Tureck's own work, for, in addition to playing Bach's music, she conducted research, recorded, lectured, and wrote about Bach. Her writings include a three-volume work, *An Introduction to the Performance of Bach,* which contains fourteen pieces of music and essays on ornamentation, phrasing, touch, and other questions of performance style.

When Tureck began her career, Bach's keyboard music was considered excellent for use as finger exercises but very stuffy and dry. Moreover, many—including Landowska—felt that Bach's music should not be performed on the piano, which did not even exist during his time, but on the harpsichord, clavichord, or organ. Tureck, on the other hand, believed that it is the conception of the music rather than the instrument it is played on that gives a performance of Bach's works authenticity. At the age of not quite seventeen, in what she later described as a kind of mystical revelation, she realized that she would have to develop an entirely new and different piano technique in order to play Bach's music properly on the piano. And she spent the next forty years developing such a technique.

At first she had great difficulty convincing others that Bach was indeed worth playing. In fact, she said in 1977 that early in her career she did not believe she would be understood until she was seventy. One early experience reinforcing this pessimism was the Naumburg Competition of 1934, in which she advanced to the finals and presented an all-Bach program as her final recital. She lost. One of the judges did not approve of her ornamentation in the *Goldberg Variations* (ornamentation itself was out of fashion then), but principally the jury refused her the much coveted Naumburg Prize because they believed nobody could (or should) make a career of Bach. Three years later, however, a year after her graduation from Juilliard, Tureck's Bach series won her the first Town Hall Award for the most distinguished performance of the season, and the award was presented to her by the president of Town Hall, Walter W. Naumburg.

SEATED AT THE KEYBOARD    [ 67 ]

At the same time she was giving all-Bach programs, Tureck was also giving more conventional piano recitals, playing Chopin, Debussy, and Scriabin. She played the Brahms B-flat Concerto with the Philadelphia Orchestra and Beethoven's Emperor Concerto with the New York Philharmonic, pieces that were still considered by many to be "men's work." The double bind of the woman musician still persisted in the 1930s. Tureck used to wear a shapeless black dress so as not to distract the audience by her appearance. Feminine sentiment was allegedly admired, but the greatest compliment was to tell a woman that she played like a man. On the other hand, masculine women were also suspect. On the whole, it was simply preferable to *be* a man. Tureck did not let this attitude stop her. One of her favorite pieces was Brahms's *Variations on a Theme by Handel,* which was supposed to be too difficult for any woman pianist except perhaps Clara Schumann. But Tureck played it with great success.

Tureck also was interested in the music of her own time. Several composers had written works for her, and she had introduced compositions by William Schuman, Aaron Copland, and other contemporary composers to both American and European audiences. In the early 1950s she founded Composers of Today, an organization intended to bring contemporary composers together with performers, and to promote the performance of new works. In the four seasons of its existence (1952-55) the group introduced works by Messiaen, Krenek, and Hovhaness to New York audiences, and presented the first concert of taped (electronic) music in the United States.

In 1953 Tureck made her London debut, and soon afterward established residence there. She also tried her hand at conducting. In 1958 she conducted the New York Philharmonic, leading the orchestra in two Bach concertos from the keyboard. The next year she formed her own chamber ensemble in London, the Tureck Bach Players, and in 1966 she founded the International Bach Society, dedicated to promoting research on and performance of Bach's works and, most particularly, to closing the gap between musicologist and performer. For a long time, Tureck believed, the tradition of how to play Bach's music was lost. By studying the sources and putting into practice what is learned, this great tradition could be revived.

In 1974 Tureck was appointed to a fellowship at St. Hilda's College, Oxford University, an honor hardly ever bestowed on a woman and especially not an American one, and subsequently she was made an Honorary Life Fellow. But in 1977 she decided to move back to the United States and to continue her multiple career of performance, writing, and study. Thanks to her, by that time no one thought it strange that an artist should devote herself so overwhelmingly to Johann Sebastian Bach.

Still another kind of specialization for pianists takes the form of teamwork—that is, pairing off with another pianist and tackling the two-piano and four-hands (on one piano) literature. Many outstanding pianists have performed as duopianists once in a while, as Bloomfield-Zeisler did with her teacher, Annette Essipoff, in London in 1888. There have been husband-wife duopianists (Robert and Gaby Casadesus of France, Ethel Bartlett and Rae Robertson of England, and briefly Teresa Carreño and her third husband, Eugene D'Albert), father-son duopianists (Rudolf and Peter Serkin of the United States), and many unfamilial pairs (Carreño and Wilhelm Backhaus, for one).

The hazards of two-piano performance are considerable. Touring pianists frequently complain about the instruments they must play on, and usually for good reason. To find *two* pianos of acceptable—let alone excellent—quality is understandably even rarer. Moreover, they really should be grand pianos and be placed so that the two performers can see one another. As with other chamber music, a certain amount of eye contact is necessary simply for the ensemble to stay together. Upright pianos, apart from their other drawbacks, make this awkward.

Another problem is tuning. Violinists can adjust the tension of their strings on the spot; with a piano this takes far more time and skill. The composer Mary Howe (see Chapter 6), who for many years gave two-piano concerts and recitals with Anne Hull, wrote very amusingly about one concert in a small southern city where the pianos provided not only were uprights but one of them was tuned at least a quarter tone higher than the other. Such incidents are funny in retrospect but harrowing at performance time.

Difficulties notwithstanding, there have been a number of long-lived and successful duopianists. Among them were two sisters, Rose (1870–1957) and Ottilie Sutro (b.1872) of Baltimore. Their father, Otto Sutro, was a patron of the arts and a founder of the Baltimore Oratorio Society. They both began piano lessons with their mother, and in 1889 they were sent to Berlin, where they studied with Karl Barth. They made their debut in London in 1894 and were highly acclaimed; the same year they returned to the United States and made their first American appearance in Brooklyn, New York, which marked the beginning of an extensive American tour. They then returned to Europe and were invited to play for Queen Victoria. A number of composers wrote works for them, notably Max Bruch, the premiere of whose concerto for two pianos (composed for them) they gave with the Philadelphia Orchestra in 1916. In 1930, by now well along in years, the Sutro sisters were still performing. In that year they undertook a series of concerts in Washington, D.C., devoted to the work of American composers.

A discussion of great women pianists would be incomplete without mentioning a few of those who made a brilliant beginning but for one reason or another never fulfilled their early promise (which, of course, applies to child prodigies in every area and quite regardless of sex). One was Hephzibah

Menuhin, born in San Francisco in 1920 and making her debut as a pianist at the age of eight;[66] after only eighteen months of formal study she played the Bach Italian Concerto, a Beethoven sonata, and Chopin's Fantasy Impromptu. She did not appear in public again for six years, and then only as the accompanist of her gifted brother, violinist Yehudi Menuhin, in sonata recitals. Her mother did not believe she should have a separate career. In 1936 Marutha Menuhin was quoted as saying that Hephzibah yearned for her own career but, "I tell her the only immortality to which a woman should aspire is that of a home and children," and in 1938 Mrs. Menuhin wrote, in an article in a woman's magazine, "We have always praised Hephzibah far more for a well-balanced, well-executed dinner cooked by her than for any concert she has ever played with her brother."[67] In 1938 Hephzibah married an Australian and gave up playing for many years. She was later divorced and resumed public appearances, most often with her brother.

In January 1978 Yehudi Menuhin gave a recital in New York that marked the fiftieth anniversary of his New York debut; with him was Hephzibah, whom the *New York Times* referred to as "his perennial accompanist." In his autobiography, published the previous year, Menuhin wrote of his sister, "She could have been a leading virtuoso touring three hundred days a year. She chose otherwise." But then, though he goes on to say she has found fulfillment in her life, her second husband and his social work, and her own music, he maintains that she prefers chamber music to "the lonely glory of solo playing," and that "She needs an object of inspiration, preferably her brother, in addition to the music; as in another sphere she needs to know she is fulfilling her husband's intentions."[68]

Ruth Slenczynski, born in 1925 in California of Polish parentage, began studying at the age of three under her father's extremely harsh tutelage, and made her debut in Oakland, California, at the age of four. A fantastically intelligent and talented child, she became, as she later recounts in her moving autobiography,[69] a virtual slave to her father, who forced her, from the age of three, to practice nine hours a day, slapped her face for every wrong note she played, and exploited her as a performer (financially and in just about every other way) until, at fourteen, she rebelled and gave up the piano entirely for a time. She married early, and her husband, George Born, pressed her (although more gently) to resume her career. Although she eventually became a successful teacher and writer of technical books about the piano, she never entirely shook off the traumas of her childhood and, as a performer at least, never reached the heights that she had so nearly scaled earlier.

Finally, there was Philippa Schuyler, born in 1931 in Harlem (New York City) of a black father and white mother. She made her debut at the age of four, playing her own compositions before the National Piano Teachers

Guild. At ten she had finished eighth grade and was giving solo recitals all over the United States, and at eleven she composed *Manhattan Nocturne* for a full symphony orchestra. At fifteen she played her composition *Rumpelstilts* (and also the Saint-Saëns G-minor Concerto) with the New York Philharmonic. She traveled widely, became a news correspondent in addition to pursuing her career in music, and was tragically killed in Vietnam at the age of thirty-five.[70]

In the late 1970s there were several promising women pianists on the American concert scene, but none had yet won world wide recognition. Ruth Laredo made her New York Philharmonic debut in 1974 at the age of thirty-seven, eight years after her first New York solo recital. A native of Detroit, she had studied with Rudolf Serkin and became, during her marriage to violinist Jaime Laredo, chiefly an accompanist for her husband. When the couple parted, she resumed her solo career. In the mid-1970s she became known for her recordings of the complete Scriabin sonatas and of Ravel's works, and she also began recording the complete piano works of Rachmaninoff.

In 1977 Ursula Oppens was one of four young artists to win the Avery Fisher Award, entitling her to an appearance with the New York Philharmonic, six other orchestras, and a $1,000 cash prize. A specialist in contemporary music (she helped found and performed with Speculum Musicae, a group devoted to new music), Oppens scored considerable success in her concert with the Philharmonic, combining two familiar works by Mozart and Rachmaninoff with two virtually unknown ones by contemporary composers Pierre Boulez and Frederic Rzewski (the latter performance was a world premiere).

At this writing it is too soon to say whether either Laredo or Oppens will be a world-famous virtuoso. The competition now is stiffer than ever, the standards no doubt higher than they were in Carreño's day, but the doors are open a little wider thanks to the "lady pianists" of the nineteenth century.

# 4 NEW ENGLAND'S "LADY COMPOSERS"

The first native American school of musical composition was that of the singing masters, the Yankee "tunesmiths" of the eighteenth and early nineteenth centuries who began fashioning music for their pupils and eventually published hundreds of songs (see Chapter 1). Except for a few isolated individuals, another group of American composers with common bonds did not arise until the third quarter of the nineteenth century.[1] Its center, too, was New England, where between approximately 1850 and 1875 more than a dozen significant composers were born. This group is frequently called the New England school (or sometimes the second New England school, the first being that of the Yankee singing masters), but it might just as well be called the school of Paine and Chadwick, its most influential exponents. From their respective posts at Harvard University and the New England Conservatory of Music, these two men exerted a powerful sway over their pupils and the entire American musical world of their time.

John Knowles Paine (1839-1906) was Harvard's first professor of music (and occupant of the first such university chair in the United States), and he ran the department of music from 1875 until his death. He also was the first American composer to write in the larger musical forms (he wrote a Mass, oratorios, and symphonies). His pupils included composers Arthur William Foote (1853-1937; chamber music, organ and choral works), Frederick Shepherd Converse (1871-1940; symphonies, operas, oratorios, etc.), Daniel Gregory Mason (1873-1953), grandson of music educator Lowell Mason, and John Alden Carpenter (1876-1951; songs, orchestral works).

George Whitefield Chadwick (1854-1931), who had studied in Germany, taught at the New England Conservatory for a half-century (he was its director from 1897 to 1931) and composed operettas, symphonies, and other orchestral works, choral works, and songs. His pupils included Horatio William Parker (1863-1919; two operas and many choral works, the best of which is *Hora Novissima;* he taught at Yale for twenty-five years), Edward Burlingame Hill (1872-1960; he later taught at Harvard);

Margaret Ruthven Lang and Mabel Wheeler Daniels (discussed later in this chapter), and also Converse and Mason. Parker's most famous pupil at Yale was Charles Ives (1874–1954), long unrecognized but today considered the most innovative and talented of the entire group.

Also active in Boston during this period was Alsatian-born Charles Martin Loeffler (1861–1935), who played first violin with the Boston Symphony for several decades and became one of the first American impressionist composers, and the first outstanding American woman composer, Amy Marcy Cheney Beach (or, as she signed all of her works, Mrs. H. H. A. Beach).

Beach was neither the first nor the only American woman to write music, but she was the first to hold her own with highly educated and, for their time, sophisticated musicians like Chadwick and Parker. Indeed, her success led one writer to conclude with great enthusiasm that the prejudice militating against women composers in Europe was absent in the United States.[2] Unfortunately this conclusion was far from valid.

Women composers, even more than performers, faced considerable odds. Part of the reason is that composition is a very difficult field, for women and men alike. From playing an instrument to writing music is just a short step, and countless musicians have taken it. But to compose in a concentrated way poses the same requirements as the serious pursuit of painting, poetry, or any other art: a certain amount of schooling and enough money to support one's efforts. The survival of a piece of music, however, requires even more. Works must be written down in order to be performed by others, and they also must be accessible—that is, they must be published. Their availability must be made known, through further performance and other means of advertising. In present-day terms that often means they should be recorded, so that they can be heard not just by the relatively small audience of a concert hall but in homes, via record players or tapes and broadcasts. All this involves convincing a number of persons—performers, publishers, recording companies—that a composition is good enough to warrant their investment of time and money.

Clearly these requirements pose problems for any would-be composer, regardless of sex, and undoubtedly they have suppressed hundreds of thousands of musical works. But for women who wished to compose, these problems were compounded by the lack of education and lack of financial support, not to mention the lack of positive encouragement. There have been no great woman composers, said critic Ernest Newman as late as 1910, because they have no opportunity, no patronage, no support for the long period of technical study that is necessary. Economic necessity leads them either to marriage or to gainful employment; neither is conducive to composition. Moreover, when they do manage to compose, they cannot get their works published or performed. Some have gotten around this difficulty by publishing under pseudonyms (masculine, or at least ambiguous), and some by financing their own performances, as Carlotta Ferrari paid for the production of her opera, *Ugo,* in Milan in 1857. But how many can afford that?[3]

Despite these handicaps, women have been composing music since the time of Sappho, who lived in the seventh century B.C. (and none of whose compositions has survived). The handful of women living before 1800 whose works did survive (though only in small part) tended to belong to one of three social groups—the convent, the nobility or near nobility, or a family of professional musicians (usually supported by a wealthy patron).[4] Only women in these circumstances were sufficiently supported—financially and in other respects—to pursue composition. The convent provided not only education but performance opportunities, usually in the form of a choir. Thus some songs by an anonymous tenth-century Benedictine nun from near Gandersheim (Germany) and some plainsong and a morality play by the twelfth-century Hildegard of Bingen have survived. Wealthy and/or politically powerful women similarly were able to acquire an education and, often, to hire musicians to perform their works. In the Renaissance a number of Italian noblewomen composed music—Maddalena Casulana, Vittoria Alioti, Isabella Leonarda, and others—as did such better-known women as Anne Boleyn, Mary Queen of Scots, Elizabeth I of England, and, later, Marie Antoinette of France, Catherine the Great of Russia, and Princess Anna Amalia of Prussia (sister of Frederick the Great).

Daughters in families of professional musicians often were taught music along with sons. One such woman was Francesca Caccini (1588–c. 1640), daughter of composer-singer Giulio Caccini; she wrote operas, opera-ballets, and ballets, and won the favor of Maria de' Medici. Another was Elisabeth-Claude Jacquet de La Guerre (1664?–1727), a famous harpsichordist who wrote an opera (*Céphale et Procris,* performed in Paris in 1694), keyboard works, cantatas, trio sonatas, a Te Deum (performed 1721), and sacred and secular vocal music; she was a protégée of France's music-loving Louis XIV.

Of course, being a member of a musical family did not guarantee either talent or success, then or now. Indeed, it carries the risk of being overshadowed by a more talented or more favored relative. This apparently happened in the eighteenth century to Mozart's sister Nannerl, who allegedly was as gifted as her brother, and several generations later to Mendelssohn's sister Fanny, who went so far as to publish some of her compositions under her brother's name.

Even when circumstances permitted a woman to compose, she still lacked social support, and sometimes she faced active opposition. Such antagonism ranged from simply not being taken seriously or treated condescendingly (women especially excel in writing children's music, said one writer, a work requiring "perfect sympathy with child-life")[5] to bald denials that a woman can have musical talent ("A woman seldom writes good music, never great music").[6]

Those who deny women's capabilities often point out that there has been no female Bach or Beethoven. Why this should be so has been a subject for speculation by leading American music journalists from the 1880s to the present day. The views presented range from wholly unsympathetic (women just do not have the talent, perseverance, concentration, dedication) to ludicrous (women cannot compose because they cannot sing bass)[7] to very sympathetic (women have not been given the same chance as men, at least not until very recently).[8] Even Fannie Bloomfield-Zeisler, who presumably realized she was the equal of practically any male pianist of her day, said that in the creative arts (i.e., composition) women are not the equal of men but they should nevertheless cultivate the very best they can muster. If they work hard, develop the greatest possible competence, and aim at clearness of thought and symmetry of form, they might perhaps become as great as men within the limits of their own sphere. "May it then be said," Bloomfield-Zeisler concluded, "She came, was heard, and conquered."[9]

If, by some lucky fluke, a woman should produce a respectable composition, it was argued that she could do so only at the expense of her "womanhood." For example, one writer pointed out that, even if matrimony and lack of strength and endurance did not deter a woman composer, it still took a considerable amount of "fight" to make one's way. Even many men found themselves temperamentally ill equipped for such battle. And if a woman *should* be suited for it, it would diminish her "womanly qualities," and then what would become of her power of writing "womanly music?"[10] Like the violinists and pianists who were suspect—or even condemned—for playing "just like a man" and condescendingly praised for their "feminine playing," the woman composer found herself damned if she did and damned if she didn't. Composing was inherently a masculine province. If women succeeded at it, they were betraying their femininity, except insofar as they expressed feminine delicacy and other approved virtues in a sentimental love song or graceful piano piece for the salon. Indeed, one present-day musicologist suggests that this is the very reason the popular nineteenth-century parlor song became a feminine genre, if not actually written by women (for men wrote them, too), then written to be sung by women and for female audiences.[11] Even when a writer proudly pointed to the many works produced by women composers, it was usually only their songs that were selected, despite the fact that they wrote in many other forms.[12]

These attitudes prevailed in Europe[13] and America alike, and if there were few women composers in nineteenth-century Europe, there were fewer still in America. Here, after all, the tradition of native composition still lay in the hands of the singing masters, none of whom was a singing mistress.

Nevertheless, by 1800 some works by women, principally songs, had been published in America, and possibly more are hidden behind masculine pseudonyms.[14] Oscar Sonneck's compendium of music published in America in 1800 or earlier[15] cites four women composers by name and one anonymous "lady of Boston." The most prolific of them was Mrs. Mary Ann Pownall (1751–96), the English actress-singer who had come to America in 1892 and collaborated on at least two books of music with James Hewitt (see Chapter 1), as well as writing numerous songs of her own. Another was Harriet Abrams (1760–c. 1825), who wrote "Crazy Jane" and other popular songs.

Women also are represented, still sparsely but in growing numbers, in the music published between 1800 and 1850. Jane Sloman, the young English pianist (see Chapter 3) who settled here, published songs and solo piano pieces into the 1850s, as well as *The Melodist,* a collection of "gems from celebrated composers" that was dedicated to her father and went into several editions.[16] Augusta Browne, who played the organ at Dr. Cox's church in Brooklyn, New York, in the late 1840s and apparently gave some organ recitals as well,[17] is represented by "Tyrolese Evening Hymn" to words by a Mrs. Hemans, published in Boston in 1828. Two more of her songs, "The Music We Love Most" and "The Mexican Volunteer's Quickstep," were among the new publications received by the *Musical Gazette* of Boston in 1847.[18]

Mrs. Hemans's sister, a Mrs. Hughes, set a number of her poems to music in the 1830s and 1840s.[19] In 1838 there appeared at least two instrumental works by women, *Victoria Waltz* with variations, for piano, by Mrs. Nixon of Cincinnati (published by Dubois & Bacon, New York), and *New Brighton Quadrilles,* also for piano, by Mrs. George Dearborn (published by J. F. Nunns, Philadelphia).[20] "Are We Almost There," a sentimental ballad by Florence Vane, was published in Boston in 1845, and undoubtedly many other songs of this kind appeared elsewhere. Somewhat later came the ballads, sacred songs, and piano pieces of Faustina Hasse Hodges (died 1895). Daughter of organist Edward Hodges (1796–1867) and an organist herself, she was active from the 1860s on, and one of her songs, "Rose Bush," supposedly sold 100,000 copies.[21]

Scarcely anything is known about these women other than their names and an occasional date of publication. Even the music itself is difficult to find, and indeed much of it may not be worth rediscovery. As for the larger forms of composition—symphonies, concertos, oratorios—women are conspicuous by their absence. Of course, not many such works were produced by American men composers between 1800 and 1850. (One of the very few was William Henry Fry, 1813–64, the first American to write a grand opera, *Leonora,* which was produced in Philadelphia in 1845.) For the most part, the American concert scene was dominated by the European repertory, and only an occasional short work by an American—usually a song or piano solo—would be performed in a program of otherwise entirely European compositions. Not until John Knowles Paine returned from years of study in Berlin (1858–61) and wrote his first large choral composition could America claim a native composer of larger works.

Most of the composers of the New England school founded by Paine went to Europe for several years' study, usually to Germany. There were two important exceptions. Arthur Foote was trained entirely in the United States (under Paine and Benjamin J. Lang), although he did travel in Europe. And Amy Marcy Cheney Beach, the first American woman to write a Mass and a symphony, did not even visit Europe until 1910, and by then she had been composing for a quarter of a century.

Amy Marcy Cheney was born on September 5, 1867, in Henniker, New Hampshire, the only child of paper manufacturer Charles Abbott Cheney and Clara Imogene Marcy Cheney.[22] She showed musical inclinations very early, already singing many songs quite accurately at the age of two and composing her first pieces at four. In 1871 the family moved to Chelsea, near (now in) Boston, and soon afterward Amy's mother, who was an excellent pianist and singer, began to teach her piano. She attended a private school and in 1875, at seven, she appeared as pianist at a church musicale, playing a Chopin waltz and, as an encore, "Mama's Waltz," which she had written at four or five.[23] In that year the family moved to Boston, where Amy resided for the next thirty-five years.

From 1876 to 1882 she studied piano with the immensely successful Leipzig-trained teacher Ernst Perabo, and from 1881 to 1882 harmony with organist Junius W. Hill. On October 24, 1883, she made her professional debut at the Boston Music Hall, playing the Moscheles G-minor Concerto with an orchestra conducted by Adolph Neuerdorff and, as a solo, Chopin's Rondo in E-flat. She played in several recitals the following year and received good reviews for her rendition of works by Bach, Beethoven, and Chopin. In March 1885 she played the Chopin F-minor Concerto with the Boston Symphony, the first of more than a dozen appearances with that orchestra over the years, and a few weeks later she appeared with the Theodore Thomas Orchestra at the Music Hall, playing the Mendelssohn Concerto in D minor. That marked the virtual end of her professional concert career for the next quarter of a century, for in December 1885, a few months after turning eighteen, she married Dr. Henry Harris Aubrey Beach, a prominent Boston surgeon. A widower in his forties (actually a few months older than Amy's father), Beach was a distinguished amateur musician, and he encouraged his young wife to concentrate on composition. Except for occasional appearances, usually to play her own works in charity benefits, she did just that.

Beach's formal training as a composer was minimal. She had studied piano and some harmony, but she had never learned theory systematically. She had, however, tried to train herself, and in the process she translated into

English the treatises of Berlioz and Gevaert on instrumentation and orchestration. At first she confined her own attempts to the smaller forms. In December 1886 the *Musical Herald* announced the publication of "Ariette," a setting of a Shelley poem that, the reviewer said, was "dainty yet sufficiently passionate" and "the guitar effect is well sustained throughout." A year later, perhaps influenced by her translations from the French, she produced the song "Jeune Fille et Jeune Fleur," which a reviewer pettishly said should be sent to a French critic, and weren't there any English poets Mrs. Beach could "employ her excellent muse upon?"[24] In 1888 she played her own cadenza for Beethoven's Piano Concerto no. 3, which she performed with the Boston Symphony and published later that year. Of the published version, her first publication of instrumental music, the reviewer said it was interesting but too long for its purpose. In sum, it was a fine piece of bravura work and an excellent study piece, but as a cadenza it violated good taste.[25]

But she continued to make progress. Of her new duet, "Sea Song," a vocal canon, Louis Elson said it betrayed considerable skill in polyphonic work.[26] Moreover, despite her youth and sex she was already recognized by Boston's musical establishment; at the commencement exercises of the New England Conservatory in 1891 Amy Beach, then twenty-three, served on the piano awards committee, along with Arthur Foote and Edward MacDowell. And in December of that year, commenting on her anthem, "Praise the Lord All Ye Nations," Elson said, "Boston at last possesses a female composer of merit able to cope with the large as well as the small forms of musical creation."[27]

This judgment was premature, but only by a couple of months. In February 1892 Beach's first large work, a Mass in E-flat (op. 5) for full chorus, soloists, orchestra, and organ, was presented by the Handel and Haydn Society under conductor Carl Zerrahn. (Later that year her Scene and aria *Eilende Wolken,* from Schiller's *Maria Stuart,* for contralto and orchestra was performed by Mrs. Carl Alves and the New York Symphony Society under Walter Damrosch, the first work by a woman composer at these concerts.)

The Mass in E-flat was, on the whole, a success. Most critics liked it, though a few quibbled about portions of it, and the audience gave the composer a standing ovation. President A. Parker Browne, in his annual report on the Handel and Haydn Society's season, said the Mass "may well be considered a wonder...and is certainly matter for hearty congratulations and great national and local pride." Philip Hale admired the comparative simplicity of the Kyrie and the Sanctus, saying, "these are more effective than certain passages where the composer apparently strained every nerve." He felt the solos were the weakest part of the work, and that there was excessive modulation throughout. The *Musical Herald* said the Mass was "well worth the study of those who decry the ability of women in the field of music." It praised the rare skill and taste shown in the use of quartet and chorus, but found the "bold free style" of the Quoniam section "difficult to associate with a woman's hand." However, the Credo, for soprano solo and chorus, was simply excellent. The *Boston Evening Transcript* called it very original and excellent.[28] Rupert Hughes felt the Mass "suffers from Mrs. Beach's besetting sin of over-elaboration, but it proclaims a great ripeness of technic."[29] And finally, the *Musical Record* praised the Mass for its directness and clearness, for the deep religious feeling that pervades it, and for the consistency and cohesiveness with which the composer's ideas are elaborated. Its themes, said the critic, will be sure to win more and more praise as they become more familiar.[30]

This enthusiastic reception notwithstanding, the Mass in E-flat, which had taken the composer three years to complete, was strictly a *succès d'estime*. It was never performed again. Nevertheless, it proclaimed Beach's ability to produce a score for large forces, and it no doubt helped her obtain the commission to write a work for the dedication of the Woman's Building of the Columbian Exposition (World's Fair) to be held in Chicago the following year. Two other women were invited to compose for this occasion—Ingeborg Bronsart of Weimar, Germany, and Frances Ellicott of London. They both wrote orchestral works while Beach wrote, in only six weeks, *Festival Jubilate,* op. 17, which was performed May 1, 1893, by a mixed chorus of 300, soloists, and an orchestra conducted by Theodore Thomas.

Though much was made of women musicians at the women's division of the exposition, Beach's was the only large-scale work for chorus and orchestra by an American woman that was played during the following four months of festivities, and even then the performance was confined to the Woman's Building. W. Waugh Lauder, special exposition correspondent for the *Musical Courier,* said of the work, "It was thoroughly scholastic... the success of the afternoon. It made a deep and satisfying impression, and gave an official seal to woman's capability in music."[31] The *Musical Herald* called the work exceedingly well written, pleasing, and musicianly.[32] And Rupert Hughes later said, "The work is as big as its name. It may be too sustainedly loud, and the infrequent and short passages of *piano* [softness] are rather breathing spells than contrasting awe, but frequently this work shows a very magnificence of power and exaltation. And the ending is simply superb."[33]

The 1890s were an exceptionally prolific period for Beach. By 1896 she had produced more than sixty shorter works for piano, violin, or voice, and several cantatas. Outstanding among the shorter works and singled out for special praise by critics were *Four Sketches* for piano, op. 15 *(In Autumn, Phantoms, Dreaming, Fireflies),* and the song "Ecstasy," op. 19, which became one of the most popular of her many songs.

Beach's next major work was her Gaelic Symphony, op. 32, whose premiere was an important event. It took place on October 30, 1896, with Emil Paur conducting the Boston Symphony Orchestra. Scored for full orchestra, it was the first symphony ever produced by an American woman, and the first such work ever performed by an American orchestra.[34] Beach's symphony, in four movements, is in the traditional mold. The first movement, *Allegro con fuoco,* is in sonata form, and it introduces the themes resembling Gaelic folk tunes for which the work is named. The second movement opens with a lilting *Siciliano,* has a brisk *Scherzo* midsection, and returns to the *Siciliano* at the end. The third movement, *Lento con molto expressione,* again has a melody of Celtic character, followed by second and third themes that undergo elaborate development. The final movement, fast and brilliant, is again in sonata form.

The Gaelic Symphony, which is rather long, is very much a work of its time, both in its incorporation of folk motifs (a popular late nineteenth-century device) and in its overall harmonic vocabulary, directly traceable to Wagner and Brahms. (One present-day writer believes all Beach's instrumental works are derivative, though probably not consciously so, and that those of her early period all echo Wagner and Brahms, whereas later she reflected elements of the styles of Debussy, Reger, and MacDowell.)[35] Certain stylistic traits of Beach's own also are present, particularly the flowing melodies (characteristic of all her work, vocal and instrumental) and the persistent use of chromaticism (use of all tones, not just those of the particular key a section is in), especially at points of climax. The symphony also shows, to some extent, Beach's perennial tendency toward overelaboration. But it further demonstrates a technical mastery that is truly surprising for a largely self-taught composer. Allegedly, conductor Wilhelm Gericke had at one time told Beach to study analytically all the best works performed by the Boston Symphony, and she had faithfully followed this advice for fourteen years. Clearly it paid off.

Unlike the Mass in E-flat, the Gaelic Symphony was performed numerous times during the next twenty years or so, not only in Boston but in New York, Brooklyn, Philadelphia, Pittsburgh, Chicago, Detroit, Buffalo, Minneapolis, San Francisco, and many smaller cities. Nevertheless, some critics continued to insist that Beach was at her best in smaller works, especially the songs and chamber pieces that she continued to turn out.[36] Among these was the Sonata in A minor, op. 34, for violin and piano, first performed by Franz Kneisel and the composer in 1897 in Boston. Elson regarded this work, along with the Gaelic Symphony, as the most important music produced by an American woman.[37]

Not everyone admired Beach's music, to be sure. Further, some of the criticism, both favorable and unfavorable, invoked the double standard by which the music of women composers was so often judged;[38] that is, it was either "too feminine" or "too masculine." For example, the *Etude* said the Violin Sonata was excellent, feminine in sentiment but worked out in a broad, masterful spirit worthy of a man.[39] (A month earlier it had praised the Gaelic Symphony on more neutral grounds, for having more "musical imagination" than her earlier works and for exhibiting both originality and profundity of thought.) Herbert Hall did not like the Violin Sonata at all; he believed Beach should concentrate on simplicity and "not draw her ideas out to an infinitive point."[40] Nevertheless, the sonata won favor with performers such as Teresa Carreño (see Chapter 3), who played it with Carl Halir in Berlin.

In March 1898 Beach appeared in a program of her own works as a benefit for Elizabeth Peabody House, Boston. She and violinist Olive Mead (see Chapter 2) played several of her works for violin and piano, among them *Romance*, op. 23. The program also included the song "Forget-me-not," to words by Dr. Beach, as well as settings of poems by Burns, Shakespeare, Heine, Goethe, and Hugo. It must have been just about this time that Beach was working on her Opus 44, three settings of poems by Robert Browning that include two of her most famous songs, "The Year's at the Spring" and "Ah, Love But a Day!" The first, relatively simple, sounds much like a Schubert lied, and the second, more chromatic, like a Brahms song.

Both these songs, which were frequently performed for many years, show several basic traits of all of Beach's vocal music: They lie well for the voice, with comfortable intervals and tessitura, and the setting of the words is skillfully handled. They are, of course, very sentimental, and, although once praised for their sincerity and depth of feeling,[41] they seem somewhat silly today. Yet they are melodic, well crafted, and eminently singable, which is undoubtedly why so many recitalists chose them for so long.

In June 1898 came the premiere of another commissioned choral work, *Song of Welcome*, written to open the Trans-Mississippi Exposition in Omaha, and in fall the Worcester Festival featured *The Rose of Avontown*, for soprano solo, women's chorus, and orchestra. Harmonically simpler than her instrumental writing, these works are less distinguished as well, and of the second one critic said, the soloist "sang a good deal better than the composition deserved."[42]

In April 1900 Beach herself appeared with the Boston Symphony in the premiere of her last big orchestral work, the Piano Concerto in C-sharp minor, op. 45. During the remaining forty-four years of her life (she was only thirty-two in April 1900), Beach continued to write songs, choral works (including one large cantata), chamber music, and piano pieces, but she never again wrote a purely orchestral piece.

The Piano Concerto was dedicated to Teresa Carreño. A long work in four movements, it has a brilliant and quite difficult piano part. The first movement, *Allegro moderato*, takes up fully one-half the length of the concerto. In modified sonata form, it presents the main theme in two forms, first lyrically by the orchestra, then passionately by the solo piano. The coda of this movement includes a richly worked out cadenza. The second movement, a brisk *Scherzo,* is a *perpetuum mobile* (perpetual motion) for the piano, with the orchestra playing two countermelodies against the piano's constantly shifting rhythms. The third movement, marked *Largo,* is a lament built on two brief ideas, one stern, the other lyrical. It proceeds without interruption into the final movement, *Allegro con scioltezza* (fast and fluent), a vivacious rondo in 6/8 time, with a quasi-bolero rhythm marking the second theme. This is the most interesting of all the movements, both rhythmically and melodically. The central section is a slow part in which, in indistinct rhythms, the piano plays a free-flowing fantasy of the main thematic material marked by drifting fragments of melody and flashbacks to earlier themes. With mounting excitement in a stretto coda (ever narrower, ever faster), the concerto concludes with extremely rapid octave passages by the piano.[43]

Like the Gaelic Symphony, the concerto was a resounding success, and it was played with major orchestras in the United States (Chicago, Pittsburgh, St. Louis, Los Angeles) and, some years later, in Europe (Berlin, Leipzig, Hamburg, with the composer as soloist). It was last performed by the Boston Symphony under Karl Muck (with Beach as soloist) in 1917, and then was reintroduced nearly sixty years later, in 1976, by Mary Louise Boehm with the American Symphony under Morton Gould. Although it has been criticized as oversentimental, a quality Tuthill and others find especially prevalent in Beach's writing for the piano,[44] it shows a mature mastery of form and undeniable lyrical talent. The composer's skill and imagination are evident throughout.

Until the end of World War I all of Beach's big works except the Mass— Gaelic Symphony, Violin Sonata, and Piano Concerto—were performed quite frequently, both in America and in Europe. The Violin Sonata was performed in Paris by Ysaÿe and Pugno in 1900, and in London by Sigmund Beel and Henry Bird in 1904. The Gaelic Symphony was performed in 1915 by the Philadelphia Orchestra under Leopold Stokowski, by New York's Manhattan Symphony under Henry Hadley in 1931, and by the Woman's Symphony Orchestra of Boston under Alexander Thiede in 1940 (and the Los Angeles Symphony performed the first movement alone in 1972). The Piano Concerto, introduced in Germany by Carreño, was often played by major orchestras there, especially during Beach's stay abroad.

An interview published in the *Etude* in 1904 gives a vivid picture of the composer. Amy Beach was then in her mid-thirties, childless, and, by virtue of her own talent and her husband's position, very much a lady of quality. Said William Armstrong:

She is a woman of charmingly simple manners....She is of medium height. Her eyes are of a grayish blue, large and smiling. Her complexion is fresh and brilliant. Her blonde hair, primly parted, is brushed back smoothly from her face. The manner of her wearing it, and the quaint style of her dress, rather that of the early seventies [i.e., 1870s] than of today, make her appear older than she in reality is.[45]

The interview, which took place at Beach's Boston home on Commonwealth Avenue, continues, "She composes when she feels the inclination moves her to it." When not writing, she studied the piano, and she was (said Armstrong) very interested in housekeeping. She spoke about the classics of the piano literature, of the neglected (at that time) works she loved, among them the Schubert impromptus and sonatas, the lesser Chopin mazurkas, Mendelssohn's Songs Without Words, some of the Liszt works no longer played. Her favorites, however, were Bach, Beethoven, and Brahms.

Those who knew her recall Amy Beach as a woman of considerable personal charm. Called "Aunt Amy" by the younger generation, she was unfailingly courteous to all and especially kind to young students (though she herself never taught). Amy Beach Clubs were formed in many towns, often initiated by a local piano teacher who admired Beach but enthusiastically joined by many others. Though her husband encouraged her to compose, one cannot help but wonder if he did not restrict the expression of her undeniable talent. His very position in upper-class Boston society— intellectual and artistic, but also somewhat stuffy—probably imposed rather rigid standards of respectability and gentility. Moreover, the Beaches seldom traveled, and so had little exposure to other worlds.

Amy Beach surely realized this, for soon after her husband's death in 1910 she undertook her first journey to Europe, and she remained there for nearly four years. Though her stay there did not greatly influence her style of composition, she did resume more frequent public performances, appearing with German orchestras in her Piano Concerto and with chamber groups in her Violin Sonata and her Piano Quintet in F-sharp minor, op. 67 (written in 1908). Though this last piece, too, has been criticized for oversentimentality, a present-day critic singled out the slow movement for its "scrumptiously Straussian melody" although he considered the rest rather dull.[46]

Beach returned to America in 1914. She had adopted a more modern style of dress and coiffure, and she resumed playing in public here. She began with a program of her own works in New York's Aeolian (later Town) Hall, which included the Violin Sonata, Piano Quintet (with the Olive Mead Quartet), and a long Prelude and Fugue for piano. For the next couple of years she traveled across the country for performances of her works, appearing in Milwaukee, Chicago, St. Louis, Toronto, Baltimore, Boston, Philadelphia, and San Francisco. Also during this period her *Panama Hymn* was accepted by the Panama Pacific Exposition as its official hymn.

In 1915 Beach gave an interview to the *Los Angeles Examiner* in which she cited "ten commandments" for young composers:

1. Perfect the technique of composition, beginning with the simplest rudiments.

2. Begin with small things—ideas that can be expressed in small forms.

3. Develop all the possibilities of a small form.

4. Learn to employ as much variety in form as possible. Avoid becoming stereotyped in expressing melodic, harmonic, or rhythmic ideas.

5. Analyze the old masters, especially their examples in the same form (as, for a fugue, Bach's *Well-Tempered Clavier).*

6. Study the string quartets of Haydn, Mozart, and the early Beethoven; analyze and learn them by heart.

7. Listen to good string quartets at their rehearsals and concerts; take along a score and follow it.

8. Hear good choral music.

9. Learn the master works of the symphony as played by fine orchestras; be thorough in studying symphonic works.

10. Remember that technique is only a means to an end. You first must have something to say. "If you feel deeply and know to express what you feel, you make others feel."[47]

Deep-feeling and emotional as Beach herself was, she believed in a firm technical foundation for expressing her sentiments. Again in an article she wrote for the *Etude* of November 1918, "To the Girl Who Wants to Compose," she stressed the need for sound technical equipment and for starting with small forms.

Though Beach told John Tasker Howard that she divided herself about equally between composing and performing, her public appearances from 1920 on became much rarer. She said,

I have literally lived the life of two people, one a pianist, the other a writer. Anything more unlike than the state of mind demanded by these two professions I could not imagine! When I do one kind of work, I shut the other up in a closed room and lock the door, unless I happen to be composing for the piano, in which case there is a connecting link. One great advantage, however, in this kind of life, is that one never grows stale.[48]

After her husband's death Beach gave up her Boston house and made New York her base, at least in winter. One of the last big pieces she composed was *The Canticle of the Sun,* op. 123, performed at the Worcester Festival in 1931 and numerous times thereafter in various New York churches (including St. Bartholomew's, which she attended). In Worcester she told Raymond Morin, "One thing I have learned from my audiences is that young women artists and composers shouldn't be afraid to pitch right in and try. If they think they have something to say, let them say it. But let them be sure to build a technique with which to say it. The technique mustn't be visible, but it must be there."[49]

Concerning the status of women composers, there were some contradictions in Beach's views, or at least in those she expressed. As early as 1898, in a letter published in the April issue of the *Etude,* Beach turned down an offer to write about women in music because, she said, she was too busy composing and, further, she felt women composers should stick to their craft. Later, in 1915, she said that she herself had never felt limited as a woman and had encountered no prejudice; she believed the opportunities for men and women were equal.[50] Certainly she had no trouble in getting her works published—in 1940 only 3 of her 150 opus numbers were still unpublished: a one-act opera, *Cabildo,* op. 149; a String Quartet in one movement, op. 89 (whose manuscript apparently is lost); and a Piano Trio, op. 150.[51] Quite a few of her works were out of print but, considering the half-century of her activity as a composer, that is not too surprising.

On the other hand, Beach could not have overlooked the fact that she was almost invariably singled out as the leading *woman* composer—not as the leading American, or New England, or even Boston composer. In July 1924 she became president of the newly founded Society of American Women Composers.[52] The following year she was represented at a Women Composers Festival held in Washington, D.C., sponsored by the National League of American Pen-Women, and she continued to be more or less active in the women composers' group for the next decade. At the very least, through her membership in the group she acknowledged her kinship with other women composers. And the very fact that they joined together and regularly arranged for performances of their works indicates a perceived need for more performance opportunities.

Always a devout Episcopalian, in the 1920s and 1930s Beach wrote a considerable amount of church music. In addition to the early Mass in E-flat she had, by 1910, written several anthems, the three-movement motet *Help Us, Oh God* (op. 50) for a cappella chorus (its last movement is one of the few fugues she wrote, and a fine one at that), and a Service in A, op. 63. She wrote a number of other anthems and motets, a Te Deum in F, a Communion service, and, in addition to *Canticle of the Sun,* the cantata *Christ in the Universe,* op. 133, for soloists, chorus, and orchestra or organ. The very last composition she produced, "Though I Take the Wings of Morning," op. 152, was also sacred, on a text paraphrasing Psalm 139. One writer thinks this is the single best work she ever produced, showing "a lack of chromaticism, a simplicity of style, plus a reticence in the piano part [that] allow the musical ideas to show through."[53]

There were also secular choral works and, of course, more songs, much in the vein of the earlier ones but none as successful as the Browning songs or "Ecstasy." Indeed, it has been said that her style—sentimental but technically sound, somewhat overcomplicated by the overuse of chromaticism but lush in musical imagination—changed but little between opus 1 and opus 152.[54] The only exceptions, Tuthill suggests, are the Variations for flute and string quartet, op. 80 (published 1916), and the unpublished (and lost) String Quartet in one movement. The former, consisting of a theme and six variations, not only displays her technical command of harmony and counterpoint, but her genuine understanding of the balance of parts in chamber music (where each instrument is equally important, an idea she had trouble conveying when one of the instruments was the piano). In the quartet, Beach for the first time departed from traditional tonality, introducing what for her was an unusual amount of dissonance.

Though Beach may have clung to essentially the same style, she continued to try her hand at new forms. Her first attempt at opera, *Cabildo,* was written in 1932, at the age of sixty-five. In 1933 she was still considered one of the leading American composers, along with others of the New England school and its descendants (with John Alden Carpenter, Howard Hanson, and others). In that year she received a medal from the Chicago International Exposition for creative work in music.

Winters Beach spent in New York in a residential hotel (her alleged love for housekeeping must have died with her husband), but in summer she returned to New England. There she went to her summer home in Centerville, on Cape Cod (bought and paid for with royalties from "Ecstasy" alone), to the MacDowell Colony in Peterborough, New Hampshire, or to a room she kept in Henniker to spend time with relatives and friends (she retained her legal and voting address there throughout her life). "Life in the woods is my greatest joy," she told John Tasker Howard, "with my friends and all that they have meant to me."[55] She was a close friend of Marian MacDowell's, to whom she dedicated her *Three Piano Pieces,* op. 128. it was at the MacDowell Colony that Beach befriended many young musicians and fellow women composers (among them Mabel Daniels and Mary Howe), and there she composed one of her last works, the Piano Trio, op. 150, in the summer of 1938.

On May 8, 1940, Beach was honored at a dinner in New York's Town Hall Club, attended by some 200 musicians, composers, and friends. Marian MacDowell (see Chapter 11), the composer Douglas Moore, and pianist Olga Samaroff (see Chapter 3) were among those who paid tribute to her. In her speech on that occasion, Samaroff said that, although women

were handicapped in music, Amy Beach had not faltered in courage and had
set an example to her personally, as well as to many other women. Both
*Romance* and the Piano Trio were played that day.[56] Four and one-half
years later Beach died, on December 27, 1944, at the age of seventy-seven.
Her music was no longer in vogue, and that, together with her persistent
old-fashioned use of her husband's name and her uncanny physical re-
semblance to a benignly smiling Queen Victoria, made her a figure of fun to
some. Yet, considering that she was largely self-taught and entirely Amer-
ican-trained, her achievements were quite remarkable for her generation,
and some of her music can hold its own in any age.

Though Beach's Gaelic Symphony was the first symphony written by an
American woman, it was not the first orchestral work by a woman performed by the Boston Symphony. That honor belonged to Margaret
Ruthven Lang, whose *Dramatic Overture,* op. 12, was performed under Artur Nikisch on April 7, 1893. At that time the composer was twenty-five
years old. Later that year her overture *Witchis* was performed in Chicago by
Theodore Thomas and his orchestra.

Margaret Lang was, like Amy Beach, born in 1867, and her orchestral
works were received with great enthusiasm in the 1890s. But there the
similarity between the two women ends. Lang was the daughter of a highly
successful and prominent Boston musician. She studied, both in Boston and
abroad, with the most eminent teachers of the time. Her works run to fifty-
seven opus numbers but, except for three overtures and a few other orchestral works, her output was confined to songs and choral music, and her last
published work appeared in 1916, when she was not yet fifty. For the remainder of her long life—she lived to the age of 104—she apparently never
composed again.

Unlike Amy Beach, Lang was no child prodigy. Her mother was a talented amateur singer and her father an eminent conductor, organist, and
teacher. Benjamin Johnson Lang, born in 1837 in Salem, Massachusetts,
served as organist for the Handel and Haydn Society of Boston from 1859
to 1896, and as its conductor from 1896 to 1898. He was instrumental in
building up two other musical organizations, the Apollo Club, a male
chorus formed in 1871, which he directed till 1901, and the Cecilia Society,
a mixed chorus formed in 1877, which he led till 1907. The latter is credited
with giving more first performances of great works (including that of
Bach's B-minor Mass) than any other Boston group. A church organist,
Lang also produced a number of compositions—songs, duets, and an
oratorio, *David*—but he allowed none of them to be published ("rightly
judging them to have no lasting merit," according to one writer).[57] He died
in 1909, leaving an estate of $600,000. One must conclude that he had a
shrewd head for business, music being an impecunious profession even
then. And money, of course, made it possible for his daughter Margaret,
who never married, to become a composer.

One of three children, Margaret Lang first studied under one of her father's pupils, and then studied piano with her father and violin with Louis Schmidt of Boston. At twelve she wrote her first piece, one movement of a piano quintet. In 1886 she went to Munich and studied violin with Drechsler and Abel, as well as composition with Victor Gluth. When she returned to Boston in 1887 she continued her musical education, studying orchestration with George Chadwick and composition with Edward MacDowell. Finding it difficult to work at home without interruption, she rented a room in the neighborhood to use as a studio. Allegedly it contained a shelf full of "rejected manuscripts," pieces with which Lang was not satisfied. During this period she also went to see individual members of the Boston Symphony to discuss the capabilities of their respective instruments, so that she might write better for them.[58]

Her father's position in Boston's musical world provided Lang with an entrée. A number of her works were performed by the Cecilia Society and the Apollo Club. The *Musical Herald* of March 1889 reports "a very pretty quartette by a young Boston composer, Miss M. R. Lang," at a recent Cecilia Club concert, and the *Musical Record* of June 1889 notes that a recent Apollo Club concert included her "The Maiden and the Butterfly," a song Rupert Hughes later described as being "as fragile and rich as a butterfly's wing."[59]

The following year the Apollo Club performed one of Lang's best works, *The Jumblies,* a series of settings of limericks by Edward Lear for baritone solo, men's chorus, and two-piano accompaniment. The *Musical Herald* critic said of them, "It is impossible to deny Miss Lang's facility in composition or the grace with which she states her ideas, and while she has constructed a rather formidable work upon Lear's innocent text, she has shown an original bent in her harmonies, and a sympathetic study of the voices."[60] A number of these settings are musical pastiches—takeoffs on forms such as the development section of a late romantic symphony, a barcarolle, a waltz—executed with great delicacy and wit. (A portion of the group was revived at a special Handel and Haydn Society concert in October 1975, in arrangements for mixed chorus, solo voice and piano, women's voices, etc.) *The Jumblies* was repeated at a Mendelssohn Glee Club concert in New York on February 10, 1891, and was most favorably received.

In February 1893 the Cecilia Society, in two concerts at the Boston Music Hall, included the song "Love Plumes His Wings," which Francis H. Jenks of the *Musical Herald* described as "very delicate and bright." A few weeks later, on April 8, the Boston Symphony performed the *Dramatic Overture,* of which the same critic wrote, "Miss Lang's work is an ingeniously devised and constructed composition with evidences of thought at every turn."[61]

The Bureau of Music of the 1893 World's Fair (Columbian Exposition) had asked for new American works, and twenty-one American composers had responded, but only four instrumental compositions were chosen for public performance. One of them was Lang's overture *Witchis,* op. 10, which was performed in August under Theodore Thomas and later was repeated by Bendix. In the next few years she wrote another overture, *Totila,* op. 23, and three arias for solo voice and orchestra (*Sappho's Prayer to Aphrodite,* for contralto, performed in New York, 1896; *Armida,* for soprano, performed by the Boston Symphony January 13, 1896; and *Phoebus' Denunciation of the Furies at His Delphian Shrine,* for baritone and orchestra).

The only other performance of a large work of Lang's appears to have been that of the Choral Music Society of Boston on January 10, 1917, performing *The Heavenly Noel,* for mezzo-soprano solo, women's chorus, organ, piano, harp, and string quartet. Philip Hale said of this work, "The music, published last year, is not too deliberately quaint, nor is it affectedly modern. It reflects the spirit of the text."[62] And the *Boston Transcript* review said, "The least pretentious proved the most distinctive and meritorious." It called the setting "freshly imagined, dexterously conducted, and abundant in unobtrusively ingenious and prettily fanciful play with the timbres of the women's voices and the heightening strings."

As it happens, neither reviewer mentioned Lang's outstanding characteristic, her highly individual treatment of harmonies and her exploration of dissonance. Unlike Beach, however, who was accused (often justly) of overcomplicating her works with unnecessary key changes and chromaticism, Lang's harmonies have, as Rupert Hughes put it, "the appearance of spontaneous ease, and the elaborateness never obtrudes itself upon the coherence of the work." Moreover, he adds, her songs "are singable to a degree unusual in scholarly compositions."[63]

After producing well over a hundred songs, Lang simply stopped composing. She lived out her life on Brimmer Street, in Boston's Back Bay, regularly attending the concerts of her beloved Boston Symphony. On her 100th birthday the Boston Symphony, under conductor Erich Leinsdorf, honored her by playing "Old Hundredth" and a Bach cantata. She died on May 30, 1972, six months before her 105th birthday.

A contemporary of Margaret Lang's who also studied piano with Benjamin Lang and composition with George Chadwick was Helen Hood, born in 1863 in Chelsea, Massachusetts.[64] She, too, went abroad to study for a time, with Moszkowski and Scharwenka in Berlin, and returned to spend the rest of her life in Boston. And she, too, was represented at the 1893 Columbian Exposition in Chicago. Although Hood wrote two suites for violin, piano pieces, a piano trio, string quartet, and a Te Deum, she was noted principally for her songs. Unlike Lang's songs, which were closer in approach to the German lied, Hood's were principally "parlor songs," graceful, melodious, sentimental ballads, popular in their time but of passing interest. She died in 1949.

Still another pupil of Chadwick's was Mabel Wheeler Daniels, who brought with her to Germany a letter of introduction to Professor Gluth from Margaret Lang. Born on November 27, 1879, in Swampscott, Massachusetts, Mabel Daniels[65] came from a musical family. One grandfather, William Daniels, was an organist and a member of the Handel and Haydn Society from 1844 to 1886; the other grandfather was a choir director. Both her parents sang with the Handel and Haydn Society, and her father, George F. Daniels, served for a time as the society's president (1899–1908).

Daniels began piano lessons at an early age and wrote her first piece, *Fairy Charm Waltz,* at ten. She had a good soprano voice, and at Radcliffe College she joined the glee club and soon was given leading roles in the operettas it presented. She became the glee club's director, and wrote two operettas for it, *A Copper Complication* (1900) and *The Court of Hearts* (1900). After graduating magna cum laude (with high honors) in 1900, she studied composition with George Chadwick (who became a close friend) and then, in 1903, went to Germany to work with Ludwig Thuille. She was the first girl to be admitted to the score-reading class at the Royal Conservatory in Munich. (Apparently five years earlier women had not even been allowed to study counterpoint at the conservatory. In 1903 they could, but few chose to. Also, the faculty actually included two women professors—and thirty-eight men.)

After two winters in Germany, where the conservatory awarded her a medal, Daniels returned to the United States and joined the mixed chorus of the Cecilia Society in order to learn more about orchestration and scores (since she herself played no orchestral instrument). During this time she also wrote a book about her experiences in Germany, *An American Girl in Munich (Impressions of a Music Student),* which was published in 1905. Less influential then Amy Fay's book (see Chapter 3), it nevertheless presents an interesting picture of the life of American students abroad.

In 1908 the Boston "Pops" under Gustav Strube performed Daniels's first work for full orchestra, *In the Greenwood.* In 1911 she won two prizes from the National Federation of Music Clubs, one for the song "Villa of Dreams" and the other for two three-part songs for women's voices with violin and piano accompaniment. She also wrote *The Desolate City,* a cantata for baritone solo, chorus, and orchestra, which Marian MacDowell asked her to conduct at a MacDowell Colony summer festival in 1913. Mrs. MacDowell was so impressed that she invited Daniels to return the following summer as a "colonist" (resident artist), and Daniels, accepting the invitation and returning many times thereafter, wrote many of her later works during her stays there. (She also became a corporate member of the Edward MacDowell Association.) The prelude *Deep Forest,* one of her most frequently performed works, was inspired by one of her summers in the New Hampshire woods. Originally written for chamber orchestra, it was first performed by the Barrère Little Symphony; later it was revised for full orchestra and in this form was performed by Serge Koussevitsky, John Barbirolli, Hans Kindler, and other important conductors. Daniels herself conducted it with the Chicago Symphony on August 1, 1915, in a program of American compositions at the Pan-Pacific International Exposition in San Francisco.

Meanwhile Daniels was active in other areas as well. From 1911 to 1913 she directed the Radcliffe Glee Club and served as music director for the Bradford Academy, and from 1913 to 1918 she was director of music at Simmons College. She later became a member of the advisory committee on music for the Boston public schools, served as a trustee of Radcliffe College, and was an active member of the Society of American Women Composers. She was a good friend of many women composers, especially Amy Beach, Margaret Lang, and Helen Hopekirk (who rode with her in her carriage during a suffragist demonstration in Boston in 1915).

In 1929 Daniels wrote *Exultate Deo,* op. 33, for mixed chorus and orchestra, for the celebration of Radcliffe's fiftieth anniversary. It was later performed by the Boston Symphony and Cecilia Society under Koussevitsky, and became one of Daniels's best-known choral works. The cantata consists of four sections: The first and last ring out in praise of God, assisted by trumpet fanfares; the second describes the instruments that shall join together in praise; and the third is a short prayer of trust in God.

Though she produced a number of other works, the next important one—and some believe the most important of all her compositions—was *The Song of Jael,* op. 37, which had its premiere at the Worcester Festival of 1940. A cantata for soprano solo, mixed chorus, and orchestra, it was based on the poem *Sisera* by Daniels's close friend, Edward Arlington Robinson, and was the first of her works to use modern idioms. The story concerns a Jewish woman, Jael, who killed the tyrant Sisera while he slept and became a heroine to her people. The music consists of three sections, essentially two hymns of triumph separated by a shorter *Andante pastorale.* The *Boston Post* critic said its outstanding feature was the striking and highly original handling of the choral sections, but there were also many effective parts in the orchestral score, and the soprano solo, performed at Worcester by Rose Bampton, was dramatic and impressive.

In her later works Daniels continued to use modern idioms, although with some caution. Among these are *Pastoral Ode,* for flute and strings, op. 40 (1940), given its premiere by members of the Boston Symphony; *Three Observations for Three Woodwinds* (1943), a short satirical piece that the composer said was not intended to be taken too seriously and which has considerable charm; *Digressions for String Orchestra,* op. 41, no. 2 (1947); and *Two Pieces for Violin and Piano* (1948). Her last completed composition was *Piper, Play On!* op. 49 (1961), a choral work based on an ancient Greek text.

For the seventy-fifth anniversary of Radcliffe Daniels had written her last big choral work, *A Psalm of Praise,* op. 46, for mixed chorus, three trumpets, percussion, and strings. It was first performed by the Harvard Glee Club and Radcliffe Choral Society under G. Wallace Woodworth in 1954, with the piano playing the string parts. Two years later it was performed by the Boston Symphony, making Daniels the first woman ever to have had three different works performed by that orchestra *(Exultate Deo,* 1932; *Deep Forest,* 1937; and *A Psalm of Praise,* 1954).

Though Daniels was active in groups of women composers, she had some mixed feelings about this issue. Concerning the premiere of *The Song of Jael* at Worcester in 1940, she later recalled with amusement that she was called to the stage to take bows with conductor Albert Stoessel and then encountered a man at intermission who said, "That Jael piece was tremendous, and what a climax with the brass and drums and cymbal all going like mad while the chorus sings 'Jael has killed Sisera!' But tell me, what was that woman doing who came on to the stage when they applauded?"

Yet Daniels herself believed that women musicians and composers are handicapped in at least two ways. First, they have more exacting time-consuming obligations than men do, by which she meant not social functions but the ordinary routines of life (domestic and other). Second, she did not believe that most women have the physical strength to compose an extended list of symphonies, operas, string quartets, and other kinds of concerted music. The sheer burden of writing down, day after day, notes, dynamics, accents, and phrasing for all the different parts of an orchestral work was extremely hard work. It was for this reason, she said, that women usually stuck to the smaller forms. Four requisites, she maintained, were indispensable to any woman composer (over and above talent): a strong constitution, perseverance, ingenuity, and above all, courage.[66]

Awarded honorary degrees in music from Tufts and Boston universities, Wheaton College, and the New England Conservatory of Music, Mabel Daniels was highly respected throughout her long life. She was kind and generous to many young musicians and students, offered several composition prizes anonymously, set up a loan fund for music majors at Radcliffe, and established a scholarship at the New England Conservatory of Music, where she also served as a trustee. She died on March 10, 1971.

The last important "lady composer" of New England, Helen Hopekirk, was a Scot by birth. Like Beach, she began her career as a pianist, and it was in that capacity that she first came to Boston, where she eventually settled permanently, devoting herself to composition and teaching.

Helen Hopekirk was born near Edinburgh in 1856 and studied with G. Lichtenstein and A. C. Mackenzie.[67] She spent two years at the Leipzig Conservatory and later studied piano with Leschetizky in Vienna. She made her debut in Leipzig in 1878 and her English debut at the Crystal Palace in

London the following year. In 1882 she married a Scottish music critic and landscape painter, William A. Wilson, and in 1883 she made her first American tour, playing with the Boston Symphony on December 8, 1883, and giving a New York recital a couple of weeks later. She continued to study and perform in Europe during the 1880s, visited the United States again during the 1890-91 season, and moved to Boston permanently in 1897. From 1892 on she had been living in Paris, concentrating primarily on composition; in fact, her Sonata in E minor for violin and piano was first played in Boston at a Kneisel Quartet concert in March 1891. The *Musical Herald* critic liked the piece, calling it "a little classic in point of dignity of form." The themes were good; the repetition of the first movement's subjects was somewhat excessive but showed a sure musical touch. The slow movement was "really imaginative." And the Finale was "vivacious," though its ideas were slight.[68]

In 1897, after her husband was severely injured in a traffic accident and could no longer work, she accepted George Chadwick's offer of a job teaching piano at the New England Conservatory. The Wilsons remained in the United States for the rest of their lives, except for one year they spent in Edinburgh (1919-20), and both of them became American citizens. Hopekirk (she retained her maiden name for professional use) taught at the conservatory for four years, and in 1901 resigned, thereafter teaching only privately at her home.

Hopekirk's first major composition was her *Concertstück* for piano and orchestra, composed in Paris in 1894 and first played in Edinburgh by the Scottish Orchestra under Georg Henschel in November of that year. The American premiere took place seven years later, on April 15, 1904, with the Boston Symphony and the composer as soloist. The form of this work is that of a piano concerto in one movement, molded on classic lines in the opening section but then becoming freer. Although the program notes describe the unifying effect of a theme presented in the prelude that appears and reappears throughout, the *Boston Transcript* critic said the piece was rich in ideas but lacked unity (though many of the themes were "charming"). Besides the Violin Sonata, several other of her compositions had been heard in America. In June 1899 her song "Under the Still White Stars," with violin accompaniment, won a prize in the *Musical Record* contest in the category of concert songs. Then in 1900 the Boston Symphony performed her Piano Concerto in D major, which was never published.

For the next couple of decades Hopekirk continued to appear regularly in recitals of chamber music or of her own works, once or twice a year. In 1904, in an interview with Edith Lynwood Winn published in the August issue of the *Etude,* she said her ancestors were Celts and she had become interested in Gaelic song. The following year she published *Seventy Scottish*

*Songs,* which went into a number of editions and was considered very successful. Her next major published work was *Iona Melodies* (1910), four short piano works that show the influence of both Edward MacDowell and Scottish folk song. In an interview published in the *Musician* in 1912, Hopekirk said that she spent each morning composing and practicing, and each afternoon teaching; also, part of each year she spent in Europe, where she devoted her time entirely to composition. In 1919 she and her husband went to spend the entire year in Scotland, and at the time of their departure a silver bowl was presented to her by her friends; among the donors' names engraved on that bowl was M. R. Lang; so presumably Margaret Lang and Helen Hopekirk were good friends.

In 1925 Hopekirk became musical adviser for the Dana Hall Music School in Wellesley. The following year her husband died, but she continued to be active, giving recitals regularly and composing. Her last public appearance, in a recital of her own compositions before the Pianoforte Teachers Society of Boston, occurred in April 1939, a month before her eighty-third birthday. She died in November 1945 at the age of eighty-nine. She appears not to have composed any large-scale works after the early concertos, but she produced another violin sonata, more than a hundred songs, and many piano pieces.

Hopekirk's attitude toward other women musicians was also somewhat ambivalent. Like so many others, she wanted to be judged not as a woman composer or a woman pianist but as an individual making a contribution. Yet in 1901 she wrote a curious letter to the *Etude* concerning piano teachers. She believed that the ability to teach was found equally in men and in women, she said, but she opposed "the thoughtless plunging into teaching, by women, that is so prevalent." She went on:

In this country there is a perfect mania to become a teacher of some sort or other among people who, in Europe, would not feel themselves demeaned by doing housework well. Many girls would be much better employed and more comfortable keeping houses orderly and nicely—say for other women who through their work lack the time for personal supervision—than in giving cheap, bad piano-lessons and swelling the ranks of the victimizers of our much-abused piano.[69]

At the same time, she was an ardent suffragist and had great respect for the compositions of Mabel Daniels.

One more pianist-composer of European birth had enough impact in New England to be mentioned with this group of women. She was Adele Lewing,[70] born in 1866 in Hanover, Gemany, where her maternal grandfather, A. C. Prell, was a cellist in the court orchestra. She began her musical studies early and made her debut as a pianist at the age of twelve. She studied at Leipzig under Reinecke, graduated with high honors from the conservatory there, and then went to America, where she first taught and gave concerts in Chicago but later moved to Boston. On May 10, 1892, she gave a concert devoted entirely to her own compositions at the Meionaon in Boston, performing some twenty-five songs and piano works. In 1893 she played another program of her own piano compositions at the Woman's Congress of the Columbian Exposition in Chicago, and a number of her songs were sung there as well. Soon afterward she went to Vienna to study piano with Leschetizky and composition with Robert Fuchs, and she remained there for three years.

In October 1896 Lewing returned to New York and announced that she would teach the Leschetizky method and accept concert engagements. Her first concerts, in Carnegie Hall and Steinway Hall in December 1896, were well received. The following July her composition *Meditation* was played at the nineteenth annual convention of the Music Teachers National Association. In 1899 she married Dr. Benjamin W. Stiefel of New York, and the following year her song "Fair Rohtraut" won the *Musical Record's* first prize for a concert song. She continued to be active, teaching and composing, until her death in 1943, at the age of eighty-two.

A woman who was influential in Boston's musical world during the latter part of the nineteenth century was Clara Kathleen Barnett Rogers, who as Clara Doria had made a name for herself as an opera singer. Born in England in 1844, the daughter of composer John Barnett, she was graduated from the Leipzig Conservatory and also studied at Berlin and Milan. She came to the United States in 1871 on tour with the Parepa-Rosa company and several years later settled in Boston. In 1878 she married Henry Munroe Rogers, a Boston lawyer, and retired from professional performance, although she continued to participate in private musicales and amateur musical clubs. In 1883 she helped form a Bach Club, in order to study cantatas, and she was active in the Manuscript Club (founded in 1888), whose chief aim was to perform the works of young, unknown composers. At one of its early meetings she performed the piano part of her own Violin Sonata in D minor, together with Charles Loeffler; the same meeting also featured a group of songs by Margaret Lang and a Suite by Arthur Foote.

Rogers's other compositions included a string quartet, a cello sonata, some piano pieces, and a large number of art songs. Of her *Six Songs* for soprano or tenor, published in 1882, the *Musical Herald,* after a detailed description of each of the songs, said, "The set as a whole is one of the most poetic and genuinely beautiful that we have seen for a long time."[71] This was high praise indeed, for during this period dozens of newly published songs were listed in every issue. Another *Six Songs* by Rogers were reviewed in the same journal in April 1884, and two months later her Scherzo in A major for piano received a highly favorable review.

William Upton also admired Rogers's songs, which he said had great spontaneity and showed consummate skill in interpreting various moods. Artistically, he felt the best of her songs were the last—especially "Sudden Light," op. 33, no. 1 (1900) and "Overhead the Treetops Meet," op. 36 (1903), which he described as "choice songs of rare flavor, showing a high grade of musicianship."[72] In 1902 Clara Rogers joined the faculty of the New England Conservatory to teach voice, and thereafter she published a number of books on singing, among them *My Voice and I* (1910), *English Diction in Song and Speech* (1912), and *The Voice in Speech* (1915). She also wrote two autobiographical books, *Memories of a Musical Career* (1919) and *The Story of Two Lives* (1932). She died in 1931.

Though Boston was an outstanding American musical center during the last quarter of the nineteenth century, it certainly was not the only home for women composers during this period. At least three women of the same era, all of them known principally for their vocal compositions, pursued active careers elsewhere. The oldest of them was Mary Elizabeth Turner Salter (1856–1938), born in Peoria, Illinois,[73] who did study for a time at the New England Conservatory and with Hermine Rudersdorff near Boston, and briefly held the job of soprano soloist in Boston's St. Paul's Church. However, she followed Rudersdorff to New York, and in 1881 she married the organist and music teacher Sumner Salter, subsequently moving with him to Syracuse, Buffalo, Atlanta, New York City, and finally Williamstown, Massachusetts, where he became director of music at Williams College. This marriage produced five children, and when domestic duties began to interfere with her concert career as a singer, Mary Salter began to compose. She had had only a few formal piano lessons as a child and no formal training in theory or composition, but she ended up writing more than two hundred songs, as well as a number of anthems and other choral works, of which about a hundred were published. Among her best-known works were *The Cry of Rachel, The Pine Tree,* and *A Christmas Song.*

The other two women were midwesterners. Carrie Jacobs Bond (1862–1946) became famous for her popular songs, two of which are still sung today—"I Love You Truly" and "A Perfect Day." The former was her first published song; the latter sold some 7 million copies in sheet music and 5 million records. Born and educated in the small town of Janesville, Wisconsin, Bond began to compose at the age of thirty-two, after her husband died and she had to support herself and her young son. She promoted her songs by singing them at parties, dinners, and other entertainments, for which she was paid $10 per appearance; when publishers rejected her material, she started her own printing business. She ended by writing some 175 songs, and publishd her autobiography, *The Roads of Melody,* in 1927. Jessie L. Gaynor (1863–1921) of St. Louis, Missouri, became famous mostly for her children's songs, although she also wrote numerous piano pieces, piano-teaching material, and vocal quartets. She studied piano with Louis Maas and theory with A. J. Goodrich and Frederic Grant Gleason, and she taught in Chicago, St. Louis, and St. Joseph, Missouri.

Of a later generation but also remembered principally for their vocal compositions (though each published many other kinds of music as well) are Harriet Ware, Mana-Zucca, and Lily Strickland. Harriet Ware (1877–1962) was born in Wisconsin and studied in New York, Paris, and Berlin. Her *Women's Triumphal March* was made the national song of the Federation of Women's Clubs in 1927, and her symphonic poem, *The Artisan,* was performed by the New York Symphony Orchestra in 1929. She also wrote cantatas, a choral cycle, many songs, and an opera, *Undine.*

Mana-Zucca (b.1887?), born Augusta Zuckerman in New York City, was a piano prodigy who made her debut with the New York Symphony at eight, studied in the United States and Europe, gave a program of her own compositions in New York in 1917, and wrote a piano concerto (performed by her with the Los Angeles and National Symphony orchestras), violin concerto, piano trio, and many short piano pieces and songs. Allegedly she published well over a thousand compositions. Her most famous song is "I Love Life," to words by her husband, Irwin M. Cassel.

Lily Strickland (1887–1958) was born in South Carolina, studied music in New York, and published many songs, choral works, and piano pieces. Her piano compositions tended to have descriptive titles *(Cherokee Indian Dances, Moroccan Mosaics, East Indian Nautches)*; one of her best-known works was the song "Lindy Lou," which became a standard encore in song recitals.

One other area of nineteenth-century American composition deserves mention, that of church music, in which surprisingly few women's names are known. Although the organist and choir director in most American Protestant churches is a woman and many of these women have composed music, little of it is published or circulates beyond their own churches. Thus, though the *Musical Herald* of November 1881 says that, contrary to popular thought, there have been many fine women hymnists, six decades later Clement Harris said that of 150 women composers listed in music dictionaries and biographical works, only about one-sixth showed any predilection for sacred music,[74] and Ellinwood's biographies of American church musicians comprise 98 men and 3 women (2 of them Roman Catholic nuns).[75] Eva Munson Smith, herself a composer, made a collection of hymns by women that was published in 1885.[76] It contains some 2,500 hymns whose *texts* were written by women (more than 820 authors are represented). The preface states that only at the last minute was it decided to include music in the book, and consequently 52 women composers of hymns are represented as well; the compiler adds that given more time she surely would have found a great many more hymn tunes by women.

One reason is undoubtedly the lack of performance opportunities other than in the church to which the composer belongs. Beach's Mass in E-flat was performed just once, but her later anthems and other sacred works, all for smaller forces, were frequently performed at New York's St. Bartholomew's, where she was a loyal parishioner. Similarly, Mabel Daniels's sacred works were performed at Boston's Arlington Street Church, which she attended regularly. The music performed at the Washington (D.C.) Cathedral, one of the nation's important Episcopal churches, between 1941 and 1951 included only two works by women, Mabel Daniels's *The Christ Child* and Mary Howe's *Song of Ruth.* [77]

Although the sheer number of women composers increased vastly from the mid-1880s on,[78] public performance of thier works did not, neither by symphony orchestras nor by groups presumably sympathetic to women, such as the Music Teachers National Association (MTNA). At the tenth annual MTNA meeting, held in Boston in 1886, a program of all-American works included compositions by Parker, Chadwick, Paine, Rohde, Maas, Buck, Foote—not one by a woman. Nor were there women performers, except for a few singers and the women's chorus. "It is an oversight that speaks volumes and puts out of sight the much vaunted American estimation of feminine talent," protested Amelia Lewis.[79]

The representation of women at the Columbian Exposition of 1893, with its separate Woman's Building and special programs of women's music, was, generally speaking, a case of "separate but less than equal." In May, the opening month of the exposition, there were thirty-seven musical programs by visiting orchestras, quartets, and choruses at the big Music Hall, performing no works by women, and two programs at the Woman's Building. At the opening of the Woman's Building there was no orchestra, just an organ, in a concert of compositions written and performed by women.[80] In two special concerts of American music presented at the Music Hall on May 23 and 24, no woman composer was represented. The only work by a woman played at the Music Hall apparently was Lang's *Witchis* overture. Yet there was no lack of women composers. In 1896 the Manuscript Society of New York, founded in 1889 to give its members (all composers) a chance to hear their own works played, had 1,000 members and practically every one of its concerts included works by women (the members included Beach, Lang, Rogers, Hood, and others).[81]

Neither the New York Philharmonic nor the Boston Symphony had performed a single work by a woman until the latter played Lang's *Dramatic Overture* in 1893. Between then and the start of World War I, works by only 3 women (Beach, Lang, and Hopekirk) were played by the Boston Symphony, as well as works by 249 men. The records for New York and Boston did not improve markedly after 1914. Boston performed Beach's piano concerto once more (1917); three works by Mabel Daniels, once each; Leginska's *Two Short Pieces for Orchestra* (1924); and three works by the Frenchwoman Germaine Tailleferre (in 1925, 1926, and 1927). New York did Mana-Zucca's *Fugato-Humoresque on "Dixie"* (1916–17 season), Marion Bauer's *Sun Splendor* (1947–48 season), and Julia Perry's *Study for Orchestra* (1965).[82]

In 1975 *Musical America* asked five of the major U.S. orchestras what works by women they had performed in the past decade. Cleveland had done none, Detroit one (Warren's *The Crystal Lake,* 1974), New York the same Warren work (1974) and two works by Ruth Crawford Seeger (1971, 1974); San Francisco had performed *Sun* by Tonia Scherchen (1973); and Los Angeles the Warren work (1965) and, in 1972, a special program devoted to women composers and performed at U.C.L.A., with works by Beach, Warren, Seeger, and three other women.[83]

Only after 1975 did women begin to be represented more, although still with the fanfare accompanying a novelty. The New York Philharmonic did a program of music composed entirely by women and led by a woman conductor, Sarah Caldwell, in November 1975. (Ironically, it was a benefit for the orchestra's pension fund that, considering the number of men versus women players, helped chiefly men.) Even as late as 1978, the performance of a work by Barbara Kolb on the regular subscription series of the Boston Symphony prompted a special interview in the Boston *Globe,* radio talks, and other publicity that rarely accompanies the first (or local premiere) performance of a piece of contemporary music. Women composers were just beginning to be heard; they were far from being "conquerors."

# 5 APARTHEID: THE ALL-WOMEN'S ORCHESTRAS

From a "lady violinist" to a "ladies' orchestra" would seem to be but a short step, but in reality it was a giant stride, and one toward a dead end, at that. That women instrumentalists should have been excluded from conventional orchestras—which might just as well have been called "gentlemen's orchestras"—is hardly surprising. Despite the increase in women instrumental players, particularly violinists, in the second half of the nineteenth century, despite the growth of music schools and conservatories, despite a spate of articles saying, "Why shouldn't women play instruments?" women were not encouraged to play professionally, either as soloists or in ensembles.

A major reason for their exclusion was economic. Any post given to a woman meant one less opening for a man. And the very fact that women had been allowed to play instruments other than keyboard instruments for only a short time led to the conclusion that few competent women players were available, especially for the woodwind, brass, and percussion sections.

In any event, women were largely excluded. The *Boston Herald* of December 12, 1878, for example, reported a real novelty: A new orchestra in Louisville was going to admit women, and a number of violinists, violists, and cellists were about to join, along with a woman cornetist. But the Harvard Symphony Orchestra, said the *Herald* reporter, "an old conservative society," would not admit women players. The Chicago Orchestra during its first season (1892–93) had one woman harpist, Mrs. Lawrence A. Winch, and one man harpist; the following season it employed Mrs. C. Wunderle as harpist (she probably was the wife of C. Wunderle, listed for both cymbals and viola).[1] The Philadelphia Orchestra, in contrast, did not employ a woman harpist (or any other woman instrumentalist) on a regular basis until the 1930–31 season. (See Chapter 10 for more recent practices in orchestral hiring.)

The harp was, as we saw, sanctioned for women, and women string players were growing in numbers. But orchestras also include brasses and woodwinds. Could women play those as well? Contrary to Victorian belief, women had been playing wind instruments for centuries. The flute was played by women in numerous ancient cultures (Sumerian, Egyptian, Greek, and Roman iconography shows women playing flutes). Early Christianity began to forbid such active music making by women,[2] although this proscription did not apply to prostitutes, nor did it affect the lower classes. Peasant women of all cultures had always made and played pipes and flutes.[3] During the Renaissance, respectable women again were permitted to play instruments—flutes, along with lutes, viols, virginals—but this applied largely to courtly ladies. A few of these women actually formed little orchestras of their own; among them was Tarquinia Molza, a composer who organized and conducted her own women's orchestra at the Italian court of Ferrara.[4] And eighteenth-century Venice had all-female orchestras made up of musically trained orphans that were named for their sponsoring charitable institution, such as the Mendicanti, heard in 1774 by Charles Burney, the English music historian.[5]

These groups were largely, if not entirely, made up of string and keyboard players. As late as 1880 Maria Bianchini of Venice, a concert flutist, was still a great novelty (though critic Eduard Hanslick pointed out that she had predecessors in Madame Rousseau in 1827 and Mademoiselle Lorenzine Meyer from about 1830 to 1840). Hanslick praised Bianchini's performance, saying that "she avoids the ugly contortions of the lips and short-breathed blowing which may so easily jeopardize the aesthetic effect of flute-playing. Managed as it was on the occasion in question, the flute is decidedly not an unfeminine instrument."[6] In response an American reader wrote to the *Musical Record* that there was a comparable lady flutist in America: Madame Emilie Schiller, a flute teacher in Chicago and "a virtuoso much admired."[7] Nine years later the same journal reported, "New York has a lady flautist, of whom great things are expected,"[8] and in 1900 it announced that a Danish flutist, Julie Peterson, was coming to settle in the United States (her name had appeared earlier in an ad placed by flute manufacturer John C. Haynes and Company, in which she was described as "a world-renowned concert flute virtuoso and teacher").[9]

If flutists and other woodwind players were rare, one would think women brass players would be scarcer still. Yet as early as 1873 Miss Nellie Daniels, cornet soloist, joined Spaulding's Concert Company,[10] and a few months later a Ladies Cornet Band, led by Georgie Dean Spaulding (with her gold cornet), played in Vermont.[11] In 1875 it was announced that Anna Berger, cornetist, would take lessons from Matthew Arbuckle,[12] and in 1879 another ladies' cornet band was organized in Tipton, Indiana.[13] In the early 1880s at least one woman cornetist, Miss Fannie Rice of Lowell, Massachusetts, advertised her services for concerts or entertainments.[14] A child prodigy, Ida Clark of Chicago (aged thirteen), appeared in 1885,[15] and in the same year Eva Hewitt reportedly "played so beautifully that she has astonished Levy and received an engagement for New Orleans, where she will be a novelty next season."[16]

By 1889 Anna Berger had profited enough from Arbuckle and her other teachers to go on tour, and she was well received at Covent Garden and London's Promenade concerts.[17] The following year the *Musical Herald* reported: "Madame Anna Teresa Berger, an American (wife of the manager Leigh Lynch) has electrified English audiences at Covent Garden by her cornet playing. She played fifty nights in succession and has accepted offers from France, Germany, and Russia."[18]

Even more unusual was the achievement of saxophone virtuoso Elise Hall (always listed in programs as Mrs. R[ichard]J. Hall), for her instrument was uncommon for men players as well. A pupil of Georges Longy (principal oboist of the Boston Symphony and founder of the Longy School of Music in Cambridge), she became manager of the (second) Orchestral Club of Boston (founded in 1899), which Longy conducted. Critic Philip Hale praised her playing at an Orchestral Club concert, commending her technical mastery, musical intelligence, and beautiful tone.[19] She was the first amateur ever to appear with the Boston Symphony Orchestra, playing the long solo in Bizet's *Arlésienne Suite* no. 1 in the subscription concerts on December 24 and 25, 1909, "because no [other] competent saxophonist" could be found.[20] A number of composers—among them Vincent d'Indy, Charles Loeffler, and Georges Longy himself—wrote compositions especially for her. Hall herself had received most of her musical education at the Paris Conservatory, renowned for its school of wind playing, and in 1909 she reportedly was taking up another instrument as well, the new doublebass clarinet.

There were others too, for by the late nineteenth century women's (brass) bands had become more common. Indeed, a letter to the *Musical Record* in 1882 claims a considerable history for this phenomenon. The writer, J. Heneage Carter of Louisville, maintains that he managed the first female brass band in the United States:

Twenty years ago [in 1862] I had a number of young girls—from ten to fourteen years of age—who were engaged to give a military drill in the performances of my company. My orchestral leader suggested that I should try and form these girls into a brass band. I almost scouted the idea, but, shortly after, a man desired me to engage him as a cornet player. I did so, and asked him to co-operate with my leader to see what they could do with the girls in brass band playing. The result was that my "young female brass band" was soon formed, and the people of the cities of New England, and other sections, abundantly testified to the popularity of my troupe. Had I not taken the celebrated Berger Family into my service, and had them taught to play brass music, the public would probably never have heard Miss Anna Teresa Berger (Mrs. Leigh Lynch) playing cornet solos... My company was known as the Carter Zouave Troupe.[21]

In 1888 the 120-woman Ladies Band of Audubon, Iowa, performed at the annual meeting of the Northwestern Band Association,[22] and by 1895 the *Musical Record,* announcing the formation of another new women's band in Michigan, commented that this "hobby" seems to prevail to a considerable extent in the West. By then Boston had had its own Ladies' Military Band for some years. Organized in 1890, it consisted of thirty "young ladies" who toured the United States and Ontario in the 1898–99 season (directed by Mr. D. W. Howard) and played at the Pan-American Exposition in September 1901.[23] Also, an ad in the *Musical Review* of October 1899 shows the Ladies' Talma Band, an eighteen-woman wind ensemble that was allegedly the chief attraction at the Boston resort, Norumbega Park.

Beginning in the late 1870s, a special variety of women's orchestra became popular. It was modeled after the Vienna Ladies Orchestra, which had first come to America on tour in 1871 and aroused considerable interest. One reviewer said:

One of the musical sensations of next season will be the female orchestra, consisting entirely of female performers, which Mr. Rullmann has brought over from Vienna, and who will make their appearance at Steinway Hall in September. Judging from their photographs, they must be quite pretty.[24]

The Vienna group was organized in 1867 by Josephine Weimlich, who at first formed a string quartet that later expanded. By 1871 it had about twenty players: four first violins, three second violins, one viola, two cellos, one double bass, one flute, one piccolo, one harp, one parlor organ, and three drums. The ensemble performed mostly light music—waltzes, movements from operettas by Strauss, von Suppé, and other popular composers of the time, and an occasional movement from a symphony. The *Metronome* critic did not like the group at all, terming them "another foreign fraud" because they lacked horns, trumpets, trombones, clarinets, oboes, and bassoons, and therefore were not really an orchestra.[25]

Originally, the Vienna Ladies Orchestra came to the United States as concert artists, but by 1873 they were roaming about the land as "lager-beer musicians," playing in restaurants and beer gardens. Moreover, common report had it that the women were very poorly paid, earning no more than $15 or $20 per week even though they played every night until after midnight.[26]

Their detractors notwithstanding, the Vienna Ladies Orchestra soon had numerous American imitators which became closely associated with German-American entertainment. In New York they played in the German music halls of lower Manhattan, such as the Bowery Garten, Atlantic Garten, and Volksgarten. In fact, they were often known by the German term for ladies' orchestra, *Damen Orchester*. Their appeal, like that of the brass bands, was based entirely on their oddity; the curiosity value of women playing cornets and double basses was such that audiences would come for that alone.[27] Moreover, if any instrument was lacking and no woman player could be found, they used one or more men instrumentalists dressed in women's clothes to preserve at least the illusion of an "all-female" ensemble. The most famous of these groups was the Ladies Elite Orchestra, which performed at the Atlantic Garten for more than thirty-five years. Its repertory varied during this long period, but for the most part it played popular songs as well as selections from opera—both grand and light—between vaudeville acts.[28]

New York had the largest number of these ensembles, but they existed elsewhere as well. Ohio had at least two, one at Schumann's Garden and the other at Meyer's Music Hall,[29] while Boston had Kampa's Ladies Orchestra, made up of six sisters,[30] and John Braham's Female Theater Orchestra, based at the Oakland Garden. Of the latter group a reviewer wrote:

Lady artists, a lady chorus, a lady ballet, an orchestra composed of ladies, lady ushers, lady doorkeepers, and lady ticket-sellers held possession of Oakland Garden, Boston, during the presentation of "An Adamless Eden." Who shall say that "Woman's rights" are not progressing?[31]

The first to deny the truth of this, in all likelihood, would have been the very performers in question, who could enter the entertainment world only through the back door. After all, blacks formed their own minstrel troupes and, as late as the 1940s, their own baseball league because that was the only way they could appear in public. Women likewise formed their own orchestras, and exploited their novelty value, in order to play their instruments and be paid for it (however little). Said one member of the Ladies Elite Orchestra, "If I had the chance to substitute for a man I should do so in a minute, and should look for more and better opportunities to follow."[32] (Nor did Jackie Robinson turn down a contract with the Brooklyn Dodgers when it finally came along.)

In the case of orchestral musicians, economic discrimination was supported by prejudices and stereotypes. If women were considered on the same level as men, they would presumably compete with men for the same jobs. But if they could not play the same instruments at all, or not as well, or if they could not play the same kind of music, their threat was automatically diminished. Thus initially women were told they were not "strong" enough to play large, heavy instruments—tubas and double basses, for example—or not "skilled" enough for some of the others (oboes and clarinets and drums). Then if they proved that they could indeed play these instruments, they were told they were not talented or dedicated enough to play serious music and had to confine themselves to the lighter repertory.

The rapid growth of American music schools and conservatories in the late nineteenth century aggravated the problem. What would become of all the women musicians they were turning out in growing numbers? They could not all become teachers, for that market would soon be glutted (and further, on the assumption that teachers would train still more musicians, the problem would be compounded for future generations).

The solution was segregation. Women could, on the one hand, form professional all-women's ensembles, which would survive, despite their alleged inferior quality, because of their novelty appeal and because they were willing to play any music, anywhere, any time, that would appeal to a paying audience. Or they could, on the other hand, remain dedicated amateurs, performing serious music if they wished (since they were not paid for playing anyway).

As a result, the late nineteenth century saw the formation of two kinds of women's orchestra. The one was professional (in that performers were paid) and played mostly popular but some serious music, often in conjunction with other kinds of popular entertainment (principally vaudeville). The other was amateur (that is, unpaid), even though its members might be highly trained and of professional caliber. Boston and New York each had several ensembles of both kinds (and some that fell somewhere between the two categories). One was the Ladies (Amateur) Orchestra of New York, which gave charity concerts in 1888 and 1889.[33] The (first) Orchestral Club of Boston, formed in 1885, included both men and women, though the latter were in practice confined to the violin section. It included some pupils of Julius Eichberg's (see Chapter 2), among them Lillian Chandler, Jennie Ladd, Georgie Pray (a cellist but playing violin here), Edith Christie, Lettie Launder, and Fannie Grebe.[34] In contrast, the Beacon Orchestral Club of Boston, conducted by violinist Marietta B. Sherman, consisted wholly of women (ten violins, two violas, one cello, one trombone, one flute, two cornets, one clarinet, and one piano).[35]

Boston also had two hybrid (semiprofessional) ensembles. The twenty-five-piece Englesbian (Lady) Orchestra, under conductor J. E. Dandlin, performed at the Brookline Town Hall on January 24, 1888, featuring as soloists Georgie Pray (on the cello), cornetist Lizzie Howe, and several men; the program announced that the group was available for concerts and other "occasions," suggesting that fees might be involved.[36] During the same year, Marion Osgood's Lady Orchestra reportedly enjoyed a successful season; all the "young ladies" in this group were said to have considerable concert experience.[37] Again, it is not clear if this ensemble was paid or not. Definitely unpaid, however, were the Ladies Philharmonic Orchestra of

Boston, formed about 1892 under Arthur W. Thayer, and the Women's String Orchestra of New York, formed in 1896 under Carl V. Lachmund.The latter consisted of twenty-eight string players, among them Jeanne Franko (see Chapter 2).[38] Both these groups were devoted to serious music exclusively, and each survived for about ten years. A typical program was that presented by the Boston women on January 23, 1900: Mendelssohn's Italian Symphony, Tchaikovsky's *Nutcracker Suite* in its Boston premiere, and Schubert's Unfinished Symphony.[39]

Of the professional ensembles, by far the most prominent and longest lived was the Fadette Women's Orchestra of Boston, which was founded in 1888 by violinist Caroline B. Nichols.[40] Named for Fanchon Fadette, the heroine of a Georges Sand novel *(La Petite Fadette)* who brought joy to her townspeople, this ensemble survived until 1920 and in all yielded more than $500,000 to more than 600 performers. It presented more than 6,000 concerts in the United States and Canada, playing symphonies, all of the classical overtures, selections from seventy-five grand operas, and numerous salon pieces and popular songs. In 1902 it began the first of its fifteen winter tours on the Keith circuit, traveling all over North America as a twenty-woman ensemble. In summer, augmented to forty players, it performed at Keith's Theatre in Boston, where it had displaced an ensemble of Boston Symphony players (all men, of course) who were understandably disgruntled at losing their summer jobs (especially since the Fadettes included a few of their own former pupils).

The Fadettes' founder and conductor, Caroline Nichols, was yet another pupil of Julius Eichberg's. Born in 1864 in Dedham, Massachusetts, the daughter of a choir director, she also studied violin with Leopold Lichtenberg and Charles Loeffler, and theory with Percy Goetschius and J. B. Claus. Her motive in founding the Fadettes was quite straightforward: to provide employment for herself and other women musicians. She began, on October 1, 1888, with a group of six players, which by 1890 had grown to fifteen. Supported by Nichols's brother-in-law, George H. Chickering (president of the Chickering Piano Company), the Fadettes gave a few recitals in Chickering Hall, and Benjamin J. Lang (see Chapter 4) was among those who praised their performance. The group soon grew to twenty: four first violins, two second violins, one viola, one cello, two double basses, one flute (doubling on piccolo), one clarinet, two cornets, two French horns (allegedly the only two women horn players in the entire United States),[41] one trombone, two percussionists (tympani and drums), and one harp.

In 1895 the group was incorporated in Massachusetts and given a charter with exclusive rights to its name. Three years later it toured the East, the West, and the South, ending with a six-week junket through Canada. Then, in the summer of 1902, Keith engaged the Fadettes for a two-week tryout in his Boston theater and promptly invited them to remain for the rest of that season. That fall they also joined the Keith winter circuit. They performed in so-called "first-class" (i.e., respectable) vaudeville theaters all over America, interspersing musical performances with comic routines and skits. In one such skit, the orchestra members would pretend to quarrel and leave the stage, one by one, forcing the conductor (Nichols) to take up first one instrument and then another in order to keep the music going. One of the group's innovations was that they would play pieces by popular request; indeed, their official program booklet eventually listed a repertory of 600 pieces from which the audience could make requests.

For a time the Fadettes also accompanied silent films at Roxy's Theatre in New York, but the musicians' union put a stop to this undertaking. Eventually Nichols retired to Boston, where for a time she trained new orchestra members. In the end, it was said, she had trained more young women for professional, wage-earning self-supporting orchestral jobs than any other individual. She died in 1939, at the age of seventy-five. In June 1952 nine survivors of the original Fadettes assembled in Boston to celebrate the fiftieth anniversary of their first season with Keith.[42] The total they looked back on was staggering: 2,025 concerts in parks and summer resorts, 3,050 concerts in vaudeville theaters, 364 in Boston alone.

The Fadettes were unique, and not just in their long life. They were the only professional women's orchestra of their time that directly and successfully competed with men's ensembles. Not only did they oust established Boston Symphony players from their summer jobs, but Caroline Nichols often found herself on the same podium as John Philip Sousa, Walter Damrosch, and Victor Herbert—all highly respected conductors. The Fadettes may have begun with purely novelty status, but they eventually transcended it.

In 1903 discrimination against women orchestral players officially ended when the Musicians Union, in order to join the American Federation of Labor, was forced to admit women for the first time (see Chapter 10 for more about the union's role). Although 31 women (and 4,469 men) were enrolled in New York at that time,[43] in the following decades only a few women harpists found their way into major orchestras, and the women's orchestra movement had by no means become obsolete. As late as 1936 *Women in Music,* edited by conductor Frederique Petrides, claimed that there were 522 women playing in 8 women's orchestras—and this did not include jazz orchestras or chamber ensembles with fewer than 15 players. The two largest women's orchestras then were the Women's Symphony of Long Beach (California), with 105 players, and the Woman's Symphony of Chicago, with 100; the Los Angeles Women's Symphony had only 70 members but was the oldest still in existence, then in its forty-fifth season.[44]

Indeed, the women's orchestra movement was far from being an exclusively eastern phenomenon.[45] Early in the 1890s San Francisco had a Saturday Morning Orchestra of twenty-six players, all women (nine violins, three violas, four cellos, two double basses, one flute, three cornets, one trombone, one harp, one snare drum, one tympani). Its first conductor was a Professor Rosenwald, but in October 1895 he was replaced by Alfred Roncovieri. The Los Angeles Women's Symphony was founded in 1893, under conductor Harley Hamilton. It began with twenty-five players, and expanded (by 1936) to seventy. In its early decades it was principally an amateur group, although it always had a few professional musicians in its ranks. It regularly gave anywhere from three to eight concerts per year, playing at first the lighter repertory but in time attempting symphonies and other classical works. The Cleveland Ladies Orchestra, on the other hand, which gave daily concerts during the summer of 1900 at Atlantic City's Royal Palace Hotel, was a professional group that stuck to the popular repertory.

The Women's Orchestra of Minneapolis, founded in 1910, consisted of twenty-nine players, twenty-two of them women. (Most likely its two bassists, two cornetists, two cellists, and one euphonium player were men, but this is a matter of conjecture.) The Women's Orchestral Club of New York, organized in 1914 under Theodore Spiering, was definitely all female; an amateur group, it was founded in order to give women ensemble practice and it survived for at least three seasons. Oddly enough, there had been, for nearly twenty years, a New York organization that should have provided such opportunities. This was the quasi-professional Women's Philharmonic Society of New York, which was founded in 1899 by Melusina Fay Peirce, sister of Amy Fay (see Chapter 3). By 1910 it had more than two hundred members, including both performers and teachers. Though all its members were professional musicians (they included pianist Amy Fay, violinist Jeanne Franko, and singer and voice teacher Eugenie Pappenheim, among others), the society seems to have functioned as a nonprofit philanthropic organization, its object both to provide performance opportunities and to give scholarships to students in piano, violin, voice, and composition. It supported both an all-women's orchestra and a chorus, and it presented four large concerts each season (usually in Carnegie Hall) as well as monthly musicales. Presumably the performers were not paid, though admission may have been charged to pay for the hall rental and other expenses. It was still alive as late as 1916, when it gave an orchestral concert. However, as the *Etude* reviewer of that occasion points out, though the all-women's orchestra included one double bass and several flutes, clarinets, and cornets, there were no "heavy" brasses (trombone or tuba), a piano being substituted to play these parts.[46]

In the 1920s a few orchestras finally began to hire women other than harpists. In 1925 the *Etude* announced that five women—four violinists and a cellist—had been engaged by the San Francisco Symphony, the first time a first-rank orchestra had made such a move, and commended conductor Alfred Hertz "for his courage."[47] Many women harpists were already being employed, and both the Cleveland and Minneapolis orchestras had a few women violinists; moreover, in smaller city orchestras many players were women.[48]

Obviously these new opportunities represented just a drop in the bucket, for women's orchestras continued to be founded all over the country. The year 1925 saw the formation of the Long Beach Women's Symphony under conductor Eva Anderson (it had 102 players and gave more than 100 concerts in its first decade); the Women's Symphony of Philadelphia (founded by trumpeter Mabel Swint Ewer, conducted by J. W. F. Leman, with 70 members), which performed the standard orchestral repertory into the late 1930s; the American Women's Symphony Orchestra of New York, organized and conducted by the Dutch composer Elizabeth Kuyper, who had led similar ensembles in Europe; and the Chicago Woman's Symphony Orchestra (100 players, at first conducted by Elena Moneak, from 1928 to 1937 by Ebba Sundstrom, and thereafter by various men conductors; it survived through the end of World War II).

In most instances women's orchestras were begun by a local musician (instrumentalist or conductor) who wanted to create performance opportunities for herself and other local women. But in at least two cases such ensembles were founded by women conductors who had led all-male orchestras elsewhere and decided to found a women's orchestra in some particular city that appeared to have a sufficient number of unemployed women instrumentalists. These two were the Boston Woman's Symphony Orchestra, established by Ethel Leginska, and the Woman's Symphony of New York, founded by Antonia Brico. Both ensembles lasted for a number of years, whereupon they admitted a few men players, renamed the group for its conductor (Leginska's Symphony Orchestra and Brico Symphony Orchestra), and soon afterward disbanded.

If playing in an orchestra was a male province, conducting was far more so. What more outspoken role of leadership could there be than leading an orchestra? "A conductor," said one woman of her profession, "controls the orchestra in order to embody the expression of the composer and to project the music itself."[49] Traditionally such control, especially over an all-male orchestra, requires a forcefulness that was encouraged only in men. Even in the late nineteenth century women conductors were extremely rare. Hermine Rudersdorff, a German soprano who settled in America in the 1870s and became a famous voice teacher, conducted the Handel and Haydn Society of Boston in the quartets of Mendelssohn's *Elijah* in 1872, and did it so well that "it was said that she could have conducted singers, orchestra, and all if given the chance."[50] (She was not.) Selma Borg, a Scandinavian, conducted one performance at Boston's Music Hall in June 1879.[51] Nor should one conclude, just because both Rudersdorff and Borg were Europeans, that the situation was any different in Europe. Amy Fay, writing about her stay in Germany from 1869 to 1875, reported:

Did you read my letter to N.S., in which I told her about Alicia Hund, who composed and conducted a symphony? That is quite a step for women in the musical line... All the men were highly disgusted because she was allowed to conduct the orchestra herself. I didn't think myself that it was a very *becoming* position, though I had no prejudice against it. Somehow, a woman doesn't look well with a baton in her hand directing a body of men.[52]

By the turn of the century only two American women had become well-known conductors, Caroline Nichols of the Fadettes and Emma Steiner, who conducted principally light opera (see Chapter 8).

In addition to superb musicianship, a successful conductor usually must have a vivid personality, which can command both the orchestra and the attention of the audience. The latter was possessed in abundance by Ethel Leginska, one of the most colorful women musicians of her time. Born in 1886 in Hull, England, and originally named Ethel Liggins, she (like many performers) changed her name to sound more exotic.[53] She began her musical career as a pianist, studying first in England and then at Hoch's Conservatory in Frankfurt. At fourteen she allegedly ran away to Vienna to study with Leschetizky, where she remained for three years and was one of the few students he consented to teach gratis. She made her orchestral debut at sixteen in London, under conductor Henry Wood. For a time she pursued a successful career as a concert pianist in Europe, and in 1912 she came to the United States, making her New York debut that fall. She appeared in New York every subsequent season through 1919, receiving very favorable reviews; Aldrich said she showed great delicacy of interpretation, was marvelous in Beethoven's Waldstein Sonata, and also played Bach, Mozart, and Schubert very well. She also was known for her all-Chopin recitals.

In 1907 Leginska had married Roy Emerson Whithorne, an American composer from Cleveland who served as her manager for a time, and in 1915 the newspapers were full of their sensational divorce suit, complete with a custody fight over their six-year-old son. Leginska claimed that Whithorne had deserted her and insisted she could earn enough to support the child. (She later lost custody of her son to her ex-husband's parents.) She gave numerous interviews to newspapers during this period, explaining that the only way a woman could succeed as a concert pianist was to stand on her own feet and emulate a man in her dress and hairstyle. Contending that the conventional bare-shouldered evening dress of women artists was a terrible handicap in concert halls (often unheated), she devised her own costume, consisting of a black silk skirt and black velvet jacket over a white brocade vest and silk shirt with a mannish collar and cuffs. She also affected a hairstyle resembling that worn by Paderewski and Liszt. Not only in her unconventional dress, which aroused both interest and much publicity, did she show her definite knack for promotion. When she caught her finger in a door in 1916, she promptly sent an X-ray of the bruised finger to *Musical America,* which published it. She also omitted taking intermission breaks during a long, difficult program at Carnegie Hall in 1916, a feat that made headlines.

In 1919, after seven seasons of constant touring throughout the United States, Leginska announced that she would retire from performing for a season and devote herself entirely to composition and teaching; at that time one journal described her as "the Paderewski of women pianists."[54] She had spent the summer of 1918 studying composition with Ernest Bloch, and during the next few years she produced a considerable number of compositions—orchestral works such as the symphonic poem *Beyond the Fields We Know* (1921), *Two Short Poems* (1922), and the four-movement suite *Quatre Sujets Babares* (1923), *Four Poems* for string quartet (given its premiere by the London String Quartet at London's Aeolian Hall, June 14, 1921), *Six Nursery Rhymes* for soprano and small orchestra (1923; given three performances by the Boston Philharmonic in 1926), and numerous songs and piano works.

In 1924 Leginska embarked on yet another career: conducting. In October she conducted the Paris Conservatory Orchestra, and in November she led (allegedly) the London Symphony, Berlin Philharmonic, and Munich Konzertverein orchestras. (In newspaper interviews and publicity releases in the United States, Leginska claimed to have been the first woman to conduct the previously mentioned ensembles, but she may have embroidered her feats somewhat; Antonia Brico also said she was the first woman to conduct the Berlin Philharmonic, in 1930, and her claim is better documented.) In any event, Leginska was back in the United States early in 1925, and proceeded to conduct the New York Symphony Orchestra at Carnegie Hall in Beethoven's Symphony no. 7 in January (first appearance of a woman on the Carnegie Hall podium), the People's Symphony of Boston in April, and the Los Angeles Symphony in August.

The following year Leginska founded a new 100-man Boston Philharmonic Orchestra (all men except for the harpist and pianist), which was intended to make good music available to the masses by charging very little for tickets (25 cents admission, 50 cents and up for seats). She led this ensemble in its first concert on October 24, 1926, in overtures by Weber and Wagner, Beethoven's Symphony no. 5, the premiere of Peterka's *The Triumph of Life,* and Liszt's Hungarian Fantasy (for which Leginska performed the piano solo as well as conducting). This concert got excellent reviews in all of the Boston papers (*Herald, Globe, Transcript,* and *Christian Science Monitor*). But the ensemble survived just one season. Nevertheless, in March 1927, Leginska offered to conduct and train, without a fee, the Boston Women's Symphony Orchestra, which made its "introductory appearance" on March 23 and gave its first real concert December 12, 1927 (to mixed reviews). This ensemble was made up of about sixty-five performers, all women, and frequently played works by women composers. The third concert, on April 14, 1928, featured Radie Britain's *Symphonic Intermezzo* (see Chapter 7) and an arrangement of a Bach Prelude and Fugue for strings by Mabel Wood Hill, as well as Leginska's own *Fantasie* for piano and orchestra (which, according to the Boston *Herald,* was "not old-fashioned," for it had "fascinating discords, and modern rhythms").

In its second season, Leginska took the Boston Women's Symphony on tour for six weeks to Chicago, St. Louis, Milwaukee, Buffalo, Cleveland, and Washington, D.C. (presenting 52 programs in 38 cities). For its February concert it played the Boston premiere of Leginska's *Triptych* for eleven solo instruments. By 1930, according to the printed program, the Boston Women's Symphony had, in its three years, played more than 200 symphonic concerts in 21 states. For its program of January 29, 1930, a few men appeared with the orchestra, and its name was now Leginska's Women's Symphony Orchestra. (Leginska later explained that when Boston women could not be found for certain parts, she could not afford to import women players from other cities and simply had to substitute local men instrumentalists.) But this turned out to be the ensemble's last concert.

Leginska did not give up, however. In 1932 she started another women's orchestra, this time called the National Women's Symphony and based in New York City. It gave its first concert in Carnegie Hall on March 12, 1932, playing Schubert's Symphony in B-flat, Glinka's Overture to *Russlan and Ludmilla,* and the Mozart Piano Concerto in A major (with Leginska conducting from the piano). It was well received but appears to have disbanded soon afterward.

Between 1930 and 1932 Leginska also found time to compose her first opera, *The Rose and the Ring,* based on a satire by Thackeray. (It was not performed until 1957, in Los Angeles.) She had done some opera conducting as well, presenting *Carmen* in English at Boston's Jordan Hall in May 1929. She then wrote another opera, *Gale,* and herself conducted the premiere, with the Chicago Civic Opera Company and John Charles Thomas in the title role, on November 23, 1935. She continued to make guest conducting appearances, but by 1939 she had moved to Los Angeles, and thereafter she devoted herself almost entirely to teaching piano. In the 1940s she established a series of public piano recitals devoted to the works of individual composers, and in the 1950s she was still presenting her pupils in musicales, often including some of her own piano pieces and songs. A woman of considerable talent and energy, she remained active until she died, in 1970, at the age of eighty-three.

Less flamboyant than Ethel Leginska but just as determined to pursue a conducting career was Antonia Brico,[55] who was born in Holland on June 26, 1902 and was brought up in California. In 1923 she graduated from the

University of California at Berkeley, where she assisted Paul Steindorff in directing the chorus and also in his work at the San Francisco Opera. She then studied piano for two years with Sigismund Stojowski in New York and went on to Berlin, where she studied privately with Karl Muck and at the State Academy of Music. She spent five years (1925–30) at its master school of conducting, becoming its first American graduate. She made her debut with the Berlin Philharmonic on February 14, 1930, conducting a Dvořák symphony, a Handel concerto grosso, and the Schumann Piano Concerto in A minor, with Valesca Burgstaller as soloist. There followed four years of conducting appearances in Germany, Poland, and other European countries, although she took time to come to America in 1930 for appearances with the Los Angeles Symphony at the Hollywood Bowl and the San Francisco Symphony.

In 1933 Brico returned to the United States, making her New York debut at the Metropolitan Opera House with the Musicians Symphony Orchestra. She conducted a second concert there but then was denied a third appearance because the baritone John Charles Thomas refused to work under a woman conductor. (Ironically, he changed his mind the very next year and worked with Leginska in Chicago.) Sporadic conducting assignments followed—one with the Detroit Symphony in 1934, others in Buffalo (New York) and California, two with the National (Washington, D.C.) Symphony in the summer of 1935, the New York Civic Opera at Brighton Beach in 1936. But with far too little opportunity to exercise her métier, Brico decided to form her own orchestra, the New York Women's Symphony, and prove once and for all that women could be competent musicians. The ensemble, consisting of eighty-six players, made its first appearance at Carnegie Hall on February 18, 1935, performing Schumann's Symphony no. 1, Handel's Concerto Grosso in D minor, and Tchaikovsky's *Romeo and Juliet* overture. Pianist Olga Samaroff addressed the audience during the intermission. The concert received excellent reviews, and two more concerts followed that spring. In 1935–36 the New York Women's Symphony undertook a full season at Carnegie Hall. In 1937 Brico publicly challenged the pianist José Iturbi, who in a speech had said that women were incapable of greatness in either music or sports, to bring a group of men musicians to compete against a group of women before a panel of blindfolded judges. "I am sure that at least half of the players selected would be women," she said, "and after this proof has been given and more women trained for orchestral work, we shall have mixed orchestras of men and women."[56] Iturbi hastily backed down, saying he had been misquoted.

In 1938, believing she had proved her point that women could play as well as men and that she should now hire simply the best available players, she admitted ten men to the orchestra and renamed it the Brico Symphony. Despite enthusiastic reviews of its concerts, the ensemble did not survive much longer. Brico continued to make guest appearances. She was the first woman to conduct the New York Philharmonic at Lewisohn Stadium (summer 1938); that same summer she was awarded an honorary doctor of music degree from Mills College, taught a master class in conducting at Golden Gate College (San Francisco), and conducted a series of municipal concerts in San Francisco and Oakland. In 1939 she led the Federal Orchestra concerts at the New York World's Fair, and she subsequently conducted a number of concerts by choral groups in the metropolitan area.

In 1942 Brico moved to Denver, Colorado, where she devoted herself largely to teaching piano and conducted whenever she could. Soon after World War II ended, she went to Europe for a five-month tour, conducting and appearing as a pianist in Stockholm, Vienna, Amsterdam, London, Prague, and Zagreb. The highlight of this trip was conducting the Helsinki (Finland) Symphony in 1946 in an all-Sibelius program at the express invitation of the Finnish composer, with whom she had become good friends.

Quite unlike Ethel Leginska, Antonia Brico believed a conductor should not present his or her own "interpretation" of a composition but should serve the composer's intention and purpose. "The music I am conducting at the moment is my favorite," she once said. "I try hard to put everything into it."[57] Self-assured but unassuming, she wore, when conducting, a simple black dress with a white collar and cuffs, designed to blend with the orchestra and background rather than stand out in any way.

For the next three decades Brico had to content herself with conducting various amateur orchestras in Denver, performing only a half-dozen times a year; the rest of her time she spent teaching and lecturing. But in 1973 the folk singer Judy Collins, a former piano pupil of Brico's, together with director Jill Godmilow made a documentary film about her old teacher. Called *Antonia: A Portrait of the Woman,* it presented a poignant picture of a talented woman musician who had no instrument to play—which is how Brico herself described her lack of an orchestra. The film aroused new interest in its subject, leading to Brico's debut as a recording artist and engagements with a number of symphony orchestras. Although delighted with her revived conducting career, Brico did not abandon her old pupils. She continued to teach piano and conducting, coach opera, and lead her old ensemble, the Denver Businessmen's Orchestra, which had renamed itself the Brico Symphony in her honor.

Brico was not reticent about describing the difficulties she had encountered. Despite the support of artists such as conductor Bruno Walter, composer Jean Sibelius, and pianist Artur Rubinstein, orchestra boards would not engage her, managers would not accept her, artists refused to work with her—solely because she was a woman. Manager Arthur Judson, the most powerful man in American music—he managed most leading conductors as well as both the New York Philharmonic and Philadelphia orchestras—

would not engage Brico as a Philharmonic guest conductor because, he maintained, the orchestra's women subscribers would not like to see a woman on the podium. Minnie Guggenheimer, who managed the Lewisohn Stadium concerts, was outraged at the idea of a woman conducting and only allowed Brico to appear because 4,000 persons had signed a petition for her appearance. Unrecognized for years, Brico in her seventies began to build a new career, determined to make the best of the years ahead, as she had of the leaner years in the past.

Besides Leginska's and Brico's ensembles, several other women's orchestras were founded in the 1930s: those of Youngstown, Ohio, in 1930, under Margaret Walter; Hollywood, California, in 1932, under Anna Priscilla Risher; Portland, Oregon, in 1934, under D'Zama Murielle; Pittsburgh (Pennsylvania), in 1935, under Carl Simonis; Little Symphony of Cleveland (Ohio), 1935, under Ruth Sandra Rothstein; and Commonwealth Symphony of Boston, 1936, under Solomon Branslavsky, the only WPA-funded orchestra consisting entirely of women;[58] Women's Chamber Orchestra of New York, 1937, under Jeanette Scheerer; and the Baltimore Women's String Symphony Orchestra, 1937, under Stephen Deak.

Two more deserve special attention, the Orchestrette Classique of New York, and the Women's Symphony Orchestra of Boston. The Orchestrette Classique[59] was founded in 1933 by Frederique Joanne Petrides and survived until 1943. An outspoken feminist where women musicians were concerned, Petrides also published a monthly newsletter, *Women in Music,* from 1935 to 1940, and used its pages to publicize the achievements of women musicians, past and present. The Orchestrette was a 30-woman chamber group that was ahead of its time in several respects. For one thing, it performed baroque music with the forces for which it had originally been composed—that is, a chamber orchestra, rather than the 100-piece symphony orchestra then used for such compositions. (Virgil Thomson, reviewing one of the Orchestrette's programs, said, "To hear the music of the great eighteenth century masters...in such appropriate acoustical frame is to begin to know something of what that music really sounded like in the ears of its makers and of its contemporary listeners.")[60] For another, it performed a considerable amount of contemporary music, often giving first performances of new works. And finally, it often performed works by women composers. Its pianist for some years was the composer Julia Smith (see Chapter 7), some of whose works it performed and whose *Hellenic Suite* was dedicated to Petrides.

The Women's Symphony Orchestra of Boston was founded in 1939 by conductor Alexander Thiede and lasted until 1944, when it was merged with the Civic Symphony Orchestra of Boston.[61] Consisting of sixty-five players, it was set up as a kind of subscription cooperative; to join, one had to subscribe to four concerts (for $4). Any leftover proceeds from subscriptions would be distributed among the active members at the end of the season. Men could subscribe but could not become active members. At least one composition by a woman would be performed at each program, and indeed the orchestra did perform Daniels's *Deep Forest* (January 16, 1940), Beach's Gaelic Symphony (March 12, 1940), and other works by women. In its third season it sponsored a composition contest that was won by Radie Britain with her symphonic poem, *Light* (performed May 25, 1941; see Chapter 7 for more about Britain).

The Boston Women's Symphony was, by and large, a community orchestra, differing from other such ensembles mainly in that it admitted only women players. Its performers included shopgirls, housewives, secretaries, music teachers, and music students, as well as some professional musicians. Seven of its members had played with the Fadettes thirty years earlier, and practically all had been members of Leginska's Symphony. The tuba player, Thelma Goodwin, had played that instrument since the age of nine (she learned from her father, also a tuba player); she was a church organist, and had eight children. The third trombone was a sixteen-year-old high school student. The first trombone, Belle Mann, was a former Fadette and had for a time conducted her own ensemble. The Boston Women's Symphony annually gave four concerts at Jordan Hall and one summer concert at the MacDowell Colony in New Hampshire. Its only male member was the conductor, Alexander Thiede, who was quoted as saying that a women's orchestra needs a male conductor because women accept criticism better from a man. In the end, although its programs were regarded as interesting and the reviews were favorable if not overwhelmingly enthusiastic, the group merged with the Boston Civic Symphony, the compositions of whose conductor, Joseph Wagner, it had often performed.

During World War II, the women's orchestra movement came to an end. Although a few of the orchestras survived the war years, principally as amateur organizations, few new ones were founded after 1945.[62] Civic and community orchestras increasingly allowed women to join them,[63] and the orchestras of smaller cities began to admit more women as well. In the major orchestras, however, women were to remain a very small minority (see Chapter 10). In 1978 Kay Gardner founded the Boston-based New England Women's Symphony, which was intended primarily to provide a podium for women conductors and perform compositions by women. It gave three concerts in its first season.

# 6 AMERICAN COMPOSERS IN EUROPEAN IDIOMS

From the very start the music of Europe dominated the concert halls of America. Serious native American music remained little more than a curiosity until the emergence of the New England school of composers in the latter half of the nineteenth century. Even then, most of these composers received their training in Europe, and when they did not, the best of what they produced was most often an amalgam of the musical language that dominated late nineteenth-century Europe, the late romanticism of Brahms and Wagner, Tchaikovsky and Dvořák.

There were, of course, a few important exceptions. Charles Ives (1874–1954), far ahead of his time, used native American idioms (hymn tunes, popular songs, marches) along with both conventional devices and innovations such as conflicting rhythms and keys, dissonant harmonies, optional parts, and the like. Charles Tomlinson Griffes (1884–1920) combined elements of Oriental music, unusual harmonies, and some impressionistic devices. And Alsatian-born Charles Martin Loeffler (1861–1935), a resident of Boston for much of his life, wrote music that reflected his European—especially his French—training, with definite leanings toward modality, chromaticism, and new tone colors, all features of impressionism.

Although Germany had been the wellspring of romanticism, which was the dominant nineteenth-century style, the search for new modes of musical expression began principally in France, and the first composer to succeed in this endeavor was Claude Debussy (1862–1918). The style he developed is generally called "impressionism," a term Debussy himself rejected but that nevertheless has some validity. Borrowed from the visual arts, impressionism is used to describe music that evokes mood and atmosphere through the use of pure tone color (the individual characteristic sounds of the different instruments) rather than traditional melody or harmony. It therefore produces an effect of vagueness of form, even when the harmonies themselves follow a very strict formal pattern. Probably the most important contribution of impressionism was its use of new harmonies and scales, which greatly expanded the tonal possibilities available to composers.

The musical form that became the principal vehicle of impressionism was the symphonic poem or tone poem, an orchestral work in a single, fairly long movement, which, however, unlike the earlier tone poems of the nineteenth-century romanticists, did not necessarily follow a specific program. Sometimes the impressionist tone poem was a description of some natural phenomenon, usually named in the title, such as Debussy's *Prélude á l'après-midi d'un faune* and *La Mer,* or Respighi's *The Pines of Rome.* Some impressionist works were more programmatic, and often they employed exotic devices—that is, elements from non-European music, such as Persian or Balinese; among these is Griffes's *The Pleasure Dome of Kubla Khan.* And still others evoke a specific national tradition, such as Debussy's *Images* (which includes *Ibéria*) and Ravel's *Rapsodie espagnole.*

By the early 1900s Debussy's influence was strongly felt. His *La Mer* (1905) was followed fairly rapidly by Ravel's *Rapsodie espagnole* (1907), and the English composer Frederick Delius, who lived in Paris from the late 1880s on, was producing orchestral works in a similar vein about the same time. The Spanish composer Manuel de Falla lived in Paris from 1907 to 1914 and was personally acquainted with Debussy, whose influence is apparent in his *Noches en los jardines de Espana* of 1916 (though later De Falla turned away from impressionism).

With these and other composers the influence of French impressionism was quite direct and was most apparent in works published from about 1905 to 1925. By the mid-1920s other influences had become important in the European mainstream, notably the neoclassicism of Prokofiev and Stravinsky, and the serial techniques of Schoenberg and others. The legacy of impressionism, while not exactly lost, had been, as it were, internalized, to be drawn on as needed for writing music that was essentially in quite another vein.

Yet just about the time that most European composers had turned to other styles, two American women composed impressionist music. Both Marion Bauer and Mary Howe had been in Europe in the early 1900s and thus had undoubtedly been exposed to at least some impressionist music. Bauer studied in France in 1906 and 1907, was in Berlin from 1911 to 1912, and again was in France from 1923 to 1926. Howe studied piano briefly in Dresden and was making almost annual journeys abroad between about 1901 and 1912. Neither woman composed any large-scale works until after 1925 or so, but when they did, the impressionist influences from their formative years were unmistakably present.

Mary Carlisle Howe was born on April 4, 1882, in Richmond, Virginia, and grew up in Washington, D.C.[1] Her father, Calderon Carlisle, was an international lawyer. Her mother, Kate Thomas, had studied voice. Educated privately, Mary became a fine pianist, and by the age of eighteen she was accompanying a good deal at private recitals. (In her milieu—wealthy and socially prominent—public performance was still frowned on, but playing at private social gatherings was quite acceptable.)

Just after Christmas in 1900 Mary went to Baltimore's Peabody Conservatory for an audition with Ernest Hutcheson, playing Schumann and Debussy. She was accepted as a student and commuted regularly from Washington to study piano with Hutcheson and later with Harold Randolph. In 1901 her father died, and Mary began to go abroad frequently with her mother. In the spring of 1904 she spent four months in Dresden, studying piano with Richard Burmeister. She continued to play in private recitals, abroad and at home, even tackling the difficult Schumann A-minor Concerto (with a second piano playing the orchestral part). During the Taft and Roosevelt administrations, she was often a guest at the White House, and she played chamber music at Washington's Friday Morning Music Club.

In 1912 Mary married her brother Mandeville's law partner, Walter Bruce Howe, and devoted the next few years to starting a family; her son Bruce was born in 1912, another son, Calderon, in 1916, and a daughter, Mary (called Molly), in 1918. At the Peabody Conservatory she had become acquainted with another pianist, Anne Hull, and in 1912 the two women gave the first of a long series of two-piano performances. At first they performed chiefly before music clubs, in private homes, and at the Peabody (from which Hull had been graduated), and from 1920 on they played with a number of symphony orchestras (on tour with the Russian Symphony under Modest Altschuler, with the Baltimore Symphony, Cleveland Orchestra, and others).

About 1920 Howe began to devote herself more and more to composing. She had returned to the Peabody to study composition formally with Gustav Strube. On March 3, 1920, at a "Manuscript Evening" held there, her *Three Preludes* for piano were performed by Colin McPhee. The following year her *Berceuse* for piano was played, and in 1922 she was graduated, passing the first formal examination she had ever taken. In 1923 Howe appeared with the National String Quartet to play her Andante and Scherzo for piano quintet. During this period, her two-piano performances with Hull continued as well; in 1924 they made their New York debut in a two-piano recital at Aeolian (later Town) Hall, performing a Bach chorale (transcribed by Anne Hull), three *Spanish Dances* (transcribed by Mary Howe), and other works for two pianos by Mozart, Schumann, Glière, and others. The reviews were universally enthusiastic.

In the early 1920s Howe had become acquainted with Amy Beach (see Chapter 4), and in 1925 the two women gave the Washington premiere of

Beach's Suite for two pianos in a benefit concert for the MacDowell Colony. Howe visited the Colony the following summer, and from about 1927 on, sponsored by Beach and another composer friend, Ethel Glenn Hier, she was a fellow there nearly every summer for the next twenty years. Though she usually stayed only for a few weeks, not wanting to leave her family for longer periods, she felt her time there was extremely productive.

Howe also attended the Festival of Chamber Music established by music patron and composer Elizabeth Sprague Coolidge in Pittsfield, Massachusetts, where she heard for the first time works by Schoenberg and Hindemith. There she met Carl Engel, chief of the Music Division of the Library of Congress. Howe helped organize the first Coolidge Festival in Washington, held on October 28, 1925, and also a Chamber Music Society that eventually became the Friends of Music of the Library of Congress. Engel became a good friend of Howe's and helped arrange performances of her works.

Just a few weeks earlier Howe had attended the premiere of her *Chain Gang Song* for chorus and orchestra at the Worcester Festival of 1925. This represented her first public success as a composer. In retrospect, she said,

The first time I heard a piece of my own orchestral writing played, I got a real kick out of it. I finally began to rate respectably as pianist and composer... This was the public rehearsal at Worcester, 1925, of my *Chain Gang Song* for chorus and orchestra, with about 275 voices and the New York Symphony [under Albert Stoessel], and there it was out of my hands and about to come to life.[2]

*Chain Gang Song* is based on three actual tunes sung by a road gang of prisoners in the western North Carolina mountains. Howe said,

It means to me, rounding a bend on horseback on a hot Southern afternoon and coming on a gang of twenty or so black convicts in striped clothes, guarded by a lean ornery looking white man with a shot gun. Iron ball and chain on many feet, and they sang while they drilled the hole for the dynamite charge. One man held and aimed the iron drill, and two more slugged at it with heavy shoulder weight iron hammers, rhythmically, so the three could know inevitably when the hammer blows would fall. The man holding the drill shifted it slightly after every impact, thus making the hole wider.[3]

*Chain Gang Song* was hailed as a strong, effective work. One critic said, "a powerful piece of writing with no trace of femininity and astonishing skill in the handling of her resources."[4]

In 1926 conductor Georges Barrère asked Howe to orchestrate three of her shorter works—*Stars* (originally for piano), Scherzo (piano quintet), and the *Chain Gang Song*—and in March 1927 he conducted his Little Symphony in New York in all three works. Barrère became one of Howe's staunchest champions; in 1930 he performed her new work, *Sand,* which he repeated the following year on a program that also included the first performance of Mabel Daniels's *Deep Forest* (see Chapter 4).

A short but quite difficult work, *Sand* is essentially a tone poem in miniature. According to Howe, it was intended to convey the consistency, grains, bulk, grittiness, and potential scattering quality of sand itself. The intriguing staccato effects she used in this piece led Leopold Stokowski to say it had given him an entirely new view of what could be done with staccato. (Stokowski conducted *Sand* with the Philadelphia Orchestra in 1934.) Though Howe herself said that her "back foot is in the garden gate of the Romantics, but I feel no hesitation in thumbing the passing modern idiom for a hitch-hike to where I want to go,"[5] she used dissonances rather sparingly. But *Sand* is very much an impressionist work, exploiting, as it does, the characteristic sounds of the instruments to evoke a desired atmosphere. So is *Stars,* transcribed for orchestra at Barrère's request and frequently performed in conjunction with *Sand.* Here the composer wished to convey the gradually overwhelming effect of a starry night, opening with a sonorous ensemble of strings and expanding to use the full orchestra. Another short tone poem from this period was *Dirge* (1931), dedicated to Harold Randolph.

About 1930 Hans Kindler, principal cellist with the Philadelphia Orchestra, asked Howe to help raise $40,000 for a new Washington, D.C., orchestra. An energetic, strong-minded woman with connections in both wealthy and musical circles, Mary Howe readily raised the required sum, and in 1931 the National Symphony Orchestra was born. For the next eighteen years Howe, together with her husband and Kindler, worked hard to support the orchestra. In addition to its Washington concerts, it undertook regular symphonic series in other cities and became known for its imaginative programs, combining music from all periods and presenting many new works. Eventually Kindler had a falling out with members of the orchestra's board and resigned (in 1948), but Howe remained on good terms with his successor, Howard Mitchell, and continued to work for the orchestra.

Kindler had performed some of Howe's works in recitals (her *Ballade fantasque* for cello and piano, and also *Canción romanesco* for string quartet).[6] Under him the National Symphony regularly performed her tone poems and also *Castellana* for two pianos and orchestra, a brilliant, showy piece. Built on four folk tunes she had learned from Spanish cousins of her father's, this work became one of Howe's most popular, and was often performed by her and Anne Hull.

In the 1936–37 season the National Symphony performed Howe's most recent orchestral work, *Spring Pastoral,* in Washington and then more than a dozen times on tour. Originally a setting of a poem by Elinor Wylie scored for women's chorus, it was then revised for orchestra. Still short (about five minutes' performance time) but longer than *Sand* or *Stars,* it is essentially a mood picture of spring, combining rich, soft string textures with the fresh timbres of woodwinds and French horn.

The two-piano recitals also continued through the 1930s, though by then Anne Hull had moved to New York and was pursuing a busy teaching career. Hull became, in effect, the New York custodian of Howe's compositions and did a great deal to promote their performance, in New York and elsewhere. Together Hull and Howe often performed *Castellana,* Howe's transcriptions of several Bach arias, and her *Three Spanish Folk Tunes (Habanera de Cinna, Petenera,* and *Spanish Folk Dance);* of these works, the transcription of Bach's aria *Sheep May Safely Graze* has become a standard work in the two-piano literature.

Howe's views on women composers were unequivocal:

Women composers should be played more than they are. I don't think conductors have a prejudice against women composers now. But no one puts women writers or women painters in a class any more, and they still do so with women composers. I know I considered it a handicap to be a woman when I started composing. I'm not a feminist. But I think I would have gotten along faster if I'd been a man.[7]

Despite Howe's wealth, social position, and connections in the musical world, she was discriminated against. In fact, the conductor William Strickland, who knew her well, believed that both her position and her sex militated against her: The former marked her as a "dilettante," and the latter prevented her from being taken seriously.

Howe had early become a member of the Society of American Women Composers (see Chapter 4), founded around 1924, and her music was regularly performed at its concerts. She also befriended and retained contact with many other woman musicians and composers. One of the first performances of her Violin Sonata was given by violinist Leonora Jackson McKim (see Chapter 2) and Mary Howe. Olga Samaroff (see Chapter 4) played Howe's *Nocturne* on her tour in 1924 and remained a friend for many years, as did Amy Beach and Ethel Glenn Hier. Conductor Antonia Brico performed *Sand* with the National Symphony at a summer concert in 1940 and another of Howe's symphonic poems, *What Price Glory,* the following summer. Howe also kept up her connection with the Friday Morning Music Club well into the 1940s.

Howe always took what she saw as her responsibilities very seriously, using her position to help raise funds for the National Symphony and many other musical enterprises. Partly in the interest of such fund raising, she organized herself and her three children into a performing group, "the Four Howes." In the late 1930s they began presenting recitals of madrigals, glees, and catches, accompanied by Mary Howe on the virginal and Calderon on the recorder. (It was for him that Mary Howe wrote *Interlude Between Two Pieces,* usually performed on the flute and piano but originally played by Calderon on the alto recorder and Ralph Kirkpatrick on the harpsichord.) A number of these programs were benefits for the MacDowell Colony, and in fact the Four Howes raised about $1,000 for the Colony.

Shortly before the United States entered World War II, Howe completed her last two orchestral works, *Paean* and *Potomac.* The former, a symphonic poem, is thought by some to be her best orchestral score; the latter, a suite consisting of a prelude and three movements, was given its premiere by Albert Stoessel with the New York Symphony at Chautauqua in 1942. Busy with Red Cross work and other volunteer activities during the war, Howe still continued to compose. In 1943 she wrote *Prophecy, 1792,* a setting of part of William Blake's "Song of Liberty," for the Army Music School Choir, which performed it at the National Gallery that September.

Throughout the 1930s, in addition to orchestral works, Howe had continued to write chamber works, choral music, and many solo songs. In April 1939 a recital devoted entirely to Howe's songs was held at Washington's Phillips Memorial Gallery. It included settings of poems by Rainer Maria Rilke, Elinor Wylie, and others, and prompted warm praise from critics:

Mrs. Howe has a remarkable talent in lyric style....She does not bend the text to the melodic line, or use any of the strategems of emotional appeal, save in one or two instances of obvious strophe form imposed by the nature of the poem. Her music grows out of the text and exists with it in artistic symbiosis.[8]

Seven volumes of her songs were published in 1959. Among the best are the settings of Elinor Wylie's poems, especially "When I Died in Berners Street," which has been called "a perfect union of text and music," and "one of the finest American songs produced to date."[9] It is every bit as good as the songs of Debussy, with which it has inevitably been compared.

Howe herself disclaimed allegiance to any school. "If I want to use dissonance," she said, "I use dissonance. If I want to express feeling, I express feeling. I write what I want to write." She admired many contemporary American composers, especially Aaron Copland, Gian Carlo Menotti, Paul Creston, and Louise Talma; she had heard some of Talma's works played at the Library of Congress and called her "a very talented young woman."[10] She also was a great admirer of Nadia Boulanger (who is discussed later in this chapter), with whom she had studied in 1933, during a year spent in France.

Howe continued to be active throughout the 1950's. In 1952 the National Symphony under Howard Mitchell gave an all-Howe program featuring *Stars, Sand, Dirge, Paean, Castellana,* and a number of the songs. The following year there was an all-Howe concert in New York at Town Hall, with Katherine Hansel, soprano, and the Howard University choir performing *Prophecy, 1792, Cavaliers, Williamsburg Sunday,* and numerous songs. Again the reviews were universally favorable. Frances Perkins of the *New York Herald Tribune* said the songs showed "notable ability for presenting the texts and musical projection of the expressive atmosphere of the poems was constantly persuasive," while the choral writing was "lucid and skilfully wrought." The *New York Times* critic agreed: "Mary Howe's musical idiom is a refreshing one. The musical structure has clarity and design throughout."

In 1954 Walter Howe died. By then her children were settled in careers of their own, and the following year Mary Howe went to Vienna, where William Strickland led the Vienna Symphony in a performance of *Stars, Sand,* and *Rock* (the last was another short tone poem, here given its premiere). The Vienna orchestra, Strickland recalled more than twenty years later, was notoriously hard on foreigners and could scarcely be expected to open its arms to a foreign woman composer. But Howe won them over readily, and, in fact, it was at the request of the orchestra's principal wind players that she composed a new Suite for wind quintet.

*Stars, Sand,* and *Rock* were again performed together by the National Symphony in Washington in February 1956 and won the composer a standing ovation by the Constitution Hall audience. Shortly before, on the fifty-fourth anniversary of her father's death, Howe wrote:

I have a certain reputation as a composer—coloured by not having to make my living and by my being a woman. (I might add also by my age being honestly known!)....I want to sort all this to protect my own inner viewpoint during my remaining years, more especially my remaining years of work....At the moment one is especially conscious of a revival of early attributes, believing oneself insecure, and having a lack of ability. And yet I do sincerely believe in many of the works perpetrated, and have had them proved in performance. The crux must be that one should *never* stop—but close in with work itself, without thought of performance, or lack of more years, or age, "or any other creature."[11]

On Mary Howe's eightieth birthday she was given a party attended by some two hundred guests at the Mayflower Hotel in Washington. Among the music performed was *Interlude Between Two Pieces* (for flute and piano), a two-piano version of *Stars,* the Violin Sonata in D, choral works, and many songs. Among the last tributes Howe received was an honorary doctor of music degree from George Washington University. She died in 1964.

The other woman who absorbed French impressionism at an early age and used its idioms in her own compositions years later was Marion Bauer, who is remembered as much as a champion of contemporary music and a teacher as a composer. Marion Eugénie Bauer was born on August 15, 1887, in Walla Walla, Washington, the youngest of seven children.[12] Her parents were of French lineage, her mother a gifted linguist and her father an amateur musician. Her first music lessons were with her oldest sister, Emilie Frances, a pianist and later a music critic.[13] Marion was educated in the West, and after graduation from high school she went to New York to live with Emilie Frances, by then established as a critic there.

Bauer's first studies in New York were with Henry Holden Huss; later she also worked with Eugene Heffley and Walter Henry Rothwell. In 1906 she went to France, where she studied piano with Raoul Pugno, the famous violinist. Through him she met Nadia Boulanger, who began to teach her harmony. In exchange Bauer gave both her and Pugno's young daughter lessons in English, thus helping to finance her year of music studies. She later said that she must have been the first American pupil of Nadia Boulanger, who was to teach a whole generation of American composers (see the later discussion in this chapter).

In 1907 Bauer returned to the United States and spent the next four years in New York, teaching piano and theory and continuing her own studies. During this time, her first published song, "Light," was introduced by the famous contralto Ernestine Schumann-Heink. In 1910 Bauer again went to Europe, this time to Berlin, and studied counterpoint and form for a year with Paul Ertel. She was still composing songs that clearly showed the influence of French impressionism, and in 1912, when she returned to America, she obtained a seven-year contract with the music publisher Arthur P. Schmidt.

Bauer continued to write songs, but she gradually expanded into piano works and then chamber music. One composition from this period is a tone poem for violin and piano, *Up the Ocklawaha* (1913), which was written for her friend Maud Powell (see Chapter 2) and describes Powell's trip up this Florida river. She also wrote *Fair Daffodils* (1913), a trio for women's voices; *The Lay of the Four Winds* (1915), for men's voices; and in 1920, *Allegretto giocoso* for eleven instruments, her most ambitious instrumental work so far.

In 1923 Bauer returned to Europe for a third time, this time to France, where she studied fugue with André Gédalge, the teacher of many celebrated composers (including Ravel, Milhaud, and Honegger). She remained in France until January 1926. But then her sister fell ill, and Bauer returned to her bedside and remained with her until her death later that year.

Very early in her career Bauer had begun to write for music journals in both Europe and America. In 1926 she replaced her sister Emilie as New York correspondent of the *Musical Leader* (an important Chicago journal), for which she reviewed an immense number of concerts and recitals; she held this post until her death. She also began what was to be an important collaboration with Ethel Peyser on popular books of music history, the first of which, *How Music Grew*, was published in 1925. *Their Music Through the Ages* appeared in 1932, and *How Opera Grew* in 1956. In addition, Bauer alone wrote *Twentieth-Century Music* (1933) and *Musical Questions and Quizzes* (1941), as well as contributing articles and chapters to Oscar Thompson's *International Cyclopedia of Music* and *Musicians and Great Modern Composers*, and writing for many music journals.

Bauer's own compositions were not radically innovative, but they were skillfully wrought. Of her *Four Songs*, op. 16 (1924), William Upton said, "In easy command of modern technique, in rich pictorial quality, in vivid play of the imagination and sustained dramatic interest, these songs may worthily take their place beside Griffes' own."[14] Like Griffes and other impressionist composers, Bauer often used "exotic" (i.e., non-Western) elements in her music, which in her case ranged from American Indian to African material. In this vein are her *Indian Pipes* (1927) for orchestra and *A Lament on African Themes* (1928) for chamber orchestra. During the same period she also wrote a Violin Sonata, op. 18 (published 1928) and a String Quartet, op. 20, first performed in 1928.

In 1926 Bauer joined the faculty of New York University, where she taught music history and composition for the next quarter of a century. Later she also taught at the Juilliard School, and she taught summer sessions at several well-known institutions, including Mills College, Carnegie Institute of Technology, and the Cincinnati Conservatory of Music. She was not in the forefront of the avant-garde in her own compositions (although her later works became increasingly dissonant), but she was extremely sympathetic to those who were. In 1932 she initiated a series of lecture-recitals with pianist Harrison Potter to "explain modern music" to the general public. Four years earlier she had begun a twenty-year stint as annual lecturer at the Contemporary Trends Series of the Chautauqua Institute in New York State. She was the only woman on the executive board of the American Composers Alliance,[15] founded by Aaron Copland in 1937, and she also served on the boards of the League of Composers (beginning in 1926) and the Society for the Publication of American Music, all organizations working to foster the cause of contemporary American music. Bauer tirelessly defended this cause in many quarters. Typical is her article, "Why Not Teach Music of Today?" in the November 1951 issue of the *Associated Music Teachers' League Bulletin*, in which she said: "It's a vicious circle! Publishers don't publish modern teaching pieces because teachers don't buy them. Teachers don't teach modern music because publishers don't publish it." And everyone, Bauer continued, was partly to blame. Teachers did not want to take the trouble to find and buy and test new music; parents complained about unusual-sounding pieces; composers did not bother to write good teaching pieces. "Dissonant sounds do not disturb the young pianist," said Bauer, "if there is a rhythmical interest or a melody that may be easily followed, or an entertaining subject or a pattern that is easy to get hold of." But children must have the chance to get used to new styles of music, or they never will be accepted. "Do no forget that... all music was modern once."

Bauer herself did continue to write teaching pieces, as well as more choral, chamber, and orchestral music. Her Viola Sonata (1935), op. 22, was often performed. Her *Symphonic Suite for Strings* was given its premiere at Chautauqua in 1941; *American Youth Concerto* for piano and orchestra was written for and performed at New York's High School of Music and Art in 1943; *China,* a setting of a poem by Boris Todrin for mixed chorus and orchestra, was performed at the Worcester Festival in 1945; and the tone poem *Sun Splendor,* originally for piano and later orchestrated, was performed by the New York Philharmonic under Leopold Stokowski in 1947. Other works include Concertino for oboe, clarinet, and string quartet (1939–43) and Symphony no. 1 (1950).

In 1951 the Phi Beta National Fraternity of Music and Speech sponsored an all-Bauer program at New York's Town Hall, which included the first performances of her Trio Sonata no. 2 for flute, cello, and piano, op. 47 (1951), commissioned and played by the Sagul Trio (Edith Sagul, Marilyn Beabout, and Mary Stretch), and her *Moods for Dance Interpretation,* op. 46 (1950), for dancer and piano. Of this program Olin Downes of the *New York Times* reported, "The music is prevailingly contrapuntal and dissonance is not absent. Yet the fundamental concept is melodic, the thinking clear and logical, the sentiment sincere and direct."[16]

Four years later Marion Bauer died, a few days before her sixty-eighth birthday. At her funeral the musicologist Gustave Reese, a long-time friend and colleague at New York University, said that in the 1920s Marion Bauer had been very much a modernist and the outstanding woman among American composers. What he omitted to say (and perhaps did not realize) was that she frequently was the only woman among a group of men. As early as 1921, when she was one of the founders of the American Music Guild (formed for hearing and criticizing each other's works), she was also its only woman member. Her *Sun Splendor* was the only composition by a woman performed by the New York Philharmonic in a quarter of a century. She was the only woman who was consistently quoted in settings such as the Yaddo Festival of Contemporary Music held in the early 1940s.

There were a number of reasons why she was accepted when other women, some of them just as competent, were not. For one thing she, like many of the young American men composers of the 1920s—and unlike many prominent women composers, including Beach and Daniels—had studied in France during the early 1920s, and from that time France replaced Germany as *the* music center. Second, her position as a working music critic gave her considerable influence; she was in a position to help or put down new works, so inevitably her favor was courted. And finally, her intelligent approach to new music—and her ability to explain it lucidly—in lectures and in her book, *Twentieth-Century Music,* earned her universal respect.

As for her own views about women, she said, "My early aspiration was not to listen to the sly remarks of intolerant men regarding women composers...that if given a reasonable chance for development, an individual talent, regardless of sex, can progress and grow."[17] Generous in helping students and younger composers, Bauer numbered many women musicians among her friends. Some of her own compositions are dedicated to Maud Powell, Amy Beach, and Ruth Crawford, among others; the last was to become one of the most innovative of all American composers.

A close friend of Bauer's from their first meeting at the MacDowell Colony in 1929, Ruth Crawford was, like Charles Ives, one of the great originals in America music, and Bauer was among the first to give her public recognition. A good many of Crawford's works give, at least on first hearing, the sense of diffuseness and vagueness that often is associated with the impressionist music of Debussy and others. Nothing could be further from the truth. In all but her earliest works, the music of Ruth Crawford (she continued to use her maiden name professionally after marriage) is very tightly organized with respect to just about every element—pitches, intervals, rhythms, meters, dynamics, instrumentation, and in vocal works, text. Though she was exposed to late romantic and impressionist music, as well as to the twelve-tone music of the Viennese school (Schoenberg and Hauer) and the expressionism of Alban Berg, she assimilated elements from all these and formed her own highly individual style. Moreover, some of the techniques she developed anticipated by twenty or thirty years the experiments of post-World War II composers in Europe and America.

The daughter and granddaughter of Methodist ministers, Ruth Porter Crawford[18] was born on July 3, 1901, in East Liverpool, Ohio, the younger of two children. Her father held many pulpits during Ruth's early childhood, and the family moved frequently, from Ohio to Missouri to Indiana, and finally, in 1911, to Jacksonville, Florida. About that time her father became ill, and three years later, when Ruth was fourteen, he died. After this her mother rented out rooms to help support Ruth and her brother, Carl.

Crawford's first music studies were with her mother, but at six she went to a professional piano teacher. She continued to study music through high school, but she was also very interested in writing, especially poetry. After graduating from high school she began to earn her own living, teaching piano at the School of Musical Art and music at a settlement kindergarten in Jacksonville. In 1920, having saved just enough money to support a year's study, she went to Chicago and enrolled in the American Conservatory there. After that first year, she supported herself by ushering and checking coats in theaters on the Loop, and, in 1921, having earned the American Conservatory's teacher's certificate, she began teaching piano and theory. At first she taught privately and then, from 1924 on, at the American Conservatory and later (1926) also at Elmhurst College. In 1923 her mother joined her in Chicago, and they lived together until Mrs. Crawford's death in 1928.

Crawford's first courses at the American Conservatory were in piano and harmony, but later she also took up counterpoint, composition, and orchestration, earning a bachelor's degree in 1923 and a master's (with highest honors) in 1929. A number of musicians Crawford met during these years had a profound influence on her music and her life. Her first teacher of harmony and counterpoint at the Conservatory, violinist Adolf Weidig, was one of the first to encourage her to concentrate on composing. Djane Lavoie-Herz, with whom Crawford studied piano for four years, regularly held musical evenings in her Chicago studio, and it was here that Crawford met the composers Henry Cowell, Edgard Varèse, and Carlos Chávez; art critic Alfred Frankenstein; Adolf Weiss, a Chicago Symphony bassoonist who had studied with Arnold Schoenberg and was enthralled with the Viennese composer's twelve-tone system; and Dane Rudhyar, a French-born composer with mystical leanings who introduced her to the music of Scriabin. It was here, also, that Crawford first heard the music of Igor Stravinsky, Paul Hindemith, Darius Milhaud, and Ralph Vaughan Williams. Frankenstein introduced her to the poet Carl Sandburg, whose children she taught piano for a time. She contributed some of the piano accompaniments for Sandburg's collection of folk songs, *The American Songbag,* and this association awakened what was to be a lifelong interest in folk music. Probably the most important new friend was Henry Cowell. It was Cowell who first helped Crawford publish some of her compositions; it was he who persuaded her to leave Chicago for New York in 1929; and it was he who introduced her to Charles Seeger.

By 1929 Crawford was considered one of the most promising young musicians in Chicago, and in fact she had already produced nearly half of her total compositional output. (In the end, she wrote but thirty-two compositions in all, and even that figure is reached only by counting each song and prelude as a separate work.) Among the earliest of her works to survive[19] are *Five Preludes* for piano (1924–25) and a *Suite for Small Orchestra* (1926), written while she was studying under Weidig. The preludes, first performed at Town Hall in New York by Gitta Gradova (and never published) are still late romantic in style, though Gaume saw in them some characteristics of Crawford's later style: a twisting and quite chromatic (moving in half-tones) melody; no key signatures, though the music is not yet atonal (it still has a tonal center, or key, and the harmonies and chord progressions are based on the traditional triads of tonal music); repeated patterns and sequences in which the repetition often is not quite exact but involves slight changes (a characteristic Crawford technique). These pieces, like most of Crawford's compositions, are quite short; Prelude no. 1 is only twelve measures long, and the longest, no. 2, consists of forty-six measures.

The *Suite for Small Orchestra,*[20] scored for flute, clarinet, bassoon, violins, cellos, and piano, consists of two movements, the first somber and slow, the second lively and jaunty. In the first movement, static ostinato patterns (figures repeated over and over) in groups of six, five, four, three, and two notes are set against sustained pedal tones (long-held notes or chords in the bass) in the cello and piano parts. The pedal tones consist chiefly of tone clusters—that is, adjacent notes that might be played by simply putting one's forearm down on the keyboard. The second movement, in contrast, trips along almost mechanically, relieved by a flowing melody full of triplets. This work, too, was never published and received what was presumably its premiere performance only in 1975 by the Boston Musica Viva chamber ensemble.

There followed another set of piano pieces, *Four Preludes* (1927–28), first performed at one of the Copland-Sessions concerts devoted to new music in New York in 1928. These compositions are more impressionist and rhapsodic in character and include the only two works Crawford ever dedicated to anyone: no. 6, to Djane Lavoie-Herz, and no. 9, to pianist Richard Buhlig, who played it in San Francisco in 1928 (as well as in New York).

Crawford's next instrumental work was a *Suite for Five Wind Instruments and Piano,* written in 1927 and revised in 1929. Neither version was ever published. It was followed in 1929 by a *Suite for Strings and Piano,* in three movements. This composition shows two other characteristic Crawford devices. First, the conventional melody or theme of several bars is replaced by a brief (four-note) motif of closely spaced pitches (all within a fourth), which is interwoven with motifs of two, three, and six notes and is reworked in each movement. Second, there is a clear suggestion of Schoenberg's twelve-tone technique, in that often all twelve tones of the chromatic scale are used within a few bars, although unlike the twelve-tone system they are not used in any fixed order.

Also in 1929 Crawford produced her first vocal works, *Five Songs,* settings of poems by Carl Sandburg. All five are for medium or low voice, suitable for either a man or a woman singer. All of them use panchromatic harmony—that is, the simultaneous sounding of chromatic notes—and tone clusters.

Crawford spent the summer of 1929 at the MacDowell Colony, and that fall she moved to New York. Soon after Henry Cowell persuaded Charles Seeger, his own former teacher, to take Crawford as a pupil. At first Seeger did not take kindly to the idea; he had a low opinion of women composers and some very radical ideas about composition. But Cowell convinced him that Crawford was no run-of-the-mill student, and Seeger finally agreed to take her on.

Seeger, whom Cowell later described as "the greatest musical explorer in intellectual fields which America has produced, the greatest experimental musicologist... [who] suggested more fruitful pathways for musical composition than any other three men,"[21] was fifteen years older than Ruth Crawford. A graduate of Harvard, he had taught at the University of California from 1912 to 1919 and there developed—at a time when Debussy's impressionism was considered the most modern kind of music—the idea of dissonant counterpoint, a technique in which dissonance (discordant, tension-filled intervals) is the desired norm, and consonance (agreeable-sounding intervals, giving an effect of rest) is undesirable, and the texture of the music is not primarily chords but a fabric of separate melodic lines. Such a texture, he believed, would make the musical structure more apparent to the listener (separate lines are easier to discern than the individual notes in a chord).

In Ruth Crawford Charles Seeger found a kindred spirit. They both were fascinated with Schoenberg's twelve-tone system, where a row of twelve tones, used in a fixed order, becomes the organizing principle of a composition. This row or series (hence the term "serial music") is used over and over throughout a work—no pitch may be repeated before all the others have sounded—but it may be varied in accordance with certain rules (notes may be moved up or down an octave, or a fifth, or the entire series may be inverted, or appear backward, or both backward and inverted). But much as they liked this system, Crawford and Seeger agreed that it was too rigid, and that the music so produced was too diffuse. The tonal organization should be more obvious to the listener.

Crawford's next compositions, produced during the winter of 1929–30, were essentially exercises in dissonant counterpoint assigned by her new teacher. In effect, the purpose was to take a single melodic line and keep it dissonant for as long as possible, using only major and minor seconds, sevenths, and ninths, and augmented fourths, and avoiding all the consonant intervals (thirds, perfect fourths and fifths, sixths, and octaves). The first of these exercises, *Piano Study in Mixed Accents* (1930), consists entirely of octave passages (no chords), the same in the right- and left-hand parts. The melodic line moves from the low end of the keyboard to the high end and down again, and there are three optional dynamic (loud-soft) patterns: (1) loud throughout; (2) soft to loud to soft; (3) loud to soft to loud. *Four Diaphonic Suites* (1930) are similar exercises, this time in dissonant two-part polyphony.

In 1930 Ruth Crawford won a Guggenheim Fellowship in composition for a year abroad, the first woman ever selected. That fall she sailed for Europe, and she spent most of her year there composing. For several months she stayed in Berlin, where she wrote *Chant,* part of her String Quartet, the song "In Tall Grass," and some unspecified shorter pieces. She went for what she called "too short a time" to Vienna, where she had long talks with Alban Berg (whose opera *Wozzeck* had impressed her profoundly), with the twelve-tone composer J. M. Hauer, and with Egon Wellesz. She met Bela Bartók in Budapest, and in Munich she heard a choral work by Werner Egk. She then spent a number of months in Paris, where she met Maurice Ravel and finished the String Quartet.

Because she did not produce a major symphonic work the Guggenheim Fellowship was not renewed, an irony since during the year abroad she produced her most remarkable composition to date, the String Quartet, which also became her best-known work. She herself recognized its value: "I am sure that the work I did during this time was by far the best I had done—a fact which I attribute not so much to Europe itself (though the experience abroad was invaluable to me in a general sort of way) as to the financial freedom to work and to the natural course of my growth."[22] The String Quartet was first performed by the New World String Quartet at the New School in New York on November 13, 1933, and was published in 1941. The third movement, marked Andante, can be performed alone by a string orchestra (a part for double bass was added for this purpose), and so it has been heard not only as chamber music but as orchestral music. In the 1970s, when so many of her compositions still were available only in manuscript (from the Library of Congress), it was performances of the Quartet and the Andante that sparked new interest in Crawford's work.

The Quartet is a remarkable piece. The first movement, *Rubato assai,* has fourteen changes of tempo (in seventy-eight measures) and twelve different time signatures. The texture is contrapuntal, with each instrument having its own dissonant line. In contrast to the generally subdued dynamics of most of her earlier works, Crawford here made more use of sudden dynamic changes and high levels, that is, suddenly soft and suddenly loud. The basic tonal material is again short motifs, not themes or melodies, and the composer notes: "The melodic line, as indicated by 'solo' in each part, must be heard continuing throughout the movement."[23] In the second movement, *Leggiero* ("Lightly"), there is more rhythmic drive, and the four instruments play "follow the leader" through five basic motifs, stated first by one and then the other. Meter and tempo remain the same throughout. The third movement, *Andante,* was called by Charles Seeger an experiment in "dynamic counterpoint." All four parts change pitch slowly and together, but they are differentiated from one another by their dynamic (loud-soft) patterns, which are so staggered that each instrument alternately emerges and then sinks back into the total mass of sound, going from very soft to very loud and then back again. The fourth movement, *Allegro possibile* ("as fast as possible"), consists of two contrapuntal lines, one played by the first violin and the other by the three remaining instruments in unison and octave doublings. Tempo and meter remain the same, but variety is achieved through changes in pitch (every possible interval is used), rhythm, and dynamics. The first violin starts with a single-note unit, which is gradually increased, one note at a time, to a twenty-one-note unit. At the same time, it begins by playing very loud and becomes softer and softer. Halfway through the movement, the entire process is repeated in reverse (and transposed up one step), so groups of fewer and fewer notes are played louder and louder. In the meantime the other three instruments play the same design in reverse, beginning with a twenty-note unit, decreasing to one note, and reversing the process at midpoint.[24]

In 1931 Crawford returned to America, and in November she married Charles Seeger. She continued to compose, producing the third of the *Three Songs of Carl Sandburg* and orchestral parts for all three of them, and *Two Ricercari,* two songs to political texts—"Sacco, Vanzetti" and "Chinaman, Laundryman," both written in 1932, settings of poems by H. T. Tsiang that were published in 1928 in the *Daily Worker* (the leading American Communist newspaper). Their choice shows Crawford's concern with social and economic conditions, an interest shared by her husband and many other intellectual liberals of this period. Sacco and Vanzetti were two Italian-Americans who were executed for the murder of a guard during a robbery, even though many believed they were innocent of the crime and had been accused chiefly because of their radical political beliefs. "Chinaman, Laundryman" concerns the miserable conditions of the exploited immigrant in his laundry sweatshop.

For "Sacco, Vanzetti" Crawford noted on the manuscript: "It is essential that the audience understand the words. If the effort to secure the pitches as written should interfere with the clear rendition of the words, these pitches should be regarded as general rather than as specific indications." Rarely do composers regard the words (especially someone else's text) more important than the music, but Crawford explicitly did. The vocal part of this song is written in declamatory style, with the word accents of speech strongly emphasized in the music. Some of the pitches are actually indefinite, marked only by an arrow pointing up or down to indicate that a pitch should be higher or lower than the preceding pitch. This technique, called *Sprechstimme* ("speaking voice"), was used early in the 1900s by Schoenberg and others.

The *Three Songs* (1930–32) also use some of these devices but are still more complex. They are scored for alto voice, oboe, percussion, and piano, a group the composer called "concertanti," plus an orchestra, called "ostinati." All settings of poems by Sandburg, they were published in 1933 and the manuscripts are dated "Rat Riddles," March 1930; "In Tall Grass," January 1931 (written in Europe); and "Prayers of Steel," November 1932.

Again the composer included instructions for performance: Accidentals (sharps, flats, natural signs) affect only those notes before which they appear (instead of all notes of that pitch within a bar); the concertanti section is complete in itself and can be performed with or without the ostinati section; the concertanti and ostinati should be rehearsed several times separately, so that the performers understand the independence of the two sections; the oboe should be a powerful one, using a broad reed.

This group was the first of Crawford's output to receive more than a local hearing. It was one of two compositions selected to represent the United States at the International Festival of the International Society for Contemporary Music, held at Amsterdam in 1933 (the other that year was Aaron Copland's *Piano Variations*).

With these songs Crawford's original work came to a halt. In 1933 Michael, her first child, was born. He was followed by Margaret (1935), Barbara (1937), and Penelope (1943). In addition, Seeger's three children from his first marriage lived with them. While raising her family, she devoted much of her time to folk music. In 1935 the Seegers moved to Silver Spring, Maryland, outside Washington, D.C., and during the next fifteen years Crawford transcribed some 1,000 songs from field recordings in the nearby Archive of American Folk Song in the Library of Congress. For many of these songs she also wrote piano arrangements and accompaniments, some of which were published in the collections of John A. and Alan Lomax, *Our Singing Country* and *Folksong: USA*. Others appeared in some of Crawford's own books for children, *Songs for Children, Animal Folk Songs,* and *American Folk Songs for Christmas*. During this period, Crawford also taught music, not only to her own children (one stepson, Pete Seeger, and two of her own children, Michael and Peggy, became professional folk singers), but at a number of local schools. She apparently had a marvelous faculty for conveying her own delight in the spontaneous vitality of folk song to others, especially to they young.

Crawford produced only one original composition during these years. *Rissolty, Rossolty* (1941), a work for small orchestra commissioned by the CBS American School of the Air and performed over the radio that year, is actually based on three folk tunes woven into a complicated pattern without, however, obscuring their dancelike quality and rustic flavor.

In 1952 Crawford returned to composition. In that year she wrote a *Suite for Wind Quintet* and submitted it to a competition sponsored by the District of Columbia chapter of the National Association for American Composers and Conductors. It won first prize and was performed on December 2, 1952, by the National Woodwind Quintet in Washington. In three movements, the quintet combines elements of Crawford's earlier style—dissonance, contrapuntal texture, chromatic motifs instead of a melody, ostinati—with later influences, especially her interest in folk music (seen in the quintet's strong rhythmic pulse) and the cool objective style of

Hindemith and other neoclassical composers (particularly seen in the treatment of the wind instruments).

This was Crawford's last complete work. In 1953 she became ill with what turned out to be a rapidly advancing cancer. On November 18, 1953, she was to appear at a children's folk festival in Washington but had to cancel at the last minute; Michael and Peggy took her place, and on that same day she died. For some years thereafter Crawford was remembered principally for her work in folk music. Her obituary in *Musical America* was typical: "folk singer, composer, leading collector of children's folk music."[25] But gradually her music began to be recognized for the milestone it was, and it surfaced in more and more concerts of "contemporary" music. *Piano Study with Mixed Accents* and the *Andante* for string orchestra found their way into New York Philharmonic concerts (in 1974 and 1971, respectively); *Suite for Piano and Woodwind Quintet* (1927/29) was played by members of the Boston Symphony at Tanglewood (1976); the *Three Songs by Carl Sandburg* turned up again in New York (1977). Gradually the musical world began to realize that Crawford had been one of the best and most original of all American composers of the first half of the twentieth century.

One of the most important influences on American composers of this very period was a French teacher of composition, Nadia Boulanger (1887–1979).[26] Trained at the Paris Conservatory, where Gabriel Fauré was among her teachers, she began to teach privately when she was only seventeen (in 1904) and five years later joined the Conservatory faculty. In 1913 her best-loved pupil, her younger sister Lili, became the first woman to win the First Grand Prix de Rome for her cantata *Faust et Hélène,* and Nadia decided to devote herself entirely to teaching and give up composition, for which she believed she had little talent compared to her sister's. Her sister died of tuberculosis five years later, and after Lili's death Nadia's pupils became, in effect, her family.

In 1920 Boulanger became a professor at the Ecole Normale de Musique, teaching harmony, counterpoint, accompaniment, the history of music, and, after Paul Dukas died in 1935, composition. She remained there until 1939. But her principal influence over American composers was exerted at a summer school of music founded at Fontainebleau (near Paris) in 1921, the American Conservatory (whose director she became in 1949). Three young Americans—Aaron Copland, Melville Smith, and Virgil Thomson—more or less independently found their way to her, and they were followed before long by Elliott Carter, Theodore Charles, Herbert Elwell, Roy Harris, Douglas Moore, Walter Piston, and Roger Sessions.[27] As Copland later said, "No one to my knowledge had ever before thought of studying composition with a woman....Everyone knows that the world has never produced a first-rate woman composer; so it follows that no woman could possibly hope to teach composition."[28] Copland wrote his *Symphony for*

*Organ and Orchestra* for Boulanger, and she was soloist in its premiere in New York (with the Boston Symphony Orchestra under Damrosch) on January 11, 1925.

Highly knowledgeable about many kinds of music, both ancient and modern, Boulanger had a gift for teaching the techniques essential to composition—harmony, counterpoint, ear training—and, whatever her own prejudices, for allowing her pupils to develop their own individual styles. Looking back a half-century, Virgil Thomson said she had "put me at ease in front of music paper. She taught me that writing music was a normal thing to do, like writing a letter. You simply put down what you mean. Her gift as a teacher was to force you to mean what you had said."[29]

Boulanger herself was by temperament, if not by training, a neoclassicist, and her favorite contemporary composer for many years was Igor Stravinsky. The detachment, the clarity, the strict forms of baroque and classical music, combined with the tonal and harmonic freedom to which the impressionists first pointed the way, had enormous appeal for her. Or, as one writer put it:

Historically Nadia Boulanger came at a very opportune moment. French music had reacted against Romanticism, and was therefore placed in a very advantageous position to welcome the new developments of the twentieth century. The school of Franck is an exception, but basically French music during the Romantic period was always looking towards ideals that one would term classical with, say, the French art of the period. In her own mind she always sought after a distillation of expression that was more in sympathy with classicism than romanticism. She was on the side of those who looked outwards, rather than in.[30]

For Boulanger the touchstone of great music was that it satisfy the mental faculties but also touch the heart. For her Stravinsky's music (at least until 1950 or so) met those requirements. For intellectual understanding she turned to old music, and in the mid-1930s she became one of the first to teach by performing and analyzing the music (especially the choral masterpieces) of Bach and Monteverdi, Schütz and Carissimi, Palestrina, Taverner, Tallis, and Binchois. A keyboard artist of concert caliber, she also continued to perform throughout the 1930s and take up a new career, conducting. (She herself said it was the need of students studying Bach by singing his cantatas that had turned her in this direction.) In 1936 and 1937 she conducted the Royal Philharmonic Orchestra of London in Gabriel Fauré's Requiem, the first woman conductor they ever had. She also was the first woman to conduct the Boston Symphony, the Philadelphia Orchestra, and the New York Philharmonic, and she came to Washington in 1938 to conduct the premiere of Stravinsky's *Dumbarton Oaks Concerto*.

Though pupils flocked to Boulanger from all over the world, she never attained the stature in France that she had elsewhere. Her closest ties were with America, which in the 1920s and 1930s she believed was about to embark on a golden age of music such as Russia had seen in the 1850s. She spent World War II in America, living mostly in the Boston area but giving concerts and recitals in many places. She returned to Paris after the war and continued to teach well into her nineties. Virgil Thomson called her "a one-man graduate school for musical Americans," one so powerful that "legend credits every United States town with two things—a five-and-dime and a Boulanger pupil."[31]

One of Boulanger's star pupils at the American Conservatory, and the only American she ever permitted to teach there, was Louise Talma, whose compositions embody much of Boulanger's teaching. Talma became the first woman to receive a Guggenheim Fellowship in composition twice (in 1946 and 1947), the first woman to be awarded the Sibelius Medal for composition (1963), and the first woman composer to be elected to the National Institute of Arts and Letters (1974). She also became the outstanding American woman neoclassical composer.

Louise Juliette Talma was born on October 31, 1906, in Arcachon, France, of American parents.[32] Her father, a pianist, died not long after her birth. Her mother, Alma Cecile Garrigue, was an opera singer but gave up her own career to direct her daughter's musical education, teaching her solfège and piano. For her formal education she brought the child to New York, where she attended high school and then studied at the Institute of Musical Art (later the Juilliard School) with theoreticians such as George Wedge and Percy Goetschius, and the composer Howard Brockway. Money was scarce, but Talma was able to go to Europe in 1926 and spend the summer at the American Conservatory at Fontainebleau. She returned there every summer for the next fourteen years (through 1939). Originally intending to become a pianist, Talma was convinced by Nadia Boulanger that she could be an outstanding composer. Winters she taught, at the Manhattan School of Music and then at Hunter College, where she began teaching in 1928 and celebrated her fiftieth anniversary in 1978 (after reaching mandatory retirement age she simply stayed on without pay).

Talma's earliest compositions were songs and piano pieces. In 1929-30 she wrote *Three Madrigals* and *La Belle Dame sans merci,* commissioned by Gerald Reynolds for the Women's University Glee Club. About this time, however, her mother became paralyzed, and Talma had to concern herself with earning enough to support them both. To keep her job at Hunter, she needed to obtain a degree (which at first had not been required); so Talma, who had attended night school for years, completed her degree requirements and by 1933 received a bachelor of music degree from New York University and a master of music degree from Columbia University. (Even so she was not made a full professor at Hunter until 1952.)

Consequently, the 1930s were a less productive period, although Talma did produce a number of songs, the song cycle *Five Sonnets from the*

*Portuguese,* and *In Principio Erat Verum* for chorus and organ. In 1943 her mother died and Talma felt freer to return to creative work, but for a time, at least, she found herself blocked. That summer she went to the MacDowell Colony and completed her Piano Sonata no. 1, which she performed in New York for the League of Composers on January 21, 1945. The following year she completed *Terre de France,* a song cycle for soprano and piano that sets five poems by French poets that pay homage to France. These songs are still tonal and even reminiscent of impressionism. They were sung over radio station WBAF in New York, with the composer at the piano, in January 1946, and again in September at the Yaddo Festival.

In 1944 Talma wrote her first big orchestral work, *Toccata for Orchestra,* which was given its premiere by the Baltimore Symphony under Reginald Stewart on December 20, 1945. Olin Downes said of it, "It reminds me more of one of the baroque eighteenth century toccatas in the variety and style presented."[33] *Toccata for Orchestra,* which won the Juilliard Publication Award in 1946, opens with a brilliant trumpet fanfare, continued by the strings and woodwinds. The theme is then stated by violins and violas; it is cast in one of the dominating rhythms of the work, a Latin figure in 4/4 time ( ♩. ♩. ♩ ). It is followed by a very soft but rhythmically spirited section, and then a *Presto* with legato triplets. About halfway through the work (which lasts about twelve minutes) a new theme is presented, first by the oboe, then by strings and brasses. The texture here is more chordal and denser, and the rhythm less syncopated. This section is followed by a return to the brilliant mood of the beginning, with its syncopated rhythm, but slower and less frantic, until the majestic end.

An excellent pianist and organist (she became a fellow of the American Guild of Organists, having decided to study organ in order to play Bach's organ works as they were intended to be played), Talma continued to write keyboard compositions as well as songs and chamber music. (These were, after all, the principal kinds of composition produced during the baroque period, whose forms—toccata, fugue, canon, cantata—attracted the twentieth-century neoclassicists.) Her *Alleluia in the Form of a Toccata* (1944), written about the same time as *Toccata for Orchestra,* features jazz rhythms and a percussive style reminiscent of Stravinsky's music. A second piano sonata, which was begun about the same time but not completed until 1955, still shows the dry, spare style and transparent texture of much of her work but incorporates some serial elements.

In the 1950s Talma became interested in twelve-tone music, a development that her long-time teacher, Nadia Boulanger, regarded as "a musical heresy."[34] Carried to their logical conclusion, Boulanger believed that the serialists, particularly the postwar composers such as Anton Webern, would dehumanize music. Talma nevertheless found their work interesting. Arthur Berger, also a former Boulanger pupil, thought it was Irving Fine's espousal of the twelve-tone idiom (in his String Quartet, 1952) that prompted Talma to adopt it, but rather than adopting the style completely she absorbed the technique of row-writing into her customary manner.[35]

Talma's *Six Etudes* for piano (1953–54), each quite short, employ a tone row for demonstrating a variety of pianistic techniques. No. 1, "Allegro— for contrasts," sets brilliant virtuoso passages against quiet, simple ones; no. 2, "Prestissimo—for staccato," has an interesting syncopated rhythm; no. 3, "Allegro—for sostenuto pedal," uses quite fast passages above a sustained pedal; no. 4, "Allegro—for wide skips," uses huge horizontal skips up and down the length of the keyboard; no. 5, "Allegro grazi- oso—for crossed hands," is a quiet, flowing piece; and no. 6, "Molto adagio—for increase of notes per beat," begins with one note per beat, two per beat, and so on, progressing to chords per beat, and then slows back to one note per beat. Nearly a quarter of a century later, Talma wrote a simi- liar work, *Textures* (1978), in which each of five interconnected sections concentrates on a different pianistic texture.

In 1955 Talma was awarded a Senior Fulbright Research grant and went to Rome for ten months to work on what was to become one of her most discussed works, the opera *The Alcestiad,* with a libretto by Thornton Wilder. She later recalled that it was a chance hearing of a piano work of hers that prompted Wilder to propose they do an opera together. "You can imagine how I felt," she said, "Since so many composers had been trying to get him to collaborate on an opera."[36] The opera, in three acts, took some- what longer to complete, and received its premiere on March 1, 1962, at Frankfurt-am-Main, Germany (in a German translation). It received eight performances and was the first time the work of an American woman had been produced by a major European opera house. Despite the warm recep- tion, it had not (by 1979) been performed again, and to Talma's particular regret, it had never been done in the original English.

In 1959 the Koussevitsky Music Foundation awarded Talma a commis- sion to write a chamber work and the result was *All the Days of My Life,* a cantata for tenor, clarinet, cello, piano, and percussion, completed in 1965. Both this and Talma's subsequent important works—*The Tolling Bell* for baritone and orchestra (1969), *Summer Sounds* for clarinet and string quartet (1973), and *Voices of Peace* for chorus and strings (1973)—are twelve-tone in construction. *The Tolling Bell,* a "Triptych" for baritone and orchestra, is dedicated to the MacDowell Colony, where Talma fre- quently worked in the summer from 1943 on (though she did return to Fontainebleau during the summers of 1949, 1951, and 1961). Like some of her other vocal works, it is based on texts from several authors (in this case Hamlet's soliloquy, the "Ah, Faustus" speech from Marlowe's *Doctor Faustus,* and a sonnet by John Donne). The work falls into three sections, the first and third meditative, the middle one more dramatic. Its framework is a twelve-tone row  (G–D–E–B–B♭–D♭–E♭–C–G♭–F–A♭–A),  but it is used in a fairly free manner. At the same time, the texture is characteristically spare and transparent. There is little doubling of parts (that is, each instrument plays its own line), and at least one writer, the composer Elaine Barkin, finds a number of techniques typical of American neoclassicism, especially that of Arthur Berger.[37]

*Summer Sounds* is also loosely serial. Its four movements are named "Dawn," "Morning," "Noon," and "Night," a departure from the neoclassic idea that only vocal music should have specific extramusical associations. This work reminds one listener of Jánaček in its use of animal and bird sounds as material, especially in the clarinet-dominated "Noon" section,[38] whereas for another critic it recalls the "night music" of Mahler and Bartók.[39]

Though honors and prizes were not slow in coming to Talma, performances were infrequent. When she was elected to the National Institute of Arts and Letters in 1974, she was given a citation that states (in part): "Many of her admirers, who had grown accustomed to seeing or hearing her referred to as one of our foremost women composers, have noticed with pleasure in recent years that she is being referred to more and more often without any qualification at all as one of our foremost composers." How much of that was owing to a growing appreciation of her work and how much to society's changing views of women is anyone's guess. Though Talma herself, like so many others, rejected being identified as a "woman composer," she clearly benefited from the wave of concerts of "women's music" of the late 1970s. Her String Quartet, for example, was given its first performance in twenty-three years when the Aviva Players, a group devoted to promoting women performers and composers, included it in a program in New York.[40] One reviewer said the piece showed its age but was eminently respectable in craftsmanship, and as a major effort by a well-known musician and teacher it should have been performed a couple of decades earlier, when it might have sounded fresher and more adventurous.[41] Neoclassicism may have been out of fashion just then, but that does not negate the value of a well-crafted, expressive composition.

The twelve-tone school exerted a more direct influence on Dika Newlin than on Talma: Newlin studied with Arnold Schoenberg for three years (1938–41), and for about twenty-five years all of her compositions were constructed on a twelve-tone row.

Dika Newlin[42] was born in 1923 in Portland, Oregon, but while she was still quite young her father, a professor of English, went to Michigan State College; so she grew up in East Lansing, Michigan. Her parents were not musicians, but her grandmother, Eva Hummer Hull, was a piano teacher, organist, and pianist, and her uncle, Alexander Hull, a composer. Dika began piano lessons at the age of six with Arthur Farwell, who encouraged her early interest in composing. At the age of eight she wrote a *Cradle Song* that was performed by the Cincinnati Symphony in 1935 (and later also by other orchestras, including the Los Angeles Philharmonic and the NBC Symphony). Academically precocious as well, she was a sophomore at Michigan State at the age of thirteen. By then she had heard of Arnold Schoenberg, who had fled Nazi Germany for America, and in her junior year she enrolled for study at the University of California at Los Angeles, where he was teaching. In the summer of 1939 she returned to complete her bachelor's degree at Michigan State and then went back to Los Angeles for two more years and a master's degree. By that time she was a dedicated Schoenberg disciple.

In 1941 Newlin went to Columbia University, which in 1945 granted her its first doctor of philosophy degree in musicology. Her doctoral dissertation, on Bruckner, Mahler, and Schoenberg, later became a standard reference work on these composers. (It was published in 1947, and a revised edition appeared in 1978.) While in New York she also studied composition with Roger Sessions and piano with Artur Schnabel. After receiving her doctorate, she taught for six years, at Western Maryland College and then at Syracuse University. She still kept in touch with Schoenberg and returned to California to work with him during the summers of 1949 and 1950. About this time she decided to write his biography and applied for a Fulbright grant to do research on his early years in Vienna. (Schoenberg himself was never to know that her application was approved, for he died in the summer of 1951.)

Newlin spent 1951–52 in Europe, mostly in Austria doing research, but also performing in Vienna and Paris, lecturing on American music in several Austrian cities, and making some recordings with violist Michael Mann. She also performed the piano part of her Piano Trio, op. 2 in Salzburg at the 1952 Festival of the International Society for Contemporary Music. Although Newlin has been called "an American composer who speaks Viennese,"[43] this was her only prolonged stay in Austria.

Upon returning to America in 1952, she became head of the newly formed department of music at Drew University in New Jersey, a post she held until 1965. She then taught at North Texas State University for eight years, returning east in 1973 to direct the Electronic Music Laboratory at Montclair State College in New Jersey. In 1976 she resigned and devoted herself fully to writing and composition for the next two years. In 1978 she accepted an invitation to develop a new doctoral program in music at Virginia Commonwealth University in Richmond.

An excellent pianist, Newlin wrote many of her most important works for that instrument, beginning with her *Sinfonia for piano* (1947), which is not yet a twelve-tone work but uses many unusual tone colors. Her Piano Trio (1948) is fully twelve-tone, based on the row: G-F-A-B-G#-D-C#-F#-E-C-

B♭–E♭. She wrote it at least partly because none of the major twelve-tone composers—Schoenberg, Berg, or Webern—had written a piano trio. It follows a structure favored by Schoenberg, which Newlin called the "portmanteau" form—that is, with all movements built into one. An introduction is followed by a first movement with three principal ideas: *Moderato grazioso,* a slow, graceful waltz; *Poco più lento,* a more passionately lyrical theme; and *Con brio alla marcia,* a lively martial theme. The second movement is a Scherzo with two trios, in which the ideas of the first movement are transformed and developed further, ending with a very slow section. The final movement combines the Scherzo and slow themes and continues to rework this material, ending with a chord that contains all twelve tones of the row.

From the same year as the Piano Trio dates Newlin's best-known orchestral work, *Chamber Symphony* for twelve solo instruments, which was dedicated to Schoenberg (it was first performed in 1949 in Darmstadt, Germany, and did not get its American premiere until 1960). Other important keyboard works are *Variations on a Theme from the Magic Flute* (1956) for piano, two variations on the March of the Priests, Act II, that portray the dark-light contrast so important in Mozart's opera; *Sonata da Chiesa* for organ (1956), a chorale prelude on "O Mensch bewein deine Sünde gross" flanked by a praeambulum in French overture rhythm and a fugue; and *Fantasy on a Row* (1957), which Konrad Wolff regards as most typical of her piano style, in that "traditional elements of music are completely fused with the present-day melodic and harmonic language." Wolff continues, "To me, this is the most Schoenbergian quality of Dika Newlin's work, setting her apart from almost all other American twelve-tone composers."[44] In this piece the first six tones of the tone row quote the opening viola recitative of Mahler's Symphony no. 10, identical with respect to both pitch and rhythm, whereas the remaining six tones emphasize the dissonant interval of the fourth plus the octave. The Postlude, which is to be played very slowly and without expressive dynamics (crescendo and decrescendo), is based on the chorale "Ach Gott, vom Himmel sieh darein" (used by Bach in his cantata BWV 2).

About 1970 Newlin became attracted to some of the newer developments in music and began to use both taped and computer-generated sounds in her own compositions. Her first important work of this kind was *Big Swamp* (1972), which includes both taped computer-generated sounds and live performance on man-made bird and animal calls. Her *Atone* (1977), for "diverse voices and instruments," uses aleatory elements (that is, some choices are left up to the performers). Newlin's advice to young composers is, among other things, "Be aware of and enter into contemporary forms of expression, such as multimedia, musical theater, group-improvised composition, electronic music, environmental music. Be aware that today *every-*

*thing* one learns and does can be part of a musical composition.''[45] In 1978 she herself was working on group-improvised composition and verbal scores, as well as continuing her work in musicology; an analysis of Schoenberg's music, an anthology of writings about film music, and a study of Schnabel's teachings were among her current projects. Her book, *The Schoenberg Diaries,* was scheduled for publication late in 1978.

Not all the European idioms that persisted into the twentieth century were new. Many composers, in both Europe and America, clung to nineteenth-century romanticism, writing highly expressive, often emotional, largely tonal music. Among these "neoromanticists" are such Americans as Howard Hanson, Samuel Barber, and Gian Carlo Menotti, and one of the most successful of women composers, Elinor Remick Warren, best known for her orchestral and choral works.

Warren[46] was born on February 23, 1906, in Los Angeles, California, which was still her home in the late 1970s. Before the age of five she was picking out pieces on the piano, and her mother, an excellent amateur musician, wrote some of them down. Soon after her fifth birthday she began piano lessons with Kathryn Cocke, who remained her teacher throughout childhood. From her she also learned harmony, general musicianship, and good working habits; she later said that her debt to her old teacher was enormous, and many years later, when she went to study with Nadia Boulanger, Boulanger was amazed to hear about Warren's excellent early training.

Warren's first songs were published when she was still a sophomore in high school. She was graduated, studied for a year at Mills College, and then went to New York "with a sheaf of songs" that were immediately accepted for publication. She also continued her piano studies, and her accompaniment teacher, Frank La Forge, introduced her to many singers, some of whom performed her songs and with some of whom she later toured as accompanist and solo pianist. Among them were Lucrezia Bori, Florence Easton, Lawrence Tibbett, and Richard Crooks, all of the Metropolitan Opera, as well as Rose Bampton, Nelson Eddy, Kirsten Flagstad, Dorothy Kirsten, and Eileen Farrell. Warren also played numerous concerts and recitals of her own, and was soloist with several symphony orchestras. One of her first large works, *The Harp Weaver,* for women's chorus and orchestra, was performed in New York in 1936 by the New York Women's Symphony under Antonia Brico.

In 1937 Warren married Z. Wayne Griffin, a Los Angeles businessman who warmly encouraged her in her career. She continued to perform after marriage, even after two sons and a daughter had been born, but her interest in composition, always considerable, began to supersede her interest in the piano (and, she later said, "I had continued composing right up until I went to the hospital, with all three children"). But she gradually gave up touring and began to write for instruments, at first orchestrating some of her many songs, and then branching out into compositions for orchestra alone, and for orchestra with chorus. Though she had earlier studied both the larger forms and orchestration, she spent a number of years continuing these studies on her own. Finally, in 1959, she decided to go to Paris to study with Nadia Boulanger, spending an intensive three months there (with daily lessons). Warren later said that Boulanger had enlarged her scope considerably, especially in the matter of orchestration, which led her to revise some of her earlier works.

Soon after Warren's return from France the well-known Chicago baritone and music patron Louis Sudler commissioned a cantata, which became *Abram in Egypt.* Set for baritone solo, chorus, and orchestra, with a text based on Genesis and the recently discovered Dead Sea Scrolls, it received its first complete performance at the Los Angeles International Music Festival on June 7, 1961. (Other composers represented on this occasion were Igor Stravinsky, Walter Piston, and Roy Harris.) An earlier orchestral work of Warren's is *Suite for Orchestra,* first performed in 1955 by the Los Angeles Philharmonic. Both works are neoromantic in style. The latter was inspired by the vast mountain panorama seen from the composer's ranch, high in the Sierras. "Although my Suite has no story or program behind it, the overtones of this pageantry of the sky and the long shadows of the towering mountains are doubtless in the fabric of the work."[47] *The Crystal Lake* (1958), a shorter work similarly inspired by the High Sierras landscape, was one of a half-dozen works by women performed by the New York Philharmonic between 1965 and 1975; it was performed in 1974, and also by the Detroit Symphony in that year.[48]

A Requiem Mass was commissioned by Roger Wagner for his Chorale and first performed by that group in Los Angeles in 1966. Set for mixed chorus, mezzo soprano and baritone solos, and orchestra, with a text partly in Latin and partly in English, it was warmly received ("Choral writing is superbly idiomatic, solos beautifully integrated, the orchestration equally effective and colorful," said Martin Bernheimer of the *Los Angeles Times).* *Symphony in One Movement* was commissioned by Stanford University and received its premiere performance there in 1971. *Singing Earth,* for high voice and orchestra, a setting of a Carl Sandburg poem, was revised in 1977–78. Also in 1977 came the first performance of another setting of a Sandburg poem, *Good Morning, America!* for narrator, chorus, and orchestra, by the Honolulu Symphony with Efrem Zimbalist, Jr., as narrator. (It had been commissioned by Occidental College.)

Warren won many honors. She was awarded an honorary doctor of music degree by Occidental College and received first prizes in every biennial contest of the National League of American Pen Women from 1964 on. In her seventies, Warren continued to be extremely active in her "rather large old house" and with her family, which by then included five grandchildren. More than 160 of her works had been published, and she was still composing.

Impressionism, neoclassicism, serialism, and neoromanticism—the principal European styles of composition of the first half of the twentieth century—engaged American women composers just as they did men. At the same time, some composers continued to use or reflect intrinsically American idioms—folk music of the South and West (including slave songs, spirituals, square dance music, etc.), jazz, and even the music of Broadway.

# 7 GRASS ROOTS—COMPOSERS IN AMERICAN IDIOMS

Musical nationalism, conventionally associated with the second half of the nineteenth century, actually has emerged in many periods. Musical composition, like any other art, represents the sum of the creator's experience. With some artists the absorption of national or folk elements is more profound than other influences, and their work inevitably reflects these elements, either by design or unconsciously.

In music such elements surface in many ways—in melodies, in rhythms, in characteristic harmonies. Composers may literally quote all or part of folk songs, or they may invent tunes that closely resemble the spirit and idioms of actual folk songs. The overall composition, moreover, need not be in any particular style. Since nationalism was most prominent in nineteenth-century Europe, it has come to be associated with the dominant musical style of that time, romanticism, but this need not be so. Both Charles Ives and Aaron Copland incorporated American folk idioms in many of their works, which otherwise show many stylistic differences.

Folk music—both song and dance—is an oral tradition, passed on by imitation from generation to generation. In order to make use of folk music formally, it must be generally known and available. In Europe the political nationalist movement spurred the collection, writing down, and arrangement of folk music, and in America much the same process took place. One of the earliest publications of music by an American woman was, as it happened, just such a compendium, in this case a collection of camp-meeting hymns made by Peggy Dow (wife of a Methodist preacher, Lorenzo Dow), which was published in Philadelphia in 1816.[1] In this province, today generally called "ethnomusicology," many American women were active, collecting and preserving camp-meeting hymns and spirituals, slave songs and Creole ballads, songs of the Appalachians and the Southwest, and American Indian music. The very first collection of slave songs published in book form, *Slave Songs of the United States* (1867), was the work of two men and one woman, William Allen, Charles Ware, and Lucy McKim Garrison. A pianist, Garrison (1842–77) wrote down some of the slave songs she had heard in the South and published two of them in *Dwight's Journal of Music* in 1862, "Roll, Jordan, Roll" and "Poor Rosy."[2]

Without recording equipment, transcribing folk music was a very tricky business. Folk songs often, if not generally, differ from one performance to the next; indeed, in some cases such performance practice is a basic feature of the music. Even in 1862 Lucy Garrison was aware of this problem:

> It is difficult to express the entire character of these negro ballads by mere musical notes and signs. The odd turns made in the throat, and the curious rhythmic effect produced by single voices chiming in at different irregular intervals, seem almost as impossible to place on the score as the singing of birds or the tones of an Aeolian Harp.[3]

Inevitably the ethnomusicologist's own musical background—at that time usually conventional European music—influenced his or her transcriptions.

Despite these difficulties, some outstanding work was done by three women who studied American Indian music.[4] Alice Cunningham Fletcher (1838–1923) did the first important work in this area, beginning about 1882. A fellow at Harvard University's Peabody Museum of American Archaeology and Ethnology, she wrote a treatise on the songs of the Omaha Indians and articles on the music of the Sioux and Pawnee Indians; her book, *Indian Story and Song from North America* (1900), was one of the earliest authoritative works on this subject.

The second woman, Natalie Curtis Burlin (1875–1921), who had studied piano and theory in Germany and France, worked among the Indians of the Southwest, particularly the Hopi and Zuñi, beginning about 1900. She published her findings in *The Indian's Book* (1907), which contained more than 200 songs of 18 tribes. Later she also collected and recorded songs of blacks in the South for the Hampton Institute (four volumes, published 1918–19).

Finally, Frances Densmore (1867–1957), who had studied piano with Leopold Godowsky and counterpoint with John Knowles Paine (see Chapter 4), became interested in Indian music at the 1893 Columbian Exposition in Chicago (where Alice Fletcher gave a talk on the subject).[5] From 1907 on Densmore worked for the Bureau of American Ethnology of the Smithsonian Institution. She investigated the music of many tribes, recording and transcribing songs, and is said to have made the most comprehensive survey and objective analysis of their music.

There were others. Josephine McGill, Ethel Park Richardson, Dorothy Scarborough, and Susannah Westmore recorded and notated the songs of southern Appalachia. Emily Hollowell, Nina Monroe, Maude Cuney Hare, and Mildred Hill recorded and transcribed black slave songs, spirituals, and Creole ballads. Allena Luce and Elizabeth Waldo collected the songs of the Southwest.[6]

All these women were *transcribing* the music of an oral tradition. They were not using elements of that tradition in their own compositions, as Ruth Crawford did in *Rissolty, Rossolty* or Mary Howe in *Chain Gang Song* (see Chapter 6). The remainder of this chapter concerns women composers who did just that.

A characteristically American musical idiom is that of the rural West and Southwest, the songs of cowboys and the dances of hoedowns, the tradition of ranch life and rodeos, which often includes Spanish-American elements as well. Unique to the United States, this idiom is clearly evident in much of the music of two natives of Texas, Julia Smith and Radie Britain.

Julia Frances Smith[7] was born on January 25, 1911, in Denton, Texas, one of seven children. She was educated at North Texas State University and the Juilliard School in New York, where she studied piano, composition (with Rubin Goldmark and Frederick Jacobi), and orchestration (with Bernard Wagenaar), graduating in 1939. She also attended New York University, where Marion Bauer was among her teachers, and where she earned her master's and doctor of philosophy degrees. Although Goldmark, her composition teacher, had also taught Aaron Copland, Smith herself never heard Copland's music until after Goldmark's death. In 1933 she attended the New York premiere of Copland's ballet, *Billy the Kid,* and was much taken with its use of American materials. She wrote her doctoral dissertation on Copland; in book form, it became one of the standard reference works on the composer.

Smith was a fine pianist, and she became pianist for the Orchestrette Classique (see Chapter 5), whose conductor, Frederique Petrides, was to introduce her to her future husband. Smith married Oscar A. Vielehr, an engineer and inventor, in 1938. He proved to be a great help to her, copying her music at times and always encouraging her in both performance and composition.[8] Smith continued to perform, both with orchestras and in recital, for the next thirty years or so. In 1957, believing that Copland's works for piano were still neglected, she gave an all-Copland piano recital in New York's Town Hall, and during the next ten years she performed these works in colleges and universities all over the United States.

Smith's first important composition, *American Dance Suite* for orchestra, based on four American folk tunes, was given its premiere by the Orchestrette Classique at Aeolian (later Town) Hall, New York, on February 10, 1936. (It was later revised, and also was reworked into a version for two pianos.) The following year the Orchestrette performed the premiere of Smith's *Episodic Suite,* originally (1935) for piano but revised (1936–37) for orchestra. Tuneful and discreetly dissonant, it shows touches of the humor that is characteristic in the best of Smith's compositions; in 1940 Smith herself conducted it with the Dallas Symphony Orchestra.[9] In 1941 the Orchestrette gave still another premiere, this time of *Hellenic Suite,* dedicated to Petrides. Based on Greek folk melodies, this three-movement suite has not been performed as much as her works based on American materials.

During this same period, Smith composed the first of her six (by 1973) operas, the two-act *Cynthia Parker.* Based on the life of a woman in early Texas history, it was produced in 1939 in Denton, Texas, with Metropolitan Opera soprano Leonora Corona in the title role. Another work of distinctly American heritage is *Liza Jane* (1939–40), written when CBS commissioned her to produce a short orchestral work based on American folk themes; it has been widely performed in both the United States and Europe.

From 1940 to 1942 Smith taught theory and counterpoint at Juilliard, and from 1944 to 1946 she taught at New Britain (Connecticut) State Teachers College. During this period, she also founded the department of music education at Hartt College of Music, in Hartford, Connecticut, where she taught from 1941 to 1946. Always interested in music education, Smith wrote many teaching pieces, a string method (with Cecile Vashaw), and a number of works for band (including *Remember the Alamo!* 1964).

Smith's other important orchestral compositions include *Folkways Symphony* (1947–48), based on folk and cowboy songs, and Concerto for piano and orchestra (1938–39, revised 1970–71). The latter, whose revised version was first given a complete performance by the Dallas Civic Symphony in 1976, is in three movements and its themes reflect both folk and jazz idioms. The first movement, in sonata form, consists of an extended introduction, a first theme marked *Alla marcia vivace* ("a lively march"), and a second, more lyrical theme. The second movement, in three-part song form, begins with a sustained horn solo. The final movement, in free rondo-sonata form, brings the work to a playful, joyous conclusion.[10]

For smaller forces Smith wrote a *Characteristic Suite* (1949) for piano, built on a twelve-tone row (her only work so constructed), of which Virgil Thomson wrote, "Her music is jolly, and even in twelve-tone syntax, easy to take";[11] the piano trio *Cornwall* (1955); and a sprightly String Quartet (1962–64), whose syncopated, dancelike rhythms, especially in the brilliant last movement, call to mind the hoedowns and other celebrations of rural America. Notable among Smith's operas are the one-act *The Gooseherd and the Goblin* (1945–46), commissioned by and performed more than thirty times by the Hartt College of Music Opera Workshop on tour; *The Shepherdess and the Chimneysweep,* a one-act Christmas opera performed many times since its premiere in 1968; and *Daisy,* a two-act opera about the life of Juliette Gordon Low (founder of the Girl Scouts of America), which received its premiere in 1973 in Miami, Florida, and was given nineteen special bicentennial performances in 1976, as well as others in succeeding years.

In the late 1960s Julia Smith, long active in a number of composers' organizations, compiled a *Directory of American Women Composers* (for the National Federation of Music Clubs, which published it in 1970). It was the first book of its kind. "I really had to stop my own work entirely to do this," she later said, "but I felt that it was important that someone do it—at least make a start toward recognition of the really fine work (in some cases) of our women composers."[12] In November 1976 Smith helped organize an international program sponsored by the National Federation of Music Clubs and devoted to works by women, held at Columbia University; her piano concerto was among the compositions performed.

Radie Britain was born on March 17, 1903, on a ranch near Amarillo, Texas.[13] She began her music studies at the age of seven at Clarendon College, in Texas, and was graduated with high honors. She then went to the American Conservatory in Chicago, where she studied piano with Heniot Levy and organ with Von Dusen, receiving her bachelor of music degree in 1920. She returned to Texas to teach at Clarendon for about four years, and then went to Europe, where she studied composition with Albert Noelte in Germany for two years and made her debut as a composer (with four songs) in Munich. She also spent one summer in Paris, where she studied organ with Marcel Dupré. After returning to America, she taught for some ten years at the Chicago Conservatory of Music. During these years, she married and had one daughter, Lerae, but the marriage did not last. In 1939 she moved to California and taught piano and composition in Hollywood for about ten years. Also in 1939, she was married to Edgard Simone, a sculptor who died in the 1950s. In 1959 she married Ted Morton, prominent in aviation; her *Cosmic Mist Symphony* (1962) is dedicated to him.

Unlike many composers who confine themselves chiefly to small forms at the outset, Radie Britain early produced a number of works for full orchestra. Her first big success was her *Heroic Poem* for orchestra, in commemoration of Lindbergh's first transatlantic flight. It won an International Hollywood Bowl Prize in 1930, and also the first Juilliard Publication Award ever given to a woman composer (in 1945). Even earlier, in 1928, Britain's *Symphonic Intermezzo* had been performed by the Chicago Woman's Symphony under Ethel Leginska (see Chapter 5). Other early orchestral works include two composed at the MacDowell Colony in 1935, *Light,* dedicated to Thomas Edison (which won a first prize from the Boston Women's Symphony and also was performed by the Chicago Woman's Symphony), and *Southern Symphony,* a larger work in four movements. Her string quartet from the same year, *Prison Lament,* was performed at the White House in 1936 at the special request of the First Lady, Eleanor Roosevelt.

More than fifty of Britain's works received international or national awards, and she herself was awarded the honorary degree of doctor of music from the Musical Arts Conservatory of Amarillo. Though she also wrote many chamber works, ballets, operas, pieces for piano, two pianos, organ, harp, violin, choral works, and songs, it is for her orchestral compositions that Britain became best known. Many of her works celebrate her native Texas, the cattle country and the southwestern desert, as can be seen from descriptive titles such as *Ontonagon Sketches* (1939), *Drouth* (1939), *Red Clay* (1946), *Cactus Rhapsody* (1953; a piano trio), and *Cowboy Rhapsody* (1956). Some of the Spanish influence important in the Southwest emerges in works such as *Rhumbando* for wind ensemble (1975). Her last large-scale orchestral work, *Cosmic Mist Symphony,* won the first national award of the National League of American Pen Women in 1964 and was performed by the Houston Symphony Orchestra under A. Clyde Roller; it is in three movements, entitled "In the Beginning," "Nebula," and "Nuclear Fission." Her *Pyramids of Giza* (1973) for orchestra was first performed in New York in 1976. Another late work, *Musical Portrait of Thomas Jefferson,* for string quartet, received its premiere in Sacramento in 1978 and received a standing ovation, and in the same year her *Fantasie* for oboe and piano won an award from the Texas Composers Guild.

Another rich American musical tradition is that of the South, particularly (although not exclusively) that of southern blacks. Slave songs, spirituals, gospel hymns, and minstrelsy not only gave rise to the popular genres of blues, jazz, and modern soul and gospel music, but were absorbed by and reflected in a large body of music produced by serious composers. According to Frederick Douglass, on many plantations slaves were expected to sing as well as to work; for teamsters and field-workers it was a means of letting the overseer know where they were and that they were moving along with their work. These work songs, often plaintive even when they were basically wild or rapturous in character, shared certain fundamental musical traits: a steady, usually 4/4 beat; considerable syncopation; four-bar phrases; simple basic harmonies; a great deal of riffing repetition; and free improvisation by the singers.[14]

Most attractive to early collectors of southern folk music was black religious music, today lumped together under the catchall term "spirituals."[15] The most common structure for spirituals was a call-and-response form, in which solo verses, sung by a leader, alternated with the refrain, sung by a group. The leader began the words of each verse, often improvising, and the others struck in with the refrain (or occasionally joined the soloist when the words were familiar). A genuine spiritual was an unceasing variation around a theme; it changed with each performance as the leader's words were elaborated on, at different points in time, singly and together, by the chorus. There was no singing in parts, as with conventional hymns or chorales. The harmony was often jagged and dissonant, with the various parts breaking in anywere; chants and hums also were used to reinforce the verse at various points.[16]

Another feature of the southern folk tradition was the minstrel show. Originally an entertainment put on by slaves for their owners, it was imitated in time by white songwriters and entertainers who regarded the black as a figure of fun. By the 1820s white men were blacking their faces with burnt cork and mimicking black songs and dances and telling jokes based on slave life. The first organized full-length minstrel show was produced in 1843 in New York by Daniel Decatur Emmett and his troupe of Virginia Minstrels, which soon had many imitators. To obtain material, white minstrels visited plantations, listened to the songs of blacks working in the fields, on steamboats and docks, and in tobacco factories. Combining this kind of music with the sentimental parlor ballads in vogue at this time produced a new musical form, the minstrel song, whose greatest exponent was Stephen Foster (1826–64).[17] His "Old Black Joe," "Swanee River," "Camptown Races," "My Old Kentucky Home," and "Old Folks at Home" (among others) became immensely popular among blacks as well as whites and, in time, joined the roster of genuine American folk songs.

After the Civil War, genuine black minstrel companies were organized. These troupes existed side by side with white companies, remaining a very popular form of American entertainment until 1910 or so. Minstrel shows included several kinds of song: sentimental ballads, spirituals and other religious songs, operatic airs, and comic songs.

Minstrelsy was one of two major vehicles carrying southern music to the North and West. The other was the touring choral group, whose first and most famous representative were the Fisk Jubilee Singers. Soon after the Civil War ended, black schools began to be founded in the South. One of the first was Fisk University in Nashville, Tennessee, opened in 1866. To help raise funds for Fisk's building program, in 1871 the school sent a small group of excellent singers on tour. After a shaky beginning, they scored their first big success in Boston in 1872 at a huge World Peace Jubilee (hence their name). Thereafter they toured all over the United States and even in Europe, raising, in only seven years, the unheard-of total of $150,000.[18]

Other schools followed Fisk's lead, sending out groups to sing spirituals and "plantation songs." The spirituals they performed were adaptations rather than the genuine article. In their formally organized concerts, much of the improvisatory nature of the true spiritual was abandoned. Nevertheless, the melodies and something of the original performance style were retained. In time more and more spirituals became widely familiar, disseminated through both performance and publication. As they were written down, the different possibilities for arrangement became apparent. Both choral and solo arrangements were written, and later even purely instrumental arrangements were made of what had originally been vocal music.

At the same time, more and more blacks, taking advantage of new educational opportunities, took up the formal study of music, which in the late nineteenth century meant principally the study of European music. In the work of these composers, trained in the traditional European forms of composition—art song and symphony, march and overture—the native idioms appeared in new guise.

Among serious composers, the first outstanding woman of her race was Florence Beatrice Smith Price, born in the South, educated at the New England Conservatory of Music, and eventually a resident of Chicago. Her work reflects her training, which was dominated by white American men steeped in European musical traditions, but it also reflects her roots in the South.

Florence Smith Price[19] was born on April 9, 1888, in Little Rock, Arkansas, where her father was a dentist. Her early musical training was given her by her mother, a soprano and pianist. For a time she attended elementary school in Chicago but she returned to high school in Little Rock, graduating at fourteen. She then went to the New England Conservatory in Boston, where she majored in piano and organ, and received her artist's diploma in organ. She also studied composition and counterpoint with George Chadwick and Frederick Converse (see Chapter 4), and as a student wrote a string trio and a symphony.

At nineteen she returned to Arkansas and took on her first teaching job, in a school that included both elementary and high school grades; later she took over the music department at Shorter College in North Little Rock. In 1912 she married Thomas J. Price, a lawyer. They had three children, a son named Thomas, who died quite young (she wrote a song, "To My Little Son," in his memory), and two daughters, Florence and Edith.

While raising her family, Price became a highly respected music teacher in Little Rock, giving private lessons in violin, piano, and organ. But in 1927, with racial tension high following a lynching, the family decided to move to Chicago, where Price continued to teach, compose, and perform whenever possible. She became a close friend of Estella C. Bonds (mother of Margaret Bonds, who is discussed later in this chapter), with whom she lived during a brief period of hard times, and she gave Margaret Bonds lessons in piano and composition. Price herself also went back to school, studying composition with Carl Busch, Wesley La Violette, and Arthur Olaf Anderson; at various times she was enrolled at the Chicago Musical College, Chicago Teachers College, Chicago University, and American Conservatory of Music, studying not only music but also languages and the liberal arts.

In 1932 Price won two Wanamaker Foundation awards, one of $500 for her Symphony in E minor and another of $250 for her Piano Sonata (the remainder of the $1,000 stipend was won by Margaret Bonds for a song). The winning symphony was performed on June 15, 1933, by the Chicago Symphony Orchestra under Frederick Stock, at the Century of Progress Exposition. Other of her orchestral works were performed by the WPA Symphony Orchestra of Detroit and the Chicago Woman's Symphony (Bonds performed the solo part of Price's Concerto in F minor with the latter in 1934),[20] and her Piano Quintet was played at the University of Illinois and by the Forum String Quartet of Chicago.

Price was prolific. She wrote art songs, spiritual arrangements, keyboard works (for piano and organ), four symphonies, three piano concertos, and a violin concerto. She made considerable use of characteristic black rhythms and melodies in her works, especially in the Symphony in E minor, a *Concert Overture on Negro Spirituals, Three Little Negro Dances,* and *Negro Folksongs in Counterpoint* for string quartet (originally for string orchestra, commissioned by conductor John Barbirolli).

Humble in demeanor and deeply religious, Price often used the music of the black church and made a number of arrangements of spirituals. Her *Two Traditional Spirituals,* "I am Bound for the Kingdom" and "I'm Workin' on My Buildin'," published in 1949, were dedicated to the black contralto Marian Anderson, who frequently performed them. The most famous of Price's arrangements was "My Soul's Been Anchored in de Lord," published in 1937 in an arrangement for voice and piano; she later made another arrangement for voice and orchestra, and both were recorded. Price's arrangements are, on the whole, simple chordal settings that allow the melody to dominate. In "My Soul's Been Anchored," however, she created a striking rhythmic setting, with both the accompaniment and the vocal part syncopated but in contrasting rhythms. Her *Three Little Negro Dances,* highly syncopated settings of "Hoe Cake," "Rabbit Foot," and "Ticklin' Toes," was originally a piano work that later was arranged for band and was frequently performed by the U.S. Marine Band. Price died in Chicago on June 3, 1953.

The second black woman composer of note was Price's one-time pupil, Margaret Bonds, who made a conscious effort both to develop black idioms in larger musical forms and to promote the music of black Americans. Margaret Bonds[21] was born in Chicago on March 3, 1913, and began her musical studies with her mother, Estella C. Bonds. A church organist and highly accomplished musician, Estella Bonds was an important figure in black artistic circles, and young Margaret met such leading artists as the sculptor Richmond Barthe, the poets Langston Hughes and Countee Cullen, the soprano Abbie Mitchell, and the popular composer Will Marion Cook. She became especially close friends with Hughes, many of whose poems she later set to music. Abbie Mitchell introduced her to the works of the black composer Harry T. Burleigh, who not only used black idioms but actually quoted spirituals in his own compositions.

In high school Bonds began to study composition with Florence Price and with another black composer, William Dawson. She also worked closely with a number of singers, earning money as an accompanist in supper clubs and shows. Among her jobs was accompanying the dancer Muriel Abbott in the Empire Room at Chicago's Palmer House. She also copied parts for black composers. She later recalled,

Our collective security stretched out a hand to visiting artists, and when composers like Will Marion Cook had an opportunity to present a Negro choir on NBC, I was sent to extract all of his choral parts, which, incidentally, he changed daily. Even now, when I write something for a choir and it's jazzy and bluesy and spiritual and Tchaikowsky all rolled up into one, I laugh to myself, "That is Will Marion Cook."[22]

Also while she was still in high school, Bonds joined the National Association of Negro Musicians, helped establish its junior division, and worked hard in it to promote black music and black musicians.

Despite the difficulties posed by the Great Depression, Bonds went to Northwestern University, one of a small minority of black students there, and by the age of twenty-one she had earned both her bachelor's and master's degrees. She then opened a school for ballet, art, and music, but in those hard times it did not thrive. In 1939 Bonds left Chicago for New York City. For a time she worked as a music editor, and she published several popular songs, among them "Peach Tree Street," "Georgia," and "Spring Will Be So Sad." In 1940 she married Lawrence Richardson, a probation officer in the New York court system. They had one child, Djane, named for pianist Djane Herz, with whom Bonds studied at the Juilliard School. She also studied composition (both at Juilliard and privately) with Roy Harris, Robert Starer, and Emerson Harper.

While in New York Bonds met Nadia Boulanger and hoped to study composition with her, but the French teacher turned her down flat. Boulanger admired the composition Bonds showed her (it was *The Negro Speaks of Rivers)* but told her she should go on as she was, and not study with anyone. No doubt Boulanger realized that Bonds had grasped European compositional techniques but her style combined these with black improvisation in such a way that her own natural direction might easily have been stifled by further study of European idioms.[23]

From the 1940s to the 1960s Bonds continued to compose, perform, and teach. She formed the Margaret Bonds Chamber Society to present black musicians in works by black composers, and she herself continued to appear on the concert stage, both as a piano recitalist and as soloist with the Chicago Symphony, Chicago Woman's Symphony, New York Symphony, and other orchestras. She served as music director and pianist for numerous theatrical productions, and she also taught at the American Theater Wing, and at various times was music director of the Stage for Youth, East Side Settlement House, and White Barn Theater.[24] Herself a resident of New York's Harlem, she was minister of music at a local church and helped establish a Cultural Community Center there.

Bonds's own compositions show the influence of the blues and jazz she heard so much during her youth in Chicago, and they often include either spiritual melodies or original melodies in spiritual style. Understandably, they also are very pianistic, and often quite difficult technically; Bonds herself was an excellent pianist. She gradually won increasing recognition— first the Wanamaker Award for a song in 1932, then a Roy Harris Fellowship, and in the 1960s several awards from ASCAP (American Society of Composers, Authors, and Publishers). She was particularly proud of the Northwestern University Alumni Medal awarded her in 1967; at the time she had attended Northwestern, black students, few in number though they were, still were barred from many university facilities.

In 1967 Bonds moved to Los Angeles, where she devoted the remaining years of her life to teaching music to inner-city children. In 1972 the Los Angeles Symphony under Zubin Mehta performed the premiere of her *Credo* for chorus and orchestra. She died a few months later.

Bonds wrote art songs, choral works, orchestral works, piano pieces, and popular songs—more than two hundred works in all. Among the best is the song *The Negro Speaks of Rivers,* a setting of Langston Hughes's first published poem, with jazzy augmented chords. In 1967 Bonds wrote,

Thirty years ago a teacher of mine objected to the music. It was "too far out," then, not only because it had a Negro spiritual flavor, but because in the last part of the song, when the poet speaks of America, it becomes very "jazzy." My teacher said that maybe it would be all right if I took out those "jazzy augmented chords." I changed not a note, because God had "gotten at me" for several hours during the song's creation, and I believed that I had recorded what He wanted me to record.[25]

Unfortunately, Marian Anderson, to whom Bonds showed the song, also did not like it; she never performed it, although she later sang a more somber setting by Howard Swanson.

Also notable is Bonds's *The Ballad of the Brown King,* originally for voice and piano and later enlarged for chorus, soloists, and orchestra. Another setting of a Hughes poem, it tells of the three kings who attended Jesus' birth and particularly of Balthazar, who is portrayed as a black (or "brown") man. Performed by the Westminster Choir in New York in December 1960, the work is in nine movements and blends a variety of traditions: spirituals, jazz, calypso rhythms, and some blues and folk styles, as well as the traditional European choral tradition (here seen in the quasi-recitative sections).

*Three Dream Portraits,* published in 1959, also settings of Hughes's poems, is a series of mood paintings imbued with jazz style. "Minstrel Man" has repeated bass patterns in the accompaniment that are reminiscent of ragtime, and there is frequent use of the lowered seventh chord found in spirituals, blues, and jazz. "To a Brown Girl Dead," a setting of a poem by Countee Cullen, is in the style of a funeral dirge, and "I Got a Home in

That Rock," a spiritual arranged for solo voice and piano (or orchestra), has an accompaniment in jazz-blues style. Other of Bonds's spiritual arrangements are "Dry Bones," "Lord, I Just Can't Keep from Crying," "I'll Reach to Heaven," "Sit Down, Servant," "This Little Light of Mine," and "Ezekiel Saw the Wheel." In addition, Bonds wrote several scores for stage works (notably *Shakespeare in Harlem),* two ballets, a symphony entitled *Peter and the Bells, Spiritual Suite* for piano, and a Mass in D minor.

Like Margaret Bonds and Florence Price, Julia Perry made some arrangements of spirituals, and like them she wrote a considerable amount of vocal music, but in her work black idioms are incorporated far more subtly, and they rarely predominate. Indeed, as a former student of both Nadia Boulanger and the Italian avant-garde composer Luigi Dallapiccola, Perry, one might argue, would be more appropriately discussed with other composers in European idioms. But like Bonds and Price, Perry was born black, and the black experience in America during the first half of the twentieth century nearly always involved, from the musical standpoint, considerable exposure to gospel, jazz, blues, and other native American idioms. Thus, even though Perry was trained along conventional—and not so conventional—European lines, her vocal settings and her use of rhythm reflect this experience.

Julia Amanda Perry[26] was born on March 25, 1924, in Lexington, Kentucky, but her family soon moved to Akron, Ohio. Her two older sisters studied violin; her physician father was a pianist; and her mother saw to it that the children practiced. Julia, who from the first wanted to be a composer, was graduated from Akron High School and in 1943 went to the Westminster Choir College in Princeton, New Jersey, where she studied piano, violin, voice, conducting, and composition. During one summer while still a student, in 1946, she went to Birmingham, Alabama, where she trained a young choir and taught it one of her own compositions. Perry received her master's degree from Westminster in 1948, having written a secular cantata, *Chicago,* for her master's thesis. She then moved to New York City and continued her studies at Juilliard. During this period, her cantata *Ruth* was performed at the Riverside Church in April 1950, and several of her compositions were published. She also worked for a time as assistant coach at the Columbia Opera Workshop, which in 1954 performed her first opera, the one-act *The Cask of Amontillado,* based on a short story by Edgar Allan Poe.

In 1951 Perry worked with the Italian composer Luigi Dallapiccola at the Berkshire Music Center in Tanglewood, and as a result she applied for a Guggenheim Fellowship to study further with him in Italy. In 1952 she went to Europe, where she also studied with Nadia Boulanger (see Chapter 6), and in that year she received the Boulanger Grand Prix for her Viola Sonata. Perry was awarded a second Guggenheim Fellowship in 1954 and returned to Italy to study with Dallapiccola again. In the summers of 1956 and 1957 she studied conducting at the Accademia Chigiana of Siena, and in 1957 she organized and conducted a series of concerts in Europe under the sponsorship of the U.S. Information Service.

In 1959, after a total of five and one-half years in Europe, Perry returned to America and devoted herself largely to composition, and some teaching. In 1967 she taught at Tallahassee's Florida Agricultural and Mechanical College, and in 1969 she was visiting lecturer at Atlanta College. In 1971 Perry suffered a paralytic stroke and was subsequently hospitalized for a number of years. By the late 1970s, she had recovered enough to leave the hospital and resume composing.

Perry's early works in particular incorporate black musical idioms. "Free at Last," published in 1951, and "I'm A Poor L'il Orphan" are actual arrangements of spirituals. In *Song of Our Savior,* for a cappella chorus, written for the Hampton Institute Choir, she used the Dorian mode (instead of the diatonic scale) and a hummed ostinato, as well as the call-and-response structure in one section. But it was not long before Perry began to combine traditions more freely. One of her most striking works is the *Stabat Mater,* composed in 1951 and dedicated to her mother. Set for contralto solo and string orchestra, it makes free use of dissonance but is still tonal, and uses modern devices such as quartal harmony (based on fourths, instead of the traditional thirds and fifths), an occasional whole-tone scale, and cluster chords (chords made up of adjacent notes). The overall work is very dramatic, almost operatic in character.

From her early concentration on vocal music, Perry turned increasingly, from the 1950s on, to instrumental compositions. By 1971 she had produced twelve symphonies, beginning with Symphony no. 1 for violas and string basses (revised in 1962) and continuing with symphonies for full orchestra, string orchestra, concert band, marching band, and orchestra with chorus. Significantly, the first major work she produced after her illness was another symphony (no. 5, 1976).

Perry's *A Short Piece for Orchestra,* revised in 1962, was performed by the New York Philharmonic in 1965. From its rather wild, loud, brassy opening it moves to an *Andante lento* featuring the woodwinds and strings in long, lyrical passages. It then accelerates to return to the first tempo, with the horns announcing a return to the tumult of the opening, punctuated by percussion. This work has a great deal of rhythmic interest, with considerable use of syncopation. More experimental in nature is *Homunculus C.F.* for ten percussionists, composed during the summer of 1960. Scored for timpani, various cymbals, snare drum, bass drum, wood blocks, xylophone, vibraphone, celesta, piano, and harp, the work is based on the chord of the fifteenth (the *C.F.* of the title)—that is, a succession of superimposed thirds with an E root (beginning on E above middle C): E–G#–B–D#–F#–A#–C#–E#. It is not in any major or minor key, and the composer herself termed the work "pantonal"—using any and all available tones. The name "Homunculus" refers to the test-tube creature brought to life by Wagner, Faust's young apprentice, attesting to the experimental nature of the piece. The work falls into four sections, the first purely rhythmic (using only unpitched percussion instruments), the second principally melodic (timpani, harp, and two cymbals), the third harmonic, and the fourth combining harmony, melody, and rhythm.

Other instrumental works of Perry's include a *Requiem for Orchestra,* also called *Homage to Vivaldi,* and based on themes by the baroque composer (1959); a number of shorter orchestral works; chamber music; a violin concerto; and two piano concertos. She also produced a number of vocal works: a three-act opera, *The Symplegades,* concerning the seventeenth-century Salem witchcraft panic, which took more than ten years to write; an opera-ballet to her own libretto based on Oscar Wilde's fable, *The Selfish Giant; Five Quixotic Songs* for bass-baritone solo, two clarinets, viola, baritone horn, and piano (1976); and *Bicentennial Reflections* for tenor solo and six instruments (1977). In 1978 she was working on a *Suite for Brass and Percussion.*

At least two other black women composers must be mentioned. Evelyn LaRue Pittman,[27] born in Oklahoma in 1910, pursued an active career in teaching, choral conducting, and composition. Much of her original work was prompted by the need for new teaching materials for her pupils and music for choral groups under her direction. The Evelyn Pittman Choir performed for twelve years during the 1930s and 1940s. Educated at Spelman College (Atlanta), the University of Oklahoma, the Juilliard School, and with Nadia Boulanger, Pittman wrote *Rich Heritage,* a collection of songs and stories concerning eminent blacks that has gone into two editions (1944, 1968); *Cousin Esther,* a folk opera performed in Paris in 1957; *Freedom's Child,* an opera about Martin Luther King, Jr., first presented by her own Woodlands High School students (from Hartsdale, New York) in Atlanta in 1972; and many arrangements of spirituals and choral works that show the influence of black church music in particular.

Lena Johnson McLin,[28] born in Atlanta in 1929 and later a resident of Chicago, where she did graduate work in theory, counterpoint, and electronic music, similarly wrote much music for her pupils and for choirs she directed. Her compositions, which include cantatas, Masses, spiritual arrangements, anthems, operas, songs, piano works, orchestral works, and electronic music, incorporate not only the older black idioms of spirituals and work songs but the twentieth-century idioms of blues and gospel, jazz and rock. Notable among her works are *The Torch Has Been Passed,* for a cappella chorus, based on a text by President John F. Kennedy concerning the achievement of world peace; *If They Ask Why You Can,* a gospel song dedicated to her brother, the Reverend B. J. Johnson III; *Let the People Sing the Praises of the Lord,* an anthem for chorus, piano (or organ), and trumpet, notable for its driving rhythms, syncopation, and quartal, often dissonant, harmonies; and *Free at Last,* a cantata about Martin Luther King, Jr., which includes five spirituals but treats them largely in the style of freely invented gospel song.

Of course, not only black composers have made use of southern idioms or become known for their arrangements of old hymns and spirituals. One of the most renowned and successful American choral arrangers is Alice Parker, whose arrangements of folk songs, carols, and spirituals were for many years performed and recorded by the Robert Shaw Chorale. Also a composer in her own right, Parker wrote principally choral music, both sacred and secular, as well as several operas.

Alice Parker[29] was born on December 16, 1925, in Boston, Massachusetts, and studied piano, organ, clarinet, and violin. She was graduated from Smith College in 1947, having majored in organ and composition, and went on to New York to the Juilliard School, where she worked with Julius Herford, Vincent Persichetti, and, most important, Robert Shaw. After getting her master's degree in choral conducting in 1949, she went to work for Shaw, whose highly successful choral group had begun touring and so brought an end to his teaching. From 1949 to 1968 Parker was employed as arranger for the Robert Shaw Chorale, producing a total of some four hundred published arrangements of folk songs, hymns, and carols, many of which have become standard works in the choral repertory. She also assisted Shaw in planning programs, writing program notes and record jacket notes, conducting section rehearsals, and with many of the musical chores involved in conducting a famous choral ensemble. At the same time, she taught music at several private schools, but from about 1965 on she devoted herself increasingly to her own composition. In 1954 Alice Parker married Thomas F. Pyle, a baritone soloist and choral singer, and later a contractor for choral singers; they had five children. Parker accompanied her husband in recitals and often composed music for him. He died in 1976.

Though she also wrote keyboard works and instrumental chamber music, it is for her vocal music that Parker became best known. Inevitably it reflects her long-time association with American idioms. For example, *Commentaries* (1978), a cantata for women's voices and full orchestra, sets five poems by the nineteenth-century New England poet Emily Dickinson as a kind of contrapuntal commentary on arrangements of sacred and secular songs of the same period, principally from the South. The music quotes an old hymn tune (with a text from a hymn collection published in Virginia in 1835), an Appalachian love ballad with old English roots, a black spiritual, a Quaker hymn, and a mountain hymn. In 1971 Parker had completed her first opera, *The Martyrs' Mirror,* a church opera first performed that October in Pennsylvania and given more than thirty performances in the next three years. Scored for soloists, two choirs, and small instrumental ensemble, it tells the story of four sixteenth-century Swiss Anabaptists who were executed for their religious beliefs. The choral score is based partly on old Mennonite hymn tunes (the Mennonites being a sect descended from the Anabaptists), combined with an instrumental accompaniment in more contemporary style.

Parker's next opera, *The Family Reunion* (1974–75), is a one-act opera set in rural America in the 1850s (and concerns just such a reunion); it quotes folk songs, marches, dances, and hymns of that period, among them "Home, Sweet Home," "Where Have You Been, Billy Boy," and "Work for the Night Is Coming." *Singers Glen* (1978), an opera in a prologue and two acts that was first performed in Pennsylvania in 1978, concerns the life of Joseph Fuchs (1778–1862) of Singers Glen, Virginia, a Mennonite who published ten editions (1832–62) of a hymn-tune collection called *Genuine Church Music;* the twenty-third edition, entitled *Harmonia Sacra,* was still in print in 1978. The opera quotes a number of hymns from the collection, and one scene is devoted to the meeting of a singing school (see Chapter 1).

Parker's other works include *Martin Luther King: A Sermon from the Mountain* (1969), a cantata based on texts from the black leader's writings, his favorite biblical texts, and spirituals; *The Time of Ingathering* (1970), for alto solo, chorus, and organ; *Melodious Accord* (1974), a cantata for chorus, harp, and brass quartet; *Songs for Eve* (1975), for vocal quartet and string quartet, a setting of twenty-eight short poems by Archibald MacLeish; *There and Back Again* (1976), for chorus and woodwind quartet; and a number of works for chorus and orchestra, notably *Gaudete: Six Latin Christmas Hymns* (1973), *The True Use of Music* (1976), and *Journeys: Pilgrims and Strangers* (1976), the last about the different heritages of America's early settlers with texts from early hymns and spirituals.

Similarly attracted to vocal music, choral conducting, and the use of American historical subjects in her compositions was composer-conductor Gena Branscombe.[30] Born on November 4, 1881, in Picton, Ontario (Canada), Branscombe lived and worked in the United States, except for brief intervals abroad, from 1896 until her death in 1977. Two of her most important compositions reflect her dual Canadian-American background, one celebrating the Pilgrims who came on the *Mayflower* and the other the early settlers of Quebec.

Branscombe began improvising on the piano from about the age of four or five, and was accompanying an older brother in public by the age of six. At fifteen she entered Chicago Musical College, where she studied piano with Florenz Ziegfeld and composition with Felix Borowski. She received her bachelor's degree in 1900, having continued piano studies with Arthur Friedheim, Hans von Schiller, and Rudolph Ganz. In 1903 she joined the college's piano faculty and began studying songwriting with Alexander von Fielitz. Four years later she moved to the state of Washington, where she headed the piano department of Whitman College for the next two years. She then went to Europe, studying composition for a year with Engelbert

Humperdinck in Berlin and piano again with Ganz (who by then had returned to Germany). Branscombe returned to America and on October 5, 1910, she was married to John Ferguson Tenney of New York. They had four daughters.

Branscombe's first important composition was *Festival Prelude* for orchestra, which was performed at the MacDowell Colony Festival in 1914, and later in New York and at the San Francisco Exposition. Five years later she composed the text and music of her next large work, *Pilgrims of Destiny,* for soloists, chorus, and orchestra, which, however, was not performed in its entirety for another decade. Branscombe herself was not of Pilgrim stock, but her maternal ancestors had come to New York (then Nieuw Amsterdam) in 1638 and settled near Fishkill, New York, until their land was confiscated during the Revolutionary War and they moved to Canada. *Pilgrims of Destiny* celebrates the courage and vision of the young English Pilgrims who sailed on the *Mayflower* and, fittingly, it received its first complete performance at Plymouth, Massachusetts (1929), by the New England North Shore Festival Chorus, augmented by local choruses, and the Boston Festival Orchestra under Arthur B. Keene. Branscombe's other large historic work, *Quebec,* a symphonic suite for tenor solo and orchestra, was taken from an opera she never finished, *The Bells of Circumstance.* It concerns the French who settled in the icy wilderness of Quebec in the early sixteenth century, and was first performed by the Chicago Woman's Symphony, with the composer conducting. It was later performed elsewhere, and broadcast both in America and Canada.

By 1921 Branscombe had become interested in conducting, and for the next ten years she studied intermittently with Frank Damrosch at the Institute of Musical Art (later the Juilliard School), Albert Stoessel and John Warren Erb at New York University, Chalmers Clifton of the American Orchestral Society, and Walter Rothwell. Her earliest compositions were songs, but she had written a number of choral works as well, both for mixed chorus and for women's voices, and in 1934 she founded her own women's chorus, the Branscombe Choral, which she led for the next twenty years. From 1923 on she also conducted the MacDowell Club Chorus (later Chorale) of Mountain Lakes, New Jersey, and she frequently appeared as guest conductor in performances of her own choral compositions in the United States, Canada, and England. In the 1940s she conducted the Contemporary Club Chorale of Newark, New Jersey, the New Jersey State Chorus, and the first organized American Women's Voluntary Services chorus, which sang in uniform throughout World War II.

One of the high points of Branscombe's conducting career came in 1941, when she was chosen by the General Federation of Women's Clubs to conduct a national chorus of 1,000 voices for its golden jubilee in celebration of women's achievements. Held in Atlantic City, New Jersey, its final concert featured works by women composers, selected by Branscombe herself.

Branscombe's own favorite among her choral works was *Coventry's Choir,* a setting of a poem by Violet Alvarez about the bombing of the great English cathedral during World War II. Scored for soprano solo, four-part women's chorus, and orchestra, it received its first complete performance by the Branscombe Choral in Town Hall, New York, on May 2, 1944. Other important choral compositions were *Youth of the World,* a cycle for women's voices and orchestra, written in the early 1930s and often performed over the years in England, Holland, and Canada, as well as many American cities; and *A Joyful Litany* (1967).

Branscombe was active in the National Federation of Music Clubs for many years, serving it in a variety of capacities. She was president of the Society of American Women Composers from 1929 to 1931 and maintained lifelong friendships with many of its members, especially Harriet Ware, Amy Beach, Mary Howe, and Mabel Daniels (see Chapters 4 and 6). Also, she was active in the General Federation of Women's Clubs and served as chairman of American Music and Folksong; in this capacity she made up numerous programs of works by women composers and American composers for use by clubs affiliated with the General Federation.

In 1973, by then in her nineties, Branscombe was asked by the organist Frederick Swann to compose an Introit, Prayer Response, and Amen for a special service at the Riverside Church, New York. This was her last commission. She died on July 26, 1977, at the age of ninety-five, and the Introit, Procession, and some of her other works were performed at her funeral.

Always a vigorous supporter of women musicians, Branscombe once said, "Having a home, a husband, and children to love and serve brings enrichment of life to a woman, but being a part of the world's work in humbly serving and loving the illumined force which is music brings fulfillment."[31] Later, in 1962, she wrote,

Had there been time, space, money, I could have done hundreds of programs devoted entirely to the works, large and small, of women composers. I have found women, in groups and individually, generous, chivalrous, efficient, and intelligent—a joy to work with....It's a good life, being a woman composer, worth all the hard work that goes into it.[32]

In publicizing Branscombe's life and work for a special U.S. Information Services article to be used abroad on radio, television, and in printed media, the writer said, "She has done perhaps more than anyone else to revitalize and expand the repertory for the nation's many women's choral groups."[33]

# 8 OPERA COMPOSERS AND CONDUCTORS

Vocal music has long been more hospitable to women musicians than instrumental music. Women singers were accepted long before women instrumentalists. Although in the earliest operas the female roles were sung by countertenors and castrati, by the early eighteenth century women were allowed onstage, and within another hundred years the prima donna was placed on a pedestal and made a public idol.

The same was true of vocal composition. Women songwriters were winning acceptance by 1800 or so, and in fact the nineteenth-century sentimental ballad—the parlor song—was intended to appeal chiefly to women and was often composed by a woman. The next logical step was a more ambitious vocal composition, with music for choruses or for several soloists, or both: oratorio or opera.

Among the first American women to compose an opera was Constance Faunt Le Roy, a granddaughter of Scottish industrialist and reformer Robert Owen. She was born in Indianapolis in 1836 and spent part of her childhood at New Harmony, the utopian colony in Indiana established by her grandfather. Her mother was a fine pianist and harpist, and her father an amateur composer. In 1852 she was sent to Germany to study harp and piano; she remained there for five years, and during this period developed an interest in composition. After returning to New Harmony, she married the Reverend James Runcie in 1861 and proceeded to write a great many songs, both words and music. She also wrote one romantic opera, *The Prince of Asturias,* which allegedly was considered for production by "a prominent eastern manager" but presumably was never performed, or if it was, only locally.[1]

Considerably more prolific and more successful was an American singer who wrote more than a hundred songs and, during the last twenty years of her life, took up the cause of opera in English and herself composed nine operas. Eleanor Warner Everest Freer[2] was born on May 14, 1864, in Philadelphia, the daughter of Cornelius Everest, a prominent teacher of music theory and church organist, and Ellen Amelia Clark Everest, a singer. Eleanor's early musical training came from her parents, who, at the suggestion of the renowned soprano Christine Nilsson, sent her to Paris in 1883 to study at the music school of Madame Mathilde Marchesi. She remained there for three years, her fellow students including Nellie Melba, Emma Eames, and Emma Calvé, who all became world-famous opera singers.

In 1886 she returned to Philadelphia and began teaching voice, the first pupil whom Marchesi ever officially sanctioned to teach her famous method. By 1889 she also was commuting to New York twice a week to teach the Marchesi method at the National Conservatory of Music. In 1891 she married Archibald Freer of Chicago, and the following year the young couple went to Leipzig, where he studied medicine and she continued her music studies and bore their only child, a daughter (Eleanor).

In 1899 the Freers returned to Chicago, where she became active in music clubs and began to study composition with Bernard Ziehn. By 1902 she had begun to compose, which occupied her fully (except during World War I, when she devoted herself to volunteer war work) until her death in 1942. At first Freer wrote many art songs—mostly settings of English poems, since she believed the repertory already included settings of the best French, German, and Italian poems but that English had been sadly neglected. The most ambitious of these was her cycle of all forty-four of Elizabeth Barrett Browning's *Sonnets from the Portuguese,* but she also set poems by Robert Browning, Coleridge, Donne, Crashaw, Herrick, Longfellow, Lowell, Milton, Shelley, Shakespeare, and Tennyson.

Shortly after World War I Freer wrote her first opera, the one-act *Legend of the Piper,* about the Pied Piper of Hamelin, completed in 1921 and first performed in 1924 in South Bend, Indiana. It was performed in Chicago in 1925, by the American Theater for Musical Productions, and again in Nebraska in 1926 on a double bill with her next opera, *Massimiliano, or the Court Jester,* also in one act. In her first opera, Freer used graceful melodies, easy rhythms, and relatively uncomplicated orchestration to present an old folk legend. In *Massimiliano,* the romantic tale of a court jester in love with a noblewoman, she used more modern harmonies but nevertheless produced very singable melodies. There followed four more one-act operas: *The Chilkoot Maiden,* based on an Alaskan legend and first presented in Skagway, Alaska, in 1927; *A Christmas Tale,* adapted from a French play; *A Legend of Spain* (performed in 1931), based on a fifteenth-century Spanish story; and *The Masque of Pandora* (1927; first performed 1930), an adaptation of a poem by Longfellow. Her remaining operas are *Preciosa, Joan of Arc,* and *Frithiof* (1929).

Another woman who studied voice with Marchesi in Paris and composition with Ziehn in Chicago just after the turn of the century was Jane Van Etten,[3] born in St. Paul, Minnesota. She also studied voice in London, where she made her debut in the opera *Faust* in 1895, and later toured in both England and the United States. In 1901 she married Alfred Burritt Andrews and retired from public performance, settling in Evanston, near Chicago. She began to study with both Ziehn and Alexander von Fielitz, and soon published some songs. Her one-act opera *Guido Ferranti*, performed in Chicago on December 29, 1914, by the Aborn Brothers' Century Opera Company, was, according to Hipsher, the first opera by an American woman presented by a well-known company. (He may have meant "serious opera," for Emma Steiner's *Fleurette* and other light operas preceded it by some years.) The libretto was based on a play by Oscar Wilde, *The Duchess of Padua*, and the music was in the style of late nineteenth-century Italian opera, as represented by Puccini and Mascagni. Though it won critical acclaim, it appears not to have been performed again.

A contemporary of Freer's and also a native of Philadelphia was Celeste de Longpré Massey Hecksher,[4] who became very prominent in that city's musical affairs. Born in 1860, she began to compose about 1890, served for a long period as president of the Philadelphia Opera Society, and wrote two operas, *The Flight of Time* and *The Rose of Destiny*. The latter was performed at the Metropolitan Opera House of Philadelphia on May 2, 1918. She also wrote an orchestral suite, *Dance of the Pyrenees*, which was performed by the New York Symphony, Philadelphia Orchestra, and Chicago Symphony, as well as songs and piano works. She died in 1928.

In the early 1900s California was the home of at least three women composers of opera. Elsie Maxwell, of San Francisco, wrote songs, instrumental music, and at least one grand opera (in English) and a comic opera. In 1909 she also was working as a music critic,[5] and in 1916 her suffragette operetta, *Melinda and Her Sisters*, with a libretto by Mrs. O. H. P. Belmont, was presented in New York at the Waldorf Astoria Hotel with a cast headed by Marie Dressler.[6]

Abbie Gerrish Jones,[7] who was born in 1863 in Vallejo and grew up in Sacramento, began her music studies with voice lessons but turned to theory and composition soon thereafter. She first published some compositions at the age of eighteen. She wrote works for piano, piano and violin, and more than a hundred songs, as well as at least six operas *(Priscilla; Abon Hasson; The Aztec Princess; The Milk-Maids Fair; The Andalusians; Two Roses)*. In 1906 her *Prelude* for piano won a prize offered by the pianist Josef Hofmann. Like Maxwell she was for some years a music critic, for the San Francisco paper *Pacific Town Talk*, the *Pacific Coast Musical Review*, and West coast correspondent for the *Musical Courier*. Her music drama, *The Snow Queen*, was performed in Cleveland and New York as well as California. She later moved to Seattle, where she died in 1929.

The third woman, Mary Carr Moore,[8] was born in 1873 in Memphis, Tennessee, and in 1885 moved with her family to California, where she studied both voice and theory. Her first opera was *The Oracle,* in which she sang the leading role in a San Francisco production in 1894. For her four-act grand opera *Narcissa,* written in 1912 and given a one-week run in San Francisco in 1925, she also staged and conducted the performance with an eighty-piece orchestra. With a libretto by Sarah Pratt Carr, it tells the story of a hero of the American Northwest, Marcus Whitman. Moore's opera *Los Rubios,* commissioned for the celebration of the 150th anniversary of the founding of Los Angeles, received its premiere on September 8, 1931. The following year came the premiere of her two-act *Davide Rizzio,* to an Italian libretto by Emanuel M. Browne about Mary, Queen of Scots. Moore also wrote choral works, songs, and instrumental pieces; her suite, *Four Love Songs,* for voice, strings, and piano, won an award from the National League of American Pen-Women in 1932. She died in California in 1957.

None of the women just described ever had an opera performed in an internationally known opera house, in either Europe or America. Yet the precedent had been set, at least in Europe. The French composer Marie Félicie Clémence de Reiset, Vicomtesse de Grandval (1830–1907), who had studied composition with Flotow and Saint-Saëns, had no fewer than five operas produced in Paris between 1859 *(Le Sou de Lise)* and 1869 *(Piccolino),* and another in Bordeaux in 1892 *(Mazeppa).*[9] Of course one cannot be sure how much her rank and wealth had to do with these performances. Perhaps she financed them herself. But this was not the case with Ethel Smyth,[10] whose first opera, *Fantasio,* to her own libretto in German, was produced in 1898 in Weimar, Germany. Born in England in 1858, Smyth studied at the Leipzig Conservatory and in Berlin, and presented several orchestral works in London in 1890. Her first major success was the performance of her Mass in London in 1893. From then on she devoted herself principally to composing operas, both serious and comic, and some songs. A militant leader in the women's suffrage movement, she also composed its theme song, "The March of the Women," and was honored in 1923 by being made a Dame of the British Empire.

An Englishwoman who worked chiefly in Europe, Smyth would have no place in this book except for the fact that her opera *Der Wald,* to her own German libretto, was the first and still (in 1979) the *only* opera composed by a woman to be presented at the Metropolitan Opera. It was performed there twice during the 1902–3 season because Maurice Grau, then manager of the company, believed it had considerable novelty appeal. Her next opera, *The Wreckers,* proved to be her single most successful work; it had librettos in French, German, and Engish. It has not been performed in America. Smyth was to write four more operas. She also became a popular conductor of her own works, appearing frequently with the London and BBC Symphony orchestras from about 1910 through the 1920s. She died in 1944.

Although the Metropolitan Opera did not perform another work by a woman during the next three-quarters of a century, on November 17, 1925, its house was the site of a special program to honor a woman on her golden anniversary as a composer and conductor of operas. Ironically, none of her works was ever produced there, nor did she ever conduct there.

The woman so honored was Emma R. Steiner, and the program included the overture to her opera *Fleurette,* composed in 1879, and scenes from two "Italian" operas of hers, *The Man from Paris* (1900) and *The "Burra Pundit."* It ended with her orchestral song, "The Flag—Forever May It Wave" (1918), dedicated to her grandfather Colonel Stephen Steiner, who led the American victory at North Point (near Fort McHenry) during the War of 1812, and incorporating some melodies from that period.

Steiner[11] was born in 1852 in Baltimore, Maryland. Her father was Colonel Frederick B. Steiner, and her mother was a fine pianist. She was writing simple tunes by the age of seven and produced a piano duet at nine, but her parents did not encourage her musical ambitions. About a year later a number of Baltimoreans interested in music advised her father to send her to Paris to study, but nothing came of the suggestion. Nevertheless, she was determined to continue and at eleven had begun working on a grand opera, *Aminaide,* for which she completed one and one-half acts. Unfortunately the score was later lost, along with many of her other belongings, in a New York City warehouse fire in 1902. But one scene of this opera had been produced at Baltimore's Peabody Conservatory, whose director at the time, the Danish composer Asger Hamerick, liked it very much. (Steiner herself did not study at the Peabody, however.)

It is not known exactly when or how Steiner managed to break away from her family and pursue a career in music. One account has it that she sang in the chorus of several touring companies and was finally asked by manager Edward E. Rice to rehearse his opera company's orchestra. Another says that she began to compose waltzes and other popular music in order to earn money and so attracted the attention of opera managers, who then asked her to assist them. However it happened, by the time she was twenty-one Steiner had left for Chicago, where one of her earliest jobs (perhaps her first) was as assistant music director to Rice in the Rice and Collier "Iolanthe" Company.

The Gilbert and Sullivan comic operas were immensely popular in America in the 1880s and 1890s, and managers formed touring companies that took each new opera from town to town. For example, the *Musical Record* of January 3, 1880, announced, under the headline "A Lady Conductor," that Miss Fannie Arnold was to bring out Sullivan's *The Sorcerer* in Brownville, Nebraska, conducting it herself. She wrote, "Tho' we are miles and miles from Boston, America's musical centre, yet in our small way we have considerable music here.'' Steiner conducted for a number of companies that presented these and other light operas. She worked three seasons with George Baker's company, unspecified periods with Grau and Fitzgerald and the Julius Howe Company, and finally one season in New York with Heinrich Conried, who the following year (1903) became the manager of the Metropolitan Opera. Conried allegedly told Steiner that he would gladly have appointed her conductor at the Met if only he had dared.

By 1902 Steiner was relatively well known. Her opera *Fleurette* had been produced in San Francisco in 1889 and in New York in 1891; a reviewer said that its music was far superior to that usually heard on the comic opera stage. The Act I finale was brilliant and effective, worthy of composers of much greater fame, clearly indicating that Steiner could undertake serious opera if she wished. As a conductor, Steiner was ''easy, self-contained, and careful,'' and the production was a success despite an unsympathetic orchestra and inferior company. Moreover, said the reviewer, the libretto, by Edgar Smith, was just plain terrible; ''more Steiner is wanted, and less Smith.''[12]

In 1894 Steiner conducted the eighty-man Anton Seidl Orchestra, one of the best of its time, in New York City in a program of her own works. In 1896 *Freund's* reported that she was seriously ill with pneumonia,[13] potentially fatal in the absence of antibiotics, but she recovered, and in 1897 it was announced that she would soon start a series of instrumental and vocal concerts with forty members of the New York Metropolitan Orchestra, leading them in works by Wagner, Flotow, Liszt, and Meyerbeer.[14] By then she herself had written at least two other operas, *Day Dreams,* based on Tennyson's *Sleeping Beauty,* and *Brigands.*

Shortly after the turn of the century Steiner again became ill, and then was troubled with failing eyesight. The doctors ordered a complete rest, which she must have interpreted to mean a radical change. She went to Nome, Alaska—in those days one of the last frontier outposts—and, carrying provisions and tools on her back, became the first white woman to go to the tin fields 100 miles northwest of Nome. She later was credited with discovering important tin deposits there. She spent ten years in Alaska, prospecting, mining, and traveling. After her return to New York she often gave lectures—illustrated by slides—on Alaska's natural resources.

In 1921 Emma Steiner presented *Harmony and Discord,* a program of her own works, at New York's Museum of Natural History. It included songs, arias, an oboe solo, and the vocal quartet from *The Man from Paris,* and received quite favorable reviews. During her career, she produced seven operas, a number of musical dramas, ballets, and many songs and dances. The score for a dance for piano and orchestra, *Gavotte Menzeli,* published in 1914, designates this work as opus no. 400. Toward the end of her life she decided to found a Home for Aged and Infirm Musicians, for which she and her friend Margaret I. MacDonald (librettist for *The "Burra Pundit"*) donated property at Bay Shore, Long Island, and to which the proceeds of her "golden jubilee" concert at the Metropolitan Opera House also were donated. By then Steiner had conducted more than 6,000 performances of more than 50 different operas and operettas. According to the *New York Times,* work and worry over the new musicians' home brought on a nervous collapse, followed by heart trouble, which eventually caused her death on February 27, 1929.

It was another fifty years before a woman appeared on the podium of the Metropolitan Opera. On January 13, 1976, Sarah Caldwell became the first woman to conduct there. She was engaged for eleven performances of Verdi's *La Traviata* that season, and the first performance, in which her good friend, soprano Beverly Sills, sang the title role, was an artistic triumph. Said one of New York's most respected critics, who also happened to be an expert on Verdi:

Until "La Traviata," the Met season lacked first-rate conductors. Miss Caldwell's arrival there—it was her debut in the house—brought a triumph for her and confirmation of her great power to animate a score and reveal its composer's intentions. By the stopwatch, and by tradition, many of her tempi must probably be counted fast—as fast, even, as the metronome markings in Verdi's score! But there was no sense of hustle—only Verdian vitality, tension, vigor, dramatic impetus. The singers were not straitjacketed. When a phrase needed to expand, or a syllable to be dwelt on, or an attack to be delayed for an instant, Miss Caldwell was there. She also showed an uncommon command of dramatically striking timbres and of instrumental balances in support of, not in competition with, the individual voices.[15]

This certainly is high praise for a woman whose first strength long had been acknowledged to be her sense of theater and skillful staging, and whose emergence as a conductor came relatively late and, she once said herself, almost by accident.

Sarah Caldwell[16] began her musical studies on the violin, and at one point in her life she nearly accepted an offer to join the violin section of the Minneapolis Symphony. But her dual interest in the theater and music won out, and she turned the offer down. Caldwell was born in 1928 in Maryville, Missouri. She grew up in Fayetteville, Arkansas, where her mother moved when her second husband, Henry Alexander, became a professor of political science at the University of Arkansas. Her mother, educated at Northwestern University and the Juilliard School, taught piano during Sarah's childhood. Sarah herself took up the violin and was giving recitals by the age of ten. At fourteen she was graduated from high school and then studied for a time at Hendrix College and the University of Arkansas. In her late teens she went to Boston to attend the New England Conservatory, and it was there she first became interested in opera.

In the early 1940s Caldwell staged Ralph Vaughan Williams's *Riders to the Sea* at Tanglewood, and shortly afterward conductor Serge Koussevitsky named her to the faculty of the Opera Workshop at Tanglewood, which was headed by Boris Goldovsky. Goldovsky, a Moscow-born pianist and conductor who had been in America since about 1930, later recalled that he had first met Caldwell about 1942 and she became his personal assistant soon afterward, working with him for about a decade at Tanglewood (during the summer), Worcester, Boston, and the New England Conservatory. In 1946 Goldovsky founded the New England Opera Theater of Boston, which he hoped to make into a permanent Boston company and in which he tried to carry out his concept of opera. Unlike many music directors, Goldovsky regarded theater as important as music, and he believed that in opera the two are intricately entwined. Although he and Caldwell eventually came to a parting of the ways, she always acknowledged that he had been a great teacher, with many ideas far ahead of his time.

In the mid-1950s the old Boston Opera House was torn down and Goldovsky abandoned his Boston ambitions and turned to a touring company, the Goldovsky Grand Opera Theater. By then Caldwell, who in 1952 joined Boston University's opera department, had begun to plan for her own Boston company, and in 1957, with only $5,000, she founded the Opera Group (later Company) of Boston. It gave its first production the following year, and in subsequent seasons, even though it presented only about four productions per season (usually a total of twelve to sixteen performances), it became known as one of the most innovative companies in the United States. Working as producer, stage director, sometime conductor, and—in a sense most important of all—fund-raiser, Caldwell presented the Boston public with many "firsts"—the first American productions of Schoenberg's *Moses und Aron* (1966) and Rossini's *Semiramide;* the first American stage appearance of the great Australian soprano, Joan Sutherland; the first *Boris Godunov* in Moussorgsky's own orchestration (1966); the first five-act *Don Carlos* in Verdi's original French edition (1972); the first complete version of Berlioz's *Les Troyens* ever staged in the United States (1972; the Metropolitan Opera followed suit two years later). By 1978 the company was operating on a $1.5 million budget, and Caldwell was trying to raise funds for building a proper opera house, having for years performed in college gyms, converted movie theaters, convention halls, and dirt-floored arenas.

According to *Boston Globe* critic Richard Dyer, who closely followed her career over the years, Caldwell's eloquent advocacy of opera as an important and exciting art took three principal forms: her musical preparation and conducting, her stage direction, and her skill as an impresario, that is, in choosing repertory and convincing patrons to underwrite her choices. Initially an indifferent conductor with little of the conventional technique of wielding a baton (she sometimes forgot an upbeat or downbeat, or could not reestablish order when the orchestra fell apart, or herself became so absorbed in the action onstage that she forgot to conduct at all), Caldwell managed to pull through and continued to attract fine musicians because of her sheer enthusiasm, her attention to tone and the shape of a melodic line, and her feeling for the pace of an opera.[17] And in time she improved, so much so that from about 1975 on she was invited to conduct symphony orchestras all over the United States and in Europe, as well as operas in New York and elsewhere.

As a stage director, Caldwell was considered by many to have no equal. At her best, her ideas enhanced the meaning of the music and drama in a striking visual way; for example, in *Moses und Aron* she placed the two main characters back to back on a slowly revolving circular platform, illustrating in one bold stroke the underlying meaning—that they represent two complementary aspects of a single personality.

Though Caldwell was asked to conduct the New York Philharmonic in a special concert celebrating women composers in 1975, and much was made, a few months later, of her being the first woman to conduct the Metropolitan Opera, she herself denied having difficulties because of her sex. This is particularly interesting in that reviews of her performances—especially in earlier days—often referred to her physical appearance in terms that not only were unflattering but were rarely (if ever) used for a man on the podium. Fortunately she chose to ignore them, and perhaps other slights as well, for her talent in creating exciting opera performances was undeniable.

Eve Queler, who in 1967 founded her own orchestra to present operas in concert form (unstaged), also said she never felt discriminated against because of being a woman, but in the same interview she stated, "I know that some orchestra managers, when approached to engage me, turned me down because 'we already have hired our woman guest conductor for the season.'"[18]

Eve Rabin Queler[19] was born in 1936 in New York and began piano lessons at the age of five. Her first ambition was to be a concert pianist, and to this end she practiced constantly, gave recitals, and entered competitions. After a year off following graduation from the High School of Music and Art (where she played French horn in the orchestra), she enrolled at both City College of New York and the Mannes School of Music. At the former she met Stanley Queler, whom she married while he was still attending law school. Unable to afford further music study for the time being, she gave up the idea of a concert career and decided to become an accompanist, taking on various assignments as pianist and organist.

In 1957 their first child, Andrew, was born, and six months later Queler was engaged as rehearsal accompanist and coach at the New York City Opera. It was a bad year for her. She had thirteen operas to learn, a small baby to care for, and little experience. She was not rehired the following year, and at this point Queler decided to return to Mannes and study conducting with Carl Bamberger. A second child, a daughter, was born, but Queler continued her studies, with Joseph Rosenstock of the Metropolitan Opera and Igor Markevitch of the Monte Carlo Orchestra.

In 1967, in part to test her conducting ability, in part to provide instrumental students with a chance to learn opera repertory (which was largely overlooked at conservatories), Queler established the Opera Orchestra of New York. At first it only rehearsed; then it performed an opera in concert form at a junior high school auditorium. As the orchestra developed, it moved to more prestigious halls, and in 1972 it made its debut in Carnegie Hall, where it continued to appear. By then, its student musicians had grown into or been replaced by professional instrumentalists, and its singers, instead of young beginners, were opera stars from the Metropolitan and other companies. In addition, instead of performing the standard repertory, Queler had begun to present rarely performed operas—Donizetti's *Parisina d'Este*, Meyerbeer's *L'Africaine*, Zandonai's *Francesca da Rimini*, Verdi's *Lombardi*, Massenet's *Le Cid*.

Oddly enough, Queler did not list herself as a conductor on her résumé until the fall of 1970, when she was appointed associate conductor of the Fort Wayne (Indiana) Orchestra. For one season she moved to Indiana, returning to New York only when she had a week or more off. But at the end of the year, rather than moving her family to the Midwest, she decided to give up the job. From that time on, she was offered more and more guest conducting assignments, in Europe and in the United States, for both staged productions of operas and, increasingly, wholly symphonic concerts. In 1975 she conducted the San Antonio Symphony, which she regarded as a breakthrough for a woman, and in the summer of 1976 the Philadelphia Orchestra at Saratoga. There followed appearances with the Hartford Symphony, New Jersey Symphony, Colorado Springs Symphony, and Cleveland Orchestra. Also, in 1978 she appeared for the first time in the pit of the New York City Opera, marking her first opportunity to conduct a fully staged production in New York. The work was Mozart's *The Marriage of Figaro,* and despite the handicap of performing with no orchestral rehearsal, the performance was a success.[20]

Conducting is a demanding job. For her Opera Orchestra Queler found she had to go through approximately fifty neglected scores for every opera she finally chose to perform. Moreover, when she began conducting purely instrumental works, she had to learn (or relearn) the symphonic literature to know it sufficiently well. She always conducted from memory.[21] "Conducting," she once said, "involves endless studying of scores. In a sense I'm lucky because I can do a lot of studying in my head and that means I can work on an opera almost any time. I can hear any part of a score at will—if I can't hear a piece at will, I know I'm not familiar enough with the music and have to to go back and study the score."[22]

In 1966, just before Queler founded the Opera Orchestra of New York, another woman, Judith Somogi, was hired as assistant conductor with the New York City Opera, but it was some years before she actually conducted a performance herself. Then, on March 17, 1974, she led Gilbert and Sullivan's *The Mikado,* the first time a woman had conducted the company.

Actually, when Somogi was first hired, her job had no title. She began as a coach, that is, a pianist who helps singers prepare their roles. She went on to conduct backstage ensembles, help prepare the chorus, play piano accompaniments during rehearsals, and occasionally help out in the orchestra, playing the celesta or another instrument.

Judith Somogi[23] was born in 1943 in Brooklyn, New York, and grew up in Lynbrook, Long Island. She first studied violin and then piano, but did not decide to become a professional musician until her last year in high school. She went to the Juilliard School, where she majored in piano, and received both bachelor's and master's degrees. During these years, she also put in a seven-year stint as organist and choir director of a local church, where she hired soloists and guest organists, conducted oratorios, and acquired considerable conducting experience. She also spent one summer at the Oberlin (Ohio) Music Theater, where she conducted *The Mikado* and Verdi's *La Traviata,* and then was hired as one of Leopold Stokowski's three assistants at the American Symphony Orchestra, which she conducted in nearly three dozen children's concerts. She also spent a summer studying chamber music at Tanglewood, played for ballet and voice classes, and served as music director of the American Savoyards, an off-Broadway Gilbert and Sullivan troupe. After she was hired by the New York City Opera, she spent three summers as assistant to conductor Thomas Schippers at the Festival of the Two Worlds in Spoleto, Italy. Then Christopher Keene, whom she had come to know at Spoleto, engaged Somogi to conduct Menotti's *Amahl and the Night Visitors* and *Help! Help! The Globolinks* at the ANTA Theater on Broadway during the Christmas season of 1971, marking her New York conducting debut.

Though her New York City Opera debut in *The Mikado* was warmly praised, Somogi really came into her own later the same season when she conducted the company in *Traviata.* In this performance, wrote *Times* critic Donal Henahan, she "met the challenge of the Verdi opera with the utmost aplomb and professionalism...and demonstrated not only intimacy with the score and technical security, but also the ability to control the pace and flow of the performance, which some conductors never learn to do with any consistency.''

In May 1975 Somogi became the first woman to conduct a Naumburg concert (a seventy-year-old series of free summer concerts) in New York's Central Park. Engagements followed with the Tulsa Philharmonic, Syracuse, Duluth, Oklahoma City, and Milwaukee Symphony orchestras, and with the Tulsa and San Diego operas. In 1977 Somogi was appointed music director of the Utica (New York) Symphony. In spring of that year she had made her conducting debut with the New York Philharmonic in a Promenades concert, of which Henahan wrote, it "left no doubts about her basic musicianship and competence as a baton wielder."[24] Somogi also continued to work with the New York City Opera, conducting a number of other productions, and she conducted the live television broadcast of Douglas Moore's *The Ballad of Baby Doe* in 1976.

When asked about her views about women conductors, Somogi once half-jokingly suggested that opera was an ideal vehicle because the conductor was virtually hidden in the orchestra pit. By the winter of 1975–76, however, she said, "When I take my bow at a New York City Opera performance, and the audience realizes that a woman is conducting, there's a kind of 'Yeah, team' response from men and women alike. Of course, part of that reaction is because the idea of a woman conducting is still so new to most people. What we need now is a whole *army* of women pursuing conducting careers."[25] And in 1977 she said she believed there was no prejudice against women in the major orchestras and opera houses or the top echelons of management, though there still might be some among smaller organizations.[26] (Actually, the opposite was true, the major orchestras being the last to engage women and the smaller ones having the largest proportion; see Chapter 10.)

Somogi's views were not shared by Alberta Masiello, a widely respected opera coach and assistant conductor at the Metropolitan Opera, which engaged her as a rehearsal pianist in 1959. Originally intending to be a concert pianist and then becoming a professional singer, Italian-born Masiello[27] came to the United States in 1939. She studied conducting with Fausto Cleva and in 1954 took her first job as assistant conductor with the Chicago Lyric Opera, where she remained for three seasons. She also coached a number of famous singers, including the great soprano Maria Callas.

Though Masiello's name had been suggested to the Metropolitan Opera management before, allegedly there was not even a ladies' room in the part of the house where coaching and rehearsals took place. But in 1959 this obstacle was somehow overcome, and Masiello was hired. She rose to the position of assistant conductor, coaching all the principal artists and playing all the rehearsals for the operas she prepared, chiefly the Italian repertory. At one time the New York City Opera invited Masiello to conduct as well as coach, and the Metropolitan Opera appears to have extended a similar invitation, but Masiello would not consider it. In 1976 she told an interviewer:

I am too old for pioneering in this respect—much too old. I think the time is coming when some lady will come through and be a great conductor. But my principle has always been that a great opera conductor really has to start from the bottom, to go backstage and try to understand all the ingredients that go into the soup....You see, I have been a pianist, a singer, a coach. I have also conducted—not very much. But I should go to the podium of the Metropolitan and conduct? No. That would be against my principles.[28]

Although both the Metropolitan and New York City opera companies—as well as some of the smaller organizations—had begun to lift their bars against women conductors, they remained remarkably slow to perform an opera by a woman composer. But in 1963 the Ford Foundation awarded a commission to Peggy Glanville-Hicks to compose a new opera for the San Francisco Opera, and in 1977 the New York City Opera presented the American premiere of Thea Musgrave's *The Voice of Ariadne,* with the composer conducting. As it happens, neither woman was American by birth, but both lived in America for extended periods and their work had considerable impact in the United States.

Peggy Glanville-Hicks[29] was born on December 29, 1912, in Melbourne, Australia, and began her musical studies at the conservatory there, studying composition with Fritz Hart. From 1929 to 1931 she studied at the Melba Conservatory, and in 1931, at nineteen, she won an open scholarship to the Royal College of Music in London, where she studied for the next five years—composition with Ralph Vaughan Williams, piano with Arthur Benjamin, and conducting with Constant Lambert and Malcolm Sargent. In 1936 she won another traveling scholarship for further studies, in Vienna with composer Egon Wellesz and in Paris with Nadia Boulanger. In 1938 Glanville-Hicks achieved her first big success when Sir Adrian Boult conducted her *Choral Suite* at the International Society of Contemporary Music Festival in London (the first time Australia had been represented at the festival).

About 1940 Glanville-Hicks moved to the United States, where she remained for the next twenty years, composing many of her major works, becoming active in the cause of contemporary music (she directed the Composers Forum concert series, featuring new works), and writing extensively (she was music critic for the *New York Herald Tribune* from 1948 to 1958, and her reviews and articles appeared in *Musical Quarterly* and other journals). During this period, she became an American citizen with a permanent residence in New York, but she also found time to travel extensively, to

Morocco, Greece, Italy, Jamaica. Her interest in Near Eastern and North African music, early awakened, developed further through these trips and began to be reflected in her own compositions. Her travels were assisted by two Guggenheim fellowships (1956, 1957), a Fulbright grant (1957–58) for research in Greek music, and a Rockefeller grant for travel and research in the Middle and Far East (1961).

Glanville-Hicks's earliest compositions, produced between 1932 and 1945, included an opera, three ballets, a flute concerto, piano concerto, sinfonia, cantata, and many chamber works, but she later withdrew nearly all of these. Instrumental works she composed in America include her *Concertino da Camera* (1945) for flute, clarinet, bassoon, and piano; Harp Sonata (1950); Sonata for piano and percussion (1951); *Three Gymnopedie* (1953) for string orchestra with solo instruments; *Sinfonia da Pacifica* for chamber orchestra; *Letters from Morocco,* a set of songs for tenor and orchestra, given their premiere by conductor Leopold Stokowski; *Etruscan Concerto* (1956) for piano and orchestra; and *Concerto Romantico* (1957) for viola and orchestra. In these and in her ballets, film scores, and vocal works, Glanville-Hicks increasingly made explicit her idea that melody and rhythm are the quintessential elements of music, and that harmony should have but a minor role, as it always has had in non-Western and ancient music. Rejecting atonality, neoclassicism, and serial techniques, she developed what she called a new kind of melody-rhythm structure.

Though her reputation as a composer had been building steadily over the years, she was not really considered fully established until she wrote her first full-length opera, *The Transposed Heads.* It was commissioned by the Louisville Opera (apparently the first opera commission awarded to a woman composer), composed in 1953, and produced on April 4, 1954, by the Kentucky Opera Company and Louisville Symphony Orchestra. It was later recorded, and it was performed again in New York in 1958 at the Phoenix Theater. With a libretto by Thomas Mann based on his novel of the same name, the opera is in six scenes, all set in India, and the music, which includes elements of Hindu melodies and rhythms, is, according to composer George Antheil,[30] among Glanville-Hicks's finest works.

Immediately afterward Glanville-Hicks was commissioned to write several ballet scores, beginning with *The Masque of the Wild Man* (1958) and *Triad* (1958). She also wrote another opera, the one-act *The Glittering Gate,* composed in 1956 and first performed in New York in 1959. Intended as a comic half-hour "curtain raiser" to precede another opera, it was performed together with Lou Harrison's *Rapunzel.* It is scored for tenor, baritone, chamber orchestra, and tape.

In 1961 Glanville-Hicks moved to Greece, and the following year she produced her next full-length opera, *Nausicaa,* with a libretto after Robert

Graves's novel, *Homer's Daughter*. It was first performed in the ancient Herod Atticus theater, at the base of Athens's Acropolis, on August 19, 1961. The production was recorded and broadcast four days later in the United States, and excerpts later were released on a commercial recording. Again using folk music, this time from various parts of Greece and enhanced with appropriate orchestration, this opera embodied the composer's theory that melody and rhythm are the all-important elements of music.

*Sappho,* commissioned for the San Francisco Opera in 1963, also drew on Greek material and had a libretto by the English novelist Lawrence Durrell. Glanville-Hicks's other important works include the ballets *Saul and the Witch of Endor, Tragic Celebration (Jeptha's Daughter),* and *Season in Hell.* As Virgil Thomson said, Peggy Glanville-Hicks "made for herself out of elements from India, North Africa, and Greece a musical idiom that has proved useful in ballet, and surprisingly so for English-language opera."[31] In 1975 Glanville-Hicks returned to Australia at the invitation of the Australian Music Centre to set up an Asian music studies program, which proved highly successful. She also continued composing and began to think in terms of new ways of uniting heard and seen elements. Among these was an exhibit called *7 Sculptures/Compositions* (1978), for which seven composers (she was one of them) each wrote a work relating specifically to a different sculpture by Pamela Boden. In the exhibit each piece is individually lighted and revolving while the composition related to it is played (on tape).[32]

Thea Musgrave,[33] whose *Voice of Ariadne* was the first opera by a woman performed by a major New York company since the Met put on Smyth's *Der Wald* in 1903, was born on May 27, 1928, in Edinburgh, Scotland. Though interested in music throughout her childhood, she originally planned a career in medicine. First enrolled as a pre-medical student at the University of Edinburgh, she decided after a couple of years to switch to music. She studied for four years in Paris with Nadia Boulanger and scored her first success with *Cantata for a Summer's Day,* performed at the Edinburgh Festival in 1955. Other important early works are the ballet suite *A Tale for Thieves* (1953), *Triptych* for tenor and orchestra (1959), and her first full-length opera, *Decision* (1964–65), which was performed several times at Sadler's Wells. (Still earlier, in 1955, she had written a chamber opera, *The Abbot of Drimmock.*) She also wrote a considerable amount of chamber music—two piano sonatas, a violin sonata, a string quartet[34]—and from 1959 to 1965 lectured on music at London University.

In the 1960s Musgrave composed three chamber concertos (nos. 1, 2, 3; 1962–66) and a Concerto for Orchestra (1967) in which she began to use devices such as not only setting one instrument in opposition to the others (as in the classic concerto, where one or more soloists contrast with the orchestra) but having one instrument woo some of the others to its side. In the Concerto for Orchestra the first clarinet rises (physically and musically) to challenge the conductor's authority and incites the other players to join the rebellion. In the Clarinet Concerto (1968; first performed by the Royal Philharmonic in 1969) the soloist moves about from one section of the orchestra to another, playing with each in turn, and sometimes attracting subsidiary soloists to form a concertante (soloists' group) in dialogue with the rest of the orchestra. In her Viola Concerto, commissioned by the BBC and written for her husband, violist Peter Mark, she carried this further: The solo viola enlists the orchestral violas on his side, and they actually rise (from their seats) in his cause and then almost overwhelm him. And in her Horn Concerto (1971), at one point the four orchestral horn players surround the soloist and engage in a kind of parodistic battle with him, while at another point the soloist summons horn calls from the horn players placed in different parts of the hall. Describing her style as "dramatic abstract," Musgrave said that her approach to instrumental music was colored by her interest in drama, and "I have gradually evolved a style where at times certain instruments take on the character of a dramatic personage, and my concern is then directed toward the working out of a dramatic confrontation."[35]

Increasingly, however, Musgrave devoted herself to theater music. Her first full-length ballet, *Beauty and the Beast,* performed by the Scottish Theater Ballet at Sadler's Wells in 1969, was a great success. In it she used taped music for the first time. It was followed by *Soliloquy* for guitar and tape (1969).

In 1970 Musgrave and her husband came to the United States, both to teach at the University of California at Santa Barbara. Her compositions, still largely unknown in America, now began to be performed more widely, and she herself began to conduct them occasionally. She later said she had begun to conduct quite by chance, after only two lessons, when *Beauty and the Beast* was to be put on in Edinburgh for a special Christmas production and the conductor could not be there. "They said I should do it," she told an interviewer later, "and I said that's crazy...but I did it. It was jumping in at the deep end but it was a challenge and I enjoyed it. One thing is in my favor. I do know the music, and that helps."[36] She conducted the Philadelphia Orchestra in her Concerto for Orchestra in 1977, but then said she would conduct only her own works. Indeed, she preferred to be involved only in their premieres, in effect establishing how she wanted the performance to go and then relinquishing the baton to others. Performances of Musgrave's instrumental works in the 1970s included the Clarinet Concerto at a 1975 New York Philharmonic concert devoted to women composers and conducted by Sarah Caldwell; a 1976 performance of *Space Play,* a concerto for nine instruments, by the Chamber Music Society of Lincoln

Center; and one of Chamber Concerto no. 1 by the Boston Symphony Chamber players in 1976.

Musgrave herself conducted the New York City Opera production of her *Voice of Ariadne*. Based on a short story by Henry James and dedicated to Benjamin Britten, the opera was first performed in 1974 by the English Opera Group at Britten's Aldeburgh Festival. Essentially a romantic ghost story, it portrays a husband who is temporarily seduced by the voice of a statue of Ariadne, which only he can hear, but who then is made to realize that his wife is his only true love. The score requires no chorus and can be performed by a small orchestra (thirteen instruments), and the voice of Ariadne, along with sounds suggesting the sea and other effects, is supplied on prerecorded tape. The New York audience gave the opera and its composer a standing ovation, and most reviewers were enthusiastic. They praised Musgrave's excellent setting of English to music, and her clever use of tape and aleatory elements. Andrew Porter pointed out the composer's skillful planning, with a well-balanced sequence of solos, duets, and ensembles. Stylistically, too, Musgrave paralleled the events of the story, moving from diatonic to troubled atonal harmonies as the characters' emotions change from clarity to confusion[37] But one critic believed the opera fell short, mainly because there was no real melody in which singers can let themselves loose.[38] The composer herself did not agree; to her, lyricism and the idiomatic handling of the voice were of basic importance, and she held that "there's even a motif for the word *Ariadne* that people will go away singing by the end of the evening."[39]

In fall of 1977 Musgrave returned to Edinburgh to conduct the premiere of her next full-length opera, *Mary, Queen of Scots*. In three acts, with a libretto by the composer, it chronicles the seven years from Mary's return to Scotland in 1561 to her flight to England in 1568, forced by her half-brother, James Stewart, Earl of Moray. Performed several more times in Britain, the opera was given its American premiere six months later by the Virginia Opera Company, under conductor Peter Mark, and it was enthusiastically received:

It is an interesting, affecting, and important work, successful on many counts: as a poetic drama, as a presentation of characters and conflicts, as a study of history, as a long stretch of imaginative and excellently written music, and as a music drama in which words, sounds, spectacle, and action conspire to stir a listener's mind and emotions. In short, it succeeds as a show, as a score, and as that fusion of both which creates good opera.[40]

But the same critic who had not liked *Ariadne* again complained that, although the dramatic qualities and setting of the language here were admirable, "the opera, as a whole, just misses, mostly because of its lack of sustained melodic flow—a fatal defect in a score that attempts to be melodic throughout."[41] The disagreement of critics, however, did not diminish Musgrave's achievement. None would deny that she had written an important work—whether or not they personally liked it—and that she merited serious attention. Musgrave herself simply said, "Opera, with its combination of elements—theatrical, dramatic—is a fascinating challenge."[42]

Of the other women who during the 1970s were writing operas, one who achieved some local success was Margaret Garwood. She received a grant from the National Endowment for the Arts for her one-act opera, *The Nightingale and the Rose,* first performed in Pennsylvania in 1973 and receiving its New York premiere in December 1978. Born in 1927 in New Jersey and trained at the Philadelphia Musical Academy, from which she received a master's degree, Garwood taught piano for many years and began composing about 1960. At first she wrote chiefly songs. Her cycle *lovesongs,* a setting of six poems by E. E. Cummings (who avoided capital letters), was performed at New York's Carnegie Recital Hall in 1964, and three ballets entitled *Aesop's Fables* (1970), commissioned by Young Audiences, were widely performed in the Philadelphia schools. In 1965 Garwood began work on her first opera, the one-act *The Trojan Women,* which was performed by the Pennsylvania Opera Company in 1967. In 1978 she was working on a third opera, based on Nathaniel Hawthorne's tale *Rappaccini's Daughter.*

Some of the composers best known for their use of experimental contemporary idioms also tried their hand at opera, among them Lucia Dlugoszewski (*The Heidi Songs*) and Beth Anderson (*Queen Christina*), whose work is discussed in Chapter 9. Other composers made attempts to combine conventional serious opera with elements of popular musical theater, resulting in works such as Myrna Lamb's *Mother Run* and Elizabeth Swados's *Nightclub Cantata.*[43]

# 9 CONTEMPORARY IDIOMS—AFTER 1950

In the second half of the twentieth century composers began to work with new modes of musical expression. Technical developments, notably the perfection and increasing sophistication of electronic equipment and of computers, enabled the creation of new kinds of sound. Pure electronic music, in which all sounds are generated by machinery and recorded on tape, attracted some composers. Increasingly, however, such material was combined with vocal and instrumental performance, both taped and live. In some instances new instruments were devised. In others instruments and human voices were used in new ways; for example, a pianist might be required not only to play the keyboard but to pluck or otherwise manipulate the piano's strings, with or without the aid of mallets or other implements. Sometimes performers were told to choose what portion of a composition they would play, or in what order they would play its sections, or they were asked to improvise. Music was combined with special stage effects and special lighting, with film and with dance, all considered integral parts of a performance. Pitches lying between the conventional half-tones of the chromatic scale—quarter tones and other microtones—were used. Melodies were broken into fragments; contrasting rhythms were made to overlap or were used simultaneously; members of instrumental ensembles were physically separated into groups and subgroups. As might be expected, every one of these techniques and styles has attracted both women and men composers.

If composition is a difficult field in which to succeed, creating music in new ways is harder yet. As Janet Baker-Carr put it:

The eye delights in new sensation. Not so the ear, which seeks patterns and is grateful for repetition. If in hearing a new piece the ear does not recognize a familiar structure or pattern, the listener is prevented from participating and responding and so is unable to find the significance or meaning of the whole....Only as the patterns and relationships become familiar does the music itself become evocative and significant. This is why most people go to concerts to hear a beautiful performance of music that they know.[1]

Relatively few people are willing to experiment, and that is true of performers and conductors as well as audiences. What are listeners to make of a piece such as Annea Lockwood's *World Rhythms* (1976), which consists of natural sounds (from pulsars, earthquakes, volcanic activity, rivers, human breathing, ocean waves) and the playing of a gong? Some would argue that this is not even music.

Some composers, to be sure, were less radical. They continued to use the human voice and traditional instruments, though not always in conventional fashion. Among the most important and successful women among them were Marga Richter, Ursula Mamlok, Joyce Mekeel, Barbara Kolb, Joan Tower, and Shulamit Ran.

Marga Richter[2] was born on October 21, 1926, in Reedsburg, Wisconsin. She received her bachelor's and master's degrees from the Juilliard School of Music in New York, where she studied composition with William Bergsma and Vincent Persichetti and piano with Rosalyn Tureck (see Chapter 3). Although at first intending to become a concert pianist, she soon turned to composition. Among her first published works were a Clarinet Sonata, first played in New York in 1948, and *Two Short Suites for Young Pianists* (1947). Her three-movement Piano Sonata, composed in 1953 but not performed until 1964, shows some typical features of her style: wide-ranging pitches, free use of tone clusters and other dissonances, and, in the third movement especially, a strong rhythmic drive, in which chordal passages alternate with running passages. An interesting contrast is provided in a later piano work, *Remembrances* (1977), a gently atonal nocturne, with a treble melody steadily supported by broken chords in the bass.

Notable among Richter's longer orchestral works are Concerto for piano and violas, cellos, and string basses (also called Piano Concerto no. 1), given its premiere in San Francisco in 1957, of which critic Alfred Frankenstein wrote, "I do not recall hearing a new piano concerto with such keen interest since the second concerto of Ravel was revealed."[3] In five short, strongly contrasting movements, the concerto was later recorded and was described by several critics as "virile" and "masculine."[4] Richter did not compose her second piano concerto for nearly twenty years. Entitled *Landscapes of the Mind I* (Piano Concerto no. 2) and composed in 1974, it received its orchestral premiere with the Tucson Symphony in 1976. In contrast to the first concerto, it is scored for full orchestra (strings and brass) plus electric guitar, electric bass guitar, and a number of unusual percussion instruments, including electric tamboura, two tomtoms, and Indian drums. It is divided into two sections, the second of which is based on an Indian raga but treated at least partly in Western style (it concludes with a climax of volume and tempo, rather than subsiding in characteristic Indian style to a quiet ending).[5]

Between these two concertos Richter wrote *Abyss,* commissioned by the Harkness Ballet and first performed in 1965 in Cannes, France; it later became part of the repertory of the Joffrey Ballet, and also has been played as an orchestral suite. Particularly notable is its first section, an extended, very lyrical viola solo, accompanied by the muted strings of the rest of the orchestra. Two other important works for strings are *Lament* (1956) for string orchestra, constructed on a single theme with variations, which builds gradually to intense crescendos on very high notes, and *Landscapes of the Mind II* (1971), for piano and violin, written for the young violinist Daniel Heifetz, a moody, impressionistic work that was extremely well received. Married to Alan Skelly and a long-time resident of Long Island (New York), Richter in 1972 became a co-founder, with Herbert A. Deutsch, of the Long Island Composers Alliance. From 1966 to 1978 she was an annual recipient of the ASCAP Standard Award, and in 1977 she received a National Endowment of the Arts grant to write a concerto, *Music for Three Quintets and Orchestra* (1978).

Ursula Mamlok[6] was born in 1928 in Berlin, Germany, where she began her first music studies in piano and theory with composer-musicologist Gustav Ernst. After emigrating with her family to Ecuador in 1939, she sent some of her compositions to the Mannes College of Music in New York and in 1942 was awarded a full scholarship to study composition there with George Szell. From that time on she made her home in the United States. Later she also studied with Roger Sessions, Edward Steuermann, Stefan Wolpe, and Ralph Shapey, and earned both bachelor's and master's degrees at the Manhattan School of Music.

Mamlok's compositions consist principally of songs and chamber music, although she did write a symphony and in 1976 she produced one large-scale work, *Concerto for oboe and orchestra*, which received its premiere at the University of Illinois in 1978. *Variations* for solo flute (1961), the trio *Stray Birds* (1963) for soprano, flute, and cello, and *Haiku Settings* (1967) for soprano and flute are among Mamlok's most frequently performed compositions. *Stray Birds*, five short songs based on writings by the Hindu poet Rabindranath Tagore and dedicated to the late President John F. Kennedy, is constructed on a twelve-tone row but is more emotional than most such compositions. Voice and instruments both reflect the quality of birdsong. A similar effect is achieved in the five *Haiku Settings*, in which both flute and voice are made to sound like the songs of a rocking gull, a nightingale, and a sparrow, the trill of a tree frog, and the spatter of rain. Among Mamlok's later works is a Sextet for flute, clarinet, bass clarinet, violin, double bass, and piano, which received its premiere in New York in 1977. Mamlok herself summed up her style of composition: "My primary concern as a composer has been the consolidation of old and new techniques which best serve to express the work at hand."

Joyce Mekeel[7], born on July 6, 1931, in New Haven, Connecticut, studied at the Paris Conservatory from 1955 to 1957 and in 1960 received her master's degree from Yale University. Her teachers included Nadia

Boulanger (see Chapter 6), Ralph Kirkpatrick, and Earl Kim. A number of her compositions are closely related to theater and ballet, including scores for productions of three Shakespeare plays (*Othello, Macbeth, Richard III*) and George Bernard Shaw's *Androcles and the Lion*. Beginning about 1970 she started to pursue two other interests, anthropology, which took her on several fields trips to West Africa, and sculpture, which led to several shows. From 1964 to 1970 Mekeel taught at the New England Conservatory, and in 1970 she joined the faculty of Boston University.

Although Mekeel wrote for ordinary instruments and the human voice, she frequently treated them in unusual ways. For example, *The Shape of Silence* (1969) for solo flute calls for the flutist to walk and to whisper as well as to blow and overblow the instrument. Her *Corridors of Dream* (1972) for mezzo soprano, alto flute, clarinet, viola, cello, harp, and conductor (who also speaks and plays percussion instruments), uses a variety of German texts (some in the original and some in translation). The first words are spoken by the flutist, partly through the instrument, over a repeated accompaniment played by the harp. Then, in the first large section, the singer performs in the manner used in Japanese Noh plays, that is, a kind of rhythmic recitation. In another section, a marching song is recited by the conductor, accompanied by winds and harp, while the singer utters a frantically rapid speech accompanied by the strings. In *Serena* (1975), for mezzo soprano, speaker, and piano, the singer performs a multilingual text while the speaker, in the background, declaims a poem, and the piano, fitted with cymbals and other devices on the strings, accompanies this dialogue. *Planh* (1975), for solo violin, presents a set of motifs that, in the space of thirteen minutes or so, exploit virtually all of the sonorities of that instrument. *Alarums and Excursions* (1978), for mezzo-soprano, flute, clarinet, piano, violin, viola, cello, and percussion (the forces of the Boston Musica Viva ensemble, for which she wrote it), again uses texts in several (six) languages, has the instrumentalists as well as the conductor declaim and/or sing, and includes a section in which the soloist utters gibberish and gesticulates wildly. The music is less a direct setting of the texts than an evocation of their feeling and atmosphere, and the overall effect is highly dramatic.

Among the most frequently performed of this group of composers, winner of both the Prix de Rome and a Guggenheim Fellowship, was Barbara Kolb.[8] She was born on February 10, 1939, in Hartford, Connecticut. Her father, music director of a local radio station, did not want her to become a professional musician. He did allow her to attend Hartt College of Music in Hartford and major in music education. But in her second year there she changed her major to clarinet, and when she decided to get a master's degree in composition, he refused to finance her studies. For several years Kolb played clarinet in the Hartford Symphony Orchestra. In 1964 she moved to New York and spent the next four years supporting herself as a music copyist. She had won a scholarship to Tanglewood in 1960 and returned there again in 1964 and 1968, studying composition with Gunther Schuller and Lukas Foss. In 1969 she won the Prix de Rome, entitling her to a year's study at the American Academy in Rome. She was the first American woman to receive this award, and she was allowed to renew it the following year. The year after that she won a Guggenheim Fellowship.

One of relatively few contemporary composers (men or women) who managed to live on commissions and grants, Kolb became, from the time her *Duo* for violin and viola won first prize in the Mu Phi Epsilon contest of 1963, quite successful. Much of her music was written on commission, most often for chamber ensembles, and each work she produced seemed to have a truly original flavor. With *Trobar Clus, to Lukas,* for chamber ensemble, she scored her first major success at Tanglewood's Festival of Contemporary Music in 1970. Named for a poetic form used by the troubadours of Provence during the eleventh and twelve centuries, this work is a kind of rondeau in which repetition functions through the recurrences of different groups of instruments rather than of melodies or rhythms. *Three Place Settings* (1968), for narrator and chamber soloists, sets three texts concerned with food (one of them from an elegant wine cookbook of 1936) in humorous fashion. *Solitaire,* for piano and vibraphone, consists of two pre-recorded tapes with piano and vibraphone that are combined into one working tape against which a live pianist plays. The music is divided into ten sections that can be played in various sequences, and some of them quote parts of a Prelude by Chopin. *Spring, River, Flowers, Moon and Night* (1975), for two pianos and tape, was inspired by an eight-century Chinese poem. The piano parts include both conventional playing and special effects directly on the strings; the tape, providing a soft background, consists of both electronically generated sounds and recorded parts for instruments such as lute, guitar, and mandolin. In *Soundings,* originally for chamber ensemble and later revised for full orchestra (it was performed by the New York Philharmonic and the Boston Symphony orchestras in 1977 and 1978 respectively), the same musical elements are developed at varying speeds by different subsections of the orchestra, so that the texture grows denser and denser and the music in effect echoes itself. *Appello* (1976), for piano, is highly organized, using a tone row (series of pitches in fixed order) in both the melody and the harmonic structure; the specific row used in all four movements is taken from Book 1A of Pierre Boulez's *Structures. Homage to Keith Jarrett and Gary Burton* (1977), for flute and vibraphone, is an extended duet that resembles the improvisatory interaction of the two jazz musicians on whose material it is based.

Joan Tower,[9] trained as a pianist, not only specialized in composing chamber music but helped found her own chamber ensemble, the Da Capo Players, which won the highly prestigious chamber music award of the

Naumburg Foundation in 1973. The five-member group (flute, clarinet, violin, cello, piano), which specialized in contemporary music and for which Tower was the pianist, gave, from the time it was founded in 1970, an annual series of concerts at Carnegie Recital Hall in New York and also toured widely; moreover, it commissioned many new works from composers.

Tower was born on September 6, 1938, in New Rochelle, New York, and was educated at Bennington College and Columbia University. She also taught at the Greenwich House Music School from 1961 to 1971, and at Columbia from 1964 to 1971; in 1972 she joined the faculty of Bard College. Her compositions include Percussion Quartet (1963; revised 1969), *Movements for Flute and Piano* (1968), *Prelude for Five Players* (1970 for flute, clarinet, piano, and either violin and cello or oboe and bassoon), *Hexachords for Flute* (1972), *Platinum Spirals* (1976) for solo violin, *Red Garnet Waltz* (1977) for piano, and *Amazon* (1977) for flute, clarinet, viola, cello, and piano.

Shulamit Ran[10] was born on October 21, 1949, in Tel Aviv, Israel, and began her music studies there. In 1963 she came to New York, where she had a full-tuition scholarship at the Mannes College of Music, and she studied composition with Norman Dello Joio and piano with Nadia Reisenberg. An excellent pianist, she had made her debut recital in Israel at the age of twelve, and her first orchestral composition was performed when she was only fourteen. Following her graduation from Mannes in 1967, she made a number of recital tours, including several in Europe. In the 1970s she continued to perform in public, mostly her own piano works, but devoted herself increasingly to composition. In 1973 she joined the faculty of the University of Chicago, and in the same year she married Clifford L. Colnot, an American arranger and composer.

Ran's first major composition was a *Capriccio* for piano and orchestra (1963), which was performed by the New York Philharmonic under Leonard Bernstein in 1963 as well as by other orchestras. Other orchestral works, also for piano and orchestra, are *Symphonic Poem* for piano and orchestra (1967), Concert Piece for piano and orchestra (1970; revised 1973), and Concerto for piano and orchestra (1978). She has also written a considerable number of chamber works and piano pieces. Typical of her style is *Ensembles for 17,* for soprano and sixteen instrumentalists, given its premiere in Chicago in 1975. A work in two movements, it interweaves the final speech from *Othello* ("loved not wisely but too well") with strong instrumental writing, so that the winds, strings, piano, and percussion convey the mood of Othello's famous speech as much as the voice itself.[11] Other important chamber works by Ran are *O the Chimneys* (1969), for voice, chamber ensemble, and tape, performed a number of times and also recorded; *Double Vision* (1976), for two quintets and piano; *Hyperbolae* (1977) for solo piano, which was performed by all participants in the

Second Artur Rubinstein Piano Competition in Israel in 1977; and *For an Actor* (1978), for solo clarinet.

Of all the new styles and techniques developed since 1950, electronic music of various kinds attracted many composers, some of whom had long been working in other styles. Among the women composers who switched gears in midstream, so to speak, was Jean Eichelberger Ivey.

Born on July 3, 1923, in Washington, D.C., Ivey[12] spent the first twenty years of her career teaching, giving concerts (piano), and producing fairly conventional compositions, basically tonal and neoclassic, with a strong affinity for the styles of Bela Bartók and Maurice Ravel. In the early 1960s, however, she became interested first in twelve-tone music (compositions based on a fixed order of all twelve pitches of the chromatic scale; see Chapter 6 for further explanation), and then in electronic music. In 1969 she founded an Electronic Music Studio at the Peabody Conservatory in Baltimore, and in 1972 she got a doctorate in music from the University of Toronto, where she had specialized in electronic music. By the late 1970s she was concentrating less on pure electronic music and more on combining it with live performance, often in very dramatic ways.

Ivey's music studies began at the age of six, when she started piano lessons and also to compose. She went on to study at Trinity College and then received two master's degrees, one in piano from the Peabody Conservatory (1946) and another in composition from the Eastman School of Music (1956). In the meantime she had been teaching part time at a number of schools in the Washington-Baltimore area and served as organist in several churches. In the 1950s she toured as a pianist, appearing in Mexico, Europe, and the United States in recitals that often included some of her own compositions. She also gave lecture-demonstrations on teaching contemporary music for groups of piano teachers throughout the United States. In 1958 she married Frederick Maurice Ivey.

By the time she became interested in electronic music Ivey had worked in practically every medium of composition. She had written for orchestra, both full and small, songs and song cycles, choral anthems, a piano sonata and many shorter piano works (some of them teaching pieces), chamber music, incidental music for plays, and film scores. One of her first and most radical departures from traditional music was *Pinball,* an impressionistic study of sounds made up entirely from the actual sounds—rattles, clicks, bells—of a pinball machine in operation. Produced at the Brandeis University Electronic Music Studio in 1965, this work is an example of *musique concrète,* that is, music made up of taped real-life sounds (such as street noises, thunder, the ocean, etc.), a concept developed by Pierre Schaeffer and other composers in France in the late 1940s. Ivey's work also served as the score for a film by Wayne Sourbeer, *Montage V: How to Play Pinball,* produced during the same year.

Ivey's next important electronic work was *Continuous Form* (1967), a composition of indeterminate length written for use during station breaks (together with another film by Sourbeer) for television broadcasts. This work has had literally thousands of performances over educational television stations, principally in New York and Boston. The music accompanies the film in nonsynchronized excerpts selected at random in such a way that no two performances are exactly alike.

By 1970 Ivey had decided to use the best of both worlds and combine taped music with live performance. Her first completed works of this nature, *Terminus,* for mezzo soprano and tape, and *Three Songs of Night,* for soprano, five instruments, and tape, had their first performance at the Peabody Conservatory in spring 1971. Ivey herself described the technical problems raised by this kind of composition:

It combines all the problems of composing for live performers and the problems of pure tape composition, with some special problems raised by their interaction....A pure tape composition is like a painting—one puts it together alone in the studio, drawing on all one's resources of equipment, imagination, and taste. Unlike traditional composition, where the composer hears his work only in his mind until, often much later, performers bring it to life, the tape studio offers ready access to sound.... Composing for live performers, on the other hand...requires an intimate knowledge of how voices and instruments behave, how performers react to each other, to notation, and to the whole performance situation, including the audience....some unpredictability is inevitable; each performance differs, grossly or subtly, from every other.[13]

Ivey considered unpredictability a drawback for live performance, not an advantage. On the other hand, she acknowledged that pure tape music lacks visual interest. Although visual elements can be supplied by lighting, the use of film, or other means, she believed that the visual experience of watching a live performer had more direct appeal. Moreover, a live performer can be inspired by audience reaction to perform better, whereas a tape remains unaffected.

Though combining tape and live performance overcomes some of these drawbacks, it raises still other problems. Synchronization between performer and tape must be carefully planned; the tape cannot adjust to the performer, and the performer also cannot adjust unless he or she is sufficiently informed and cued. A new set of problems relate to the equipment needed. Playback equipment may differ; the engineers may not understand the composer's instructions; the balance between stereo channels or other amplifiers may vary; what sounds loud in one hall may be too soft in another, and so on.

Ivey found all these difficulties challenging. Both *Terminus* and *Three Songs of Night* were given numerous performances, and both were used on an all-Ivey recording issued in 1974, along with *Aldebaran* (1972), for viola and tape, and the earlier, purely electronic *Cortege—for Charles Kent* (1969), the first piece to be composed in the Peabody Conservatory Electronic Music Studio. Two important live-tape works followed, *Hera, Hung from the Sky* (1973), for mezzo soprano, winds, percussion, piano, and tape, which had been commissioned by the Collegium Musicum of the University of North Dakota (first New York performance, 1974), and *Testament of Eve* (1976), a monodrama for mezzo soprano, orchestra, and tape, given its premiere by the Baltimore Symphony Orchestra in April 1976. The latter, with a text by the composer, tells the story of Eve's rejection of pleasure in preference to the Spartan quest for knowledge outside the Garden of Eden. The score is conceived as a debate between Lucifer, who appears as a disembodied voice on a tape that also includes electronic sounds, and Eve, personified by the live voice. The dialogue is vivid, accompanied by picturesque electronic colors and impressive climaxes (aided by the two dozen percussion instruments called for in the orchestra). The vocal part contains quite difficult intervals, timbre changes, and meters. Though Ivey originally had written the text nearly ten years earlier, she did not complete the music until she was promised a performance by conductor Sergiu Comissiona, and she specifically tailored the vocal part for soloist Elaine Bonazzi, who had recorded two other works of hers.

Unlike Ivey, Pauline Oliveros[14] was from the start attracted to unconventional kinds of music, and she became one of the most versatile experimenters. Born on May 30, 1932, in Houston, Texas, she later recalled that as a young child she had enjoyed listening to her grandfather's crystal radio over earphones, and also used to tune her father's radio to the whistles and white noise between stations. She also remembered listening, in the 1940s, to popular radio programs for their sound effects—the squeaking door on "Inner Sanctum" and others. In 1952 Oliveros moved to San Francisco. She studied there with Robert Erickson and worked as a free-lance musician, and then, beginning about 1957, she became involved with group improvisation. In 1961 she began to work at the San Francisco Tape Center, where she remained for five years; in 1966 she was appointed director of the Tape Music Center at Mills College, and the following year she began teaching electronic music at the University of California at San Diego, where she later became director of the Center for Music Experiment.

Before she began to work with electronic music, Oliveros composed for conventional instruments, using no particular system or style. Group improvisation, in which an ensemble of musicians simply produces music as a group, as it occurs to them, made her feel free to write whatever she pleased (she once said, "I simply listened until I heard the next sound to write down").[15] Although the electronic generation of sounds fascinated her, she believed, like Ivey, that pure tape music performances lacked visual interest.

Consequently she began to experiment with using dancers, actors, live musicians, film, and lighting effects in combination with taped music. Also like Ivey, she became interested in *musique concrète,* and in this vein created a series of works for amplified boxes (*Applebox,* 1964; *Applebox Double,* 1965; *Applebox Orchestra,* 1966; *Applebox Orchestra with Bottle Chorus,* 1970). At the same time she experimented with real-time tape compositions, that is, compositions of electronically generated sounds recorded as soon as they are produced, without being mixed with other sounds or otherwise altered through splicing the tape. Outstanding among her early works of this nature is her *I of IV* (1966).

Another area that attracted Oliveros was sound sculpture, that is, the creation of sound-producing sculpture. Such devices produce, mix, and process sound and light at the same time. Notable among her works in this vein is *In Memoriam Nicola Tesla, Cosmic Engineer* (1968), which was commissioned by the Merce Cunningham Dance Company and was widely performed. In it Oliveros, according to her colleague, composer Gordon Mumma, "has the performers conduct an acoustical analysis of the performance space. For the closing section the space is subjected to a sea of low-frequency sounds which establish physically imposing standing waves and structural resonances in the building itself."[16]

Still another experimental area in which Oliveros became involved was astro-bio-geo-physical applications of electronic music. With the development of ultrasensitive electronic equipment, many previously unknown natural activities (astrophysical, biophysical, or geophysical in nature) could be detected, and the sounds and lights they emitted could be recorded and used as part of a musical presentation. For example, in Oliveros's *Valentine* (1968), for four card players, both the heartbeats of four persons playing a game of Hearts and the sounds of the card table they play on are amplified. Combined with these sounds is an amplified narration of a historical text on the making of playing cards, and a series of projected images (the Queen of Hearts changing to the Queen of Spades, and others). Oliveros said of this work:

The interest of this piece depends greatly on the players' real involvement in the game of Hearts and their peripheral interest in the hearing of their own heartbeat bio-feedback loop while the game is in progress. If the players' interest is real, audience sensitivity should increase, and the players' heart rates should change significantly with various events during the game.[17]

Multimedia presentations—performances in which more than one artistic medium (music, dance, film, acting, sculpture) functions—continued to engage Oliveros in the late 1970s, a time when she was also increasingly devoting herself to Tibetan Buddhism. Her *Horse Sings from Cloud,* presented in New York in 1977, featured the composer herself sounding chords on an accordion and sustaining a particular note along each chord. The accordion part began with a single note and evolved into chords of increasing complexity, moving slightly up the scale, and the single note picked out from the chord often quivered slightly in pitch. Whether or not this presentation constituted music was apparently questioned even by the composer, for at this time she told an interviewer that she had not been working with musical ideas for some time but on her "mode of consciousness."[18] Six months later she presented *Rose Moon,* a ritual choral work commissioned and performed by Neely Bruce's Wesleyan Singers (an experimental choral ensemble). The music consists not only of choral singing but the sounds of running feet, percussive choral chanting, solo singing, and verbalizing. Theater entered into the presentation as well. As *New York Times* reviewer John Rockwell described the performance:

There is a circular space with a center point and a cross, forming a mandala. Around the outer circle are runners, who pass eight "cuers" per revolution, each of whom marks the runner's passage with a percussive stroke. The next inner circle is a procession of figures walking counterclockwise, led by Miss Oliveros, who shakes a "moon rattle" and passes it periodically to the cuers. The next circle is four groups of three figures who chant and enact theatrical tableaux representing the elements. And at the center, inside a black and white tentlike structure, Mr. Bruce and his wife stand nude and intone the names of the moon from all the known languages and make nonverbal sounds of an emotional origin.[19]

In addition, three "lunatics" (including the designer and choreographer) express disorder by wandering at random through the pattern.

Also the director of an electronic music center but far more conventional in approach, and composing non-electronic as well as electronic works, was Daria Semegen.[20] Born in West Germany on June 27, 1946, she came to America at the age of four, and by the age of six she had begun both studying piano and composing. Semegen was interested also in acting and theatrical production, but she nevertheless committed herself to music and for four years attended the Eastman School of Music. She studied composition with Robert Gauldin, Burrill Phillips, and Samuel Adler, receiving her bachelor's degree in 1968. She then won a one-year Fulbright scholarship to the Warsaw (Poland) Conservatory, where she studied composition with Witold Lutoslawski and electronic music at Warsaw University with Wlodzimierz Kotonski. Subsequently she went to Yale to study composition and electronic music with composer Bulent Arel and theory with Alexander Goehr.

Semegen completed her master's degree in 1971 and that summer went to the Columbia-Princeton Electronic Music Center, where she worked for the next five years, studying and teaching. During that period, she also worked for two years as sound engineer for the Boulton Collection of World Music, where she edited and technically supervised materials that were later released as recordings. In 1974 she was appointed to the faculty of the State University of New York at Stony Brook, where she was named assistant professor of music and associate director of the Electronic Music Studios, as well as designer of the university's professional recording project.

Semegen's non-electronic compositions include *Suite for Flute and Violin* (1965), *Silent, Silent Night* (1965) for tenor voice and piano (to a text by William Blake), *Three Pieces for Piano* (1966), *Triptych for Orchestra* (1966), *Quattro* (1967) for flute and piano, *Study for 16 Strings* (1968), and *Music for Violin Solo* (1973). Her electronic works include the film score *Out of Into* (1971), in collaboration with Bulent Arel for an animated film by Irving Kreisberg, *Electronic Composition no. 1* (1972), and *Arc: Music for Dancers* (1977). This last work, commissioned by the Mimi Garrard Dance Theatre of New York, combines electronic music, dance, and lighting with computer technology; it was performed in New York in May 1977 and at a number of electronic music festivals throughout the United States in that year and in 1978.

Electronic music has obvious advantages as an accompaniment for staged presentations—for theater, dance, and film—since it requires only the presence of playback equipment, and its lack of visual interest is amply compensated. Among the electronic composers who became known for her compositions for theater and film was Pril Smiley.[21] Born on March 19, 1943, in Mohonk Lake, New York, she began composing electronic music in 1963 at the Columbia-Princeton Electronic Music Center, where she eventually became an instructor and then associate director. From 1968 to 1974 she also served as electronic music consultant to the Lincoln Center Repertory Theatre in New York, and from time to time she worked as a free-lance percussionist.

Between 1966 and 1978 Smiley composed scores for nearly two dozen theater productions, not only for Lincoln Center but for several Shakespeare Festivals (in New York, Connecticut, and Canada) and for other companies. She also composed scores for film, television, and dance (including one free-style skiing ballet). One of Smiley's first successful electronic works was *Eclipse* (1967), which was runner-up in the First International Electronic Music Competition at Dartmouth College in 1968. This work was composed for four separate tracks, to be heard as though, for example, music was being played from all four corners of a room. All the elements of this work—rhythm, timbre, loudness, and duration of pitches—were very precisely determined. In her own description of the work, Smiley said:

In many ways the structure of *Eclipse* is related to the use of timbre. There are basically two kinds of sounds in the piece: the low, sustained gong-like sounds (always either increasing or decreasing in loudness) and the short, more percussive sounds, which can be thought of as metallic, glassy, or wooden in character. These different kinds of timbres are usually used in contrast to one another, sometimes set end to end so that one kind of sound interrupts another, and sometimes dovetailed so that one timbre appears to emerge out of or from beneath another. Eighty-five percent of the sounds are electronic in origin; the non-electronic sounds are mainly pre-recorded percussion sounds—but subsequently electronically modified so that they are not always recognizable.[22]

Both *Eclipse* and another of Smiley's electronic works, *Kolyosa* (1970), were commercially recorded and performed many times. Also, both works were used by Vladimir Ussachevsky (considered one of the founders of electronic music) as part of his extensive lecture-demonstration tours throughout the United States. Smiley was awarded a National Endowment for the Arts Grant in 1974 and a Guggenheim Fellowship in 1975–76.

A composer who became known principally for works written for the dance is Lucia Dlugoszewski, who in 1960 became associated with the Erick Hawkins Dance Company. In addition, she also produced compositions for films, plays, and the concert stage.

Dlugoszewski[23] was born on June 16, 1931, in Detroit, Michigan. Her parents were Polish-born, her father an engineer and her mother a painter. She was educated at Wayne State University, where she was a pre-medical student, majoring in science and philosophy. At the same time, she wrote poetry (her book, *A New Folder,* was published in 1969) and studied piano and composition at the Detroit Conservatory of Music. About 1950 she went to New York, where she studied at the Mannes College of Music and also privately with Grete Sultan, who introduced her to dancer-choreographer Erick Hawkins. She also studied composition with Felix Saltzer and Edgard Varèse; the latter in particular she considered an important influence, because she believed he was one of few who understood the profound relationship between science and music. Another important influence was the philosopher F. S. C. Northrop, who taught at Yale and with whom Dlugoszewski collaborated on a long article on esthetics.[24]

Dlugoszewski did not use synthesizers and other electronic equipment to generate sounds. Rather, she used traditional instruments in unconventional ways, and sometimes she invented new instruments. The most important of her inventions was a timbre piano (1951), a piano that can be muted in a variety of ways and can be struck, plucked with plectra, or stroked with bows. For this instrument she wrote numerous works, among them *Archaic Timbre Piano Music* (1953–56) and *Instants in Form and Movement* (1957) for timbre piano and chamber orchestra. In 1958 she created an "orchestra" of 100 new percussion instruments: wood, glass, paper, metal, skin, plastic ladder harps, tangent rattles, unsheltered rattles, closed rattles, wave rattles, a quarter-tone gong, and square drums (on which the performer can change the pitch somewhat by playing in the corners); Dlugoszewski herself performed on these. Her compositions for this ensemble include *Suchness Concert* (1958–60), *Clear Places* (1958–61), *Geography of Noon* (1964), and *A Zen in Ryoko-In* (a film score).

At the same time, Dlugoszewski continued to write for conventional instruments and ensembles. One of her best-known works is *Space Is a Diamond* (1970) for solo trumpet, which Virgil Thomson described as "an eleven-minute trumpet solo unaccompanied that seems virtually to exhaust the technical possibilities of the instrument without becoming didactic."[25] In *Angels of the Utmost Heavens* (1976), for brass quintet, the virtuosic potentialities of the instruments are similarly exploited, and they "bleat and gurgle and flare and snort from the depths of their registers to their highest extremes."[26] In *Abyss and Caress* (1975), a fifteen-section work for a standard chamber ensemble of seventeen players, the piano is prepared with odd materials to create special sound effects, and the string players sometimes use glass and comb bows on their instruments. "The result," said one reviewer," is quite unlike anything. A good many of the sounds are extreme, in pitch, timbre, and dynamics. They are common enough in contemporary music, it is true, but the composer has put them through a cycle of white-hot intensity."[27] Given her long-standing interest in poetry, it is not surprising that Dlugoszewski composed a number of works including narration, and she also wrote an opera, *The Heidi Songs* (1970), with a libretto by the poet John Ashbery.

A composer who turned from largely traditional styles to aleatory music (in which elements of the music are determined by the performer rather than the composer) and to graphic notation, in which the conventional musical staff is replaced by drawn indications of how a work is to be performed, is Netty Simons.[28] Born in New York City on October 26, 1918, the youngest of five children, she began studying music at the age of six with her oldest sister, who was a pupil of Walter Damrosch. She then studied piano and composition at Manhattan's Third Street Music School and presented her first concert at the age of thirteen.

Always attracted to contemporary composers, such as Ernest Shelling and Henry Cowell, Simons became increasingly interested in composition and enrolled at New York University, where her teachers included Percy Grainger and Marion Bauer (see Chapter 6). In 1933 she interrupted her studies there to accept a one-year scholarship at Juilliard to study piano with Alexander Siloti. She then returned to New York University and for the next three years studied composition with Stefan Wolpe, who, she later said, was probably the greatest single influence on her. During these years, besides composing and performing, she presented music broadcasts over New York radio station WHN and also taught, both privately and at the Third Street School. In 1936 she married Leon Simons, an inventor, and they had two children, a son and a daughter. From 1949 she again worked with Wolpe, and from 1965 to 1971 she wrote and produced radio broadcasts of new music for the New York municipal radio station WNYC and the University of Michigan station WUOM.

Simons's early compositions are characterized by an extreme economy of means and imaginative control of tone color. They are principally chamber works, among them her earliest published work, *Duo for Violin and Cello* (1939), a String Quartet (1950), Quartet for flute and strings (1951), *Piano Work* (1952), *Night Sounds* (1953), for piano, and *Set of Poems for Children* (1949), for winds, strings, and narrator, originally composed for her own children. She also wrote two later works "for children," *Puddintame* (1972), for one or more players plus narrator, which sets a series of limericks interspersed with a short refrain and employs a graphic, color-coded notation, and *The Pied Piper of Hamelin* (1972), for narrator, flute, piano, and violin orchestra, setting Robert Browning's version of the folk legend.

Simons's *Too Late, The Bridge Is Closed* (1972), for strings, is devised for any number of players and also can be performed as a theater piece or ballet. Its graphic score resembles a linear maze, with colored lines to indicate dynamics, articulation, and occasionally duration, and letters for the seven basic pitches. Although requiring careful study of the performance directions, this work gives the players considerable choice and leeway. Also notable are four aleatory works, *Design Groups I* (1966) for one to three percussion players, *Design Groups II* (1968), a duo for any combination of high-and low-pitched instruments, *Silver Thaw* (1969), for any combination of one to eight players, and *The Great Stream Silent Moves* (1974), for piano, harp, and percussion.

Still another area of experimentation has been that of microtonal music, that is, music using intervals smaller than a half-tone, with pitches that lie between the conventional notes of the chromatic scale (white and black keys of the piano). Though only specially tuned keyboard instruments can produce these notes, they are easily accessible on some wind and all stringed instruments. Tui St. George Tucker, born in California in 1924 and a resident of New York since 1945, began experimenting with quarter tones in 1955. (A quarter tone lies midway between a half-tone interval, for example, midway between C and C-sharp, or C-sharp and D natural). At first trained as a violinist, Tucker later became a virtuoso performer on the recorder, for which she wrote many of her works. Her first successful quarter-tone composition was *The Bullfinch Sonata* (1960) for solo recorder; she later devised a fingering chart for playing quarter tones on this instrument. Tucker also worked as a conductor, both choral and instrumental, but by the late 1970s she largely confined her conducting to her own compositions. Her works include two piano sonatas, *Little Pieces for Quarter-tone Piano*, two string quartets, a violin sonata, works for recorder (alone, with voices, and with other instruments), *Lift Up Your Heads, Ye Mighty Gates,* for oboe, bassoon, and clarinet, and a considerable number of choral works and songs.

Two composers who have experimented with machine-generated sound in their compositions are Laurie Spiegel, who became known for her computer music, and Suzanne Ciani, who worked with analog synthesizers. Spiegel,[29] born in 1945 in Chicago, studied at Shimer College (Illinois), Oxford University, and the Juilliard School, and privately with composers Jacob Druckman and Emmanuel Ghent. She learned to play a number of plucked stringed instruments, notably five-string banjo, folk and classical guitar, and Renaissance and baroque lute. In 1975 she received a master's degree from Brooklyn College.

At first Spiegel composed for classical guitar and other traditional instruments, but about 1970 she turned to electronic music, and about three years later she chose the greater control and compositional complexity made available by computers. In computer music a program replaces a score. In effect, a score is a set of instructions for turning musical ideas into actual sound. Rather than writing such instructions in conventional (or unconventional) notation for performers to carry out, a computer composer writes a program, a set of instructions for a computer involving anything from specific pitches to a general set of relationships or processes for composing them. The computer then can generate the sounds directly itself, or control equipment such as an analog synthesizer that in turn generates sounds, or print out a "score" consisting of specific notes it may have helped compose by following certain general rules. (A simple example of the last method would be a program instructing the computer to play or store in its memory a canon in four voices made of a single melody that the composer has typed, played on a keyboard, or had computed.) The computer memory functions as traditional staff paper does, for storage, editing, and performance instructions, but unlike conventionally written notation it permits tremendous flexibility in the arrangement of the musical information it stores.

In the late 1970s computer music was still most often tape-recorded, but as ever smaller and less expensive machinery was devised, live-performance use of computers became increasingly feasible. In addition to performing pre-programmed compositions, computers also can be played "live" as other instruments are, by instructing them as to the nature of the sounds to be produced, which the composer-performer may generate by means of keyboards, knobs, switches, or other input devices. In the most recently developed and sophisticated computer systems, the actual sound—or literally, the wave motion of the speaker cone that ultimately "performs" the sound—is computed, a process called digital synthesis. Such computers actually have sufficient speed and memory capacity to permit producing an entire composition in real time—that is, producing and performing a composition at virtually the same time that the program for it is being fed into the computer. In 1978 such systems were still quite rare. More common were "hybrid" systems, which use analog oscillators to generate the actual wave forms of sounds, thereby having to compute larger parameters of sound (pitches, dynamics, etc.). Such hybrid systems were the first practical way of improvising or performing entire compositions on computers in real time.

For a number of her compositions Spiegel used a hybrid system called the GROOVE (for *G*enerating *R*eal-Time *O*perations *O*n *V*oltage-controlled *E*quipment) system. Notable among them are *The Orient Express* (1974), a work giving the illusion of continuous acceleration; *The Expanding Universe* (1975), a slow, continuous but highly structured meditative piece; *Drums* (1975), a rhythmic study of xylophone-like sounds, reflecting her interest in African and Indian rhythms; and *Patchwork* (1976), a composition exploring the relationships among four short melodic motifs and four basic rhythmic patterns, manipulated in a contrapuntal fashion reminiscent of the baroque motet, which one reviewer described as "an extremely pretty and pleasing contrapuntal effort."[30] Because Spiegel's works were principally tape music, they often were performed in conjunction with film, dance, theater, and other visual productions. In 1978 Spiegel also was experimenting with computerized real-time synthesis of visual images, recorded on film; she was exploring the idea of visual music, dealing with counterpoint, tension and resolution, groups of elements, and the like.[31]

Suzanne Ciani,[32] born on June 4, 1946, began studying piano at the age of six. She went to Wellesley College and then got a master's degree in composition at the University of California at Berkeley. It was in California that she began to compose for and perform on a Buchla Synthesizer, a voltage-controlled electronic instrument developed by Donald Buchla. Until the development of these small machines in the 1960s, made possible by the rapid development and widespread use of transistors, electronic music could be created only in tape studios on large, expensive equipment. The small voltage-controlled synthesizer in effect combines the separate components of the tape studio in a single cabinet. The different components, called modules, are electrically interconnected and manipulated so that they perform together. There are two fundamental kinds of module, those that generate basic electric signals (oscillators and noise generators) and those that process or modify the signal in some way (envelope generators, random voltage generators, ring modulators, and filters).[33] To perform on such a synthesizer, one must first set up a "patch" by interconnecting the modules in chosen configurations by means of patch cords, and then one plays the instrument by activating switches, turning knobs, sliding levers, and touching pressure-sensitive plates, which in a sense are like keyboards but do not have the mechanical action of a conventional keyboard. The musical signal is sent out through loudspeakers, often in multiple channels to allow the performer to manipulate the movement of the sound in space.

Ciani's first encounter with the Buchla Synthesizer was at a new electronic center at Mills College, where she could rent a studio with a synthesizer for a modest fee. Soon afterward she took a course in computer music at Stanford University with Max Mathews, and then she began to give concerts in Berkeley and elsewhere in the San Francisco area. In 1969 she got her first paying assignment, composing twenty-three ads for a department store. After graduating from Berkeley in 1970, she went to work in the Buchla factory, hoping to learn enough about the instrument so that she could build her own. Meanwhile, she also wanted to buy her own synthesizer, so in order to earn money she composed scores for educational films, sound effects for commercials, and any other assignments that paid.

More and more interested in her own compositions and in live performance, Ciani in 1974 moved to New York. Although she continued to produce music for television and radio commercials and film scores, she also found more opportunities for concert performance. In 1977 she joined a rock band called New Age, in the belief that electronic music presented a unique opportunity to combine elements of serious music with the more widespread appeal of popular styles. Among Ciani's important works for the Buchla Synthesizer are *Koddesh-Koddeshim* (1972), *New York, New York* (1974), *Lixiviation* (1974), and *New York II* (1975); her most successful popular electronic arrangement was the one she made for the *Meco Star Wars* album (1977), the popular disco version of the score from the motion picture *Star Wars*.

Carrying the idea of multimedia performance even further were the creators of sound environments, entire settings into which the listener enters and is surrounded by sound from various sources, as well as film, dance, sculpture, and the like. Among those who created this kind of work was Beth Anderson,[34] who was born on January 3, 1950, and grew up in Kentucky. After two years as a piano major at the University of Kentucky, she moved to California and completed her bachelor's degree at the University of California at Davis. She then earned two master's degrees from Mills College, one in piano and another in composition. Throughout this time she also taught piano and voice, and performed.

Anderson's earliest compositions were songs and piano works, but in California she began to work increasingly with tape, usually combining taped sounds with live instruments and voices. Among the important works she produced there were the opera *Queen Christina,* performed at Mills College in 1973, the oratorio *Joan,* produced in 1974, and two string quartets of 1973 (entitled *Music for Charlemagne Palestine* and *I Am Uh Am I).* Also from this period dates her first sound environment, *Hallophone* (1973), for two saxophones, steel guitar, voice, tape, slides, and dancers.

The following year she collaborated with sculptor Paul Cotton on *The Messiah Is Come,* described as a "human sculpture with internal and external sound sources."

As much concerned with verbal ideas as with musical ones, Anderson found novel ways of combining them. For example, a series of compositions she described as "text-sound pieces" (*Torero Piece,* 1973; *Ode,* 1975; *The People Rumble Louder,* 1975; *I Can't Stand It,* 1976) are actually poems, but, as one reviewer said, "In the most musical of these works, practically everything that makes music music—a coherent pitch vocabulary, patterned rhythms—was present."[35]

Anderson also was active in encouraging other experimental composers. In 1973 she became co-editor and publisher of *Ear Magazine,* a musical and literary journal that included new music, poetry, drawings, and photographs, and two years later she moved to New York, where she continued publishing an East Coast edition of *Ear.* In 1976, together with composer Doris Hays, she organized an eleven-week course at the New School in New York called "Meet the Woman Composer," in which the works of eighteen contemporary women were performed and discussed.

Without the perspective of time it is impossible to assess with any accuracy the lasting value of experimental works. Contemporary music is, after all, not a finite body; it is being written at this very moment. But it is not the purpose of this book to pass judgment on what is great music, or even to decide whether a work is or is not music. Rather, it is to chronicle the very active participation of women in American music, and certainly today's musical avant-garde includes both men and women in every area.

For the younger women composers working in the late 1970s, allegedly the social climate has been freer, and many—if not most—emphatically deny that they have encountered either more or different problems on account of their sex. At least one of them, however, suggested that composing music performed by machines rather than human musicians is especially attractive to women for two basic reasons. First, it enables the composer to take a musical idea through to a form in which it can actually be heard without having to persuade musicians, managers, and others that the music is worth performing; machines certainly are "non-sexist," and so they are "politically" liberating for composers. And second, they enable relatively fast (if not instant) feedback for composers, who through them can hear their own compositions performed and so can learn from their own successes and failures.[36]

# 10 TODAY'S ORCHESTRAS, CONDUCTORS, AND INSTRUMENTALISTS

There are very few areas today within the musical world in
which a woman need apologize for her sex. The time has
long passed when a woman appearing as a concert soloist—pianist, violinist, singer—required special treatment as
a kind of curiosity. The orchestral ranks are now open to
her in all but a very few ensembles. . . . There are many
reasons these days for not going into music as a career, but
being female is not one of them.

—Alan Rich, *Careers and Opportunities in Music* (1964)

The oldest of the top six American orchestras is the New York Philharmonic, founded as the Philharmonic Society of New York in 1842. By 1847
it allowed women to be "associate members," which entitled them to attend
rehearsals. Some of these associate members were professional musicians,
but the majority were nonprofessionals who simply liked music (or, in some
cases, professed to). By the mid-1850s most of the associate members were
women, and it was their fund-raising and publicity efforts that kept the society going. They did not, however, go so far as to run the organization.
Women did not sit on the society's board until the 1920s, their way paved
first by two wealthy and socially prominent women, Mrs. Edward Henry
Harriman and then Mrs. Vincent Astor.[1] The first regular woman *player*
(that is, with a full season's contract) in the New York Philharmonic was
Orin O'Brien, a double bassist hired in 1966. In earlier years the society had
used women harpists, but not on a regular contractual basis.[2] (The Symphony Society of New York, founded in 1878 and merged with the New
York Philharmonic in 1928, had a regular woman harpist as early as 1891;

at this time it was one of the country's four major orchestras, the others being the Philharmonic, the Chicago Orchestra, and the Boston Symphony).[3]

Although it took 124 years to admit a woman, New York was only slightly slower than the nation's other major orchestras. Soon afterward it added a few more women, first cellist Evangeline Benedetti (1967), and, by 1976, seven others. The Boston Symphony, founded in 1881, hired its first woman, bassoonist Ann C. de Guichard, in 1945, and the Philadelphia Orchestra, founded in 1900, hired harpist Edna Philipps in 1930.

The principal role women played in American orchestras for a hundred years or so, and one they have not yet relinquished, was as patronesses and supporters. Very early on the New York Philharmonic instituted the practice of "Public Rehearsals." Held on the Friday afternoon before each concert, these rehearsals, which until about 1870 were genuine practice sessions with halts for corrections, gave regular subscribers a chance to hear any work twice in a short period of time and so to know it better. Moreover, it enabled ladies to attend performances without a gentleman escort, which in those days was not possible for an evening performance.[4]

Over the years the "symphonic ladies," as they were called, made themselves indispensable. Not only did they raise money to support their orchestras, but they provided a strong and active community base through their concern with music education, the promotion of ticket sales, and the generation of publicity. Shortly after the United States entered into World War II, their activities were even more formally organized and expanded through the founding of the American Symphony Orchestra League, which in 1944 found a highly dynamic leader in Helen M. Thompson.[5] Ironically, just as women acquired the opportunity to play in American orchestras as replacements for men in the armed services, it was their supportive role that was enlarged and formalized. Indeed, in 1976 an entire book, *Music Angels,* was published about women's support of music.[6]

Nevertheless, during World War II competent instrumentalists were much in demand, and by 1945 many women had found openings in formerly closed ranks. The conductor of the Chicago Woman's Symphony, for example, reported that by January 1945 two dozen of its players had found paying orchestral jobs, some of them as first chair in a leading orchestra (principal horn in the Chicago Symphony, principal cello in Houston and New Orleans, and others).[7] For the most part, however, these jobs proved to be temporary, ending when the men returned home.

Why? Apart from the old prejudices against women instrumentalists discussed in Chapters 2, 3, and 5, there were other reasons. The dim view taken by some conductors was certainly one. In 1916 Josef Stransky, conductor of the New York Symphony, said he would not object to women in orchestras but they would have to be "better players than the men who apply for the same positions."[8] Nearly thirty years later Sir Thomas Beecham, commenting testily on the increasing numbers of women musicians, said, "I do not like, and never will, the association of men and women in orchestras and other instrumental combinations....As a member of the orchestra once said to me, 'If she is attractive I can't play with her and if she is not I won't.'"[9]

Not all the prejudice was so straightforward. In 1933, for example, British composer Ethel Smyth pointed out that the BBC Orchestra, the only one of several London orchestras to hire women in appreciable numbers (twenty in 1931),[10] had never seen fit to hire a woman cellist.[11] In America Leopold Stokowski, declared as early as 1916 that not hiring women constituted a terrible waste of "splendid power," but he himself did not engage one until 1930—and the first nonharpist (cellist Elsa Hilger) only in 1936—although his reign over the Philadelphia Orchestra had been undisputed since 1912. (He later vindicated himself, for the American Symphony Orchestra, which he founded in 1962, from the beginning included many women and also many blacks and members of other minority groups.)

Other reasons were put forward. Women could not rehearse regularly because of their duties at home. It was difficult for them to travel, and when they did there were no appropriate facilities for them.[12] Even in the late 1970s this was occasionally true; on tour the women members of the Boston and New York orchestras sometimes found no dressing room or no toilet facilities. Oddly enough these handicaps had long been overcome by the managers of opera, theater, and ballet companies, where women were essential to the performance. Orchestral music can, of course, be performed entirely by men; operas and plays and ballets rarely are.

Yet another excuse was offered by Helen Thompson, who after twenty-five years with the American Symphony Orchestra League became manager of the New York Philharmonic; Thompson maintained that fewer women audition for orchestra jobs, and therefore fewer were accepted. Perhaps many felt that there was no point in trying.

It was not only men who kept women out of orchestras. Music critic Alan Rich reported that in 1944, at a Boston Symphony fund-raising meeting attended largely by women, the president said that if not enough money was raised the orchestra would have to reduce both the number of players and the length of its season, as well as "lower its standards" by hiring women players; allegedly the last alternative was greeted with a horrified gasp.[13] Nevertheless, only eight years later the Boston Symphony hired its third permanent woman player, and at the head of a section at that. She was Doriot Anthony Dwyer, the orchestra's principal flute, who was still in that position at this writing.

How had Dwyer managed to overcome the barrier? By dint of great talent and extremely hard work. A great-grandniece of feminist Susan B. Anthony, Dwyer preferred to play down her sex. "It's a rough life being a musician, whether you are a man or a woman. Period!" she said.

Dwyer[14] was born in 1922 in Streator, Illinois. She began to study flute at eight with her mother, Edith Maurer Anthony, a professional flutist who had toured the Chautauqua circuit and played under Ethel Leginska in Chicago but had abandoned her performing career with marriage and the arrival of four children. All four children learned to play an instrument, but only Doriot, the third, became a professional musician. As a child, Dwyer had to listen to the weekly broadcasts of symphony orchestras and of the Metropolitan Opera, but it was not until she heard Rossini's *William Tell Overture* performed at a Chicago concert that she really decided to become a professional flutist. After four years in the high school band and another four years at the Eastman School of Music, where she studied with Joseph Mariano and was graduated in 1943, Dwyer obtained her first paying job with the National Symphony in Washington, D.C., under Hans Kindler. One of few conductors at that time who was sympathetic to women players, Kindler hired Dwyer as second flute, a post she held from 1943 to 1945. Meanwhile she commuted to Philadelphia for regular lessons with William Kincaid of the Philadelphia Orchestra, one of the world's greatest flutists.

In 1945 Dwyer left Washington for New York, attended Columbia University for the half-year residence period then required to join the New York union, and then took a number of touring engagements. She then went to the Los Angeles Philharmonic, where she played second flute for six years and also taught at Pomona College. Summers she played at the Hollywood Bowl under various conductors, including Bruno Walter, who gave her her first chance as principal flute (elsewhere she was not even allowed to audition for first chair). In 1952 Dwyer learned that Georges Laurent, Boston's principal flute, was retiring, and decided to apply for an audition there. She always signed her letters "Miss Doriot Anthony" so that her unusual first name would not be mistaken for a man's, and frequently she would get no answer at all. But Boston decided to give her a hearing.

She prepared rigorously for two months, practicing until late at night. She memorized everything she planned to play—a Mozart sonata, a Bach partita, Ravel's *Daphnis et Chloe,* and numerous shorter works. She decided that she would play a perfect audition, and then if she still did not get the job she would abandon orchestral work and seek a solo or chamber music career.

Several other women had been invited to apply for the Boston job, and they all were heard on a single midsummer day at Tanglewood. Dwyer played for Laurent, for concertmaster Richard Burgin, and for conductor Charles Munch. Her hard work paid off, because she got the job.

It was a post she had wanted badly, and she continued to work hard at it, constantly trying to improve. During these years she married, had a daughter, and was divorced. She taught at the New England Conservatory, and then at Boston University and the Berkshire Music Center at Tanglewood, but she tried to restrict her teaching commitments so she could continue to practice and perform, both with the orchestra and in solo recitals and guest engagements with other ensembles. Her appointment originally had made headlines, but in 1976 she declared, "Now the controversy I caused is forgotten." Not entirely. In the late 1970s there still were very few women principal players in major American orchestras, though by 1977 Boston had one other, Marylou Speaker, leading the second-violin section, and a total of eleven women (strings, harp, and flute, but still no brass or percussion) and ninety-two men.[15]

Employment discrimination on the basis of sex alone is today illegal, and the powerful American musicians union denies its existence entirely, but the union's role in this respect does not seem to have been an active one. American musicians' unions date from Civil War days. One of the first was the Boston Musicians Union, founded in 1863, which admitted as full members all musicians living in or near Boston able to pay $10 plus an initiation fee (or, for $2, allowed them to become associate nonvoting members). Further, members had to be able (that is, not infirm) to pursue music as a profession and be under the age of forty-five. The union had another category, the honorary member, for which the requirements were simpler: Anyone who donated $100 or more to the Relief Fund was an honorary member. The Relief Fund was in fact the basic purpose of the early unions—to help support musicians out of work for prolonged periods. Although the constitution of the Boston union referred to members as "he," nowhere did it explicitly specify the sex of members.

By the turn of the century this and other local musicians' unions had been absorbed or replaced by the much larger Mutual Musical Protective Union. Originally chartered in 1864, it became affiliated in July 1903 with the American Federation of Labor, which required that it admit women, and from that time on it always included some women members. The first women to join what is today called the American Federation of Musicians were harpists from the New York Metropolitan Opera; by mid-1904, 31 women had joined the union, which had a total of about 4,500 members. Each member had to pay a $100 initiation fee and take an examination of musical ability; only two or three applicants failed to pass. Ten of the new women members belonged to the Ladies Elite Orchestra of the Atlantic Garten (see Chapter 5).

The admission of women to the union was controversial enough to rouse public interest, and therefore the *Musical Standard* decided to collect the "Opinions of Some New York Leaders on Women as Orchestral Players," which it published in its issue of April 2, 1904. Most of the opinions printed were unfavorable. Gustave Kerker, musical director at the Casino, felt women and men should not play together. "Neither sex will benefit from such an arrangement," he said, *"except in the matter of wages"* (author's italics). Although women were ideally suited to play the harp, Kerker said, nature never intended them to play winds or brasses. They lack the lip and lung power to hold notes and therefore play out of tune. They do not look pretty playing brasses. Also, women cannot be depended on to work hard, rehearse regularly, or meet similar requirements.

William Furst, music director of the Belasco Theater, agreed that as harpists women were desirable but as wind players they were impossible. They cannot compete with men, and they cannot learn to read music easily. Occasionally you hear a good female violinist or cornetist, but "as a rule the fair sex is too fond of fancy playing to be of actual value to a serious musical organization."

Nahan Franko, concertmaster of the Metropolitan Opera and brother of violinist Jeanne Franko (see Chapter 2), said that union membership would encourage women to become musicians and he would hire any he found capable, but he did not expect to find any for some years to come. But in ten years, he predicted, "we shall see mixed orchestras in theaters and opera houses."

The only wholly positive opinion was expressed by Charles Eschert, who, as director of the Atlantic Garten orchestra, had considerable personal experience with women players. He maintained that only lack of opportunity kept women out of metropolitan orchestras. Said he:

They would fill the positions quite as well as men. They are hard workers, they are punctual, they keep their minds on the work at hand, and ought really to receive higher salaries than men who do fill similar positions, since women are considered an attraction outside their musical powers. The outcome of this latest advancement for women will be the formation of many mixed orchestras.

Joining the union was a big step. In 1917 the only major American orchestra not yet unionized was the Boston Symphony (it held out until 1942). Almost all theater orchestras (one of the biggest sources of employment) were unionized, as were many orchestras playing in cafés, hotels, restaurants, movie theaters, and dance halls.[16] However, despite predictions of "mixed" orchestras in the near future, very little happened in this direction. In the spring of 1938—thirty-five years after women were first admitted to the union—a Committee for the Recognition of Women in the Music Profession was formed to promote the granting of full employment opportunities to women instrumentalists, and on May 18 of that year 150 women members of Musicians Local 802 (the New York local) met to discuss their problems.[17] Not much appears to have come of this meeting, but there is no doubt that union or no union, women musicians still faced greater odds against being hired than men. Although just the previous year conductor Otto Klemperer had engaged twenty-year-old Ellen Stone as first

horn for the Pittsburgh Symphony, this was an isolated case in a major orchestra. Wind players in particular faced persistent discrimination. Leona
May Smith, the foremost woman trumpeter of this period, was featured as a
soloist at Radio City Music Hall and worked both with Fred Waring's
Pennsylvanians and the Goldman Band, two of the nation's leading popular
ensembles. Yes, she said in 1938, there *is* a future for women musicians, but
they must somehow overcome the common critic's attitude: "This is a com-
mendable performance, considering the player is a woman." The best
steady income for a woman musician, Smith concluded, was teaching.[18]
Though Smith played first trumpet with the National Orchestral Association, performed with the Chautauqua Symphony, and won a number of
awards, she devoted most of her time in succeeding years to teaching brass
instruments to high school students.

Just what were the economic stakes? In 1911 violinist Maud Powell said
that the average orchestral player earned $2,000 a year, but really good
wind players (oboe, clarinet, trumpet, trombone, or horn), who were in
short supply, might make anywhere from $35 to $75 per week.[19] In October
1925 the *Etude* reported on violinists' salaries. The Chicago Civic Opera
paid string players $119 per week plus rehearsal fees (an average of $155 per
week) for a twenty-two week season, or more than $3,000 per season. Sym-
phony players received similar pay. A violinist in a first-class hotel dance
orchestra earned $90 per week, whereas in jazz orchestras the pay was $100
to $150 per week. As for teaching, a violinist could expect $1.50 to $2 per
lesson in smaller towns, but up to $5 in large cities. A concert engagement,
on the other hand, might yield anywhere from $50 to $1,000.[20] The difference in pay between a symphony job and private teaching was, therefore,
considerable, and fortunate indeed were those women who were hired.

They added up to little more than a handful. Cleveland hired four women
in 1923, San Francisco five in 1925, Minneapolis a few the same year. Baltimore hired five women string players in 1937. The lesser orchestras were
more open. For example, the Civic Orchestra of Chicago, founded in 1918,
included twenty-four women by 1921, one of them a clarinetist;[21] during the
same time the much richer Chicago Orchestra had only a single woman
harpist, and not every year, either.

The underlying reason for job discrimination in any field is economic.
And the difference between a major and a lesser orchestra is also purely economic. Indeed, in 1979 America's 1,400 orchestras were classified on
just that basis—by the size of the annual budget, the minimum annual salary, the length of the season, and the number of players employed. According to this system of classification, the smallest are the *college* and *community* orchestras, about 1,000 in all, with budgets under $50,000 Then
come the *urban* orchestras ($50,000 to $100,000) and the *metropolitan* orchestras ($100,000 to $500,000). None of these could afford to pay players

very much, nowhere near a living wage. Consequently fewer men accepted jobs in them, and more women were willing to settle for them. Finally, there are *regional* orchestras ($500,000 to $1.5 million) and, at the top, thirty-one *major* orchestras (over $1.5 million), which provide a full season's employment. In 1978 eleven of the "majors" worked the year round. Clearly these were the most desirable employers. The New York Philharmonic, for example, which in 1976 paid a minimum of $23,000 per year for a fifty-two-week year, including a forty-nine-day paid vacation, might have as many as one hundred highly qualified players show up to audition for a single opening.[22]

Music is rarely a lucrative profession. For every diva or conductor who makes a fortune, there are thousands of musicians who cannot find employment at all. According to the 1960 census, musicians and music teachers earned an average of $4,757 per year versus a median of $6,778 for all professions; this was only $7 more than the average experienced male laborer over the age of fourteen. Of forty-nine professional groups, musicians and music teachers ranked fortieth in national income. Between 1940 and 1960, when American production workers in manufacturing raised their earnings by 150 percent, orchestral players' earnings rose only 80 percent. Strenuous concerted efforts, both by the musicians union and the International Conference of Symphony and Opera Musicians, greatly improved earnings between 1963 and 1971, the average annual salary rising from $4,147 to $9,893 in that period,[23] but by and large musicians were only beginning to keep up with the overall rate of inflation.

Though accurate statistics are hard to come by, it is estimated that about 42 percent of the players in urban and community orchestras—who are either not paid at all or only on a per concert basis—are women. According to the American Symphony Orchestra League's report on women in symphony orchestras, published in *Symphony News* in April 1976, orchestras with the highest budgets, longest seasons, and most generous salaries tend to have the fewest women players, and on the average, the best of the major orchestras had fewer than 10 percent women players.[24]

The same article also stated that the use of blind auditions—in which applicants are hidden from the judges by a screen—greatly increased the number of women hired. In 1976 one-third of all the major orchestras used a screen for preliminary auditions, and three orchestras—all with a high percentage of women players—used a screen in their final auditions. Needless to say, this system also could be expected to help black and other minority-group musicians (of either sex).

How are orchestra musicians chosen? Traditionally, each orchestra had its own system for filling vacancies. For many years the decision was wholly up to the principal first violinist, or concertmaster, second in power only to the conductor. However, some orchestras were ruled entirely by their conductors, whereas others had a small group of musicians, usually long-time members of the orchestra, who chose any candidate they liked. Thus, if an applicant was a favorite student of a player who in turn was a favorite of the orchestra management, the audition might be a mere formality.

Moreover, until the mid-1960s vacancies were rarely publicized. Word of mouth was the only form of advertising, and jobs often were filled before any outsider even knew they were available. As a result, some sections were filled entirely by the pupils of the first-chair player. Unfair as this system might seem, it often yielded superior results. Most of the first-class musicians of a good orchestra, like other musicians, do some teaching, but they tend to be quite selective with their pupils; moreover, the most talented students flock to such players. Consequently their pupils generally are of a very high caliber.

Beginning in the early 1960s, however, pressure from minority groups, government agencies, civil rights organizations, and the newly founded International Conference of Symphony and Opera Musicians forced orchestras to convert to a system of selection that had at least more semblance of fairness. In 1974 New York Times critic Donal Henahan described the new auditioning system adopted by the Metropolitan Opera. Weeks before preliminary auditions, notice of a vacancy was sent to the players' committee (a group selected by the orchestra to act as its representative), and ads were placed in the union periodical, and perhaps also in other media. Test music was sent to candidates in advance of their preliminary audition. For the final audition, judges sat scattered about the hall, to discourage conversation among them, and the candidates played behind black cloth screens. The candidates were forbidden to speak or to tune up from behind the screen, to avoid the possibility of using prearranged signals that revealed their identity to judges. Each judge had one vote, and the panel of judges was made up of conductors and first-chair players, as well as any members of the relevant orchestra section who wanted to participate. Henahan, who attended one such audition, pointed out that the system was not as "blind" as it sounded. Judges did chatter among themselves, and the black curtain screening the candidates was not quite opaque, so that the outlines of the players were discernible. The results for this orchestra, at least, were not markedly favorable to women: In 1977 the Metropolitan Opera had ninety-seven players, ten of them women.

In recent years players who believed themselves discriminated against occasionally instituted legal action. In 1969 two black musicians charged that the New York Philharmonic hired substitutes and extra musicians on the basis of cronyism, and that many of those hired were pupils of orchestra members. Further, they pointed out, only one New York Philharmonic player was black, indicating that blacks were discriminated against in the hiring of permanent member as well as free-lancers. The New York City Human Rights Commission upheld their charge of cronyism but dismissed allegations of discrimination against these two musicians because, it ruled, discrimination in matters regarding artistic judgment is too difficult to prove.

More dramatic was the case of Elayne Jones, who sued the San Francisco Symphony for denying her tenure. Jones, a timpanist, became the only black woman to occupy a first chair in a major American orchestra when she joined the San Francisco Symphony in 1972. She had been professionally active for nearly twenty-five years, most notably at the New York City Opera and in the American Symphony Orchestra. She was recommended for the San Francisco opening by Seiji Ozawa, the orchestra's newly appointed music director. In May 1974 the players' committee, which under the San Francisco Symphony's union contract was the most powerful such committee in the nation, voted to deny tenure to Jones and one other player, a Japanese bassoonist (male), Ryohei Nakagawa. Conductor Ozawa formally dissociated himself from this decision, saying he wanted to keep both players. The union charged coercion, and a poll of the entire orchestra upheld the committee's vote, but both players were invited to re-audition for another trial appointment. Nakagawa took the opportunity and failed the audition; Jones refused and instead brought suit. Reinstated for one year, she agreed the following summer to withdraw the suit if a new vote could be taken by a new committee. That vote was taken in late August 1975, and Jones again was denied tenure. Further, this time Ozawa publicly agreed with the committee decision. And again the legal outcome was indecisive. Because "artistic judgment" was involved, it could not be determined if Jones was actually incompetent, or if she was a victim of discrimination, or if, perhaps, she had become a pawn in a battle for power between Ozawa and the orchestra.[25]

A similar accusation of "cronyism" might be invoked in cases where a husband and wife are engaged by an orchestra. This situation is less rare than one might think. In 1977 the Buffalo Symphony (one of the thirty-one "majors") had seven married couples among its members, and the St. Louis Symphony, a "major" with a fifty-two-week season, had twelve (Cleveland had four, San Francisco three, and Philadelphia and Los Angeles each two).[26] Moreover, at Buffalo nearly one-third of the players were women, and at St. Louis twenty-eight of ninety-nine were, both comparatively high proportions. This variety of cronyism appears to favor women, and it is these orchestras that brought up the American Symphony Orchestra League's survey average to a whopping 24.9 percent women in the major orchestras in the 1974–75 season (versus 18.3 percent ten years earlier).[27] Obviously there are advantages and disadvantages—both personal and professional—in employing a married couple. However, it is interesting to note that during a time when many American colleges and universities (comparable because they, too, are nonprofit institutions employing highly trained professionals) still expressly forbade the simultaneous employment of married couples, some symphony orchestras sanctioned it.

Also during this period the number of women orchestra managers rose considerably. Again according to league statistics, between 1964 and 1974 the number of women managers of metropolitan orchestras never dropped below 11 percent and at times was as high as 33 percent. In the urban and community categories, it ranged from 25 to 54 percent, and in the 1973–74 season more than half of all urban and community orchestra managers were women. However, another writer points out that no major metropolitan or urban orchestra listed in the 1974 directory had a woman music director, and although about one-third had women managers most of these were urban orchestras with low budgets and short seasons.[28] In the major orchestras only one—the New York Philharmonic—had a woman manager (Helen Thompson).

In the concert management field, approximately one-third of managers were women, and slightly fewer than one-third of newspaper music critics were women.[29] One of the most innovative concert managers was Susan Wadsworth, whose Young Concert Artists, founded in 1961, concentrated on presenting little-known young musicians in "informal" concerts in order to bridge the gap between their conservatory and full-fledged concert careers. Among the musicians she helped get started were Pinchas Zukerman, Murray Perahia, Anthony Newman, the Tokyo String Quartet, and Ani Kavafian.[30]

Orchestra management has engaged women since the second half of the nineteenth century. The league cites as the first woman manager of a major orchestra Mrs. Anna Millar, who ran Theodore Thomas's Chicago Orchestra from 1893 to 1897, setting up all its engagements as well as making travel, transportation, and billeting arrangements.[31] But she was not the first. Norma Knüpfel, born in Detroit in 1858, went to California as a child and there married a wine merchant, H. J. A. Stuhr. She organized charity concerts, in both Los Angeles and San Francisco, and later directed a three-year series of concerts of the San Francisco orchestra. She was widowed, remarried, and widowed again. She then took up directing the foreign tours of the Leipzig Philharmonic, which still engaged her in April 1901, and that fall she settled as an independent manager, with offices in New York and Leipzig.

Another nineteenth-century manager was May Valentine, the manager-conductor of a touring opera company. Still another was May Beegle, born in 1887, who organized the Pittsburgh Orchestra Association in order to bring orchestras to Pittsburgh on tour; in 1923 she also founded a concert series there. Lenore Armsby founded the San Francisco Symphony in 1909 and managed it for some years thereafter; Adella Prentice Hughes organized the Cleveland Orchestra in 1918 and ran it until the 1930s; Mrs. L. A. Irish managed the Los Angeles Philharmonic during the 1930s and 1940s. More recent women managers include Ruth O. Seufrert of the Kansas City Philharmonic, Helen Black of the Denver Symphony, Mrs. Hugh McCreery of the Seattle Symphony, Helen Thompson of the New York Philharmonic, and Cathy French of the New Jersey Symphony.

Among the founders of orchestras was Mrs. Davenport Engberg, who started an orchestra and turned over its management to her husband while she concentrated on training its musicians and conducting it. Engberg founded her orchestra in 1911 in Bellingham, Washington, a city of 30,000, and by 1916 it had eighty performers, about half of them women. In May 1917 the *Etude* published her article, "How to Start A Local Symphony Orchestra," and described her as the only "lady conductor" of a symphony orchestra in the world.

Engberg began her career as a violinist, and appeared as soloist with several West Coast orchestras. She claimed that only a violinist could become a conductor; only a violinist could understand the all-important string sections, and only a teacher of violin would have enough students to supply the string sections. She herself gave individual lessons to any section members who needed help.

Her article includes a detailed description of the orchestra's budget. The principal initial expense was for new instruments that had to be purchased—six violas, four cellos, two double basses, and percussion instruments. Music was purchased for a total of about $9,000, and the YMCA auditorium was hired for weekly rehearsals, for $1 per week. A theater rented for a concert cost $140. The orchestra still, after six years, had no oboist or bassoonist; during rehearsal these parts were played by other instruments and for concerts players were imported, for a fee of $60 to $100. The local musicians' union was paid $5 per player, or approximately $125.

Over the years these costs rose, but the orchestra managed to survive without special help until the fifth season, when a wealthy local music lover put up $500 to cover the accumulated deficit. Until then Engberg's husband, a pharmacist, donated his services as manager (and also those of his store's stenographer). At the beginning of the sixth season a proper board was formed. It is not reported how many concerts were given each season, but works such as Schubert's Unfinished Symphony, Beethoven's *Egmont Overture,* and the Prelude to Wagner's *Lohengrin* are mentioned as part of programs.

In the 1930s at least two women founded urban orchestras that they themselves conducted, and which survive today. One was Bertha Roth Walburn Clark, who founded the Knoxville (Tennessee) Orchestra, a fifty-piece ensemble. The other was Grace Kleinhenn Thompson Edmister, who in 1932 founded the Albuquerque Civic Symphony, today called the New Mexico Symphony Orchestra.[32]

Bertha Roth was born on December 8, 1882, in Ohio and graduated from the Cincinnati College of Music in 1902, an accomplished violinist. She married Jamie Walburn and bore two children, Elsa Walburn Stong, who became a pianist, and Lenore Walburn Bryan, a cellist. About 1910 she moved to Knoxville, Tennessee, and soon became active in the city's musical life. She taught violin and voice, coached local opera groups, and founded a Ladies String Quartet. In 1923 she put together a Philharmonic Orchestra, which, however, foundered for lack of funds. In 1925 she tried again and organized the Walburn-Clark Little Symphony (several years after Walburn died, she married flutist-cellist Harold Clark), an ensemble of twenty to twenty-five members.

At first the programs were few in number and modest in content. By March 3, 1927, however, the orchestra presented a full-length symphony (Mozart's Symphony no. 39) in celebration of its new name, the Knoxville Symphony Orchestra (devised to win more financial support). Some years later, in 1935, the orchestra was officially chartered by the State of Tennessee and Bertha Clark, still its conductor, for the first time began to be paid for her services. A symphony society to establish a firmer financial base was organized in October 1941, and the first concert under its aegis was given on December 7, 1941 (the day the Japanese attacked Pearl Harbor).

During the war years Clark continued to maintain her orchestra, performing regularly throughout the state (even at the camp for conscientious objectors at Gatlinburg). After the war, on April 9, 1946, she made her farewell appearance as conductor (although she and her husband continued to play in the orchestra until 1962). The following season Lamar Stringfield served as conductor and established a "pops" series, which won the orchestra a huge following. In 1947 he was replaced by David Van Vactor, who served as music director and conductor until 1972. Under his tenure the orchestra grew to a standard full size—85 to 100 players, many of them faculty members of the University of Tennessee. In 1974 Bertha Clark died. By then the orchestra was under Arpad Jou, who in 1977 was replaced by Zoltan Rosynai. Its budget today is more than $250,000 per year, and it presents seven subscription concerts, two pops concerts, and three pairs of children's concerts each season; in addition, its Women's Guild supports and maintains a Youth Orchestra.

Grace Kleinhenn was born on August 2, 1890, near Defiance, Ohio, and began her music studies with local teachers. At nine she began studying at Defiance College and continued there until she received her bachelor's degree in 1908. Later she studied at the American Conservatory in Chicago and the Juilliard School in New York. She began teaching piano at the age of fifteen and continued for a number of years. In 1912 she married Lewis B. Thompson, a choir director and cellist; they had two children, Robert and Marilyn. But in 1918, Grace Thompson was stricken with tuberculosis, and in a desperate effort to save her life she was taken to New Mexico. She eventually recovered, and in 1923 she began to teach piano and theory at the University of New Mexico. She founded its department of public school music education, and in 1925 she was made head of the university's entire music department. During these years, she became interested in the music and dances of the local Indian tribes and the early Spanish settlers, and she transcribed some of it. From these endeavors grew a four-day pageant, "The First American," produced not only in Albuquerque (annually for some years) but also in a shorter form in New York and in Ohio.

In October 1932 some members of the Rotary Club of Albuquerque decided to provide their city with a civic orchestra, an idea long entertained by a number of local musicians. Pointing to the success of similar organizations in Tulsa and Tucson, the Rotarians decided to establish an orchestra of thirty-five to fifty players, primarily local, and charge a very low admission to concerts (twenty-five cents at the outset) in order to make good music available to everyone. The cost would be underwritten by "patrons" from local businesses and professionals. The committee then asked Grace Thompson, as head of the university music department, and William Kunkel, a fine flutist and also teaching at the university, to form the orchestra. Thompson, who by now had considerable experience conducting the student orchestra, was appointed conductor, and Kunkel assistant conductor. (Kunkel had been principal flute in John Philip Sousa's band for four years, was a band instructor in the army during World War I, and had played with the Cincinnati Symphony as well.)

The new civic orchestra gave its first concert in the university gymnasium on November 30, 1932. There were fifty-eight players, forty-three of them men (including the conductor's husband in the cello section and their daughter Marilyn as harpist). A number of the players had considerable experience; the rest were students and amateurs. Mrs. John D. Clark, "concert-master" [sic], had studied with Jacques Hoffman in Boston and played for four years in the second Orchestral Club of Boston under Georges Longy (see Chapter 5), and was one of the leading violin teachers in Albuquerque. Guy Eaglesfield, principal double bass, came from Tucson to play with the orchestra; he was an orchestra and band instructor there. Cornetist A. J. Schminke had played in Victor Herbert's orchestra for many years, and also in many theater orchestras. Myrlin Payne, violinist, was formerly with the Pittsburgh Symphony and had conducted community orchestras and bands in Kansas.

At its first concert the orchestra played to an audience of 2,000, presenting both classical and semiclassical works. They played Schubert's

Overture to *Rosamunde,* Mozart's Jupiter Symphony, portions of Bizet's *L'Arlésienne Suite* no. 2, Strauss's *Blue Danube Waltz,* and, assisted by New York baritone Robert Castle (spending the winter in New Mexico), arias from Gounod's *Faust* and Verdi's *A Masked Ball.* The concert was a resounding success, and three more were presented during that first season. The following summer Grace Thompson went to the Juilliard School, studying orchestral arranging and conducting with Julius Schmid. She continued to present four or five concerts a year, the admission price being held to 25 cents and the costs underwritten by the city's businesses. The number of players grew to about seventy, and guest artists were regularly imported. In addition to regular programs, the orchestra played on various special occasions, such as the dedication of the first 50,000-kilowatt radio station in Albuquerque, and for the centenary of the San Pedro Mine in 1940 (for that it played underground, inside the mine).

In 1941 Grace Thompson appeared for the first time as piano soloist with the orchestra, performing Constant Lambert's *Rio Grande* for piano, orchestra, and chorus. By then her marriage to Thompson had ended, and the following year she married William R. Edmister, an Ohio businessman, and moved with him to Columbus. She left a healthy organization behind her. William Kunkel took over as conductor for one season, and then was succeeded by several other conductors. Edmister remained in Columbus until 1959, for most of that time teaching at St. Mary's of the Springs College. She visited Albuquerque a number of times and occasionally conducted one of the orchestra's performances. After her husband's death she moved to New York to live with her sister, but in 1970 she decided to return to Albuquerque, where she continued to help the orchestra, now renamed the Albuquerque Symphony. In 1972 its conductor, Yoshima Takeda, invited her to be guest conductor at the orchestra's fortieth anniversary concert, and she conducted it in Schubert's *Rosamunde* overture, with which she had opened the first concert. In 1975 she became one of six New Mexicans receiving the first Governor's Award for achievement in the arts, and the following year she received the highest honor of her alma mater, the Pilgrims' Medal of Defiance College, the seventh graduate so honored (President Dwight D. Eisenhower was one of the others). In 1978 her friends honored her on the sixtieth anniversary of her arrival in New Mexico in 1918 (on a stretcher, given three months to live). She was always grateful to New Mexico and said that one major reason for establishing the orchestra was "because I wanted to give something to that part of the country that had given me my health."

The New Mexico Symphony Orchestra grew still more in the 1970s, becoming a "metropolitan" orchestra. From an initial budget of $500 in 1932, it expanded to $75,000 in 1970 and $450,000 by 1977. In the 1975-76 season it presented 26 regular concerts in Albuquerque and 22 elsewhere in New

Mexico, as well as 187 more ensemble concerts, residences, and demonstrations (about half in Albuquerque). Of these, 149 were especially for children, and 200 took place in parks, libraries, community centers, and other informal settings. The estimated annual audience in 1977 was 100,000.

Not many American orchestras have women conductors. Even in the late 1970s the majority of women who aspired to conducting resigned themselves to choral work or to a low-budget orchestra. One entirely self-taught woman began, in the 1960s, to hire a New York hall from time to time, paying musicians to play under her baton and charging no admission. Considered a recluse and an eccentric, Charlotte Bergen[33] originally began in music as a cellist and gave two well-received recitals in Town Hall. She was educated privately and later said, "I spent 35 years of my life in a little room on the third floor, playing the cello." Her father died in 1936 and thereafter she remained at home, caring for her mother until her death. By then she had gone into the dairy business on the family estate in Bernardsville, New Jersey, building a barn, buying cows, and putting in a pasteurizing plant. The enterprise was successful, but music continued to attract Bergen, and she became increasingly interested in conducting. She began in the local church, where she formed a choir. Then for a time she hired Town Hall in New York once a year for a performance of Monteverdi's *Orfeo.* About 1970 she began to rent Carnegie Hall at least once a season, and by the 1976-77 season she was presenting four concerts a year there. By then Bergen was thought to be in her seventies or older. At one concert she put on Beethoven's *Missa Solemnis,* of which a reviewer wrote, "Miss Bergen's unfussy approach worked best in the more stable stretches, which sometimes accumulated real power."[34] Another program, devoted to Mozart, presented the Jupiter Symphony and a piano concerto with Malcolm Frager as soloist; the orchestra was made up of members of the American Symphony Orchestra. "It's the fulfillment of my life," Bergen told an interviewer. "I consider what I'm doing [is] inviting people to listen to what we're playing.... To me, music is too precious to sell. I respect people who have to sell music to make a living...but it happens that I don't have to. And so, why should I?"

With all respect, one doubts that Bergen could in fact make a living in this way, for few women have succeeded as orchestral conductors. Several had brief flurries of success in Europe in the 1930s. Ruth Kemper, an American, joined the faculty of the Salzburg Conservatory in 1930 and in April 1931 conducted a regular orchestral concert in Vienna, which included Brahms's first symphony, a Chopin concerto, and MacDowell's *Indian Suite.*[35] In the same year another American, Carmen Studer, led the Vienna Symphony in a concert that included Abram Chasins's piano concerto, with the composer as soloist.[36] Married to the eminent conductor Felix Weingartner, Studer in

1933 became the first woman to conduct a major orchestra in France.[37] But as leaders of male orchestras these women represented exceptions, along with Antonia Brico and Ethel Leginska (see Chapter 5) and Nadia Boulanger (Chapter 6).

Choral conducting was somewhat more open to women. In 1926 Margarete Dessoff (1874-1944), a German choral conductor who first came to the United States in 1923, became the first woman to conduct a major New York choral concert, in which she led the Schola Cantorum.[38] She herself had founded both a woman's chorus and a mixed chorus in New York, which in 1929 merged and became the Dessoff Choirs, a long-lived ensemble. She also led other groups, as well as teaching and coaching. But in 1936 an automobile accident cut short her career, and soon afterward she retired.

In the Midwest, Mary Willing Megley became the first woman to conduct the Toledo Music Festival in 1924, leading a 50-piece orchestra and a chorus of 385.[39] About 1919 she had become the regular conductor of the Toledo Choral Society, which throughout the 1920s she led in annual concerts of Handel's *Messiah,* assisted by members of the Detroit Symphony Orchestra.[40] In the 1930s Gena Branscombe became a highly respected choral conductor and founded her own women's chorus (see Chapter 7).

Still more successful was a conductor of the next generation, Margaret Hillis,[41] who founded the Chicago Symphony Chorus and went on to conduct both choral and orchestral programs. Hillis was born in 1921 in Kokomo, Indiana, started piano lessons at the age of five, and by eight knew she wanted to conduct. She studied a number of orchestral and band instruments in high school, playing baritone horn in the band and later double bass in the orchestra at Indiana University. She also made her conducting debut in high school, as assistant conductor of the school orchestra. After earning her bachelor's degree in composition at Indiana, she went to the Juilliard School to study choral conducting with Robert Shaw and Julius Herford, and later became assistant conductor of Shaw's Collegiate Chorale. In 1950 she organized the Tanglewood Alumni Chorus and presented it in a full series of concerts in New York. The group soon became known as the American Concert Choir and Orchestra, and gave a series of concerts and recordings. It concentrated on performing choral works with a small orchestra, a repertory that large ensembles usually ignore entirely; in 1958 it was invited by the U.S. State Department to represent the nation at the Brussels World Fair.

In 1957 music director Fritz Reiner had asked Hillis to organize a permanent chorus worthy of regular performances with the Chicago Symphony, and it began to perform in the 1957-58 season. Made up mostly of professional singers joined by some devoted and talented (and unpaid) amateurs, the chorus in its first decade appeared in more than a hundred regular subscription concerts, as well as performing with the orchestra on tour in New York and elsewhere. Meanwhile Hillis also taught (at the Union Theological Seminary and Juilliard School), founded the American Choral Foundation, and worked at various times as a conductor and choral director with the American Opera Society, New York City Opera, Santa Fe Opera, and Cleveland Orchestra Chorus. In 1962, after twelve years of residence in New York, she moved back to the Midwest.

Inevitably Hillis's involvement with training choruses for choral-orchestral performances led her to orchestral conducting. In 1976 she became the first woman to conduct a regular Chicago Symphony subscription concert, in the world premiere of Alan Stout's *Passion* for chorus, soloists, and orchestra. By then she had often conducted the Chicago orchestra for special occasions and in pops concerts, and had substituted for the regular conductor (Rafael Kubelik) in 1972 for performances of Handel's *Jephtha*. In 1977 she made headlines when she stepped in at the last minute to replace ailing conductor Georg Solti and conducted the Chicago Symphony, appearing in New York, in the very long and difficult Symphony no. 8 of Gustav Mahler. (It is nicknamed "Symphony of a Thousand" because it uses such large forces: enlarged orchestra, double chorus, eight soloists, and a children's chorus.) Her performance was widely praised. During the late 1970s Hillis also worked as resident conductor of the Chicago Civic Orchestra and music director of the Elgin (Illinois) Symphony Orchestra (a community orchestra), accepted an increasing number of guest conducting assignments, and served as professor of conducting and head of the choral department at Northwestern University.

A contemporary of Hillis's, who confined herself entirely to choral conducting, was Lorna Cooke de Varon, who in 1978 celebrated her thirtieth anniversary as director of choruses at the New England Conservatory of Music.[42] Born about 1922 in Illinois, she moved with her parents to Rhode Island at the age of fifteen, and remained in the Boston area from the time she went to Wellesley College. While a student at Wellesley, she studied theory and harmony with Nadia Boulanger (see Chapter 6), as well as voice, piano, and organ with other teachers. She went on to get a master's degree from Radcliffe College, where she studied choral conducting with G. Wallace Woodworth. She then became assistant professor of music at Bryn Mawr College and conducted the chorus there. She spent two summers studying choral conducting with Robert Shaw at Tanglewood, and in 1953 she joined the Tanglewood faculty, with which she spent a number of summers; she was in charge of the Tanglewood Festival Chorus, and she taught choral conducting to many students. In 1947 she had joined the faculty of the New England Conservatory and a year later became its director of choruses. Her 135-voice chorus, founded in 1950, sang and recorded with the Boston Symphony Orchestra and premiered the works of contemporary composers such as Irving Fine, Daniel Pinkham, and Donald Martino. From the late 1960s on it began to tour abroad as well, making several tours of Europe, an exchange tour to the Soviet Union, and in 1978 a tour of Israel. "Working with student singers has great frustrations and rewards," she told an interviewer in 1978. "My one regret about my career is that I never founded an adult chorus." With young singers, she pointed out, one must be careful at any sign of fatigue lest their voices be injured, but because many works are new to them there is a rewarding freshness and excitement to their performances.

In orchestral conducting a small number of women were establishing themselves in the 1960s and 1970s, mostly with smaller orchestras.[43] Margaret Harris, who made her debut as a pianist in 1946 at the age of three (she played fourteen classical selections before a church audience in Chicago) and appeared for some years as a soloist in Europe and the United States, became in 1971 the first black woman to conduct the Chicago Symphony. The following year she appeared with the Los Angeles Philharmonic in the premiere of her own piano concerto. Her conducting career began on Broadway, where she became known for her work in a number of successful musicals, among them *Hair, Raisin,* and *Two Gentlemen of Verona.* Another black conductor, Joyce Johnson, also began on Broadway. An excellent trumpeter, she became assistant conductor and principal trumpet of the Oakland (California) Symphony Orchestra, where she was responsible for conducting rehearsals, youth and pop concerts, and one regular subscription concert each season. She also founded the Sinfonia of Northern California, a chamber orchestra, which she conducted. Another woman active in California in the 1970s was Frances Steiner, who began her career as a cellist and performed under conductors Eugene Ormandy, Pablo Casals, and Alexander Schneider. She studied conducting and composition with Nadia Boulanger and became music director of the Compton (California) Civic Symphony; she also formed a chamber ensemble, the Baroque Consortium.

Beatrice Brown, a violinist who studied conducting with Serge Koussevitsky, Leopold Stokowski, and Hermann Scherchen, became one of the first women to hold a permanent conducting post when she took over the Scranton (Pennsylvania) Philharmonic in 1962. In that same year she received the following reply from a manager whom she had asked to handle her career:

For reasons unknown to us, we have never been able to interest managements [of orchestras] in women conductors. There seems to be no logical reason for this, but the situation exists, nevertheless. We are perfectly certain that many women conductors are far superior to the males but since we have had no luck at all in handling women conductors, it seems useless to encourage you to have any kind of a career with us.[44]

Brown continued as music director with the Scranton orchestra for a decade, and later took over the Ridgefield (Connecticut) Symphonette. Carolyn Hills, who did postgraduate study in conducting at the International Academy Mozarteum in Salzburg (where she was the only woman and the only American accepted), founded the New York Music Society, and became head of the United Nations International School in New York, and also music director of the Livingston (New Jersey) Symphony Orchestra.

All of these women seemed to agree that conducting is an extremely difficult and competitive field for anyone, considering the combination of skills, talent, and personality it requires, the limited number of conducting posts available, and the straitened finances of many (perhaps most) American orchestras. But most of them also felt that it was at least twice as difficult for women to succeed in this traditionally male-dominated profession. Even so, some headway was made. In May 1978 the Juilliard School received a $3 million grant to endow a training program for young American conductors. Four to six musicians were to be chosen annually by audition, and, it was specifically stated, female candidates would be welcome. And in the summer of 1978, one of the five fellowships for studying conducting at the Berkshire Music Center at Tanglewood—among the most sought after fellowships in the world of music—was given, for the first time in a dozen years, to a woman (organist Patricia Handy of Baltimore).

Among the younger orchestral conductors beginning to become known in the late 1970s was Victoria Bond,[45] the first woman admitted to Juilliard as a doctoral candidate in conducting (she received her degree in 1977). Born on May 6, 1949, Bond began composing music at the age of five. She attended the Mannes School of Music in New York and received her bachelor's degree at the University of Southern California, where she studied composition with Ingolf Dahl. She then returned to New York and the Juilliard School, where she studied composition with Roger Sessions and conducting with Sixten Ehrling. Initially she was interested chiefly in conducting performances of her own works, but she soon found herself pursuing it for its own sake. At Juilliard she became conductor of the Juilliard Repertory Orchestra, as well as assistant conductor of the Contemporary Music Ensemble and the Juilliard Orchestra. Meanwhile she also continued to compose, producing songs, orchestra works, and chamber music. In 1977 she was commissioned by the Pennsylvania Ballet to compose a full-length work to open their season, *Equinox.*

Unlike some older women conductors, Bond believed that conducting was indeed open to anyone with enough talent. In an article published in 1976, in which women musicians were asked for their "advice," she said:

I would encourage anyone, man or woman, who is interested in conducting to pursue it. It is a long road, since there are many skills which must be mastered before you even hope to stand before an orchestra, but it is tremendously rewarding....In the beginning no one believed that I would "make it" and assumed that I would quit because it was a field that just wasn't open to women, but I think that I can safely say now that I have proved to them that they were wrong. It can be done, and I know because I am doing it.[46]

On May 6, 1978, Bond made her most important appearance to date when she conducted the Pittsburgh Symphony Orchestra, and a few months later she was appointed conducting assistant of that orchestra and music director of the Pittsburgh Youth Symphony. She also served as music director of the New Amsterdam Symphony Orchestra in New York City.

For those instrumentalists who choose solo careers rather than orchestral jobs the path is also rough, for both men and women. At least one such woman, pianist Susan Starr, maintained that there is active prejudice against women, whether they are soloists or orchestra players. Starr herself, after graduation from the Curtis Institute in 1961, auditioned before one of the top managers. He was very impressed with her and said, "If only you were a man I'd sign you in a minute." She was able to obtain a manager only after winning several competitions, a Bronze Medal in the First International Mitropoulos Competition in New York and Second Prize in the renowned Tchaikovsky Competition in Moscow (in 1962; she was one of twelve finalists, half of them women).[47] But pianists and violinists were discussed at length in Chapters 2 and 3. What about some of the other instruments?

In the late 1970s a small number of performers, mostly women in their thirties, seemed to be succeeding in a solo career, augmented by work in chamber ensembles and other activities. One was harpist Heidi Lehwalder,[48] who won the Avery Fischer Award in 1976. Born in 1950 in Seattle, she was given a harp at the age of seven by her mother, a Seattle Symphony cellist who loved chamber music and was always looking for a good harpist. Heidi took to the instrument and was encouraged to try a solo career, by both her family and Milton Katims, music director of the Seattle Symphony. She avoided playing in an orchestra except for three years during her teens, when she played with the Youth Symphony of Seattle; she knew that most orchestral harpists do not like to do solo work and there were relatively few solo harpists around. She herself made forty-seven solo appearances with the Seattle Symphony. She spent several summers at Rudolf Serkin's summer school and festival in Marlboro, Vermont, and in time became a mem ber of its touring chamber ensemble, Music from Marlboro. Through it she became friends with two other members, flutist Paula Robison and her husband, violist Scott Nickrenz, and in 1972 the three musicians formed the Orpheus Trio, which was soon giving as many as forty concerts per season. The Fischer Award entitled Lehwalder to a concert with the New York Philharmonic. Of her performance, Peter Davis said she displayed more aggressive assertiveness than most harpists, and with her the delicacy and refinement customarily associated with harp music took second place to structural clarity, forceful musical gestures, and a willingness to take technical chances; he deemed her a "resourceful and sensitive musician as well as a thoroughly accomplished virtuoso."

Paula Robison,[49] flutist of the Orpheus Trio, was in the late 1970s one of the most successful solo flute recitalists of either sex. Born in 1941 in Nashville, Tennessee, and raised in Los Angeles, she began piano studies at an early age. At eleven she was given a flute, which she later said she knew at once would be her instrument. She played all through high school, in student orchestras and little recitals. She attended the University of Southern California and then was heard by flutist Julius Baker, who persuaded her to study with him at Juilliard. Accepted as a scholarship student, she stayed at Juilliard for four years, graduating in 1963. Soon after she married cellist Robert Sylvester, but they were divorced six years later. Meanwhile she studied with the great French flutist Marcel Moyse, and then went to Marlboro. In 1964 she was a prizewinner in the Munich Flute Competition, and two years later, in 1966, she won first prize at the Geneva International Competition, the first American ever to win this honor. Even so, she still had doubts about succeeding as a soloist. But, she later said, "I could have done the safe thing and joined an orchestra. If I had done that, mine wouldn't have been such a rocky road. But I took the risk."

For a time Robison played some solo recitals with pianist Samuel Sanders, and then she and Sylvester formed a chamber group with violist Scott Nickrenz, his pianist wife Joanna, and violinist Donald Wellenstein. The Nickrenz and Sylvester marriages both dissolved, and in 1971 Robison was remarried, to Nickrenz. In 1970 the Chamber Music Society of Lincoln Center had been formed and its director, Charles Wadsworth, invited Robison to be one of its eleven resident artists. In 1978 she was still with the society, as well as giving about a hundred solo recitals a year, frequently performing at festivals such as Spoleto and Marlboro, and also recording and teaching.

Not permanently affiliated with a chamber group but often appearing as a guest artist with established groups, as well as in solo recitals and with orchestras, was an almost exact contemporary of Robison's, violist Karen Ann Phillips.[50] Born on October 29, 1942, in Dallas, Texas, Phillips attended schools there and in 1960 went to the Eastman School of Music, from which she received a bachelor's degree in 1964. She then spent a summer at Yale's Summer School of Music, a year at Philadelphia's Curtis Institute, and two years at Juilliard, from which she received a postgraduate diploma in 1967. From 1969 to 1971 she was an "Affiliate Artist" with the Los Angeles Music Center, and from 1971 to 1972 with the Worcester (Massachusetts) Arts Association; in these capacities she gave several hundred recitals, lectures, workshops, and demonstrations at schools, service clubs, church groups, and women's clubs.

Throughout the 1970s Phillips pursued an active career as soloist, becoming known especially for her performances of contemporary music (much of it extremely difficult from a technical standpoint) and frequently giving premieres of new works for her instrument. A number of composers wrote pieces specifically for her, among them Morton Feldman, Netty Simons, Marga Richter, David Bedford, Claire Polin, and Elisabeth Lutyens. In an article on "Today's Viola"[51] Phillips described some of the difficulties of the new literature: Luciano Berio's *Sequenza VI* calls for random wide sliding of the fingers and quick alternation between the ordinary and the harmonic positions; Tonia Scherchen's *Lien* demands six different kinds of pizzicato (plucking of the strings); David Bedford's *Spillihpnerak* (the title is Karen Phillips's name spelled backward) calls for a kind of bowing in which the hairs of the bow are loosened, the bow is reversed, and the body of the viola slips between the hairs and wood of the bow, so that the hair can move across all four strings (enabling the player to sound four notes at the same time).

In addition to performing, Phillips herself composed (songs for voice and piano, orchestral works, and chamber music). She also taught, made many recordings, and in 1975 began a weekly half-hour radio program on New York's municipal station, "Overture to Women," devoted to women musicians and composers. "The people who have the worst time," Phillips once told an interviewer, "are the women composers who express themselves on music paper and sit all day in their ivory towers putting ink on paper and don't understand why their music isn't performed." Phillips believed women composers need all the help they can get, and her radio program, for which she worked without pay, was a step in that direction.

Summarizing the work of the instrumental soloist, trumpeter Carole Dawn Reinhart, an American woman who toured widely in the 1960s and 1970s, said there are three main qualifications for success: excellent training, a great deal of varied performing experience, and a "strong desire-almost-to-obsession" to succeed. Musicianship, she believed, is also important, but it can be developed through training and experience. As for innate talent, it is generally overrated, the individual work required far exceeding any natural ability. And finally, she added: "As a woman trumpeter I have the advantage of being a novelty and often have been used for this purpose. It's much more difficult to be taken seriously. That can only be accomplished through performing not *as well* but *better* than men."[52]

Unfortunately, an honest statement like Reinhart's can be—and often has been—dismissed by saying it is simply an excuse, that if this or that woman *really* played as well as this or that man, she would have an equal chance of getting his job. Because musical ability is to some extent a matter of subjective judgment, such arguments are difficult to counter. And it is for this reason that so many women musicians are reluctant to admit that they face job discrimination. It is simply too hard to prove, and they fear that if they admit lack of success, it will be blamed on their inferior ability. Yet when more than half of all music students are female, and some 45 percent of all American women are in the labor force, surely something other than lack of ability must be keeping the representation of women in the top echelons of professional music down to 10 to 15 percent.

# 11 TEACHING MUSIC

When we come to the regular music-lessons of the children,
we see that this is nearly all done by women, and rightly
so, because this is woman's sphere. Probably if parents
were asked why they engaged a lady teacher in preference
to a man, the general answer would be that it was cheaper.
Unfortunately this is true, but it is not just. Work of equal
merit should receive equal compensation, regardless of sex.
But, in truth, pay is not the determining factor in this case.
Women teach children because they are better fitted for the
work than men. They are in closer touch with childhood,
and can therefore work along the line of the child's
sympathies....Of course, some of our women teachers will
work with more advanced students, but that is a work
which men can do equally well—in some cases, perhaps,
better.

—Daniel Batchellor, *Etude,* September 1901

In 1977 there were about 2,400 members in Local No. 9-535—the Boston
local—of the American Federation of Musicians. Very few of them made
their living exclusively from music, and nearly all of the 350 or so members
whose work was primarily in classical (as opposed to popular) music were
also teaching, either privately or at one or more schools, conservatories, or
universities.[1] Much the same was true for composers; practically none could
make a decent living from composition alone. As composer Nancy Van de
Vate pointed out, colleges and universities are the patrons of the twentieth
century, and teaching positions are the principal means of financial support
for contemporary composers.[2] Composer Shulamit Ran agreed; earn whatever credentials you need to get a good teaching position, she advised, for
you cannot earn enough to live from composition alone.[3]

It is as teachers that women musicians have been most visible. Women began to teach music in America in the eighteenth century, or perhaps even earlier. Though the masters of the singing schools were invariably men, private music teachers frequently were women, as is evident from the advertisements carried in eighteenth-century newspapers and journals. Elisabeth von Hagen and Sophia Hewitt both advertised themselves as music teachers in the early 1800s (see Chapters 1 and 3). Moreover, music was part of the curriculum at many of the private schools for girls at this time. For example, at Mme Addiks's Female Academy at 97 Chestnut Street in Philadelphia, "music either on the piano or harp" was offered.[4]

The practice of holding musical conventions, where music teachers met annually and exchanged information, was begun by Lowell Mason in Boston in the late 1820s and was well established by the late 1830s. And women participated along with men; the 1838 meeting was attended by ninety-six men and forty-two women.[5] Nor was the teaching of music, by then widespread in the Boston public schools as well as in private schools, confined to the East Coast. By 1856 San Francisco had a Mrs. G. Waldo teaching music (along with twenty-three men teachers), and two years later it boasted seven women teachers (and thirteen men).[6]

By the mid-nineteenth century full-scale conservatories of music were being established, among them the Chicago Conservatory and Peabody Institute of Music (both founded in 1857), the New England Conservatory, Chicago Musical College, and Cincinnati Conservatory (all founded in 1867), and the Philadelphia Conservatory (1877).[7] Smaller, shorter-lived institutions had preceded them; for example, a Miss Wieth opened a music school in Chicago in 1838.[8] And finally, universities began to offer music courses—Harvard in 1862, Northwestern in 1865, Oberlin in 1867 (though it already had a chair of sacred music, established in 1835).[9]

Though there are no exact figures available, it seems safe to assume that for every woman who taught in a music school of some kind there were at least a half-dozen who taught privately, in their own homes or their pupils' homes. Teaching, especially teaching of the young, was considered both respectable and appropriate for a woman, and an occupation she could pursue part time without neglecting her family obligations. Moreover, music was considered one of the social graces, along with embroidery and French, and so was particularly appropriate for a woman teacher. Women were considered patient and sympathetic, important qualities for a teacher. On the other hand, women teachers often did not regard their work as a permanent or serious occupation, and even when they taught primarily to earn their livelihood, their qualifications were sometimes very minimal. Then (as today) there was no objective standard to separate the good from the indifferent or poor teacher. In part because of this lack of standards and in part owing to traditional sex stereotypes, teaching music tended to have low status. As Belle Squire pointed out in the *Etude* in 1907, if music teaching was genteel enough for women, the man who taught was showing that he lacked something. And music teaching did indeed become a predominantly female occupation. It is estimated that in 1870 60 percent of all music teachers were women;[10] by 1909 the *Etude* believed that figure to be 75 to 80 percent.[11]

Although the numbers of private teachers are inexact, the record for the conservatories is better preserved, and indeed, a number of conservatories were founded and directed by women in the second half of the nineteenth century. Among these were the Hershey School of Musical Art, founded in Chicago around 1876 by singer and voice teacher Sara B. Hershey (later the wife of Clarence Eddy),[12] the National Conservatory of Music in New York, founded in 1885 by Jeannette Thurber, and, perhaps most important, the Cincinnati Conservatory of Music, founded in 1867 by Clara Baur and directed, after her death, by her niece, Bertha Baur.

Cincinnati, with a large German population, was a music center very early on, and it had had music schools for some time. About 1830 Mr. and Mrs. W. Nixon founded a Musical Seminary; Mr. Nixon wrote *A Guide to Instruction on the Pianoforte* (1834), and young ladies attending the seminary were taught theory, in addition to voice and piano.[13] The Cincinnati Conservatory, however, was a much more ambitious undertaking.[14] Clara Baur (1835–1912), a native of Stuttgart, Germany, wanted to establish a music school on the lines of the great European conservatories. She herself had studied piano and theory at the Stuttgart Music School and began to teach piano while in Cincinnati on an extended visit to her brother Theodore, who had settled there. During this visit, she also studied voice with Caroline Rivé, mother of Julia Rivé-King (see Chapter 3). Deciding to establish a music school in Cincinnati, Baur returned to Europe about 1858 to study the teaching methods at her old school in Germany and also in Paris. She returned to America and in 1867 began her school in a few rooms rented from the Misses Nourse's School for Young Ladies.

From the first Baur established separate departments and hired both European and American musicians for her faculty. The teachers and students presented frequent concerts, and the school also included a teacher-training course (so-called normal training) to prepare students for teaching. A children's department (for teaching youngsters after school hours) was opened in 1870. Cincinnati was one of the first conservatories to set up a residence for women students, and it was one of the first to conduct a special summer school, for both local students and those coming a considerable distance. Drama, literature, and languages were taught, as well as harmony, counterpoint, composition, voice, church music, and the various instruments. The school even had a placement bureau to help its graduates find jobs. By 1902 more than 1,000 students were enrolled, and the faculty numbered more than 50. Among the artists who often visited the conservatory were Lilli Lehmann, Franz Kneisel, Leopold Stokowski, and Enrico Caruso (who called it his "little home").

Clara Baur's niece, Bertha Baur (1858–1940), originally intended to become a physician, but in June 1876, immediately after graduation from high school, she came to visit her aunt. Somehow she was persuaded to give up her original ambition and stay on as her aunt's assistant, which she remained for more than thirty-five years. (Allegedly she also was persuaded to remain unmarried, for the sake of the family and the school.) When Clara died, she bequeathed the school and its directorship to her niece, and in her able hands it continued to prosper. The instrumental departments were expanded, and players from the Cincinnati Symphony frequently came to teach their respective instruments. The opera department grew as well, with entire productions being mounted. In 1930 Bertha Baur retired from active management of the school and presented it as a gift to the City of Cincinnati through the Institute of Fine Arts.

In 1878 Cincinnati had acquired a second conservatory, the Cincinnati College of Music. Its directorship was offered to Theodore Thomas, by then well on his way to becoming one of the most respected musicians in the country. He accepted and gave the school a good start, establishing an orchestra, quartet, and chorus, but he felt the school was too commercially oriented—it accepted anyone as a pupil, for any length of time—and after two years he resigned.[15] The college survived and thrived, and after decades of rivalry it merged, in 1955, with the conservatory.

Several other women founded music schools or departments. May Garretson Evans, a music critic for the *Baltimore Sun,* wanted the Peabody Conservatory to organize a preparatory department (to teach music after regular school hours to children enrolled elsewhere). She prepared a detailed plan for such a department, but, since nothing came of it, she and her sister opened a school of their own in 1894. It proved so successful that in 1899 their school was merged with the Peabody and became its preparatory department. Evans herself headed the department until 1929, when she retired.[16]

The Manhattan School of Music in New York was founded by Janet Daniels Schenck in 1917, and she served as its director until 1956. A graduate of the New York School of Social Work and the American Institute of Applied Music, Schenck had studied music abroad as well; the pianist Harold Bauer was among her teachers. She taught on a volunteer basis at a settlement house on New York's upper East Side until World War I, when all but essential community services were discontinued to fund the war effort. Rather than disappoint the hundred or so students who studied at the settlement house, she set about to organize a school of music and in

1917 founded the Neighborhood Music School. In 1918 Schenck persuaded Bauer and the cellist Pablo Casals to become the first members of the school's Artist Auxiliary Board, and she engaged a talented faculty. In 1938 the school, which by then attracted students from the entire metropolitan area, changed its name to the Manhattan School of Music, and today it is a full-sized conservatory, granting degrees up to the doctorate. Schenck died in 1976, at the age of ninety-three.

Another New York musical institution, the Music School of the Henry Street Settlement, owed its existence to Grace Harriet Spofford (1887–1974). A graduate of Smith College and the Peabody Conservatory, from which she held diplomas in both piano and organ, Spofford taught at Peabody from 1914 to 1924 and then served as dean of the Curtis Institute in Philadelphia until 1931. In 1935 she became director of the Henry Street Settlement Music School, where she remained until 1954.[17]

Perhaps best known of all these women music educators was Angela Diller (1877–1968), born in Brooklyn, New York, and educated at Columbia University, where she studied with Edward MacDowell and Percy Goetschius, and also in Germany.[18] From 1899 to 1916 she headed the theory department of New York's Music School Settlement, and then was in charge of music education for five years at the David Mannes School (now the Mannes College of Music). In 1921 she and another teacher at Mannes, Elizabeth Quaile (1874–1951), founded their own school, the Diller-Quaile School of Music, still in existence. The two women also collaborated on a famous piano-teaching series, the Diller-Quaile books, which are still used today. Diller alone also wrote several other books on theory and harmony.

The majority of students in the conservatories were girls. In 1888, for example, the New England Conservatory graduates were: in piano, twenty-five women, three men; in voice, twenty-nine women, three men; in organ, four women, three men. This disproportion was said to be even more marked in western (i.e., midwestern) schools of music.[19] In 1902 New England graduated fifty-six women and twelve men. Like the Cincinnati Conservatory, it had a residence for out-of-town women students; an ad in the *Musical Herald* of March 1886 announced that its new home on Franklin Square had "elegant accommodations for 500 lady students."

Today women students continue to outnumber men in American conservatories. In 1964 it was estimated that women constituted about 60 percent of the total;[20] at the University of California at Berkeley between 1966 and 1969, 58 percent of music majors on the undergraduate level were women (but women comprised only 28 percent of the graduate students and 0 percent of the tenured faculty).[21]

At the Cincinnati Conservatory the men teachers outnumbered the women considerably. Not so at the Detroit Institute of Music, founded in 1894, where women teachers outnumbered men eight to five: piano, four women;

violin, one woman, one man; viola, one man; cello, harmony, and composition, one man; normal classes (music education), one woman; ensemble classes, one woman, two men.

Women may have outnumbered men as music teachers in the 1890s, but nonetheless they took a back seat in the affairs of the Music Teachers National Association (MTNA), which held its first annual meeting in 1877 (though women often did play a more prominent role in the local chapters). Thus the fourth annual meeting of the MTNA, held in Buffalo in the summer of 1880, did not include a single woman's name in either its very detailed program or its list of officers. In contrast, at the annual meeting of the Music Teachers State Association of Indiana, held in Franklin in June 1880, the program included a presentation on "How to Keep Pupils Interested" by piano teacher Miss R. R. Ebright and another on what music teachers should know and teach by Mrs. W. E. Bates of the Columbus (Indiana) Conservatory.[22]

In 1884 the MTNA, in an attempt to set standards for music teachers, established an American College of Musicians, which was to certify teachers on the basis of examinations. The committee for this college, made up of the leading music teachers in the association, included four women: pianist Amy Fay (see Chapter 3); two prominent midwestern voice teachers, Clara Brinkerhoff and Sara Hershey Eddy; and a New York voice teacher, Mme L. Cappiani (originally Luisa Kapp-Young), who served as the only woman examiner for the college. Through the 1890s the MTNA continued to be run by men, even though most of its members were women. In the local associations, however, women often held office, and the programs of the national conventions occasionally included a woman performer or two (notably pianist Fannie Bloomfield-Zeisler, who appeared a number of times).

In 1897 the MTNA added a "Woman's Department," directed by Florence Clinton Sutro (1865–1906). Sutro, a former pupil of William Mason and Dudley Buck, was an excellent pianist and also a composer. A woman of talent and means who had long been active in local music clubs, she married Theodore Sutro, a prominent New York lawyer, in 1884, and she later published a book, *Women in Music and Law* (1895). For the MTNA annual convention held in New York in June 1897, Sutro set up a program of papers and compositions by music club women. At the end of this program a meeting was held, and she was elected president of a temporary federation of these musical societies and was urged to form a permanent federation of all clubs in the United States devoted to music.[23]

Local music clubs had sprung up all over America during the second half of the nineteenth century. They served a number of purposes. For those women who loved music but could not, for one reason or another, attempt a professional career, the club was a rewarding outlet. At the very least it fulfilled a social function. For music teachers and other professionals in small towns and rural areas, the club provided performance opportunities and a chance to work with other musicians, amateur and professional. And the clubs played a role in their communities, for not only did they present concerts by members but they raised money to buy instruments and import singers and instrumentalists (sometimes entire orchestras). Last but by no means least, the clubs were educational for their members. A whole series of meetings would be devoted to the study of a single composer's works, a single musical form, or a period of music history—subjects not universally taught in rural (or even urban) nineteenth-century America. Members were encouraged to perform and also to compose, and their compositions were performed. In her book Florence Sutro declared that America had several thousand women composers; in large part they were members of music clubs.

The events of the Columbian Exposition (Chicago World's Fair) of 1893 included an eight-session assembly of women's music clubs from all over the United States. Out of this grew a movement to organize the clubs nationally.[24] Rose Fay Thomas, wife of conductor Theodore Thomas and sister of Amy Fay, had long been active in music clubs in Chicago and favored the formation of a national body. But somehow ill feeling sprang up between her and Florence Sutro, and she had enough supporters so that not Sutro but Thomas's candidate, Mrs. Edwin T. Uhl, was elected president of the new federation. One of the unfortunate aspects of their disagreement was that it was aired through a number of letters printed in national music journals, which, although it gave the music clubs movement publicity, portrayed it in the light of a petty squabble.

Nevertheless, the National Federation of Music Clubs did get off the ground, and it grew and continues to function to the present day, a strong supporter of women musicians and composers. Fanny Morris Smith, writing in the *Etude* of July 1909, chronicled some of its activities at that time: It offered a bureau of reciprocity, which published a list of members of all clubs in the federation who were willing to give recitals for either expenses only or a small fee; a program exchange, which made available to all clubs a well-prepared scheme of programs; a plan of study, making available programs of study of various aspects of music; a circulating library of scores; and a well-tested constitution and bylaws prepared for new clubs. In addition, in 1907 the National Federation inaugurated a competition for American composers, offering cash prizes in three categories of composition.

In succeeding years these activities were considerably expanded. By 1977 the federation had an estimated 600,000 members in 4,500 local music clubs, and 50 state associations, as well as some individual members. Dedicated to fostering young talent, it held annual Junior Festivals, offered five $1,500 biennial awards in Young Artist Auditions, conducted annual

Student Auditions, sponsored composition contests on all levels (adult, young composer, junior), and granted numerous awards and scholarships. It was an active promoter of American music, sponsoring an annual February Parade of American music. It issued several publications, the most important of which was *Music Clubs Magazine,* and it sponsored a national music week each year. And finally, to help American women musicians specifically, it sponsored a Decade of Women (1975–85), chaired by composer Julia Smith (see Chapter 7), which helped promote performances of works by American women composers.

Although music clubs and teachers' organizations could raise standards and educate popular taste, it is on an individual basis that a music teacher can have the greatest impact, and few had more than a Russian-born pianist who taught at the Juilliard School for a half-century. She was Rosina Lhevinne (1880–1976),[25] a child prodigy who had studied at the Moscow Conservatory, winning its Gold Medal in 1898. That same year she married Josef Lhevinne and immediately stopped playing in public, aside from occasional appearances in two-piano performances with her husband, until after his death. In the meantime she devoted herself to furthering his career as a concert pianist and to assisting him with his students. By the outbreak of World War I the Lhevinnes were living in Berlin, and after the war they emigrated to the United States. They both joined the faculty of the Institute of Musical Art (later the Juilliard School). Actually, it was Josef Lhevinne who had a separate contract with the school, but she always took over his students during his frequent tours, and after he died, in 1944, she was asked to stay on her own account.

Lhevinne always maintained that it was her husband who was the great musician and the great teacher. Though they sometimes disagreed on various fine points, even in front of a pupil, they usually conducted their arguments in Russian and presented a united front in English. When he died, Rosina Lhevinne resolved to carry on what she regarded as "his tradition," but she became a brilliant success on her own. Her most renowned pupil was Van Cliburn, who won the Tchaikovsky Competition in 1958, the first American ever to do so. Her other famous pupils included John Browning, Daniel Pollack, Misha Dichter, Olegna Fuschi, David Bar-Illan, and Garrick Ohlsson. In addition to these well-known names, hundreds of others benefited from her untiring devotion to bring out the best in her pupils.

Lhevinne's approach to music was very open-minded. Rather than insisting on particular techniques or interpretations, she emphasized beautiful tone. She tried to pass on the great romantic tradition of nineteenth-century piano playing, as represented by Anton Rubinstein, Sergei Rachmaninoff, and Josef Hofmann, all of whom she had known personally. She also resumed, after 1945, her own career as a performer, appearing as soloist in several concertos at the Aspen Music Festival (beginning in 1956) and more often in chamber music concerts, especially (for about a decade) with the then newly formed Juilliard Quartet. In 1961, at the age of eighty-one, she appeared with the New York Philharmonic, playing the difficult Chopin Concerto in E minor. Many of her pupils came to hear this performance, some fearing that their beloved teacher might have overreached herself; but she played beautifully, demonstrating that she could still practice what she taught. Lhevinne continued to teach well into her nineties. When she finally died, at ninety-six, Peter Mennin, then president of Juilliard, said, "She was quite simply one of the greatest teachers of this century. With her passing, a whole concept of teaching and performing goes with her."

Another European-born musician who devoted herself to the survival of the works of her composer-husband after his death, and who also found a new teaching career late in life, was Vally Weigl.[26] Born in Austria in 1894, she studied musicology at the University of Vienna with Guido Adler, piano with Richard Robert, and composition with Karl Weigl, whom she later married. After completing her studies, she began to teach as Robert's assistant and also at the University's Musicological Institute. Summers she worked with visiting students who came to the Salzburg Festival. She also performed, usually together with her husband in chamber and piano duo recitals.

In 1938 the Weigls and their young son moved to New York, where they continued to compose and perform. Karl Weigl died in 1949, and his widow took up the task of collecting and disseminating his music. Around this time a serious fall, resulting in orthopedic surgery and a long recovery period, turned her to a new career. At mid-life she enrolled in Columbia University and in 1953 earned a master's degree in music therapy, rehabilitation through the use of music for patients with physical and emotional illnesses. Weigl did her on-the-job training at Columbia Presbyterian Psychiatric Institute, and at the same time taught at the American Theater Wing. She then worked for ten years at New York Medical College, where she became chief music therapist and inaugurated a dance therapy department. She also lectured widely in Europe and America, taught for fourteen years at Roosevelt Cerebral Palsy School, and directed research projects concerned with psychiatric patients and residents of an old-age home. In 1975 she was engaged to teach at the New School for Social Research in New York.

Throughout these years Weigl went on composing, principally choral works, chamber music, and songs. Her compositions, which have been widely performed and published, include the clarinet trio *New England Suite* (1954); the song cycle *Nature Moods* (1956), for soprano, clarinet (or flute), and violin; *Requiem for Allison* (1971), for soprano and string quartet, a brief work in memory of a student shot by the National Guard at Kent State University in 1970; and *The People, Yes!* (1976), a chamber cantata setting poems by Carl Sandburg.

Becoming a world-famous teacher, like Lhevinne, or mastering a specialty such as music therapy, like Weigl, is not in everyone's grasp. At the top of the pecking order for music teachers is the institution of higher learning—the college or university that grants degrees up to a doctorate, or the top-flight conservatory (such as Juilliard, Eastman, Peabody, and Curtis). In these composers and performers alike find a reliable income and assured professional status. And there are fringe benefits, too. The academic institution provides access to experienced performers and opportunities for recitals where new music can be introduced, before audiences more tolerant than the average symphony subscription audience. Moreover, an academic affiliation makes it easier for composers to obtain grants and fellowships. Indeed, some awards are so constituted that they virtually require an institution to "administer" the grant.

Though women students in these institutions still outnumbered men in the 1970s, their faculties were predominantly male. In an article concerning the status of men and women engaged in teaching music on the college level,[27] Adrienne Fried Block (herself a professor of music) indicated that the disparity between the number of women trained and the number of women employed was enormous. Though women earned 55 percent of all bachelor's degrees in music, 47.6 percent of all master's degrees, and 16.3 percent of all doctorates, they made up only 21.4 percent of music faculties on the college level. Moreover, those women who did get such appointments tended to cluster about the lower academic ranks (lecturer and instructor, rather than associate or full professor); the ratio of men to women hired was about four to one, but the ratio of men to women full professors was nine to one.

Besides rank, there is still another pecking order in college and university teaching: Teaching composition and conducting have far more status than teaching piano or school music education (that is, preparing teachers to teach music). The former two were still virtually exclusively male preserves; the latter were considered relatively "appropriate" for women. Even within those enclaves where more women were employed, the men held the higher ranks. Thus, although 32 percent of all music education faculties were women, women held only 18 percent of the full professorships in this field; similarly, though 49.2 percent of all piano faculties were women, only 12 percent of the full professors of piano were women. Less than 5 percent of all conducting appointments were held by women, and only 4 percent of all composition teachers were women. (In 1975 a total of sixty-seven women held college-level teaching positions in composition in the United States.)[28]

Nevertheless, a number of women composers pursued outstandingly successful academic careers. Among them were Marion Bauer and Louise Talma (see Chapter 6), and some of the women composing electronic music, which often requires elaborate technical facilities available only at an institution (Jean Eichelberger Ivey, Pril Smiley, Daria Semegen, and others;

see Chapter 9). Two other notable composer-teachers are Miriam Gideon and Vivian Fine.

In 1975 Miriam Gideon[29] became the second woman composer to be elected to the American Academy and Institute of Arts and Letters (the first had been Talma, in 1973). The first public performance of a work by Gideon had taken place more than forty years earlier, in 1933. Since then her compositions have been performed in the United States, Europe, and Latin America, by leading orchestras, chamber ensembles, and soloists.

Gideon was born on October 23, 1906, in Greeley, Colorado. She had revealed her talent for music by the age of fourteen, and at that time went to live with a musician uncle, Henry Gideon, in Boston. She received her bachelor's degree from Boston University in 1926, with a major in piano, and soon afterward began to compose. Gideon then moved to New York, which became her permanent home. She studied piano with Hans Barth and composition privately with Lazare Saminsky (1931–34), and then with Roger Sessions (1935–43). In 1944 she accepted her first faculty appointment at Brooklyn College, where she remained for ten years. Meanwhile she had enrolled at Columbia University, where she earned a master's degree in musicology in 1946; later she also got a doctorate of sacred music (in composition) from the Jewish Theological Seminary of America, whose faculty she joined in 1955. In 1971 she also became a professor at City College of the City University of New York, from which she retired in 1976. In 1949 Gideon married Frederic Ewen, a professor of literature, author, and translator; they had one son.

Gideon's principal compositions are chamber music (with and without voice), keyboard works, song cycles, and choral music (including two sacred services). She preferred to avoid any particular musical style or system (despite her long period of study with twelve-tone composer Roger Sessions she did not choose to write strictly serial music); when pressed, she described her style as "free atonality." For example, one of her earlier works, *The Hound of Heaven* (1945), for baritone, oboe, and string trio, sets several lines of Francis Thompson's poem of the same name that concern profound experiences that mar (in order to make) the human being. Instrumental interludes are interspersed with the text, some of whose phrases are repeated. The oboe is treated almost as a separate voice. The texture, George Perle wrote in a detailed analysis of this work, is strikingly personal, characterized by lightness, the sudden exposure of individual notes, constantly shifting octave relationships. Repetition is used a great deal, but it is rarely exact, differing slightly in pitch or in register or some other element.[30]

It is interesting to compare this work with *Rhymes from the Hill* (1968), a song cycle for mezzo soprano, clarinet, marimba, and cello, setting five poems from *Galgenlieder* ("Gallows Songs") by the German poet Christian

Morgenstern. Here the voice and chamber ensemble are made to express the ironic ideas and mood of the poems. Gideon herself described the songs (in part):

1. Songs of the Gallows Gang. Nocturnal shrieks and sinister sounds of nature are heard in the clattering of the marimba and the wail of the clarinet....5. The Sigh—a tribute to love. Skating on the ice, the sigh becomes so overheated by amorous thought that the ice melts and he disappears. Tremolos on the marimba, grace notes on the clarinet, and glissandi on the cello are used to depict this ironic tragedy.[31]

A New York reviewer wrote of this work that it "is beautifully crafted and a success on its own unpretentious terms. The vocal lines are sensitive, the accompanimental colors glow, and all goes together splendidly."[32]

Always very careful in her setting of texts, Gideon carried this even further in her *Songs of Youth and Madness* (1977), for soprano and orchestra. In this setting of four poems by the nineteenth-century poet Friedrich Hölderin, whose thwarted love for a married woman led him into insanity, Gideon alternated the words (by separate verse or by entire poem) in English translation with the original German. Each version of the text has its own music—and the two often are quite different—thereby adding a second dimension to the whole. Gideon also wrote two earlier works for orchestra, *Lyric Piece* (1941), for string orchestra, and *Symphonia Brevis* (1954), and in 1969 she received the National Federation of Music Clubs award for her contribution to symphonic music.

Vivian Fine,[33] born on September 28, 1913, in Chicago, Illinois, became known for her performances of contemporary piano music (she gave many lecture-recitals on "new" music), for her compositions (including a number for the dance), and for her teaching. Besides extensive private teaching, she was at various times on the faculties of New York University (1945–48), the State University of New York at Potsdam (1951), the Connecticut College School of Dance (1963–64), and Bennington College (1964 on).

Fine began to study piano at the age of five and soon after obtained a scholarship to study at the Chicago Musical College. From 1925 to 1931 she attended the American Conservatory, studying piano with Djane Lavoie-Herz, harmony and composition with Ruth Crawford (1925–29; see Chapter 6), and counterpoint with Adolf Weidig. She was only twelve when she began to study with Crawford, who after six months or so asked her to write a piece. Fine later said, "It had never occurred to me to write music before. I wrote it and could see that she liked it. I became so intrigued with composition that I have never stopped since then."[34] She always regarded Crawford as having had an important place in her development, not only as a "role model"—for she was the first woman composer Fine encountered—but for a time, at least, as a specific influence on her style. One of Fine's earliest works, *Four Pieces for Two Flutes,* shows her mastery of dissonant counterpoint,[35] and indeed all her compositions until about 1937 were totally atonal. Crawford also introduced her to Henry Cowell, who later published some of Fine's works in his *New Music.*

In 1931 Fine left Chicago for New York, where she studied piano with Abby Whiteside and composition with Roger Sessions. In 1935 she was married to Benjamin Karp, a sculptor who later taught at New York University; they had two daughters, but Fine never stopped composing, even when her children were young. In 1937 Fine wrote her first ballet score, *The Race of Life,* for Doris Humphrey, a humorous piece based on a series of drawings by James Thurber. There followed *Opus 51* (1938), for Charles Weidman and his dance company, and then two ballets for Hanya Holm, *Tragic Exodus* (1939) and *They Too Are Exiles* (1939). Later Humphrey wrote about Fine: "She has an uncanny sense of what to choose as sound and that *sine qua non* for dance composers, a complete understanding of body rhythm and dramatic timing."[36] With the completion of *Alcestis* (1960), commissioned by Martha Graham, and *My Son, My Enemy* (1965), written for José Limón and his company, Fine had written at least one work for each of the leading dance companies in America over a period of two decades. Several of the ballets were later arranged into independent orchestral works, notably *The Race of Life* and *Alcestis.*

When she first began to write ballets, from 1937 to the mid-1940s, Fine's style became less dissonant, and tonality became evident from time to time. From 1945 on, however, she returned to an almost totally atonal style. Many of her compositions reveal her finely tuned sense of humor. For example, in 1956 she took an article from the gardening column of the *New York Times* and set it for soprano, tenor, flute, violin, clarinet, cello, and harp. Entitled *A Guide to the Life Expectancy of a Rose,* this work sets the text in such a way—through exaggerated stresses on unstressed syllables and similar devices—that the down-to-earth seriousness of lines such as, "There are no tables of life expectancy, and it is impossible to quote any real statistics as to the longevity of a rosebush" is transformed into high comedy.[37]

Enormously prolific despite a continued heavy teaching schedule, Fine wrote songs and chamber works, choral and orchestral pieces. Notable among her later compositions are *Paean on the Sound "I"* (1969), for brass ensemble, women's chorus, and narrator, which has been recorded; *Two Neruda Poems* (1971), for voice and piano; *Missa Brevis* (1972), for four cellos and taped voice; *Concerto for Piano, Strings, and Percussion* (1972); and two works celebrating the feminist cause, *Meeting for Equal Rights, 1866* (1976), for orchestra, chorus, soloists, and narrator, and *The Women in the Garden* (1977), a chamber opera for five soloists and nine instruments, written with the assistance of a grant from the National Endowment for the Arts.

The *Two Neruda Poems, Missa Brevis,* and piano concerto were performed in an all-Fine program in New York on April 15, 1973, prompting Donal Henahan of the *New York Times* to write:

The 10-part mass was full of melismatic slides, microtones, and other currently popular devices but it left an impression of distant times and cool cathedrals. The composer also gave the first performance of her Concerto for Piano, Strings and Percussion (1972), in which she functioned as a one-woman band. Although heavily in debt to Cowell, Ives, and Cage, the Concerto was absorbing in its aural sensitivity and its tongue-in-cheek manner (a parody, perhaps, but of whom?)....The Neruda songs made a delicious pair, "La tortuga" crawling along in hushed beauty and "Oda al piano" closing the concert with a witty melodrama. The singer silenced the pianist (Miss Fine) by gently closing the lid, removing the music, and, finally, dropping the key covering. The final chord was played woodenly but expressively by Miss Fine, a marvelous straight-woman.[38]

There were a number of all-Fine programs in succeeding years, principally at universities and colleges throughout the country.

*Meeting for Equal Rights, 1866,* a setting of nineteenth-century American writings on the subject of women, was first performed in April 1976 by the Oratorio Society of New York at Cooper Union. The score again shows Fine's sense of humor: Horace Greeley's sententious statement that a woman's place is in the home is set to music more than faintly reminiscent of Brahms's famous *Lullaby,* and the male chorus shouting that women should be "Obedient, meek, patient, forgiving, gentle, and loving" is set to insipidly sentimental music. The opera *The Women in the Garden,* first performed in San Francisco in 1978, sets writings of Emily Dickinson, Isadora Duncan, Gertrude Stein, and Virginia Woolf.

To Fine, teaching and composing were inextricably entwined in the 1970s. "All my composer friends teach," she said, "and there is a great deal of musical activity going on in the universities. I enjoy teaching immensely. My only reservation is that I put so much energy into it that I don't leave enough for my composing."[39]

This indeed is the pitfall for all composer-teachers, and one that Dorothy James [40] was not able to avoid. In fact, she described herself as an "occasional composer,"[41] in that most of her works had been written for high school and college performances, some being commissioned for specific occasions. James was born on December 1, 1901, in Chicago, and she taught theory, literature, and composition at Eastern Michigan University from 1927 (when it was Michigan State Normal College) until 1968; the school awarded her an honorary doctorate in 1971.

Like Fine, James attended the Chicago Musical College and the American Conservatory where she studied composition with Louis Gruenberg and counterpoint with Adolf Weidig, and obtained both her bachelor's and master's degrees. Later she also studied with Howard Hanson at the East-man School of Music, Healy Willan at Toronto, and Ernst Krenek at the University of Michigan. Her works include *Three Symphonic Fragments* (1931), for orchestra, first performed by the Rochester Philharmonic in 1931 and dedicated to Marian MacDowell (James eventually spent four summers at the MacDowell Colony); *Paola and Francesca* (1930-34), a three-act opera; many choral works, including two for children's chorus *(The Jumblies,* 1935; *Paul Bunyan,* 1938); and songs, chamber music, and keyboard works. James continued to be active after her retirement from the university. Compositions she produced thereafter include *Motif* (1970), for organ and oboe, and *Patterns* (1977), for solo harp.

Another woman who combined teaching with composition and wrote many works for school performance was Emma Lou Diemer.[42] Born on November 24, 1927, in Kansas City, Missouri, she received her bachelor's and master's degrees in composition from Yale and her doctorate from the Eastman School of Music. She studied composition with Richard Donovan, Paul Hindemith, Bernard Rogers, Howard Hanson, Roger Sessions, and Ernest Toch, and piano with Wiktor Labunski and organ with David Craig-head.

After several years as a composer-in-residence and consultant in the Washington-Baltimore area, Diemer taught theory and composition at the University of Maryland (1965-70) and then joined the faculty of the University of California at Santa Barbara. At the same time, from the age of thirteen on, she served as organist in various churches. In the 1970s she still combined teaching and composition with presenting organ and piano recitals, and lecturing on contemporary music.

Diemer's compositions, which numbered several hundred by 1978, include works for orchestra and band, chamber ensemble, organ, piano, chorus, solo songs, and song cycles. Among them are symphonies, concertos (piano, flute, harpsichord), and overtures. Among her best-known earlier works are *Youth Overture* (1959), *Symphony Antique* (1960), and *Festival Overture* (1961), all for orchestra; *Three Madrigals* (1960), for mixed chorus with piano or organ; and *Dance, Dance My Heart* (1967), for mixed chorus, organ and percussion. Known for her well-crafted effective style, Diemer in the 1970s began to experiment with newer modes of expression, including some electronic and computer music. In this vein are her Trio for flute, oboe, harpsichord, and tape (1973) and Quartet for flute, viola, cello, harpsichord, and tape (1974).

Nancy Hayes Van de Vate also pursued a dual career, teaching and composing. In the 1970s she added still another, founding the League of Women Composers, which she headed for a number of years, in order to help other women develop their talents and find more recognition.

Van de Vate[43] was born on December 30, 1930, in Plainfield, New Jersey. She began her undergraduate work at the Eastman School of Music as a piano major, studying with Cecile Genhart, but decided to complete it at Wellesley College, where she majored in theory and got her bachelor's degree in 1952. She went on to get a master's and eventually a doctorate in composition, writing a Concerto for piano and orchestra (1968) as her doctoral dissertation. In 1957 Van de Vate moved to the South. She taught piano privately from 1957 to 1963 and then began to teach on the college level, first at the University of Mississippi and then at Memphis State University (1964–66). Meanwhile she had become a member and officer of the Southeastern Composers' League. In 1968 she moved to Knoxville, Tennessee, where she taught at Knoxville College and Maryville College, and played viola in the Knoxville Symphony Orchestra. In 1975 she joined the faculty of the University of Hawaii.

Van de Vate's compositions include many chamber works and some songs, as well as choral and orchestra pieces. Notable especially are her Sonata for viola and piano (1964) and *Six Short Pieces* (1969), for solo viola, *Quintet for Brass* (1974), which won first place in the Delius Composition contest, String Trio no. 1 (1974), *Three Sound Pieces* (1973), for brass and percussion, and *Concertpiece* for cello and small orchestra (1976).

In 1975 Van de Vate described the position of women in academic music (that is, in college and university music departments) as a "well-documented disaster." Moreover, she pointed out, unless a musician lived in a large metropolitan area, the university offered practically the only avenue for development and opportunities for performance. Although federal law prohibited the arbitrary exclusion of women from college music departments, its provisions were not being enforced. The number of women in all ranks of academic life had increased by less than 1 percent between 1970 and 1975. It was time that these conditions changed, Van de Vate said, and that women themselves become more assertive in their work and the musical profession more receptive to them.[44] In 1976, asked to advise young women who were considering a career in composition, Van de Vate was very specific:

Young women entering the field should obtain as much formal training as possible in rigorous programs. Later they should go to professional meetings and meet their colleagues; enter composition contests, especially those using anonymous entries; perform their works if necessary; write articles for professional periodicals; in other words, use the same means as their male colleagues do to capture public attention.[45]

Many other composer-teachers might be mentioned, from Ethel Glenn Hier (1889–1971), charter member of the Society of American Women Composers and long-time teacher of piano and composition in Cincinnati and then New York, to young women just beginning their careers at the time of Hier's death. Esther Williamson Ballou (1915–73), who began by accompanying and composing for modern dance, had a distinguished teaching career from 1943 until her death, at the Juilliard School, Catholic University, and then American University in Washington, D.C. Claire Polin, born in 1926, pursued a multifaceted career as a flutist, composer, and musicologist; she wrote many chamber works (among them three string quartets and a brass quintet) as well as two symphonies. Elaine Barkin, born in 1932, earned bachelor's, master's, and doctoral degrees and taught at various schools, in 1974 accepting an appointment at the University of California at Los Angeles; she also served as associate editor of a distinguished journal, *Perspectives of New Music,* and frequently wrote about contemporary composers. Principally a composer of chamber music, her own works include a String Quartet (1969), *Plus ça change* (1972), for strings and percussion, and *Sound Play* (1974), for solo violin.

Also becoming known for her chamber compositions was Eleanor Cory,[46] born in 1943 in Englewood, New Jersey, and educated at Sarah Lawrence College, Harvard University, the New England Conservatory, and Columbia, where she received her doctorate in composition in 1975. She taught at various colleges in the New York metropolitan area from 1971 on, served as associate editor of the *Contemporary Music Newsletter* from 1972 to 1977, and in 1978 was appointed to the faculty of Yale University to teach theory and composition. Her compositions include *Combinations* (1974), for piano; *Tempi* (1971), for clarinet and tape; Trio for clarinet (bass clarinet) cello, and piano (1973); *Epithalamium* (1973), for solo flute; Trio for flute, oboe, and piano (1977; and *Counterbrass* (1978), for French horn, trumpet, trombone, piano, and percussion.

Judith Lang Zaimont,[47] born in 1945 in Memphis, Tennessee, was educated in New York, at the Juilliard School, Queens College, the Long Island Institute for Music, and Columbia University. She also studied privately for a year with André Jolivet in Paris. After seven years of appearances as a duopianist with her sister Doris, throughout the United States and on radio and television, in 1967 she became resident composer and accompanist for the Great Neck (Long Island) Choral Society. In 1970 she began to teach as well, first at New York City Community College, then at Queens College, and from 1978 at Adelphi University. She also frequently appeared as a guest lecturer on twentieth-century composition before various music teachers' groups.

Zaimont's compositions are principally songs, choral works, and piano pieces. Notable among them are a *Sacred Service for the Sabbath Evening* (1976), for baritone solo, chorus, and orchestra; *Greyed Sonnets* (1975), five songs for soprano and piano to texts by women poets, which a *New York Times* reviewer described as "strongly emotional, suiting the texts, yet carefully constructed";[48] and *Songs of Innocence* (1974), for soprano, tenor, flute, cello, and harp, commissioned by the Gregg Smith Singers; and a Concerto for piano and orchestra (1972). By 1978 Zaimont was working on a number of commissioned compositions, among them a wind quintet, a string quartet (for the Primavera String Quartet), and *Songs for Soprano and Harp* (for the New York State Music Teachers Association).

A principal means of funding musical composition are commissions, grants, or fellowships, or, after the fact, the award of a prize. Composers who teach in order to support themselves are nearly always pressed for time to compose. A grant or fellowship can release them from teaching hours; a commission guarantees payment and performance for a work that would otherwise be composed on speculation, as it were. The award of a prize confers prestige, status, and publicity, both on the composer and on the institution where he or she is employed.

In the mid-1970s Carol Neuls-Bates conducted a study of four foundations that give grants in music—the John Simon Guggenheim Memorial Foundation, the National Endowment for the Humanities, the American Council of Learned Societies, and the Martha Baird Rockefeller Fund for Music. The results of her study, presented before the annual meeting of the College Music Society in February 1975, and later published,[49] showed what had long been suspected: A much smaller percentage of women than men received foundation support. The highly prestigious Guggenheim Fellowships recognized more than 200 composers between 1925 and 1973, of whom only 3.4 percent were women. However, it was more generous to women scholars engaged in music research, so that the total participation of women in the Guggenheim programs during those forty-eight years was 6.2 percent. The National Endowment for the Humanities (totally tax supported), which in 1967 began to give fellowships to enable humanists to improve their skills in teaching, interpreting, and communicating the humanities, gave several categories of grants; between 1967 and 1973 the representation of women in music was 13.2 percent.

The American Council of Learned Societies channels funds from the Ford Foundation, the Carnegie Corporation, and the National Endowment for the Humanities to humanist scholars in three kinds of program. The proportion of awards in music that went to women between 1968 and 1973 was 20.5 percent. The Martha Baird Rockefeller Fund for Music made awards in performance at the postgraduate level for a variety of projects and also in musicology. Of the musicology awards granted between 1962 and 1973, 15.7 percent went to women. Of the performance grants, the majority (nearly two-thirds) of the *vocal* awards went to women, but women received fewer than one-third of the *instrumental* awards.

Finally, the table in Appendix A shows the distribution of funds for music by the National Endowment for the Arts (also totally tax funded), which gives grants principally to composers, between 1971 and 1977; the figures come from the organization's own annual reports.

A study of awards and prizes reveals a similar pattern. Indeed, some have been openly restricted to men. Back in 1916 the Sinfonia, a Boston musical society, announced its fourth annual prize competition for a choral work with orchestra: "The composer must be a male and an American citizen who has received the major part of his musical education in America."[50] The Pulitzer Prize in music, awarded since 1943, had still (in 1979) never been given to a woman.

American women composers have still one other strike against them—the fact that they are American. European music continues to be highly valued in the United States, and still makes up the bulk of programs of serious music. Periodically there have been movements and organizations to combat this tendency and help American composers obtain at least a hearing. In the mid-1970s, when considerable public attention was focused on America's bicentennial, there were a number of attempts to celebrate American artistic achievement, including two historical surveys of American music undertaken by commercial record companies. One, the Nonesuch Treasury of Americana (Nonesuch H7-14, two records), included an assortment of serious and popular music; not one woman composer was represented. The other, much more ambitious series, A Recorded Anthology of American Music (New World Records; forty-three records by September 1978), represented only two women—Amy Beach with her Violin Sonata and Ruth Crawford Seeger with *Three Songs*. The impression given clearly was that there *were* no other American women composers.

There have been two notable exceptions to the prevailing pattern. One is represented by the various prizes of the National Federation of Music Clubs, which have frequently gone to women composers. The other is the fellowships offered by the MacDowell Colony, which have been awarded to an extraordinary number of women composers. Of the composers and musicians discussed in this book, twenty-six were MacDowell Colony Fellows between 1914 and 1978, and eight of them spent five or more summers there (Marion Bauer, Amy Beach, Mabel Daniels, Ethel Glenn Hier, Mary Howe, Dika Newlin, Julia Perry, and Louise Talma).[51] To these women the MacDowell Colony gave a space and time they could devote entirely to work, without thought of other obligations. And many did highly productive work there.

The MacDowell Colony[52] was officially established after the death of composer Edward MacDowell in 1908 by his widow, Marian Nevins MacDowell (1857–1956), who carried out her husband's wish that their farm in Peterborough, New Hampshire, become a haven of tranquillity for other artists, as it had been for him. Two dozen studios were constructed in remote parts of the wide-flung property (today there are 400 acres), and to augment the Memorial Fund supporting the Colony, Marian MacDowell, a fine pianist, carried on vigorous fund-raising for many years in order to ensure the Colony's continued existence. Every winter she toured America, giving concerts of her husband's works, speaking in public of his life and his ambition to create a working place not only for composers but for poets, painters, sculptors, novelists, and playwrights. In this way she raised 80 to 90 percent of the Colony's financial support during its early years. And every summer she personally supervised the building of roads and eventual construction of more than forty houses and cabins.

Each MacDowell Fellow receives room and board (in one of several central buildings) and the exclusive use of a private studio equipped for his or her art. The average length of stay is two months. Some of the studios are equipped with heat, enabling their use during the winter. None is within sight or sound of another, and phone messages are delivered only in emergencies. Lunch and firewood are delivered daily, so an artist may work uninterrupted all day long. In Marian MacDowell's time, Fellows were selected largely on the basis of her personal judgment, though she did have an official admissions committee. Since the early 1950s, however, applications have in fact been reviewed by a Composers Admissions Committee made up of composers, teachers, and critics, who rank all applicants on the basis of works they submit; the latter are supposed to include at least one work in a larger form (string quartet, sonata, or orchestral work).

A similar but less well-known working community for artists and writers is Yaddo, a 400-acre estate near Saratoga Springs, New York. An artistic center during the lifetime of its original owners, Mr. and Mrs. Spencer Trask, it was later set aside under the direction of the Yaddo Corporation. Like the MacDowell Colony, it offers room, board, and studio space for a period of a month or two (on the average). During the 1930s and early 1940s Yaddo became known in the musical world especially because it sponsored an annual festival of contemporary American music, in order to give young composers a chance to hear their works performed.

As in other fields where women were long excluded or, if allowed entrance, were not taken seriously, in music one elusive but nonetheless real difficulty they faced was their exclusion from the "old boy network," which functions to perpetuate the status quo. Instrumental teachers (male) help their students (male) to get orchestra jobs; professors (male) tell their students (male) of competitions they might enter, fellowships that are available, teaching jobs in their own departments or other universities; conductors (male) select programs of new works (by men). Because these are usually quite informal procedures, they are difficult to pin down, let alone combat. However, one measure women in fields such as business management have taken is to organize their own cooperative network, and this is precisely what women composers began to do in the mid-1970s. Nancy

Van de Vate was among the first to recognize the need for an organization whereby composers could exchange information and perhaps also act collectively, and in 1974 she founded the League of Women Composers (in 1979 renamed International League of Women Composers). Its aims were to obtain more commissions, recordings, and orchestral performances for women composers, to ensure that state and federal tax revenues were not allocated exclusively to men composers, and to obtain more foundation support for women.

In 1976 a second organization was founded by Tommie Ewert Carl (with Judith Lang Zaimont as vice-president). At first named Female Composers of America and then renamed American Women Composers, Inc., it issued an ambitious statement of purposes and goals that included serving as a business organization to assist women composers in the areas of live performance, publication, and recording, sponsoring specific performances of new works, and holding annual workshops. Among the first steps the new organization took was to set itself up as a publisher of new music and as a recording agent. Though it is too soon to assess their impact, both of these organizations were far more sophisticated in approach than the Society of American Women Composers to which Amy Beach, Mary Howe, and others belonged in the 1920s.

The principal pitfall for all such groups is that they combat discrimination by instituting a kind of separatism and thereby perpetuate the very image that most women composers reject outright—that is, their identification as "women composers" and not purely "composers." However, until society has changed enough so that women have a truly equal chance for achievement in all traditionally male-dominated areas—medicine, engineering, and business, as well as music—they may represent a necessary temporary compromise.

# National Endowment for the Arts Music Program, 1971-77[a]

| Year | Program | Awards | Total Awards | % Grants to Women | % Money to Women |
|---|---|---|---|---|---|
| 1971 | Composer-Performer Program | | $48,568 | | |
| | 5 men | | | | |
| | 0 women | | | 0 | 0 |
| | 22 organizations | | | | |
| | Jazz fellowships | | $ 18,470 | | |
| | 25 men | $ 17,120 | | | |
| | 1 woman | 1,350 | | 3.8 | 7.3 |
| 1972 | Jazz Fellowships/ Composers | | $ 31,600 | | |
| | 33 men | | | | |
| | 0 women | | | 0 | 0 |
| | Special Projects/Jazz | | $ 86,420 | | |
| | 4 men | | | | |
| | 0 women | | | 0 | 0 |
| | 14 organizations | | | | |
| | Travel-Study/Jazz | | $ 15,760 | | |
| | 2 women | $ 1,000 | | 5.7 | 6.3 |
| | 33 men | 14,760 | | | |
| | Kodaly Training Program | | $ 67,800 | | |
| | 1 man | $ 25,000 | | | |
| | 8 women | 28,800 | | 88.8 | 53.5 |
| | 1 organization | 14,000 | | | |

[a] The figures given, taken from annual reports of the National Endowment for the Arts (NEA) for 1971 through 1977, include only those categories in which grants are awarded to individuals.

| Year | Program | Awards | Total Awards | % Grants to Women | % Money to Women |
|------|---------|--------|--------------|-------------------|------------------|
| 1973 | Composer/ | | | | |
| | Librettist Fellowships | | $ 71,611 | | |
| | 20 men | $ 68,361 | | | |
| | 2 women | 3,250 | | 9 | 4.5 |
| | Jazz/Category 1 | | $ 63,009 | | |
| | 58 men | | | | |
| | 0 women | | | 0 | 0 |
| | Jazz/Category 3 | | $ 10,965 | | |
| | 18 men | $ 9,465 | | | |
| | 3 women | 1,500 | | 14.3 | 13.7 |
| | Jazz/Category 4 | | $ 46,230 | | |
| | 6 men | $ 5,750 | | | |
| | 1 woman | 3,500 | | 14.3 | 38 |
| | 9 organizations | 36,980 | | | |
| 1974 | Composer/Librettists/Translators | | $356,725 | | |
| | Category 1 | | $304,080 | | |
| | 74 men | $280,080 | | | |
| | 7 women | 24,000 | | 8.6 | 7.9 |
| | Category 2 | | $ 35,250 | | |
| | 15 men | $ 30,750 | | | |
| | 1 woman | 2,000 | | 11.1 | 9.2 |
| | 1 husband/wife team | 2,500 | | | |
| | Category 3 | | $ 17,395 | | |
| | 7 men | $ 14,145 | | | |
| | 3 women | 3,250 | | 30 | 18.7 |
| 1974 | Jazz/Folk/Ethnic | | $419,287 | | |
| | Category 1 | | 71,200 | | |
| | 56 men | $ 68,700 | | | |
| | 4 women | 2,500 | | 6.6 | 3.5 |
| | Category 3 | | $ 10,620 | | |
| | 21 men | $ 9,920 | | | |
| | 2 women | 700 | | 8.7 | 6.6 |
| | Other | | $122,730 | | |
| | 5 men | 7,000 | | | |
| | 3 women | 5,500 | | 37.5 | 44 |
| | 8 organizations | $110,230 | | | |
| 1975 | Composer/Librettists | | $416,175 | | |
| | Category 1 | | 371,665 | | |
| | 102 men | $348,915 | | | |
| | 6 women | 22,750 | | 5.5 | 6.1 |

| Year | Program | Awards | Total Awards | % Grants to Women | % Money to Women |
|------|---------|--------|--------------|-------------------|------------------|
| | Category 2 | | $ 24,000 | | |
| | 9 men | $ 22,000 | | | |
| | 1 woman | 2,000 | | 10 | 8.3 |
| | Category 3 | | 20,510 | | |
| | 16 men | $ 17,535 | | | |
| | 3 women | 2,975 | | 15.8 | 14.5 |
| | Jazz/Folk/Ethnic | | $671,208 | | |
| | Jazz Category 1 | | 149,980 | | |
| | 70 men | $140,980 | | | |
| | 3 women | 9,000 | | 4.1 | 6 |
| | Jazz Category 3 | | 16,300 | | |
| | 19 men | $ 15,300 | | | |
| | 1 woman | 1,000 | | 5 | 6 |
| | Jazz/Other | | 26,500 | | |
| | 0 men | | | | |
| | 1 woman | $ 1,500 | | 100 | 100 |
| | 1 organization | 25,000 | | | |
| | Folk/Ethnic | | | | |
| | Category 1 | | 5,500 | | |
| | 3 men | | | | |
| | 0 women | | | 0 | 0 |
| | Folk/Ethnic | | | | |
| | Category 3 | | 2,860 | | |
| | 3 men | | | | |
| | 0 women | | | 0 | 0 |
| | Folk/Ethnic | | | | |
| | Other | | 26,300 | | |
| | 0 men | | | | |
| | 1 woman | $ 1,300 | | 100 | 100 |
| | 1 organization | 25,000 | | | |
| 1976 | Composer/Librettists | | | | |
| | Category 1 | | $353,050 | | |
| | 164 men | $330,450 | | | |
| | 10 women | 22,600 | | 5.7 | 6.4 |
| | Category 2 | | $ 36,250 | | |
| | 8 men | 26,650 | | | |
| | 3 women | 9,600 | | 27 | 26 |
| | Category 3 | | $ 11,100 | | |
| | 8 men | 10,000 | | | |
| | 1 woman | 1,000 | | 11 | 9 |
| 1976 | Jazz/Folk/Ethnic | | | | |
| | Jazz/Category 1 | | $218,700 | | |
| | 69 men | $207,700 | | | |
| | 4 women | 11,000 | | 5.4 | 5 |

| Year | Program | Awards | Total Awards | % Grants to Women | % Money to Women |
|---|---|---|---|---|---|
| | Jazz/Category 2 | | $148,100 | | |
| | 44 men | | | | |
| | 7 women | 18,300 | | 13.2 | 12.3 |
| | 2 organizations | 129,800 | | | |
| | Jazz/Category 3 | | $ 26,330 | | |
| | 23 men | 20,255 | | | |
| | 7 women | 6,075 | | 23.3 | 23 |
| | Folk/Ethnic | | | | |
| | Category 3 | | $ 6,000 | | |
| | 6 men | | | | |
| | 0 women | | | 0 | 0 |
| | Folk/Ethnic | | | | |
| | Pilot Category | | $ 46,790 | | |
| | 11 men | 41,990 | | | |
| | 2 women | 4,800 | | 15.4 | 10 |
| 1977 | Jazz/Folk/Ethnic | | $843,092 | | |
| | 111 men | $257,940 | | | |
| | 12 women | 30,475 | | 9.8 | 10.6 |
| | 81 organizations | 554,677 | | | |
| | Composer/Librettists | | $470,000 | | |
| | 123 men | 439,600 | | | |
| | 9 women | 30,400 | | 6.8 | 6.5 |

# Applicants for NEA Music Awards and Awards Made, 1972-75

| Year | Area[a] | Number of Applicants | | Number of Awards Made[b] | |
|------|---------|-------|--------------|-------|--------------|
| | | Total | Women (%) | Total | Women (%) |
| 1972 | JFE[c] | 96 | 7 (7.3%) | 72 | 2 (2.7%) |
| 1973 | CLT | 35 | 5 (14%) | 22 | 2 (9%) |
| | JFE | 164 | 7 (4%) | 86 | 4 (4.6%) |
| 1974 | CLT | 266 | 39.5[d] (14.8%) | 108 | 11.5[d] (10.6%) |
| | JFE | 265 | 21 (7.9%) | 91 | 9 (9.9%) |
| 1975 | CLT | 515 | 59 (11.4%) | 137 | 10 (7.3%) |
| | JFE | 231 | 24 (10.4%) | 108 | 6 (5.5%) |

[a] JFE stands for Jazz/Folk/Ethnic categories; CLT for Composer/Librettist/Translator programs.

[b] Awards to individuals only (organizations not included in this tally).

[c] Only Jazz/Folk/Ethnic awards were made in 1972, plus Kodaly Training Program grants (not included here).

[d] The 0.5 refers to one-half of a husband-wife team, Ruth and Thomas Martin.

# NOTES

## Chapter 1

1. John Cotton's tract was entitled "Singing of Psalms a Gospel ordinance, or a Treatise wherein are handled these four particulars. I. Touching the duty itself. II. Touching the matter to be sung. III. Touching the singers. IV. Touching the manner of singing." It is quoted by F. L. Ritter, *Music in America*.

2. Letter to Josiah Flynt, March 27, 1661, in Massachusetts Historical Society Collection, 1st Series, VI (1799), p. 106.

3. The Reverend Thomas Walter published *Grounds and Rules of Musick explained* in 1721, and is quoted in the *History of the Handel and Haydn Society of Boston*, vol. 1, p. 19.

4. David P. McKay and Richard Crawford, *William Billings of Boston*, p. 37.

5. Karl Krueger, *The Musical Heritage of the United States*, pp. 17–18.

6. The *Euterpiad*, April 15, 1820. The practice of excluding women persisted for years. Ritter, writing in the 1880s, said that most of the many amateur vocal societies then in existence (about three-fourths of them German-American) excluded women. New York's Liederkranz Society, founded in 1847, began to admit women in 1856, two years after a splinter group had withdrawn and formed the all-male Arion Society. Milwaukee's Musikverein, founded in 1849 and one of the oldest, most influential of these groups, consisted of a male chorus, an orchestra, and a mixed chorus that performed only on special occasions. A rare exception was the Musical Fund Society of Philadelphia, founded in 1820, which included all of that city's prominent musicians and music patrons, and resolved only "that no female professional members be admitted without a written certificate from some lady of established character in this city" (Jane Campbell, *Old Philadelphia Music*, p. 192).

7. John Tufts's collection of c. 1714, Thomas Walter's collection of 1721, and Thomas Bailey's collection of 1769.

8. Ritter, *Music in America*, p. 238.

9. The organ originally was purchased for the Brattle Street Church, which, however, refused to install it, and then was offered to King's Chapel. An Englishman, Edward Eustace, was hired as organist at a salary of twenty pounds per year.

10. Orpha Ochse, *The History of the Organ in the United States*, p. 14.

11. *History of the Handel and Haydn Society*, vol. 1, pp. 27–28.

12. Ritter, *Music in America*, p. 103.

13. Quoted by Henry M. Brooks, *Olden-Time Music*, p. 100. Elisabeth von Hagen, her husband, and her children performed in New York as early as 1789; they moved to Boston in 1796.

14. Paul Eric Paige, "Musical Organizations in Boston: 1830–1850," p. 34.

15. A. Loesser, *Men, Women, and Pianos,* p. 449. Miss Wrighten was the daughter of Mary Ann Pownall (also discussed in Chapter 1). At this concert she and her sister also sang, with their mother, and her four-year-old brother Felix appeared as well. Another early pianist was a Mrs. Sully, who performed in Charleston in 1794 and 1795 and in Boston on September 13, 1796 (see Oscar Sonneck, *Early ConcertLife in America, 1731–1800,* pp. 29, 31, 227 ff., 305).

16. Her death, however, is recorded in the State of Maine Archives: She died on August 31, 1846, in Portland, at the age of forty-six.

17. The second-born, John Hill Hewitt (1801–90) ran away from home, became interested in music while at West Point, studied law for a time, and eventually composed some three hundred songs, as well as an oratorio; from 1828 on he lived principally in Baltimore. The second son, James Lang Hewitt (1807–53), became a music publisher in Boston, as did the third son, Horatio Nelson Hewitt. The youngest son, George Washington Hewitt, entered a disastrous publishing venture in Philadelphia and later settled in Burlington, New Jersey, where he composed many piano pieces and taught; his mother spent her last years with him. Sophia's sister Eliza became a music teacher and eventually also went to live with brother George. John's oldest son, Horatio Dawes Hewitt, became a musician and composer, and he wrote some comic operas; he died in 1894. George's son, Hobart Doane Hewitt (1852–1932), taught piano and violin in Burlington and was for a number of years associated with the Philadelphia publishing firm of Theodore Presser, which published many of his compositions. (See also John Tasker Howard, "The Hewitt Family in American Music.")

18. Quoted by Ritter, *Music in America,* p. 121.

19. Irving Lowens, *Music and Musicians in Early America,* p. 201. Though it was customary for established local musicians (of whom Graupner was *the* leader) to assist newcomers, Graupner's name is conspicuously absent among the assisting artists at Hewitt's concerts, nor were tickets to these events sold at his music store. Further, at an important concert in which Graupner led the orchestra and the highly regarded organist George K. Jackson played selections from Handel's works, the phrase "Mr. Hewitt has declined" was printed on the program.

20. Harold Earle Johnson, *Musical Interludes in Boston, 1795–1830,* pp. 84, 99. The solo part of this concerto by the German pianist-composer Daniel Steibelt (1765–1823) was rivaled in popularity only by Kotzwara's *Battle of Prague.*

21. John Rowe Parker, *Musical Biography: Or Sketches of the Lives and Writings of Eminent Musical Characters,* pp. 193–96.

22. Byron Adams Wolverton, "Keyboard Music and Musicians in the Colonies and United States of America Before 1830."

23. Virginia Larkin Redway, *Music Directory of Early New York City.* New York: New York Public Library (1941). See also Howard, "The Hewitt Family in America."

24. The same advertisement appeared in the June 3 issue of this journal, which was the leading music periodical in Boston at that time.

25. *Euterpiad,* April 8, 1820.

26. Johnson, *Musical Interludes,* pp. 107, 144. Loesser (p. 466) only says that she *may* have given this performance and says nothing about her later playing of works by Beethoven.

27. *Euterpiad,* June 10, 1820. In the same ad, which was repeated on June 17, June 24, and July 1, Mrs. Hewitt (presumably Sophia's mother) announced her intention of opening an academy for the French language for young ladies as soon as she could form a class of eight to ten scholars, and also offered private lessons at ladies' houses or at her own. Further, a young man probably one of Sophia's brothers—perhaps James Lang, then aged thirteen—also got into the ad: "A smart active lad who writes a good hand and understands arithmetic wants a situation in a store apply as above."

28. *History of the Handel and Haydn Society,* pp. 76–77.

29. Johnson, p. 140.

30. Ibid., pp. 18–19.

31. *Euterpiad,* May 11, 1822.

32. Ibid., May 25, 1822.

33. *Columbian Centinel,* August 14, 1822.

34. John Rowe Parker, *Euterpiad,* May 11, 1822.

35. George Thornton Edwards, *Music and Musicians of Maine,* pp. 26, 17.

36. Ibid., p. 58.

37. Ibid.

38. Brooks, *Olden-Time Music,* pp. 179–181.

39. John Tasker Howard, *Our American Music,* p. 86. Wolverton ("Keyboard Music and Musicians"), however, says he died August 1, 1827, in Boston.

40. Unsigned article reprinted from the *Providence Journal* in *Dwight's Journal of Music,* April 16, 1859, p. 20.

41. *History of the Handel and Haydn Society,* p. 98.

42. Paige, "Musical Organizations in Boston: 1830–1850," p. 54.

43. *History of the Handel and Haydn Society,* p. 101.

44. Ibid., pp. 102 f.

45. Ibid., p. 116. The society eventually did give him a raise, to $75 per quarter, in January 1834, but continued to have problems with Zeuner, who proved to be very hard to get along with. In April 1834 the society's president actually resigned on account of a quarrel with the organist. Moreover, the society accepted his resignation, realizing it would be easier to replace a president than a competent organist who also composed. Indeed, the society's very next concert, on May 18, 1834, featured, in addition to the customary oratorio selections, an organ concerto, duet, cavatina, and recitative and aria—all composed by Zeuner. Bad temper notwithstanding, in 1838 Zeuner was elected president of the society, but after nine months he resigned, and later he moved to Philadelphia, where he eventually committed suicide in 1857.

46. Edwards, *Music and Musicians of Maine,* p. 261.

47. *History of the Handel and Haydn Society,* p. 105.

48. *Eastern Argus,* July 15, 1833, and August 2, 1833.

49. Paige, "Musical Organizations in Boston: 1830–1850," p. 426.

50. *History of the Handel and Haydn Society,* pp. 141 f.

51. Harold Earle Johnson, *Hallelujah, amen!,* pp. 68–69.

52. *Dwight's Journal of Music,* April 15, 1859.

53. A dramatic account of her decline appears in U.S. Works Progress Administration, *History of Music in San Francisco,* vol. 2, p. 116. An accompanying photograph shows she had dark eyes and brows, an oval face with delicate, birdlike features, and a slightly aquiline nose. She wore her dark hair parted in the center, flat on top and puffed out at the sides.

54. Newspaper clipping, source unidentified, Boston Public Library.

55. *Folio,* October 17, 1885.

56. Ibid., January 1869.

57. *Musical Record,* October 1878.

58. James M. Tracy, in the *Folio,* 1888. She did not play every Saturday at the Music Hall, but about once every three weeks. The Arlington Street Church records list her as organist and show that she was paid from 1865 through 1867. In 1979 this venerable Boston church hired the second woman organist in its 250-year history, Joyce Painter.

59. Virginia Penny, *The Employments of Women,* pp. 76–77.

60. Mary Chappell Fisher, "Women as Concert Organists," and Everett E. Truette, "Women as Organists," *Etude,* September 1901.

61. Leonard Ellinwood, *The History of American Church Music,* pp. 202, 232–33.

62. Raymond Morin, *The Worcester Music Festival,* p. 34.

63. On p. 147.

64. John Rockwell, *New York Times,* May 4, 1976.

65. Marie MacConnell, quoted by Mary Chappell Fisher, *Etude,* July 1909, p. 484.

*Chapter 2*

1. Joseph Singer, in the *Musical Register,* reprinted in the *Musical Record,* November 26, 1881.

2. *Dwight's Journal of Music,* June 9, 1877.

3. *Boston Evening Transcript,* May 9, 1877.

4. A child prodigy who lived from 1839 to 1911, she was considered the first really great woman violinist and the only woman ever to become the most famous member of a musical family (she originally performed together with her father, brother Franz, and sister Amalie). She came to the United States only once, in 1899.

5. Reprinted in *Freund's Weekly,* May 22, 1884. The *Musical Record* of June 1884 said, "More than five hundred ladies are studying the violin in Boston, while many others are proficient soloists" (p. 6).

6. Henry Charles Lahee, *Famous Violinists in America,* p. 300. The fever had also spread across the Atlantic. The *Etude* of December 1894 reported that of 2,000 female pupils at the London Guildhall School of Music, 300 were studying the violin.

7. Renee B. Fisher, *Musical Prodigies: Masters at an Early Age,* pp. 175–76.

8. *Etude,* September 1901.

9. Frederic Louis Ritter, *Music in America,* p. 140.

10. Paul Eric Paige, "Musical Organizations in Boston: 1830–1850," p. 76.

11. Richard Dyer, *Boston Globe,* June 25, 1977.

12. *Musical Gazette,* April 26, 1847, p. 54.

13. For information about Urso up to about 1873 I have relied on Charles Barnard, *Camilla: A Tale of a Violin.*

14. *Dwight's Journal of Music,* February 14, 1863.

15. Ibid., March 2, 1867.

16. Ibid., March 16, 1867.

17. *Dexter Smith's Musical, Literary, Dramatic and Art Paper,* September 1874.

18. *Dwight's Journal of Music,* January 7, 1869. She was among the first violinists to perform this work in America.

19. Ibid., December 12, 1874.

20. Etude, November, 1891.

21. Raymond Morin, *The Worcester Music Festival,* pp. 2–3. The Worcester County Music Association, an outgrowth of the musical "conventions" begun in the 1830s, was formed in 1863. In 1865 it began to present annual festival concerts in which large works were performed and to which notable artists were invited from all over the world. The festivals remained an important event in American music up to the beginning of World War II.

22. Ibid., p. 23.

23. Ibid., p. 28.

24. Ibid., p. 35.

25. *Dexter Smith's,* January 1874, p. 7.

26. The Concerts Classiques were reported in *Dwight's Journal of Music. Dexter Smith's...Paper,* September 1874, in the interview quoted, precedes it with the following: "We found the brave little lady almost fully recovered from the effects of the ugly accident, which is still fresh in the minds of the public, and which but for her heroism and presence of mind, would probably have proved fatal."

27. *Musical Record,* June 21, 1879.

28. *Musical Herald,* July 1880.

29. *Musical Record,* December 1884.

30. *Freund's Weekly,* June 1891.

31. *Musical Herald,* April 1893.

32. *Folio,* September 1883, p. 325.

33. *Etude,* January 1891.

34. *Musical Record,* November 1891.

35. Judith Tick, "Why Have There Been No Great Women Composers, or Notes on the Score of Sexual Aesthetics," *International Musician,* July 1975, p. 6. The entire paper, in manuscript, came into the hands of musicologist Susan Kagan and was reprinted in *Signs,* Spring 1977, vol. 2, no. 3, pp. 731-34.

36. Letter to the *Musical Courier,* March 1898,

37. *Etude,* September, 1901.

38. Adella Prentiss, in the *Musical Record,* June 1900.

39. *Dwight's Journal of Music,* April 7, 1860.

40. Morin, *The Worcester Music Festival,* p. 29.

41. *Dwight's Journal of Music,* March 2, 1878.

42. Quoted by Morin, *The Worcester Music Festival,* pp. 42–43.

43. *Musical Record,* April 12, 1879, p. 20.

44. Maria Milanollo (1832–48) was a superb performer but died too soon to fulfill her early promise. Teresa Milanollo (1827?–1904) was so affected by her sister's death that she retired for a time but eventually resumed her career. She did not, however, play in public after her marriage in 1857 to a French army officer named Parmentier. She composed an Ave Maria for men's voices, a *Grande Fantasie* for piano, and a number of works for violin.

45. *Musical Record,* June 28, 1879, p. 194.

46. Her only rival on the international circuit was an Italian, Teresina Tua (1867-1955), who married and retired several times, taught at the Milan Conservatory, and eventually entered a convent.

47. Information about Powell comes from Lahee and other standard sources, and for some details I am indebted to Neva Garner Greenwood of Falls Church, Virginia, who has for several years been collecting all available information about this great violinist.

48. Theodore Thomas, *A Musical Autobiography,* vol. 2, *passim.*

49. George Lehmann, *Etude,* September 1901.

50. *Musical Herald,* April 1887, p. 112.

51. *Folio,* November 1890, p. 398.

52. Henry T. Finck, *My Adventures in the Golden Age of Music,* p. 313.

53. *Musical Record,* March 1898, p. 95.

54. George Lehmann, head of the violin column, *Etude,* January 1907.

55. *Etude,* November 1918. Also F. H. Martens, in *Dictionary of American Biography,* vol. 15, pp. 149–50.

56. Reprinted in *Ladies' Home Journal,* February 1896.

57. *Etude,* July and August 1909.

58. Ibid., August 1909.

59. Ibid., November 1918.

60. According to Neva Garner Greenwood, who spoke with family members and checked contemporary newspaper reports, Powell prided herself on not disappointing audiences by canceling. She had been advised to rest but insisted on finishing her tour.

61. At least, so it was reported in the press. However, at sometime the violin was either owned or borrowed by the French violinist Renée Chemet, and in October 1925 Turner sold it, stating its history along with the bill of sale. Somehow it fell into the hands of Henry Ford and presently is in the Ford collection at Greenfield Village, Dearborn, Michigan.

62. Sidney Homer, *My Wife and I,* p. 28.

63. *Musical Herald,* August 1882. Her most recent translation, in 1882, had been of Brahms's *Nänie.*

64. *Folio,* February 1877.

65. Arthur M. Abell, "The Arma Senkrah Tragedy," *The Musical Courier,* October 17, 1900, p. 33.

66. Although Mary Park Clements, a long-time friend of Jackson's in her later years, says she was born February 20, 1874 (letter to the author, June 24, 1978). Her scrapbooks and other papers were left to the Maryland Historical Society and Library of Congress.

67. *Musical Record,* January 1900.

68. Philip Hart, *Orpheus in the New World,* p. 36.

69. *Freund's Weekly,* October 1885.

70. *Folio,* April 1888.

71. W. S. B. Mathews, in the *Etude,* February 1897, lists the Musical College, Chicago Conservatory, Gottschalk School, Metropolitan Conservatory, and American Conservatory, and the Spiering, Listermann, and (new) Chicago Symphony quartets. In 1912 it was estimated that there were at least 2,000 teachers of the violin and other non-keyboard instruments in New York City, and they had some 20,000 pupils.

72. Mr. and Mrs. Adolf Hahn, violinists who played together and as soloists, both began their studies at the Cincinnati College of Music and were married in 1898. Their

repertory for joint performances included the Bach and Mozart double concertos and many arrangements of works made especially for them *(Musical Record,* August 1, 1899, p. 364).

73. *Musical Record,* February 1890.

74. Maida Parlow French, *Kathleen Parlow: A Portrait.* The author was a cousin of the violinist. Kathleen Parlow taught at Mills College, in California, and later at the Toronto Conservatory.

75. The *Etude* of December 1917 announced that there was a great demand for girl violinists to play in orchestras, for vaudeville, and in concerts, and good violinists had no trouble getting jobs. Presumably they, like World War II's "Rosie the Riveter," were laid off when the men returned home.

76. Winn's statement appeared in an article entitled "Music and Matrimony," in the *Musical Record,* December 1900.

77. Quoted in *Women in Music,* vol. 2, no. 8, June 1937.

78. Fisher, p. 177.

79. *Etude,* May 1921.

80. Donal Henahan, *New York Times,* February 9, 1976.

81. In 1978, as first recipient of the Philip M. Faucett String Prize, she gave a recital, of which Allen Hughes wrote (in the *New York Times,* March 23, 1978): "She is a virtuoso whose affinity for her instrument and its literature seems so complete as to make them inseparable. Tonally, technically, musically and expressively, her playing is so right that one automatically attends to what she is doing, respects it, and, generally, feels in accord with it."

82. Donal Henahan, *New York Times,* November 9, 1978.


## *Chapter 3*

1. Quoted by A. Loesser, *Men, Women, and Pianos,* p. 509.

2. Brooks, *Olden-Time Music,* p. 99. Another early performance was that of nine-year-old Lucy Moller, who appeared with her father, John Christopher Moller, in Philadelphia in 1792 and 1793.

3. Loesser, *Men, Women, and Pianos,* p. 449.

4. Ibid., p. 453. Brooks (p. 100) quotes her ad from the *Columbian Centinel,* 1799.

5. Ibid., pp. 472 f.

6. Paul Eric Paige, "Musical Organizations in Boston: 1830–1850," p. 347. A small book of unknown authorship, *A Biographical Sketch of Jane Sloman the Celebrated Pianiste* (Boston: Dutton & Wentworth, 1841) gives a little more information about her childhood.

7. Marc Pincherle, *The World of the Virtuoso, p. 23.*

8. Most of the biographical information about Carreño is based on Marta Milinowski, *Teresa Carreño, "By the Grace of God," passim,* and Victor Chapin, *Giants of the Keyboard,* pp. 138–46.

9. This was the single most famous work of Philadelphia composer Septimus Winner (1827–1902), who often wrote under the pseudonym Alice Hawthorne, a rare (perhaps unique) example of a male composer taking a woman's name for the purpose of publication. The reverse was much more common. (See Charles Eugene Claghorne, *The Mocking Bird.)* However, James Weldon Johnson (in "Negro Songmakers,"

*The Negro in Music and Art,* ed. Lindsay Patterson) wrote in 1930 that Winner originally heard the tune from Richard Milburn, a black barber, guitarist, and whistler who worked on Lombard Street in Philadelphia and used to perform it in public. The title page of the original publication, by Winner and Shuster in 1855, said "Melody by Richard Milburn, written and arranged by Alice Hawthorne," but in the 1856 edition, published by Lee & Walker, Milburn's name did not appear.

10. Teresa Carreño, "Individuality in Piano Playing," *Etude,* 1909, p. 805.

11. Milinowski and Chapin agree; further, *Freund's,* April 10, 1884, quotes Carreño herself from an article of hers in the *Chicago News.*

12. The biographical details in the preceding paragraphs are based on Milinowski.

13. On a program that also included Beethoven's Appassionata Sonata, a Chopin Prelude, Polonaise, and Tarentelle, a Schubert Impromptu, and shorter works by Mendelssohn, Rubinstein, and Schumann, among others! (W.S.B. Mathews, *A Hundred Years of Music in America,* pp. 116-17.)

14. James Huneker, in the *Etude,* January 1888, p. 2.

15. Charles Wolff, in the *Musical Record,* May 1891, p. 3.

16. Teresa Carreño, *Possibilities of Tone Color by Artistic Use of Pedals.* Like many musicians, however, she was less successful in teaching her own children, though at least two of them were undeniably gifted. Teresita Tagliapetra made her debut as a pianist in 1901 but, although talented, she proved too undisciplined for a successful concert career. Giovanni Tagliapetra, Jr., became an opera singer, but he, too, proved too temperamental and undisciplined to fulfill his early promise. Eugenia and Hertha appear not to have tried to play professionally; both eventually married Germans and remained in Germany.

17. Quoted by Henry Charles Lahee, *Famous Pianists in America,* pp. 302-13.

18. *Musical Record,* December, 1900, p. 523.

19. *Etude,* August 1917.

20. Ruth Payne Burgess, "Reminiscences of Teresa Carreño," *Etude,* November 1930.

21. Egbertina Remy, "Teresa Carreño as Teacher," *The Associated Music Teacher League, Inc.,* November 1951, p. 3.

22. The statement appeared in an editorial in *Freund's,* May 16, 1885.

23. *Dwight's Journal of Music,* May 15, 1875; July 1876; April 14, 1877; September 1, 1877.

24. There are several brief accounts of her early life and career. I have relied on those of Janet M. Green (*Musical Biographies,* pp. 145–46), F. O. Jones (*Handbook of American Music and Musicians,* pp. 145–46), Lahee (*Famous Pianists,* pp. 318–21), and Albert E. Wier (*The Piano; Its History, Makers, Players, and Music,* p. 406), among others.

25. Mathews, *A Hundred Years of Music in America,* p. 116.

26. *Dwight's Journal of Music,* April 14, 1877, p. 5.

27. Ibid., October 27, 1877, p. 117.

28. "G." in a letter to the editor, *Musical Record,* February 8, 1879, p. 290.

29. *Musical Record,* February, 1879.

30. *Dwight's Journal of Music,* April 26, 1879. Such transcriptions were common practice throughout the nineteenth century. Beethoven himself transcribed his Violin Concerto for piano, and as late as 1918 or so one of the most popular piano recital

pieces was Ernest Hutcheson's transcription of the *Ride of the Valkyrie* (from Wagner's *Ring*), preserved in a legendary recording by Olga Samaroff.

31. *Musical Herald*, August 1883, p. 212.

32. Raymond Morin, *The Worcester Music Festival, Its Background and History 1858-1946*, p. 47.

33. *Folio*, June 1881.

34. *Etude*, May 1899, p. 134.

35. Loesser, *Men, Women, and Pianos*, p. 539.

36. Annette Essipoff (1851-1914), a Russian, was a pupil of Leschetizky's and also was married to him for a time. A brilliant virtuoso, she toured Europe and America, and then returned to Russia to teach at the St. Petersburg Conservatory. Prokofiev was one of her pupils.

37. *Freund's*, November 15, 1883.

38. Ibid., March 1885. A.L., or Amelia Lewis, was the pen name of Amelia Louise Freund, mother of publisher Harry E. Freund and one of the wittiest, most outspoken reviewers of this period.

39. *Etude*, April 1887, p. 51.

40. Ibid., December 1894.

41. Ibid., January 1888, p. 2.

42. Leschetizky was the most renowned piano teacher of his time. The pianist Harold Bauer, in his autobiography (*Harold Bauer, His Book*, p. 135) tells of dining at Leschetizky's home in Vienna just after a large class had met. As the young women were leaving, Leschetizky looked at them and said, "Just think! Some fellow must be found for each one of these girls, and his sole reason for existence will be to nullify their studies and ruin their careers."

43. By Francis Williams, in *Freund's*, July 12, 1890.

44. *Freund's*, January 3, 1891.

45. Bauer (p. 87) says that the artist was greeted with yells, catcalls, and the like. She began to play and was forced to stop. Lamoureux then announced to the audience that the performance would proceed, so they might as well stop making noise and listen to what they had paid to hear, but some of the rumpus continued.

46. *Etude*, February 1896. Actually, her repertory was even larger. Between 1891 and 1924, when she appeared just about annually with the Chicago Symphony, she played, in addition to these concertos, ones by Grieg, Henselt, Moszkowski, Mendelssohn, Liszt, Mozart, and Tchaikovsky.

47. "Fannie Bloomfield Zeisler," *Dictionary of American Biography*, pp. 647-48.

48. *Etude*, November 1929.

49. Ibid., December 1908.

50. Ibid., August 1909.

51. Ibid., April 1910.

52. Much of this material is based on Mathews, *A Hundred Years of Music in America*.

53. *Dwight's Journal of Music*, March 3, 1877.

54. Susan Andrews Rice, *Etude*, May 1891, p. 91.

55. Amy Fay, *Music-Study in Germany*, p. 168.

56. Biographical details for Aus der Ohe are based on Lahee, *Famous Pianists;* Wier, *The Piano;* and *Baker's Biographical Dictionary of Musicians*, 5th ed.

57. *Freund's,* February 1889.

58. James Huneker, *Etude,* January, 1888.

59. *Musical Herald,* February 1888, p. 44.

60. *Etude,* January 1925.

61. Much of the biographical detail about Samaroff comes from her autobiography, *An American Musician's Story, passim.*

62. Milinowski, *Teresa Carreño, "By the Grace of God,"* p. 308.

63. *Etude,* January 1917.

64. For information about Tureck I have relied heavily on an unsigned article in the *New Yorker Magazine,* October 10, 1977, pp. 36–38.

65. Allan Kozinn, *New York Times,* October 9, 1977.

66. Wier, *The Piano,* p. 398.

67. U.S. Works Progress Administration, *History of Music in San Francisco,* vol. 5, pp. 80–87; the two quotations appear on p. 83 and p. 87.

68. Yehudi Menuhin, *Unfinished Journey,* pp. 319–20.

69. Ruth Slenczynska and Louis Biancolli, *Forbidden Childhood, passim.*

70. Renée B. Fisher, *Musical Prodigies: Masters at an Early Age,* pp. 73 ff.

## Chapter 4

1. Several other groups were active in eighteenth-century America, but they were quite isolated from the mainstream. The most important were two German-speaking religious groups in Pennsylvania, those of the Cloister at Ephrata, and the Moravians of Bethlehem, Lititz, and Nazareth, who composed hymns and other sacred music in the prevailing European idioms of their forebears. (A branch of Moravians also moved to North Carolina, settling in Salem, now Winston-Salem.)

2. Louis C. Elson, *The History of American Music,* pp. 293–94.

3. Newman wrote for London's *Musical Times,* and is quoted in the *Etude,* August 1910.

4. Leigh K. Scruggs, "Creative Women in Music," p. 8.

5. *Musical Record,* February 1896.

6. H. R. Hawed in *Music and Morals,* quoted in the *Musical Herald,* October 1884, p. 247.

7. Leo R. Lewis, in *Music,* July 1896.

8. These arguments were still alive in February 1973, when *High Fidelity–Musical America* published two articles under the title, "Why Haven't Women Become Great Composers?" (pp. 46–52). One, by Grace Rubin-Rabson, said they hadn't "the ultimate creative spark"; the other, by Judith Rosen, said they had been too long squelched by men.

9. Fannie Bloomfield-Zeisler, "Women in Music," pp. 1–3.

10. *Musical Record,* November 11, 1882, p. 113.

11. Judith Tick, "Women as Professional Musicians in the United States, 1870–1900," pp. 115 f.

12. The *Etude* of September 1901 gives a long list of works by women who produced many kinds of music, but only their songs are listed (p. 312).

13. Elson said that Carl Reinecke, long-time director of the Leipzig Conservatory, believed there is a point beyond which women cannot progress, in both performance

and composition, and Svendsen of Norway and Gade of the Copenhagen Conservatory expressed similar views (pp. 293-94).

14. Many women published under masculine pseudonyms or simply used initials. Among them were Dame Ethel Smyth (1858-1944), whose Mass came out under "E. M. Smyth"; Helen Guy Rhodes (1858-1936), who used the pseudonym Guy d'Hardelot; Augusta Holmès (1847-1903), whose early songs came out under Hermann Zenta; and Carrie Williams Krogmann of Boston (1863-1943), who wrote more than 1,000 semiclassical works under various names, including Paul Ducelle, Karl Kleber, and Victor Hope.

15. Oscar George Theodore Sonneck, *A Bibliography of Early Secular American Music* (original ed.).

16. Simeon Pease Cheney, *The American Singing Book,* p. 103. According to Otto Ebel (*Women Composers*), she married a man named Torry.

17. This information was given to the author by Judith Tick, author of the unpublished Ph.D. diss. "Women Composers in the United States Before 1870." Mrs. Hemans probably was the English poet Felicia Hemans (see also note 19 below).

18. She later married a man named Garrett and moved to Washington, D.C. By 1875 she had written some 200 works, including fantasies, waltzes, and songs. (See John W. Moore, *Complete Encyclopedia of Music,* p. 22.)

19. Presumably she also is the "Sister of Mrs. Hemans" who composed two hymns, "Evening Prayer to the Virgin" and "The Messenger Bird," included in Eva Munson Smith's *Woman in Sacred Song,* where the poet is listed as Mrs. Felecia Dorothea Hemans.

20. *Musical Review,* 1, no. 11 (1838): 120.

21. Tick, "Women Composers" dissertation. Also, Otto Ebel, *Women Composers,* p. 69.

22. Biographical information about Amy Beach is available in standard works such as Gilbert Chase, *America's Music,* p. 378; John Tasker Howard, *Our American Music,* pp. 319-23; Claire Reis, *Composers in America,* p. 21; L. C. Elson, *The History of American Music,* pp. 294 ff; Albert E. Wier, *The Piano; Its History, Makers, Players, and Music.* Of special interest are the articles by Walter Jenkins ("Mrs. H. H. A. Beach") in the *Dictionary of American Biography,* Supplement 3 (1973), pp. 41-43, and Burnet C. Tuthill (" Mrs. H. H. A. Beach") in the *Musical Quarterly,* pp. 297-310, as well as an unpublished Ph.D. diss. by E. Lindsey Merrill, "Mrs. H. H. A. Beach: Her Life and Music."

23. *Folio,* April 1875, p. 123.

24. *Musical Herald,* December 1887, p. 382.

25. Ibid., December 1888, p. 352.

26. Ibid., May 1891, p. 93.

27. Ibid., December 1891, p. 35.

28. All these are quoted in *History of the Handel and Haydn Society,* vol. 2, pp. 16-19.

29. Rupert Hughes, *Contemporary American Composers,* p. 437.

30. *Musical Record,* March 1892, p. 8.

31. *Musical Courier,* May 10, 1893, p. 14.

32. *Musical Herald,* August 1893, p. 206.

33. Hughes, *Contemporary American Composers,* pp. 426-27.

34. Alice Mary Smith (1839–84), an English composer, had written a symphony, as well as four orchestral overtures, five cantatas, a clarinet concerto, and many smaller works. Louise Farrenc (1804–75) of France wrote mostly keyboard and chamber music but also produced three symphonies and two overtures, and Augusta Holmès (1847–1903), also French, wrote several large orchestral works but no symphony as such.

35. Merrill, "Mrs. H. H. A. Beach," p. 121.

36. Even feminists like Fanny Morris Smith (*Etude,* March 1901) expressed this conventional wisdom.

37. Elson, *The History of American Music,* p. 295. Merrill, "Mrs. H. H. A. Beach" (p. 29) also regards it as the best of her instrumental works.

38. Tick, "Women as Professional Musicians" (article), p. 114, says just about all music by women was praised or blamed on the basis of masculine/feminine, but the author has not found this totally true.

39. March 1897.

40. *Musical Record,* May 1, 1899, p. 230.

41. William T. Upton, *Art-Song in America,* p. 304.

42. Raymond Morin, *The Worcester Music Festival.*

43. Mary Louise Boehm, notes on jacket of Turnabout recording QTV-S 34665 (May 1976).

44. Tuthill, "Mrs. H. H. A. Beach," p. 304; also Merrill, "Mrs. H. H. A. Beach," p. 17.

45. *Etude,* February 1904, p. 51.

46. Andrew Porter, *New Yorker,* November 24, 1975, p. 154. The work was performed by the Chamber Music Society of Lincoln Center.

47. Appeared in the *Los Angeles Examiner,* June 28, 1915; reprinted in the *Musical Courier,* July 7, 1915. A year later, in an article on piano she wrote for the *Etude* of October 1916, Beach repeated the same dictum for pianists—that is, technique is a vital basis for expressive playing.

48. Howard, *Our American Music,* p. 321.

49. Morin, *The Worcester Music Festival,* p. 135.

50. In the *Etude,* January 1915, p. 14.

51. The trio was performed in 1974 at Boston's Gardner Museum in an all-Beach program, and again in New York in 1976 in a program of American music by the Bergson Trio. Reviewing the latter, Patrick J. Smith (*New York Times,* April 5, 1976) described the work as "far from negligible in its forthrightly direct rhapsodics, although now and then it exudes a whiff of the palm-leafed salon." He was probably referring to the unabashedly late-romantic last movement. The middle movement, marked Lento espressivo, includes a playful, almost Ivesian treatment of motifs from children's songs that is highly original.

52. In 1927 the members included, among others, Gena Branscombe, Mabel Daniels, Marion Bauer, Ulric Cole, Ethel Glenn Hier, Mabel Wood Hill, Mary Howe, Mary Turner Salter, Lily Strickland, and Harriet Ware.

53. Merrill, "Mrs. H. H. A. Beach," p. 54.

54. Jenkins, "Mrs. H. H. A. Beach."

55. Howard, *Our American Music,* p. 322.

56. *Musical Leader,* May 25, 1940, p. 9.

57. Leonard Ellinwood, *The History of American Church Music,* pp. 221–22. Lang played the piano from an early age, studied in Europe with Satter, Jaell, and Liszt, and made his debut at the age of fifteen in a Mendelssohn Quintette Club concert. In 1862 he organized several concerts in which he conducted a large orchestra, soloists, and a chorus. He was organist at the Old South Church and South Congregational Church before going to Kings Chapel, and he was among the organists who gave recitals in the 1860s at the Boston Music Hall (as did Lillian Frohock; see Chapter 1). His last public appearance was at Boston's Symphony Hall on February 12, 1909, when he took part in a 100-year memorial service for Abraham Lincoln. (See also Thomas Ryan, *Recollections of an Old Musician,* pp. 85–86.)

58. Mrs. Crosby Adams, "Musical Creative Work Among Women," *Music,* January 1896, p. 170.

59. Hughes, *Contemporary American Composers,* p. 434.

60. *Musical Herald,* January 1891, p. 10.

61. Ibid., May 1893, p. 157.

62. In the *Boston Herald,* January 11, 1917.

63. Hughes, *Contemporary American Composers,* p. 435.

64. The principal sources for information about Helen Hood are Elson, *The History of American Music,* p. 306, and Janet M. Green, *Musical Biographies,* p. 388.

65. An excellent biographical account of Daniels is in Madeleine Goss, *Modern Music Makers,* pp. 61–69. Daniels's personal papers, including correspondence, programs, and scores, are in the Manuscript Section of the Schlesinger Library, Radcliffe College, Cambridge, Massachusetts.

66. Mabel Daniels, in *The Christian Science Monitor,* April 22, 1961.

67. In addition to Elson, *The History of American Music* (pp. 307–8), biographical information about Hopekirk is found in Constance Huntington Hall and Helen Ingersoll Tetlow, *Helen Hopekirk, passim.*

68. *Musical Herald,* April 1891, p. 67.

69. *Etude,* September 1901, p. 318.

70. A short biography appears in the *Musical Record,* March 1900, p. 144.

71. *Musical Herald,* January 1883, p. 24.

72. William Upton, *Art-Song in America,* p. 110.

73. A book about Mary Salter, *In Memoriam,* author unknown (but probably her husband), was privately published in 1939; a copy is in the New York Public Library Music Division.

74. Clement Antrobus Harris, "Women Composers of Religious Music," p. 5.

75. Ellinwood, *The History of American Church Music.*

76. Eva Munson Smith, ed., *Woman in Sacred Song.*

77. Ellinwood, *The History of American Church Music,* p. 195.

78. Tick, "Women as Professional Musicians" (article), p. 105, says that the percentage of women in the New York Manuscript Society (a professional composers' organization) doubled between 1892 and 1898. In 1899 the name was changed to the Society of American Musicians and Composers, and all the newly appointed officers and directors were men (*Musical Age,* June 1, 1899, p. 7).

79. In *Freund's Weekly,* June 26, 1886, p. 6.

80. The composers represented, in addition to Amy Beach, were Julia Rivé-King, Mrs. J. T. Draper, Eleanor Smith, Mrs. Nellie Bangs Skelton, Gertrude Griswold,

Helen Hopekirk Wilson, Marie Antoinette, and Cécile Chaminade (*Musical Courier,* May 31, 1893, p. 16).

81. *Freund's Weekly,* January 1896.

82. This information is based on lists of works performed appearing in: Frédéric Louis Ritter, *Music in America,* pp. 362-67; M. A. De Wolfe Howe, *The Boston Symphony Orchestra 1881-1931,* Appendix C; H. Earle Johnson, *Symphony Hall, Boston,* Appendix; James Gibbons Huneker, *The Philharmonic and Its Seventy-fifth Anniversary: A Retrospect,* pp. 49-130; John Erskine, *The Philharmonic Society: Its First Hundred Years,* pp. 66-168; and Howard Shanet, *Philharmonic, A History of New York's Orchestra,* pp. 496-738.

83. *High Fidelity-Musical America,* June 1975, p. 21.

### Chapter 5

1. Philo Adams Otis, *The Chicago Symphony Orchestra,* appendixes listing orchestra personnel to 1924.

2. Sophie Lewis Drinker, *Music and Women,* pp. 106 f, 178 ff.

3. Ibid., pp. 5, 8, 9.

4. Don Burns, "The Distaff'd Composers," pp. 16-17, 32-37.

5. See *Women in Music,* vol. 1, no. 3, September 1935. Burney wrote, "It was really curious to see, as well as to hear, every part of this excellent concert performed by females, violins, tenors, bases, harpsichords, and double bass."

6. Hanslick in *Neue Freie Presse* (Vienna), quoted in *Dwight's Journal of Music,* April 10, 1880, and also in the *Musical Record,* March 27, 1880, p. 395.

7. *Musical Record,* April 17, 1880, letter from George B. Nind, Iowa.

8. Ibid., March 1889.

9. Advertisement in the *Musical Record,* April 1897.

10. *Dexter Smith's Musical, Literary, Dramatic and Art Paper,* December 1873, p. 165.

11. Ibid., March 1874.

12. Ibid., March 1876. Arbuckle (1828-83), virtuoso cornetist and bandmaster, published a cornet method book.

13. *Musical Record,* December 1879, p. 206.

14. *Folio,* 1880, 1881, 1882.

15. *Musical Herald,* May 1885.

16. *Freund's Weekly,* August 22, 1885. Levy was a famous (male) brass virtuoso.

17. *Musical Record,* October 1889.

18. *Musical Herald,* March 1890.

19. *Musical Record,* March 1900. Some thirty-five years earlier Alphonse Sax, inventor of the saxophone, had written a treatise claiming that playing wind instruments was highly beneficial for the lungs and women should be encouraged to do so in women's orchestras. (*Gymnastique des Poumons,* Paris, 1865).

20. *Musical America,* February 26, 1910, p. 15.

21. *Musical Record,* June 13, 1882, p. 538.

22. *Folio,* June 1888.

23. *Etude,* August 1901.

24. *Musical Bulletin,* June 1871, p. 125.

25. *Metronome,* October 1871, p. 55.

26. *Dexter Smith's...Paper,* June 1873.

27. Judith Tick, "Women as Professional Musicians in the United States 1870–1900" (article), p. 100.

28. Ibid., pp. 100-01.

29. *Musical Record,* October 21, 1882, p. 43.

30. Ibid., December 16, 1882, p. 205.

31. *Musical Record,* August 1884, p. 4.

32. "Opinions of New York Leaders on Women as Orchestral Players," *Musical Standard,* April 2, 1904.

33. *Freund's Weekly,* March 5, 1889.

34. *Musical Herald,* March 1885 and January 1886.

35. Ibid., February 1890.

36. *Folio,* February 1888, p. 10.

37. Ibid., May 1888, p. 176. Osgood was also an Eichberg pupil, and this ensemble survived for several seasons. It played at the Plattsburgh (New York) Music Festival in May 1889 (reported in *Freund's Weekly,* June 1889) and in 1891 appeared at the YMCA Hall in Brooklyn, New York (Tick, "Women as Professional Musicians" [article], p. 101).

38. *Freund's Weekly,* September 30, 1896, p. 6.

39. *Musical Record,* March 1900, p. 137.

40. Information about the Fadettes comes principally from *Women in Music,* February 1936, and Blanche Naylor, *The Anthology of the Fadettes.*

41. *Freund's Weekly,* September 30, 1896. p. 6.

42. Reported in the *Christian Science Monitor,* June 3, 1952.

43. Tick, "Women as Professional Musicians" (article), pp. 103-4.

44. *Women in Music,* vol. 1. no. 7, March 1936. The other five were the Philadelphia Women's Orchestra (60), Orchestrette Classique of New York (24), Portland Women's Symphony (35), New York Women's Symphony (85), and Women's Little Symphony of Cleveland (43).

45. The principal sources of information about these organizations are contemporary music journals and all the issues of *Women in Music.* A summary appears in Frederique Petrides, "Women in Orchestras," *Etude,* July 1938, pp. 429–30, 474.

46. *Etude,* April, 1916.

47. Ibid., June 1925, p. 383.

48. Ibid., August 1925, p. 591.

49. Beatrice Brown of the Ridgefield (Connecticut) Symphonette, quoted by Barbara Jepson, "American Women in Conducting," *Feminist Art Journal,* Winter 1975/76, p. 16.

50. Johnson, Harold Earle, *Hallelujah, amen!* p. 113.

51. Boston Public Library scrapbook, Boston Music Hall.

52. Amy Fay, *Music-Study in Germany,* p. 117.

53. Biographical information about Leginska comes chiefly from the clipping files of the New York and Boston Public libraries, and the history of the Boston Women's Symphony from a clipping file in the Boston Public Library.

54. *Musical Courier,* July 1919.

55. Biographical material about Brico comes chiefly from a clipping file in the New York Public Library, an article in *Current Biography* (September 1948), and articles in the *New York Times* (September 15 and 19, 1974; May 19, 1975; March 4, 1977), *Boston Globe* (February 8, 1976), and *Opera News* (February 14, 1976, p. 14).

56. *New York World Telegram,* February 5, 1937.

57. *Current Biography,* September 1948, p. 10.

58. *Women in Music,* June 1937, reported that as of April 1, 1937, the WPA Music Project included 2,253 female musicians and had featured some of them as guest conductors with major orchestras.

59. Information about this orchestra is principally from *Women in Music, passim.*

60. *New York Herald Tribune,* October 16, 1940.

61. Information from the Boston Public Library clipping file on the Boston Women's Symphony.

62. One of the last and most extraordinary women's orchestras the author knows of was that of the Birkenau concentration camp of Auschwitz, movingly described by one of its survivors, Fania Fénelon, in *Playing for Time,* trans. Judith Landry (New York: Atheneum, 1977). Created in 1944 and functioning for about one year, it was conducted by Alma Rosé, a niece of Gustav Mahler's, and included a bizarre assortment of players: ten violins, one flute, reed pipes, two accordions, three guitars, five mandolins, drums, and cymbals. The forty-nine women engaged in playing and copying music for this ensemble in large part owed their lives to it, for they were given a heated room and blankets (though no extra food) and were released from the arduous physical labor required of ordinary inmates.

63. Some had done so for a long time. The Civic Orchestra of Chicago already had twenty-four women during the 1921–22 season (one clarinet and the others string players).

## Chapter 6

1. Biographical information about Mary Howe comes largely from Madeleine Goss, *Modern Music Makers,* Mary Howe's autobiography, *Jottings,* and conversations and correspondence with her friend Anne Hull in 1977 and 1978 and her son Calderon (1978). Information about programs comes from Mary Howe's papers, preserved on microfilm in the New York Public Library Music Division (programs, reviews, letters, etc.).

2. Howe, *Jottings,* p. 89.

3. Ibid.

4. Emile Bauer, *Musical Leader,* October 15, 1925.

5. Howe, *Jottings,* p. 89.

6. This last piece was written in what Mary Howe called "an access of musical spleen" (*Jottings,* p. 85). She had entered a number of competitions without results. Finally one year the League of American Pen-Women's Music Division offered a prize for a chamber work to be played at the big dinner or lunch of their convention. "Imagine," wrote Howe, "five hundred women lunching and trying to make them swallow chamber music. I thought violently to myself, 'I bet I can write a piece that's sobbing and sloppy enough to win that prize, serve them right!' " So she wrote *Cancion romanesco* and it won. "I was really ashamed," she said, but went on to say

it had since been played beautifully by several string quartets, so maybe "it had or has its uses."

7. Interview published in the *Washington Post,* December 26, 1952, p. 25.

8. Ray C. B. Brown, *Washington Post,* April 16, 1939.

9. Reviews from *Music Clubs Magazine* and *Musical America,* quoted in Howe, *Jottings,* p. 170.

10. Interview, *supra,* n. 7.

11. Howe, *Jottings,* pp. 141–42.

12. For biographical information about Marion Bauer I have relied chiefly on Claire R. Reis, *Composers in America,* Madeleine Goss, *Modern Music Makers,* Irwin A. Bazelon, "Woman with a Symphony," and David Ewen, *American Composers Today,* pp. 20-22; also, an interview with her friend of thirty years, Harrison Potter (on June 20, 1978), and letters from two of her former students, J. Vincent Higginson and composer Julia Smith.

13. Emilie Frances Bauer also was born in Walla Walla, Washington. She studied with Miguel Espinosa and at the Paris Conservatory, and then taught piano and voice in Portland, Oregon. She went east about 1896, teaching and writing in Boston for a time, and then moved to New York. From 1902 to 1903 she edited a women's page in the *Etude.* For many years she also wrote for the *Musical Leader, Concert-Goer,* and other periodicals, as well as publishing her own compositions under the pseudonym Francesco Nogero.

14. William T. Upton, *Art-Song in America,* p. 145.

15. The others, in addition to chairman Copland, were Douglas Moore, Elie Siegmeister, Quincy Porter, Roy Harris, Wallingford Riegger, Virgil Thomson, Roger Sessions, Goddard Lieberson, and Bernard Wagenaar (according to Julia Smith, *Aaron Copland,* p. 181).

16. *New York Times,* May 9, 1951.

17. Bazelon, "Woman with a Symphony," p. 6.

18. For biographical and critical information about Ruth Crawford Seeger I have relied heavily on an excellent unpublished doctoral dissertation by Mary Matilda Gaume, "Ruth Crawford Seeger: Her Life and Works." Gaume (born 1910) taught music and musicology for many years and did exhaustive research for her dissertation, studying all of Crawford's scores in the Library of Congress and contacting Charles Seeger and many musicians who had known her well.

19. One earlier work, a violin sonata performed at least once in New York and once in Chicago, was destroyed by Crawford around 1923, and presumably other compositions of her early years were similarly discarded.

20. Although Gaume believes it is significant that almost all of Crawford's chamber works are entitled "Suite," on the Delos recording of this work it is called *Two Movements for Chamber Orchestra.*

21. Henry Cowell, *American Composers on American Music,* p. 119.

22. Gaume, "Ruth Crawford Seeger," p. 19.

23. Ibid., p. 178.

24. Robert P. Morgan, record jacket notes, Nonesuch H-71280.

25. *Musical America,* December 15, 1953. Charles Seeger lived for another twenty-five years. When he died in 1979 at ninety-two, the *New York Times* obituary named his surviving children and his third wife but made no mention of Ruth Crawford.

26. Alan Kendall, *The Tender Tyrant: Nadia Boulanger, passim.*

27. Of the women discussed in the present book, the following composers studied with or at least were advised by Nadia Boulanger: Marion Bauer, Mary Howe, Louise Talma, Elinor Remick Warren, Margaret Bonds, Julia Perry, Evelyn LaRue Pittman, Peggy Glanville-Hicks, Thea Musgrave, and Joyce Mekeel, as well as conductors Lorna Cooke de Varon and Frances Steiner.

28. Aaron Copland, *Our New Music: Leading Composers in Europe and America,* pp. 217–19.

29. Interview with Richard Dyer, *Boston Globe,* July 24, 1978.

30. Kendall, *The Tender Tyrant,* pp. 90–91.

31. Quoted by Kendall, ibid., p. 77.

32. For biographical information about Louise Talma I have relied on Goss, *Modern Music Makers,* pp. 383–91; a biographical questionnaire filled out by the composer for the American Music Center, New York; and a curriculum vitae sent by her to the author in 1978.

33. *New York Times,* May 5, 1946.

34. According to Virgil Thomson, writing in 1962; quoted by Kendall, *The Tender Tyrant,* p. 69.

35. Arthur Berger, "Stravinsky and the Younger American Composers."

36. Interview with Raymond Ericson, *New York Times,* February 4, 1977.

37. Elaine Barkin, "Louise Talma: 'The Tolling Bell.'"

38. Donal Henahan, *New York Times,* March 18, 1976.

39. Joseph Horowitz, *New York Times,* February 7, 1977.

40. On February 28, 1978, at Christ and St. Stephens Church, New York.

41. Donal Henahan, *New York Times,* March 2, 1978.

42. I have relied on the following sources for biographical information about Dika Newlin: the composer herself (correspondence, 1978); *New Jersey Music and Arts,* May 1953, pp. 9–10; Konrad Wolff, "Dika Newlin."

43. Wolff, "Dika Newlin."

44. Ibid.

45. In a letter to the author, February 2, 1978.

46. Biographical information is based on the composer's own brochure, listing published works, and a letter to the author, February 20, 1978.

47. Quoted on the record jacket, Composers Recordings Inc., CRI 172.

48. *Musical America,* June 1975, p. 21.


## Chapter 7

1. Gilbert Chase, *America's Music,* p. 209.

2. Eileen Southern, ed., *Readings in Black American Music,* p. 139.

3. Quoted by Eileen Southern, *The Music of Black Americans,* p. 200.

4. For basic information about these women I have relied on Gilbert Chase, *America's Music,* pp. 405–6; John Tasker Howard, *Our American Music: A Comprehensive History; Baker's Biographical Dictionary,* 1965 ed.

5. Reported in the *Etude,* August 1893.

6. Miriam Stewart Green, "Consider These Creators," p. 11.

7. For biographical information about Julia Smith I have relied on the following: John Vinton, ed., *Dictionary of Contemporary Music*, pp. 687–88; Howard, *Our American Music*, p. 569; Mary Craig, "Julia Smith: Composer and Ambassadress of U.S. Music"; program notes by the composer for Columbia University concert, November 7, 1976.

8. Letter from Julia Smith to the author, December 30, 1975, written shortly after her husband's death.

9. Julia Smith, *Aaron Copland*, p. 10.

10. From program notes by the composer for Decade of International Women concert, November 7, 1976, at Columbia University's McMillin Theatre, New York City.

11. *New York Herald Tribune*, May 15, 1950, quoted by Howard, *Our American Music*.

12. Letter from Smith to author.

13. Biographical material for Radie Britain is based on Claire R. Reis, *Composers in America*, pp. 51–52; Madeleine Goss. *Modern Music Makers: Contemporary American Composers*, pp. 347 f; letter from composer to author, April 27, 1978.

14. From Douglass's *My Bondage and My Freedom* (1855 ed.), quoted by Southern, *Readings*, pp. 83 f.

15. According to Eileen Southern in her excellent book, *The Music of Black Americans*, the much larger body of the blacks' social music—work songs, play songs, dance songs, story songs, songs of social comment, satirical songs, field hollers, and street cries—was largely ignored. Spirituals were an amalgamation of many elements—the psalmody of the early American churches, later Protestant hymnody, Anglo-Saxon ballads, and even French band music. They were sung during actual worship services in church; for funerals and other sorrowful occasions; and for shouts, a religious dance in which the dancers moved in a circle, using a kind of rhythmic shuffling step with a jerking, hitching motion, accompanied by a group of singers who also provided percussion accompaniment by clapping their hands or hitting their knees or thighs.

16. Zora Neale Hurston, "Spirituals and Neo-spirituals," in Lindsay Patterson, ed., *The Negro in Music and Art* pp. 15–17.

17. Southern, *Music of Black Americans*, p. 213.

18. Ibid., pp. 100–4.

19. Most of the biographical information about Florence Price is based on Mildred Denby Green's dissertation, "A Study of the Lives and Works of Five Black Women Composers," and Marie Joy Yuhasz, O.P., "Black Composers and Their Piano Music."

20. Margaret Bonds, "A Reminiscence" (1967), in Patterson, *The Negro in Music and Art*, pp. 190–93.

21. For biographical information about Bonds I have relied on her "Reminiscence," Green's "A Study...of Five Black Women Composers" (diss.), and Yuhasz, "Black Composers and Their Piano Music."

22. Bonds, "Reminiscence."

23. Green, "A Study...of Five Black Women Composers" (diss.), p. 143.

24. Hildred Roach, *Black American Music: Past and Present,* p. 113.

25. Bonds, "Reminiscence," p. 192.

26. For information about Julia Perry I have relied on Green, "A Study...of Five Black Women Composers" (dissertation); Southern, *Music of Black Americans;* Howard, *Our American Music,* p. 613; letter from the composer to the author, April 24, 1978.

27. Green, "A Study...of Five Black Women Composers" (dissertation), pp. 195–213.

28. Ibid., pp. 255–85.

29. Information about Alice Parker comes principally from program notes and a letter written by the composer to the author, May 1978.

30. For information about Gena Branscombe I have relied on Goss, *Modern Music Makers,* pp. 82–90; Reis, *Composers in America,* pp. 47–48; Howard, *Our American Music,* p. 634; "Showcase" (no author), *Music Clubs Magazine,* Special Issue, 1962; and information informally compiled by Laurine Elkins-Marlow for a doctoral dissertation in progress ("Gena Branscombe: American Composer and Conductor," Ph.D. diss., University of Texas at Austin, 1978).

31. Goss, *Modern Music Makers,* p. 87.

32. *Music Clubs Magazine,* p. 9.

33. Ibid.

## Chapter 8

1. Edward Ellsworth Hipsher, *American Opera and Its Composers,* pp. 321–22.

2. For information about Eleanor Everest Freer I have relied on Hipsher, ibid., pp. 183–89; Eleanor Everest Freer, *Recollections and Reflections of an American Composer;* Agnes Greene Foster, *Eleanor Everest Freer—Patriot and Her Colleagues.*

3. Hipsher, *American Opera,* pp. 353–55.

4. Ibid., pp. 256–58, and the *Etude,* May 1928.

5. *Musical America,* July 17, 1909.

6. *Etude,* April 1916.

7. *Musical America,* July 24, 1909; Edwin N. C. Barnes, *American Women in Creative Music,* pp. 9, 10; program notes, *Sacramento Souvenir* (Music and Art), 1907.

8. Information about Mary Carr Moore comes from John Tasker Howard, *Our American Music,* and contemporary papers and journals.

9. Grandval is listed in *Baker's Biographical Dictionary,* 1965 ed.; see also the *Etude,* July 1909, p. 446.

10. *Baker's Biographical Dictionary,* 1965 ed.; Milton Goldin, *The Music Merchants,* p. 110.

11. Information about Emma Steiner has been exceptionally difficult to obtain. A pamphlet by Margaret I. MacDonald (*The Greatest Battles Ever Fought Are the Silent Ones Fought by Women*), published on March 17, 1918, is the only source of biographical information about her I could locate, but it conflicts in some details with paragraphs published in music journals from time to time, notably the *Musical*

*Record,* January 1897, p. 2; the *Folio,* March 1891, p. 90; the *Etude,* March 1897; *Women in Music,* November 1935; Frederique Petrides, "Women in Orchestras," the *Etude,* July 1938; and the *New York Times* obituary, datelined February 27, 1929.

12. *Freund's Weekly,* August 29, 1891.

13. Ibid., February 12, 1896.

14. *Etude,* March 1897.

15. Andrew Porter, *New Yorker,* January 26, 1970, p. 90.

16. Information on Caldwell is largely based on Donal Henahan, "Prodigious Sarah," *New York Times Magazine,* October 5, 1975, and Robert Jones, "Walking into the Fire," *Opera News,* February 14, 1976.

17. Richard Dyer, *New York Times,* January 11, 1976.

18. Interview with Raymond Ericson, *New York Times,* January 7, 1977.

19. Ibid., also Greta Walker, *Women Today: Ten Profiles,* pp. 75–89.

20. Joseph Horowitz, *New York Times,* April 24, 1978.

21. Ericson interview.

22. Walker, *Women Today,* pp. 87–88.

23. Biographical information about Somogi comes from Allen Hughes, *New York Times,* March 15, 1974; Raymond Ericson, *New York Times,* May 8, 1977; press release from Herbert Barrett Management, New York, April 12, 1977.

24. *New York Times,* June 4, 1977.

25. Quoted by Barbara Jepson, "American Women in Conducting," p. 18.

26. Ericson, *New York Times,* May 8, 1977.

27. Based largely on Deborah Seabury, "La Maestra," *Opera News,* February 14, 1976.

28. Ibid.

29. Material about Glanville-Hicks comes from a 1969 brochure from Broadcast Music, Inc., New York; Howard, *Our American Music,* p. 566; and from the composer herself.

30. George Antheil, "Peggy Glanville-Hicks," *Bulletin of the American Composers Alliance,* vol. iv, no. 1, 1954.

31. Virgil Thomson, *American Music Since 1910,* [1971], p. 12.

32. Letter from the composer to the author, June 1, 1978.

33. Information about Musgrave is based on Susan Bradshaw, "Thea Musgrave," *Musical Times* (London), December 1963; Shirley Fleming, *New York Times,* September 25, 1977; Andrew Porter, *New Yorker,* November 24, 1975; *Time,* October 10, 1977, p. 72.

34. Humphrey Searle and Robert Laton, *Twentieth Century Composers,* vol. 3: *Britain, Scandinavia, and the Netherlands,* p. 118.

35. *Opera News,* February 14, 1976.

36. Quoted by Fleming, *New York Times,* September 25, 1977.

37. Andrew Porter, *New Yorker,* October 24, 1977.

38. Harold C. Schonberg, *New York Times,* October 2, 1977.

39. Quoted by Fleming, *New York Times,* September 25, 1977.

40. Andrew Porter, *New Yorker,* May 1, 1978.

41. Harold C. Schonberg, *New York Times,* March 31, 1978.

42. *Opera News,* February 14, 1976.

43. Composers of opera discussed in other chapters (because they are notable principally for work in other forms) are Amy Beach (Chapter 4); Ethel Leginska (Chapter 5); Louise Talma (Chapter 6); Julia Smith and Alice Parker (Chapter 7); Miriam Gideon and Vivian Fine (Chapter 11).

### Chapter 9

1. Janet Baker-Carr, *Evening at Symphony,* p. 141.

2. Biographical information comes from the composer herself.

3. *San Francisco Chronicle,* December 12, 1957.

4. Unsigned review, *Long Player,* May 1958; Oliver Daniel. *Saturday Review,* December 26, 1959.

5. R. L. Cherry, *Tucson Tonight,* May 25, 1976, reprinted in part in *High Fidelity/Musical America,* July 1976.

6. Biographical information from the composer herself, and from Broadcast Music, Inc., *The Many Worlds of Music,* Issue 4, 1977, p. 31.

7. Biographical information from record jacket notes, Delos 25405, *Premiere Performances by Boston Musica Viva,* and the composer herself.

8. Biographical information about Kolb is based on interviews with Donal Henahan (*New York Times,* November 17, 1976) and Richard Dyer (*Boston Globe,* February 18, 1978); jacket notes of Turnabout TVS 34487 and Desto 7143; and John Vinton, ed., *Dictionary of Contemporary Music.*

9. Information from the composer herself.

10. Information about Ran comes from the *Instrumentalist,* December 1976; curriculum vitae at American Music Center, New York, and University of Chicago; letter from composer to author, July 9, 1978.

11. *High Fidelity/Musical America,* July 1975, p. MA-29.

12. Information about Ivey comes from the composer herself; also Joseph McLellan, *Washington Post,* November 10, 1974; Sam di Bonaventura, Program Notes, Baltimore Symphony Orchestra (for *Testament of Eve*), April 21–22, 1976; Jean Eichelberger Ivey, "Observations by Composers," in Elliott Schwartz, *Electronic Music: A Listener's Guide,* pp 230–33.

13. Ivey in Schwartz, *Electronic Music,* p. 231.

14. Information about Oliveros is based principally on: biography by Barney Childs, in Vinton, *Dictionary of Contemporary Music;* Pauline Oliveros, "Observations by Composers," in Schwartz, *Electronic Music,* pp. 246–49; John Rockwell, *New York Times,* September 23, 1977 and March 26, 1978.

15. Quoted by Childs, in Vinton, *Dictionary of Contemporary Music,* p. 530.

16. Gordon Mumma, in Jon H. Appleton and Ronald C. Perera, eds. *The Development and Practice of Electronic Music,* pp. 329–30.

17. Oliveros, in Schwartz, *Electronic Music,* p. 248.

18. John Rockwell, *New York Times,* September 23, 1977.

19. Ibid., March 26, 1978.

20. Biographical information about Semegen comes principally from the composer and from Broadcast Music, Inc., *The Many Worlds of Music,* Issue 4, 1977, pp. 41–42.

21. Information about Smiley comes from the composer herself.

22. Record jacket notes, Electronic Music, vol. iv, Turnabout TV 34301.

23. Biographical material about Dlugoszewski comes from Vinton, *Dictionary of Contemporary Music,* pp. 185–87; Thomson, *American Music Since 1910,* p. 139; Broadcast Music, Inc., *The Many Worlds of Music,* Issue 4, 1977, p. 17.

24. Published in *Main Currents,* 1971.

25. Thomson, *American Music Since 1910,* p. 139.

26. George Gelles, *New York Times,* April 11, 1976.

27. Raymond Ericson, *New York Times,* December 10, 1975.

28. Biographical information about Simons comes mainly from the composer and from Broadcast Music, Inc., *The Many Worlds of Music,* Issue 4, 1977, pp. 43, 46.

29. Information about Spiegel comes from the composer.

30. John Rockwell, *New York Times,* September 19, 1976.

31. Letter from Spiegel to the author, August 30, 1978.

32. Information about Ciani comes from the composer and an interview with Helen Epstein, *New York Times,* June 21, 1974.

33. Joel Chadabe, in Appleton and Perera, *The Development and Practice of Electronic Music,* pp. 139-40, 143.

34. Information about Anderson comes from the composer.

35. Robert Palmer, *New York Times,* May 16, 1978.

36. Spiegel letter, August 30, 1978.

### Chapter 10

1. Howard Shanet, *Philharmonic, a History of New York's Orchestra,* pp. 107-8.

2. *Ibid.,* p. 347.

3. *Musical Herald,* November 1891.

4. Frédéric Louis Ritter, *Music in America,* p. 277.

5. Philip Hart, *Orpheus in the New World,* pp. 120-21.

6. Lubov Keefer, *Music Angels: A Thousand Years of Patronage.*

7. Jerzy Bojanowsky, "Championing the Woman Orchestral Player," *Musical Courier,* January 15, 1945. Hope Stoddard ("Fine Musicianship Knows No Sex," in *Independent Woman,* November 1947) said women had broken into eighteen major orchestras, on the following instruments: sixty-six violin; twelve viola; twenty-one cello; seven double bass; four piccolo; seven flute; four oboe; one English horn; five bassoon; three French horn; two trombone; two percussion; twenty-one harp. But she contended that most think a woman must play better than a man to get the same job.

8. *Etude,* February 1916.

9. Thomas Beecham, "The Position of Women," *Vogue's First Reader.* He also maintained that "there are no women composers, never have been, and possibly never will be."

10. *Etude,* April 1931.

11. Ethel Smyth, *Female Pipings in Eden,* pp. 10-11.

12. Sophie Lewis Drinker, *Music and Women: The Story of Women in Their Relation to Music,* p. 239.

13. Alan Rich, *Careers and Opportunities in Music,* p. 129; Renée B. Fisher, *(Musical Prodigies: Masters at an Early Age,* p. 176) agrees.

14. Information about Doriot Dwyer comes principally from *Opera News,* February 14, 1976; interview with Richard Dyer, *Boston Globe,* January 15, 1978; *Christian Science Monitor,* October 7, 1952; and Helen Epstein, "Notes from the Orchestra Pit," *MS,* March 1977.

15. In 1979, there were still eleven women and ninety-five men.

16. *Etude,* April, 1917.

17. *Women in Music,* June 1, 1938.

18. Leona May Smith, "Is There A Career for Women Musicians?"

19. Maud Powell, "The Violinist."

20. It is interesting to compare this with figures released by the American Federation of Musicians for 1967: The average annual salary for a member of a major symphony was $6,900 for thirty-seven weeks; in a small ensemble, up to $200 per concert; in a dance band, $60 to $300 per week.

21. Philo Adams Otis, *The Chicago Symphony Orchestra: Its Growth and Development 1891-1924,* p. 351.

22. *New York Times,* December 21, 1975, p. 36, and December 19, 1976.

23. Hart, *Orpheus in the New World,* pp. 110, 115-16.

24. A summary published in *Music Journal,* January 1972, gave the following figures: New York Philharmonic, 3 women, 103 men; Philadelphia Orchestra, 9 women, 99 men; Boston Symphony Orchestra, 8 women, 93 men; Chicago Symphony, 4 women, 100 men; Cleveland Orchestra, 14 women, 94 men.

25. Information about the Elayne Jones case is based on the following sources: *New York Times,* August 2, 1974, and August 27, 1975; Richard Dyer, *Boston Globe,* September 21, 1975; Helen Epstein, "Notes from the Orchestra Pit," *MS,* March 1977.

26. *New York Times,* February 6, 1977.

27. *Symphony News,* April 1976.

28. Jean Bowen, "Women in Music—Their Fair Share," p. MA-20.

29. Ibid.

30. Helen Epstein, "Selling Tomorrow's Big Names Today," *New York Times,* Febuary 15, 1976.

31. *Freund's Weekly,* May 13, 1896.

32. Data on Clark is based on material put together by Katherine D. Moore from Clark's and her own files. Sent to the author June 24, 1979 (Mrs. Moore was a pupil of Clark's, played in the orchestra from 1927 to 1972, and wrote much of its publicity.) Information about Edmister is based on a letter from her to the author, March 8, 1978; a telephone interview, February 14, 1978; and clippings from contemporary New Mexico papers *(Albuquerque Advance, Albuquerque Journal, New Mexico State Tribune)* and the *Defiance* (Ohio) *Crescent News.*

33. Information about Bergen comes mainly from an interview with Joseph Horowitz, *New York Times,* January 14, 1977.

34. Joseph Horowitz, *New York Times,* November 8, 1976.

35. *Etude,* April 1931.

36. Ibid., October 1931.

37. Ibid., April 1933.

38. Ibid., March 1927.

39. Ibid., July 1924.

40. Ibid., February 1972.

41. Information about Hillis comes from the 1978 *Program Notes* of the Chicago Symphony Orchestra; *Pan Pipes,* May 1976, p. 22; *Time,* August 2, 1976; Donal Henahan and Raymond Ericson, *New York Times,* November 2, 1977.

42. Interview with Richard Dyer, *Boston Globe,* March 28, 1978.

43. For much of the information in the succeeding paragraphs, on Harris, Johnson, Steiner, Brown, and Hillis, I have relied on Barbara Jepson, "American Women in Conducting."

44. Quoted by Jepson, ibid., p. 14.

45. Information about Bond comes mainly from *International Musician,* vol. 74, no. 1, July 1975; Herbert Kupferberg, "Women of the Baton—The New Music Masters," *Parade,* May 14, 1978; and Bond herself.

46. "Career Alternatives in Music. Some Advice from Outstanding Women Musicians," *Instrumentalist,* December 1976, p. 34.

47. Susan Starr, "The Prejudice Against Women."

48. Information about Lehwalder comes mainly from an interview with Raymond Ericson, *New York Times,* September 9, 1977, and a review by Peter G. Davis, *New York Times,* September 11, 1977.

49. For Robison I have relied on an interview with John Gruen, *New York Times,* January 9, 1977, and the biography issued by her manager, Kazuko Hillyer International, Inc., June 1977.

50. Most of the information about Karen Phillips comes from her.

51. *Instrumentalist,* March, 1975.

52. Ibid., December 1976, p. 37.

## Chapter 11

1. Richard Dyer, "Can a Classical Musician Make a Living in Boston?" *Boston Globe,* June 12, 1977.

2. Nancy Van de Vate, "Every Good Boy (Composer) Does Fine," *Symphony News,* December 1973/January 1974.

3. In answer to a questionnaire sent by the author, July 1978.

4. According to an ad in *Daily Aurora,* quoted by Robert A. Gerson, *Music in Philadelphia,* p. 366.

5. Frédéric Louis Ritter, *Music in America,* pp. 261 ff.

6. United States Works Progress Administration, *History of Music in San Francisco,* vol. 1, p. 196.

7. Karl Krueger, *The Musical Heritage of the United States,* pp. 24-25.

8. Lubov Keefer, *Music Angels: A Hundred Years of Patronage,* pp. 166-67.

9. Krueger, *The Musical Heritage of the United States,* p. 25.

10. Judith Tick, "Women as Professional Musicians in the United States 1870-1900," p. 97.

11. *Etude,* August 1909.

12. F.O. Jones, ed., *Handbook of American Music and Musicians,* p. 32.

13. A. Loesser, *Men, Women, and Pianos,* p. 478.

14. For information about Clara and Bertha Baur and their school, I have relied on Bertha Baur, "The Cincinnati Conservatory of Music," *Musical Observer,* May 1913, and Helen Board, *Bertha Baur: A Woman of Note.*

15. Theodore Thomas, *A Musical Autobiography,* pp. 80, 180.

16. *Women in Music,* vol. 5, no. 4, April 1940.

17. Information about Schenck and Spofford comes from files in the Sophia Smith Women's History Archive at Smith College.

18. Albert E. Wier, *The Piano; Its History, Makers, Players, and Music.*

19. *Etude,* November 1888, p. 166.

20. John Owen Ward, *Careers in Music,* p. 111.

21. Jean Bowen, "Women in Music—Their Fair Share," p. MA-20.

22. *Musical Herald,* June 1880, p. 143.

23. *Musical Age,* March 17, 1898.

24. Irving L. Sablosky, *American Music,* p. 105-6.

25. Raymond Ericson, *New York Times,* November 11, 1976; Harold C. Schonberg, *New York Times,* November 11 and 21, 1976; Robert K. Wallace, *A Century of Music-Making: The Lives of Josef and Rosina Lhevinne, passim.*

26. Information about Weigl comes principally from the composer herself.

27. Adrienne Fried Block, "The Woman Musician on Campus: Hiring and Promotion Patterns."

28. Nancy Van de Vate, "Notes from a Bearded Lady: The American Woman Composer," *International Musician,* vol. 74, no. 1, 1975.

29. Biographical information about Gideon comes chiefly from the composer and from Broadcast Music, Inc., *The Many Worlds of Music,* Issue 4, 1977.

30. George Perle, "The Music of Miriam Gideon," *American Composers Alliance Bulletin,* vol. 7. no. 4, 1958.

31. Record jacket, Composers Recordings, Inc., CRI SD 286.

32. Allen Hughes, *New York Times,* December 18, 1975.

33. Biographical information about Fine comes principally from the composer.

34. Interview with Joan McKinney, *Oakland Tribune,* April 2, 1975.

35. Wallingford Riegger, "The Music of Vivian Fine," p. 2.

36. Doris Humphrey, "Music for an American Dance," ibid., p. 5.

37. Riegger, ibid., pp. 2-3.

38. *New York Times,* April 17, 1973.

39. McKinney interview.

40. Information comes principally from the composer.

41. Letter to the author, January 27, 1978.

42. Information comes from the composer.

43. Information comes from the composer.

44. Van de Vate, "Notes from a Bearded Lady."

45. *Instrumentalist,* December 1976, pp. 36-37.

46. Information comes from the composer.

47. Information about Zaimont comes from the composer.

48. Raymond Ericson, *New York Times,* November 20, 1975.

49. Carol Neuls-Bates, "Foundation Support for Women in Music," *The Status of Women in College Music: Preliminary Study,* College Music Society Report no. 1 (1976).

50. *Etude,* May 1916.

51. The record is held by Mabel Daniels, who was there twenty-four times between 1914 and 1947. The others were Ballou, Emilie Frances Bauer, Branscombe, Britain, Cory, Crawford, Diller, Garwood, Gideon, James, Kolb, Mekeel, Polin, Semegen, Tower, Tureck, Weigl, and Zaimont. (The source is the MacDowell Colony's unpublished list of Fellows.)

52. Information comes from the Colony's 1978 brochure and also Rollo Walters Brown, "Mrs. MacDowell and Her Colony."

# BIBLIOGRAPHY

## Books

Aldrich, Richard. *Concert Life in New York 1902-23*. Edited by Harold Johnson. New York: G. P. Putnam's Sons, 1941.

Applebaum, Samuel and Sada. *The Way They Play*. Neptune City, N.J.: Paganiniana Publications, 1972.

Appleton, Jon H., and Perera, Ronald C., eds. *The Development and Practice of Electronic Music*. Englewood Cliffs, N.J.: Prentice-Hall, 1975.

Bachmann, Alberto. *An Encyclopedia of the Violin* (1925). Reprint. New York: Da Capo Press, 1966.

Baker-Carr, Janet. *Evening at Symphony: A Portrait of the Boston Symphony Orchestra*. Boston: Houghton Mifflin, 1977.

*Baker's Biographical Dictionary of Musicians* (5th ed.). Rev. by Nicolas Slonimsky. New York: G. Schirmer, Inc., 1958, with Supplement, 1965.

Barnard, Charles. *Camilla: A Tale of a Violin*. Boston: Loring, 1874.

Barnes, Edwin N.C. *American Women in Creative Music*. Washington, D.C.: Music Education Publications, 1936.

Bauer, Harold. *Harold Bauer, His Book*. New York: W.W. Norton, 1948.

Bauer, Marion. *Twentieth Century Music*. New York: G.P. Putnam's Sons, 1947.

———, and Peyser, Ethel. *How Music Grew*. New York: G. P. Putnam's Sons, 1939.

Beecham, Sir Thomas. "The Position of Women." *Vogue's First Reader*. Garden City, N.Y.: Halcyon House, 1944.

Berger, Arthur. *The American Composer Speaks*. Edited by Gilbert Chase. Baton Rouge: Louisiana State University Press, 1966.

Bingley, William. *Musical Biography* (2 vols., 1834.) Reprint (2 vols. in 1). New York: Da Capo Press, 1971.

Board, Helen. *Bertha Baur: A Woman of Note*. Philadelphia: Dorrance & Co., 1971.

Bond, Carrie Jacobs. *The Roads of Melody*. New York: D. Appleton & Co., 1927.

Brooks, Henry M. *Olden-Time Music; A Compilation from Newspapers and Books*. Boston: Ticknor & Co., 1888.

Campbell, Jane. *Old Philadelphia Music*. Philadelphia: City Historical Society, 1926.

Carreño, Teresa. *Possibilities of Tone Color by Artistic Use of Pedals*. Cincinnati: John Church Co., 1919.

Chapin, Victor. *Giants of the Keyboard.* Philadelphia: J. B. Lippincott Co., 1967.

Chase, Gilbert. *America's Music.* 2d ed. rev. New York: McGraw-Hill, 1966.

————, ed. *The American Composer Speaks.* Baton Rouge: Louisiana State University Press, 1966.

Cheney, Simeon Pease. *The American Singing Book.* Boston: White, Smith & Co., 1879.

Claghorne, Charles Eugene. *The Mocking Bird: The Life and Diary of Its Author, Septimus Winner.* Philadelphia: The Magee Press, 1937.

Coolidge, Arlan R. "Maud Powell," *Notable American Women 1607–1950,* 3:90–92. Cambridge, Mass: Belknap Press of Harvard University Press, 1971.

Cowell, Henry, ed. *American Composers on American Music.* New York: Frederick Ungar Publishing Co., 1933; renewed 1961.

Daniels, Mabel. *An American Girl in Munich (Impressions of a Music Student).* Boston: Little, Brown & Co., 1905.

*Dictionary of American Biography.* Edited by Dumas Malone. New York: Charles Scribner's Sons, 1943, vol. 20.

————, Supplement 3. Edited by Edward T. James, 1973.

Drinker, Sophie Lewis. *Music and Women: The Story of Women in Their Relation to Music.* New York: Coward McCann, 1948.

Ebel, Otto. *Women Composers: A Biographical Handbook of Woman's Work in Music.* 3rd ed. Brooklyn: Chandler-Ebel Music Co., 1913.

Edwards, George Thornton. *Music and Musicians of Maine.* Portland: Southworth Press, 1928. Reprint AMS Press.

Ellinwood, Leonard. *The History of American Church Music.* New York: Morehouse-Gorham Co., 1953.

Elson, Arthur. *Woman's Work in Music.* Boston: L. C. Page, 1904.

Elson, Louis C. *The History of American Music.* New York: Macmillan, 1904.

————. *Woman in Music.* New York: The University Society, Inc., 1918.

Erskine, John. *The Philharmonic Society of New York: Its First One Hundred Years.* New York: Macmillan, 1943.

Ewen, David. *American Composers Today.* New York: H. W. Wilson, 1949.

Fay, Amy. *Music-Study in Germany.* Edited by Mrs. Fay Pierce. New York: Macmillan, 1880.

Ffrench, Florence. *Music and Musicians in Chicago.* Chicago: F. F. Ffrench, 1899.

Finck, Henry T. *My Adventures in the Golden Age of Music.* New York and London: Funk & Wagnalls Co., 1926

Fisher, Renée B. *Musical Prodigies: Masters at an Early Age.* New York: Association Press, 1973.

Foster, Agnes Greene. *Eleanor Everest Freer—Patriot and Her Colleagues.* Chicago: Musical Art Publishing Co., 1927.

Freer, Eleanor Everest. *Recollections and Reflections of an American Composer,* 1929.

French, Maida Parlow. *Kathleen Parlow: A Portrait.* Toronto: Ryerson Press, 1967.

Gerson, Robert A. *Music in Philadelphia.* Philadelphia: University of Pennsylvania Press, 1940.

Goetschius, Percy. *Mrs. H. H. A. Beach.* Boston: Arthur P. Schmidt, 1906.

Goldin, Milton. *The Music Merchants.* New York: Macmillan, 1969.

Goss, Madeleine. *Modern Music Makers; Contemporary American Composers.* New York: E. P. Dutton & Co, 1952.

Green, Janet M. *Musical Biographies.* 2 vols. Part of *American History and Encyclopedia of Music.* Edited by W. L. Hubbard. New York: Irving Square, 1908.

Hall, Constance Huntington, and Tetlow, Helen Ingersoll. *Helen Hopekirk.* Cambridge, Mass.: private printing, 1954.

Hall, Jacob Henry. *Biography of Gospel Songs and Hymn Writers.* New York: Fleming H. Revell Co., 1914.

Hart, Philip. *Orpheus in the New World.* New York: W. W. Norton & Co. Inc., 1973.

Hewitt, John Hill. *Shadows on the Wall, or Glimpses of the Past. A Retrospect of the Past Fifty Years.* Baltimore: Turnbull Brothers, 1877.

Hipsher, Edward Ellsworth. *American Opera and Its Composers.* Philadelphia: Theodore Presser, 1927.

*History of the Handel and Haydn Society.* 2 vols. Vol. 1 edited by Charles C. Perkins (Chaps. 1-3) and John Sullivan Dwight (Boston: Alfred Mudge & Son, Printers, 1883-1893). Vol. 2 edited by William Frothingham Bradbury (Boston: Handel & Haydn Society, 1911).

Hixon, Donald L., and Hennessee, Don. *Women in Music: A Biobibliography.* Metuchen, N.J.: Scarecrow Press, 1975.

Homer, Sidney. *My Wife and I.* New York: Macmillan, 1939.

Hood, George. *History of Music in New England with Biographical Sketches of Reformers and Psalmists.* Boston: Wilkin Carter & Co., 1846.

Howard, John Tasker. *Our American Music: A Comprehensive History.* 4th ed. New York: Thomas Y. Crowell, 1965.

Howe, M. A. De Wolfe. *The Boston Symphony Orchestra 1881-1931.* Boston: Houghton Mifflin, 1931.

Howe, Mary. *Jottings.* Washington, D.C.: privately published, 1959.

Hughes, Rupert. *Contemporary American Composers.* Boston: L. C. Page & Co., 1900.

Huneker, James. *Overtones: A Book of Temperaments.* New York: Charles Scribner's Sons, 1904.

————. *The Philharmonic and Its Seventy-fifth Anniversary.* n.d.

*In Memoriam Mary Turner Salter.* n.d.

Johnson, Harold Earle. *Hallelujah, amen! The Story of the Handel and Haydn Society of Boston.* Boston: Bruce Humphries, 1965.

————. *Musical Interludes in Boston, 1795-1830.* New York: Columbia University Press, 1943. Reprint AMS Press.

————.*Symphony Hall, Boston.* Boston: Little, Brown Co., 1950.

Jones, F.O., ed. *Handbook of American Music and Musicians.* Canaseraga, N.Y.; Jones, 1886.

Keefer, Lubov. *Music Angels: A Thousand Years of Patronage.* Baltimore: 1976.

Kendall, Alan. *The Tender Tyrant: Nadia Boulanger.* Wilton, Conn. Lyceum Books, 1976.

Kolodin, Irving. *The Metropolitan Opera 1883-1966.* 4th ed. New York: Alfred A. Knopf, 1966.

Krehbiel, Henry Edward. *The Philharmonic Society of New York: A Memorial.* New York and London: Novello, Ewer & Co., 1892.

Krueger, Karl. *The Musical Heritage of the United States.* New York: Society for the Preservation of the American Musical Heritage, Inc., 1973.

Ladd, George Trumbull. *Why Women Cannot Compose Music.* New Haven, Conn.: Yale Publishing Association, 1917.

Lahee, Henry Charles. *Annals of Music in America.* Boston: Marshall Jones Co., 1922.

———. *Famous Pianists in America.* Boston: L. C. Page & Co., 1901.

———. *Famous Violinists in America.* Boston: L. C. Page & Co., 1899.

———. *The Organ and Its Masters.* Boston: L. C. Page & Co., 1903.

Lang, Paul Henry, ed. *One Hundred Years of Music in America.* New York: Grosset & Dunlap, 1961.

Loesser, A. *Men, Women, and Pianos.* New York: Simon & Schuster, 1954.

Lowens, Irving. *Music and Musicians in Early America.* New York: W. W. Norton & Co., Inc., 1964.

McCusker, Honor. *Fifty Years of Music in Boston.* Boston: Trustees of the Public Library, 1938.

MacDonald, Margaret I., ed. *The Greatest Battles Ever Fought Are the Silent Ones Fought by Women.* March 17, 1918.

McKay, David P., and Crawford, Richard. *William Billings of Boston.* Princeton, N.J.: Princeton University Press, 1975.

Maine Archives, *Register of Deaths,* vol. 4, p. 1218.

Mangler, Joyce Ellen. *Rhode Island Music and Musicians 1733-1850.* Detroit: Information Service, Inc., 1965.

Mathews, W. S. B. *A Hundred Years of Music in America.* Chicago: G. L. Howe, 1889. Reprint AMS Press.

Menuhin, Yehudi. *Unfinished Journey.* New York: Alfred A. Knopf, 1977.

Milinowski, Marta. *Teresa Carreño, "By the Grace of God."* New Haven, Conn.: Yale University Press, 1940.

Moore, John W. *Complete Encyclopaedia of Music.* Boston: Oliver Ditson Co., 1876.

Morin, Raymond. *The Worcester Music Festival, Its Background and History 1858-1946.* Worcester, Mass.: Worcester County Music Association, 1946.

Mueller, John H. *The American Symphony Orchestra.* Bloomington: Indiana University Press, 1951.

Mumma, Gordon. "Live Electronic Music." In Appleton and Perera *(supra).*

Naylor, Blanche. *The Anthology of the Fadettes.* Boston: 194?

Ochse, Orpha. *The History of the Organ in the United States.* Bloomington: Indiana University Press, 1975.

Odell, George C. D. *Annals of the New York Stage.* 5 vols. New York: Columbia University Press, 1931.

Osburn, Mary Hubbell. *Ohio Composers and Musical Authors.* Privately published, 1942.

Otis, Philo Adams. *The Chicago Symphony Orchestra: Its Organization, Growth, and Development 1891-1924.* Chicago: Clayton F. Summy, 1924.

Parker, John Rowe. *Musical Biography: Or Sketches of the Lives and Writings of Eminent Musical Characters.* Boston: Stone & Fovell, 1824.

Patterson, Lindsay, ed. *The Negro in Music and Art (International Library of Negro Life and History)*. New York, Washington, D.C., and London: Publishers Company, Inc., 1967, 1968.

Penny, Virginia. *The Employments of Women: A Cyclopaedia of Woman's Work*. Boston: Walker, Wise & Co., 1863.

Pincherle, Marc. *The World of the Virtuoso*. Translated by Lucile H. Brockway. New York: W. W. Norton & Co., Inc., 1963.

Reis, Claire. *Composers in America: Biographical Sketches of Living Composers with a Record of Their Works, 1912-1937*. 1st ed. and rev. ed. New York: Macmillan, 1938, 1947.

Rich, Alan. *Careers and Opportunities in Music*. New York: E. P. Dutton & Co., Inc., 1964.

Ritter, Fanny Raymond. *Lyre, Pen, and Pencil: Essays, Studies, Sketches*. Edited by Millie W. Carpenter. New York: Edward Schuberth & Co., 1891.

Ritter, Frédéric Louis. *Music in America*. Rev. ed. New York: Charles Scribner's Sons., 1890.

Rivé, Caroline. *Madame Rivé's System of Sight Singing, based upon Rodolphe's solfeggi*. Cincinnati: John Church & Co., 187?

Roach, Hildred. *Black American Music: Past and Present*. Boston: Crescendo Publishing Company, 1973.

Rosenberg, Deena, and Rosenberg, Bernard. *The Music Makers*. New York: Columbia University Press, 1979.

Ryan, Thomas. *Recollections of an Old Musician*. New York: E. P. Dutton & Co., 1899.

Sablosky, Irving L. *American Music*. Chicago and London: University of Chicago Press, 1969.

Samaroff Stokowski, Olga. *An American Musician's Story*. New York: W. W. Norton & Co., Inc., 1939.

Sargeant, Winthrop. *Geniuses, Goddesses, and People*. New York: E. P. Dutton & Co., Inc., 1949.

Sax, Alphonse, Jr. *Gymnastique des Poumons. La Musique Instrumentale au point de vue de l'Hygiène et la Création des Orchestres féminins*. Paris: 1865.

Schwartz, Elliott. *Electronic Music: A Listener's Guide*. New York and Washington, D.C.: Praeger Publishers, 1973.

Searle, Humphrey, and Laton, Robert. *Twentieth Century Composers*. Vol. 3: *Britain, Scandinavia, and the Netherlands*. New York, Chicago, San Francisco: Holt, Rinehart & Winston, 1972.

Seeger, Charles, "Ruth Crawford." In Cowell (see *supra*).

Shanet, Howard. *Philharmonic, A History of New York's Orchestra*. New York: Doubleday & Co., Inc., 1975.

Slenczynska, Ruth, and Biancolli, Louis. *Forbidden Childhood*. New York: Doubleday & Co., Inc. 1957.

Smith, Eva Munson. *Woman in Sacred Song*. Boston: D. Lothrop & Co., 1885.

Smith, Julia. *Aaron Copland*. New York: E. P. Dutton & Co., Inc., 1955.

Smyth, Ethel. *Female Pipings in Eden*. London: Peter Davies, Ltd., 1933.

Sonneck, Oscar George Theodore. *A Bibliography of Early Secular American Music*. Revised by William Treat Upton. Washington, D.C.: Library of Congress, 1945. Reprint. New York: Da Capo Press, 1964.

————. *Early Concert-Life in America (1731-1800).* Leipzig: Breitkopf & Härtel, 1907. Reprint. Musurgia Publishers, 1949.

————. Early Opera in America. New York: G. Schirmer, 1915.

Southern, Eileen. *The Music of Black American Music.* New York: W. W. Norton & Co., Inc., 1971.

————. *Readings in Black American Music.* New York: W. W. Norton & Co., Inc., 1971.

Stoddard, Hope. *Symphony Conductors of the United States of America.* New York: Thomas Y. Crowell Co., 1957.

Stoeving, Paul. *The Violin: Its Famous Makers and Players.* Boston: Oliver Ditson Co., 1928.

Sutro, Florence. *Women in Music and Law.* New York: Authors' Publishing Company, 1895.

Thomas, Theodore. *A Musical Autobiography.* 2 vols. Edited by George P. Upton. Chicago: A. C. McClurg & Co., 1905. Reprint of vol. 1. New York: Da Capo Press, 1964.

Thomson, Virgil. *American Music Since 1910.* New York, Chicago, and San Francisco: Holt, Rinehart & Winston, 1971.

Towers, John. *Woman in Music.* Winchester, Va., 1897.

Trotter, James M. *Music and Some Highly Musical People.* Boston: Lee & Shepard, 1881 (1878). Reprint. Johnson Reprint Corp., 1968.

United States Works Progress Administration, Northern California. *History of Music in San Francisco.* 7 vols. San Francisco, 1939-42.

Upton, George P. *Musical Memories 1850-1900.* Chicago: A. C. McClurg & Co., 1908.

————. *Woman in Music.* 6th ed. Chicago: 1899.

Upton, William T. *Art-Song in America.* Boston: Oliver Ditson Co., 1930.

Urso, Camilla. *Violin-Playing and the Paris Conservatory.* In vol. 1. *The Music of the Modern World.* Edited by Anton Seidl. New York: D. Appleton & Co., 1895.

Van der Straeten, E. *The History of the Violin.* 2 vols. London: Cassell & Co., Ltd., 1933.

Vinton, John, ed. *Dictionary of Contemporary Music.* New York: E. P. Dutton & Co., Inc., 1974.

Walker, Greta. *Women Today: Ten Profiles.* New York: Hawthorn Books, Inc., 1975.

Wallace, Robert K. *A Century of Music-Making: The Lives of Josef and Rosina Lhevinne.* Bloomington: Indiana University Press, 1976.

Ward, John Owen. *Careers in Music.* New York: Henry Z. Walck, Inc., 1968.

Wier, Albert E. *The Piano; Its History, Makers, Players, and Music.* New York: Longmans, Green and Co., 1941.

Willhartitz, Adolf. *Some Facts About Woman in Music.* Los Angeles: Out West Co., 1902.

## Dissertations

Elkins-Marlow, Laurine, "Gena Branscombe: American Composer and Conductor." Ph.D. dissertation, University of Texas at Austin, 1978.

Gaume, Mary Matilda. "Ruth Crawford Seeger: Her Life and Works." Ph.D. dissertation, Indiana University, 1973.

Green, Mildred Denby. "A Study of the Lives and Works of Five Black Women Composers in America." D. Mus. Ed. dissertation, University of Oklahoma, 1975.

Merrill, E. Lindsey. "Mrs. H. H. A. Beach. Her Life and Music." Ph.D. dissertation, University of Rochester Eastman School of Music, 1963.

Paige, Paul Eric. "Musical Organizations in Boston: 1830-1850." Ph.D. dissertation, Boston University, 1967.

Tick, Judith. "Women Composers in the United States Before 1870." Ph.D. dissertation, City University of New York, 1978.

Wolverton, Byron Adams. "Keyboard Music and Musicians in the Colonies and United States of America Before 1830." Ph.D. dissertation, Indiana University, 1966.

## Clipping Files and Scrapbooks in the Boston Public Library, Music Division

Boston, Concert Life in, 4 vols. in 9, 1896-.

Boston, music in, 1845-1914.

Boston, Nadia Boulanger in, 1938-39.

Boston Conservatory of Music, programs of faculty and pupils' recitals, 1870-80.

Boston Musical Fund Society, programs, 1847-55; Boston Musical Education Society, 1840-56.

Boston Musicians Union, Constitution of the (1863; rev. 1865).

Boston Orchestral Club, programs and reviews, 1885-91; 1899-1911.

Carnegie Hall, New York, programs, 1892-1929.

Eichberg, Julius, clippings, programs, music mss. 1843-94.

Leginska, Ethel, programs and reviews.

*U.S. Secular Songsters,* collection of music (up to 1851).

Women's Symphony Society of Boston and Women's Symphony Orchestra, clippings and programs, 1939-42.

Yaddo, music at, clippings, 1932-46.

## Periodicals

*Boston Musical Gazette,* 1838-46.

*Boston Musical Times,* 13 vols. 1860-70.

*Dexter Smith's Musical, Literary, Dramatic and Art Paper,* 14 vols, 1872-78.

*Dwight's Journal of Music.* 41 vols. 1853-81.

*Etude Music Magazine.* 75 vols. Philadelphia. 1883-1957.

*Euterpiad or Musical Intelligencer.* 3 vols. Boston, 1820-22.

*Folio.* 42 vols. Boston, 1869-95.

*Freund's Musical and Dramatic Times,* 1875-80; *Freund's Daily,* 1882, 1883; *Freund's Weekly: A Review of Music and Drama,* 1883-91; *Freund's Musical Age,* 1893-96; *Freund's Weekly,* July-November 1893; *Freund's Musical Weekly,* December 1893-January 1896, Numerous vols., all published in New York, Harry E. Freund, publisher.

*Massachusetts Musical Journal* (orig. *Boston Musical Journal*), 1855-57.
*Metronome.* 3 vols. Boston, 1871-74.
*Music.* Chicago, 1891-1902.
*Musical Age* (successor of *Freund's Musical Weekly*). 59 vols. New York, 1896-1908.
*Musical America.* New York, 1898-99; 1910-65 (succeeded 1965 *Music Trades; after High Fidelity/Musical America.*
*Musical Bulletin.* 7 vols. New York, 1870-73.
*Musical Courier.* 164 vols. New York, 1880-1962.
*Musical Gazette.* Boston, 1847.
*Musical Gazette.* Boston, 1854-55.
*Musical Herald.* 14 vols. 1880-93.
*Musical Record.* 22 vols. Boston, 1878-1900.
*Musical Record and Review.* 3 vols. Boston, 1901-3.
*Musical Review.* 3 vols. New York, 1879-81.
*Musical Review and Record of Musical Science.* 2 vols. New York, 1938.
*Music Review.* 2 vols. Boston, 1898-1900.
*Music Trades,* New York, 1900-1911 (John C. Freund, editor).
*Women in Music.* New York, 1935-40.

## Articles

Adams, Mrs. Crosby. "Musical Creative Work Among Women." *Music* 9 (January 1896): 170.
"After God Comes Papa." *Stereo* (Spring 1972).
Barkin, Elaine. "Louise Talma: 'The Tolling Bell.'" *Perspectives of New Music* 10, no. 2 (Spring/Summer 1972): 142-52.
Bazelon, Irwin A. "Woman with a Symphony." *Baton* 30, no. 3 (March 1951): 4-7.
Berger, Arthur. "Stravinsky and the Younger American Composers." *The Score and I.M.A. Magazine,* no. 12 (June 1955): 38.
Block, Adrienne Fried. "The Woman Musician on Campus: Hiring and Promotion Patterns." *High Fidelity/Musical America* 25, no. 6 (June 1975): MA-22-23.
Bloomfield-Zeisler, Fanny. "Women in Music." *American Art Journal* 58, no. 1 (October 17, 1891): 1-3.
Bojanowsky, Jerzy. "Championing the Woman Orchestral Player." *Musical Courier,* January 15, 1945.
Bond, Carrie Jacobs. "Music Composition as a Field for Women." *Musical Standard* 16, no. 342 (October 23, 1920).
Bowen, Jean. "Women in Music—Their Fair Share." *High Fidelity/Musical America* 24, no. 8 (August 1974).
Bradshaw, Susan. "Thea Musgrave." *Musical Times* 104, no. 1450 (December 1963): 866-68.
Brown, Rollo Walters. "Mrs. MacDowell and Her Colony." *Atlantic Monthly* (July 1949): 42-46.
Burns, Don. "The Distaff'd Composers." *Music Journal* 32, no. 3 (March 1974): 16-17, 32-37.
"Career Alternatives in Music: Some Advice from Outstanding Women Musicians." *The Instrumentalist* 31 (December 1976): 34 ff.
Craig, Mary. "Julia Smith: Composer and Ambassadress of U.S. Music." *Musical Courier,* July 1959, p. 7.

Crothers, Stella Reid. "Women Composers of America." (Biographical series.) *Musical America,* vol. 10, nos. 4–26 (1909); vol. 11, nos. 1–22 (1910).

Eichberg, Julius, "Violin Techniqs." *Town and Country,* April 1879.

Gilbert, Steven E. "'The Ulta-modern Idiom': A Survey of *New Music.*" *Perspectives of New Music* 12, nos. 1 and 2 (Fall/Winter 1973, Spring/Summer 1974).

Graham, Shirley. "Spirituals to Symphonies." *Etude* 54, no. 11 (November 1936): 691 f.

Green, Miriam. "Women: From Silence to Song." *American Music Teacher,* September/October 1974.

Green, Miriam Stewart. "Consider These Creators." *American Music Teacher* 25, no. 3 (January 1976): 9–12.

Harris, Clement Antrobus. "Women Composers of Religious Music." *Musical America,* December 25, 1939, p. 5.

Howard , John Tasker. "The Hewitt Family in American Music." *Musical Quarterly,* January 1931.

Jepson, Barbara. "American Women in Conducting." *Feminist Art Journal,* Winter 1975/76, pp. 13–18.

Johnson, Tom. "Lucia Dlugoszewski." *High Fidelity/Musical America* 25, no. 6 (June 1975): MA-5-6.

Kagan, Susan. "Camilla Urso: A Nineteenth-Century Violinist's View." *Signs* 2, no. 3 (Spring 1977): 727–34.

MacBridge, Jessie, and Watson, Dorothy DeMuth. "American Women Composers Hold Festival in Washington." *Musical America,* 52, no. 9 (May 10, 1932): 20, 40.

"Margaret Hillis." *Panpipes* 68, no. 4 (May 1976): 22.

Mathews, W. S. B. "Personal Glimpses of Teresa Carreño." *Music* 11 (1896): 142 ff.

Möller, Heinrich. "Can Women Compose?" *Musical Observer* 15, nos. 5 and 6 (May and June 1910): 9–10, 11–12.

Morini, Erica. "Women as Musicians." *Who Is Who in Music,* Chicago, 1940–41, pp. 76–77.

*Musical Leader,* May 25, 1940.

Neuls-Bates, Carol. "Sources and Resources for Women's Studies in American Music. A Report." *Notes* 35, no. 2 (December 1978).

Oliveiros, Pauline, "And Don't Call Them 'Lady' Composers." *New York Times,* May 13, 1970.

*Opera News,* February 14, 1976.

"Opinions of Some New York Leaders on Women as Orchestral Players." *Musical Standard* 21, no. 535, April 2, 1904: pp. 217–18.

Paige, Raymond. "Why Not Women in Orchestras?" *Etude,* January 1952, pp. 14–15.

Perle, George. "The Music of Miriam Gideon." *American Composers Alliance Bulletin* 7, no. 4 (1958).

Petrides, Frederique. "Women in Orchestras." *Etude Music Magazine* 16, no. 7 (July 1938): 429 ff.

Phillips, Karen. "Women Musicians Offer Advice." *Music Journal* 32, no. 3 (March 1974): 18 ff.

Powell, Maud. "The Violinist." *Delineator,* October 1911, p. 274.

Riegger, Wallingford. "The Music of Vivian Fine." *American Composers Alliance Bulletin* 8, no. 1 (1958).

Saenger, Gustav. "Maud Powell." *Musical Observer* 8, no. 4 (New York, August 1913).

"Salute to an American Woman Composer [Julia Smith]." *Music Clubs Magazine* 49, no. 2 (Winter 1969/70): 8.

Scheibert, Beverly. "Equal Opportunities in Church Hiring." *Diapason,* August August 1976, p. 2.

Scruggs, Leigh K. "Creative Women in Music." *Music Clubs Magazine* 55, no. 2 (Winter 1975/76): 8-9.

Seabury, Deborah. "La Maestra." *Opera News,* February 14, 1976.

Smith, Leona May. "Is There a Career for Women Musicians?" *Metronome,* January 1938, p. 48.

Starr, Susan. "The Prejudice Against Women" *Music Journal* 32, no. 3 (March 1974): 14 ff.

Stoddard, Hope. "Fine Musicianship Knows No Sex." *Independent Woman,* November 1947.

Tick, Judith. "Women as Professional Musicians in the United States, 1870-1900." *Yearbook for Inter-American Research in Music* 9 (1973): 95-133.

————.Why Have There Been No Great Women Composers, or Notes on the Score of Sexual Aesthetics?" *International Musician* 74, no. 1 (July 1975): 6.

Tuthill, Burnet C. "Mrs. H. H. A. Beach." *Musical Quarterly,* July 1940.

Van de Vate, Nancy. "Notes from a Bearded Lady: The American Woman Composer." *International Musician* 74, no. 1 (July 1975).

————."The American Woman Composer: Some Sour Notes." *High Fidelity/Musical America* 25, no. 6 (June 1975): MA-18-19.

————."Every Good Boy (Composer) Does Fine." *Symphony News,* December 1973/January 1974.

Winn, Edith L. "Maud Powell as I Knew Her." *Musical Observer* 19, no. 3 (March 1920): 58-59.

Wolff, Konrad. "Dika Newlin." *American Composers Alliance Bulletin* 10, no. 4 (December 1962).

Yuhasz, Sister Marie Joy, O.P. "Black Composers and Their Piano Music." *American Music Teacher* 19, no. 4 (February/March 1970): 24-26.

# INDEX

Terms in this index, whether they consist of one word or of several words, are in strict alphabetical order, letter by letter, up to the comma in cases of inversion. Subentries are in order of first appearance. Where individuals are noted principally in one area but also were (are) proficient in another, they are listed separately under the appropriate entry; for example, Julia Rivé-King, principally a concert pianist, also composed music and so is listed separately under Composers, women.

18; Powell, 31-32; Morgan, 35;
Jackson, 36; Campbell, 38; Rivé-
King, 51; Fay, 60; Cottlow, 62;
Samaroff, 62; Sutro sisters, 68;
Paine, 76; Lang, 87; Hood, 88;
Daniels, 89; Hopekirk, 91; Lewing,
93-94; Rogers, 94; Brico, 112; Bauer,
117, 124; Howe, 117, 118; Britain,
149; Branscombe, 190-91; Faunt Le
Roy, 163
Gerst, Augusta Cottlow, *See* Cottlaw,
Augusta
Gevaert, François Auguste, 77
Ghent, Emmanuel, 196
Gideon, Miriam, 234-35, 242 n.51
Gilbert and Sullivan, 167, 173
Gilman, Sarah H., 16
Gilmore, Patrick S., 32
Gisela Weber Trio, 39
Glanville-Hicks, Peggy, 175-77
Gleason, Frederic Grant, 96
Gleason, Harold, 19, 20
Godmilow, Jill, 113
Godowsky, Leopold, 146
Goehr, Alexander, 191
Goetschius, Percy, 136, 228
Golden, Anna, 40
Goldman, Edwin Franko, 38
Goldman Band, 206
Goldmark, Rubin, 147
Goldovsky, Boris, 170
Goodrich, Alfred John, 96
Goodwin, Thelma, 115
Gospel song, 158-59
Gottschalk, Louis Moreau, 44, 45
Gottschalk School, 39 n.71
Gradova, Gitta, 128
Graever, Mme J., 50
Graham, Martha, 236
Grainger, Percy, 194
Grandval, Marie Félicie Clémence de
Reiset, 166
Grants and fellowships, 241-42, 245-49.
*Also see* specific names
Grau, Maurice, 166
Grau and Fitzgerald, 168

Graupner, Catherine Hellyer (Hillier),
5, 9
Graupner, J. C. Gottlieb, 5, 9, 11
Great Neck Choral Society, 240
Grebe, Emma, 31
Grebe, Fannie, 104
Greenwich House Music School, 186
Gregg Smith Singers, 241
Grieg, Edvard, Piano Concerto in A
minor; and Carreño, 46, 47; and
Bloomfield-Zeisler, 58
Griffes, Charles Tomlinson, 116, 117
Griffin, Elinor Remick Warren. *See*
Warren, Elinor Remick
Griswold, Gertrude, 97 n.80
GROOVE, 197
Group-improvised composition, 142.
*See also* Improvisation
Gruenberg, Louis, 237
Guggenheim Fellowship, 130-31, 136,
156, 176, 184, 185, 193, 241
Guggenheim Memorial Foundation,
241
Guggenheimer, Minnie, 114
Guichard, Ann C. de, 201
Guildhall School of Music, 19 n.6


Haffley, Eugene, 124
Hagen, Elisabeth von (Mrs. P. A.), 7,
44, 225
Hahn, Adolf, 39 n.72
Hahn, Mrs. Adolf, 39
Hale, Philip, 77
Hall, Elise (Mrs. Richard J.), 101
Hall, Herbert E., 37
Hallam and Henry, 8, 9
Hallè, Lady. *See* Normann-Neruda,
Wilma
Hamerick, Asger, 167
Hamilton, Harley, 107
Handel, George Frederick, *Messiah,* 5,
10, 25, 216
Handel and Haydn Society (Boston),
6-7, 8, 10, 11-17, 108; and Beach, 77;
and Lang, 87; and Daniels, 89

**About the Author**

Christine Ammer's earlier books include *Musician's Handbook of Foreign Terms* and *Harper's Dictionary of Music.*